O9-BSU-490

DOMINOES AND BANDWAGONS

DOMINOES
AND
BANDWAGONS

Strategic Beliefs and Great Power Competition in the Eurasian Rimland

Edited by

Robert Jervis & Jack Snyder
Columbia University

New York Oxford
Oxford University Press
1991

Oxford University Press

Oxford New York Toronto
Delhi Bombay Calcutta Madras Karachi
Petaling Jaya Singapore Hong Kong Tokyo
Nairobi Dar es Salaam Cape Town
Melbourne Auckland

and associated companies in
Berlin Ibadan

Published by Oxford University Press, Inc.,
200 Madison Avenue, New York, New York 10016

Library of Congress Cataloging-in-Publication Data
Dominoes and bandwagons: strategic beliefs and great power competition
in the Eurasian rimland / edited by Robert Jervis, Jack Snyder.
p. cm. ISBN 0-19-506246-9
1. United States—Foreign relations—Soviet Union.
2. Soviet Union—Foreign relations—United States.
I. Jervis, Robert, 1940-. II. Snyder, Jack L.
JX1428.S65D66 1991 327.47073—dc20 90-33070

2 4 6 8 9 7 5 3 1

Printed in the United States of America on acid-free paper

For William T. R. Fox,
a pioneer who taught us that a realistic strategy
is the most solid contribution
to international peace and security

Preface

Soviet-American geopolitical rivalry during the cold war was fueled in large measure by the domino theory, the notion that the outcome of contests in the periphery would produce a chain reaction affecting vital interests. Underpinning this idea was the related image of an intensely hostile superpower opponent. Such ideas were central to the rationale for American military interventions in the Third World.

Now that the bipolar hostility of the cold war has eroded, what will become of the domino theory as a spur to global American involvement? Domino arguments were absent from the Bush administration's list of justifications for the military intervention in Panama. President Bush argued that protecting the Canal, saving American lives, and ousting a drug-runner were sufficient reasons in themselves to intervene, not that they entailed important precedents, reputational questions, or spillover effects. Domino arguments reappeared, however, in Bush's arguments for sending troops to Saudi Arabia and embargoing the Iraqi economy: Sadam Hussein, like Hitler, would push on to further aggression unless his occupation of Kuwait were to be rolled back. Thus, the evidence appears mixed.

The fear of falling dominoes also continues to play a role in Soviet thinking. With dominoes already fallen in Eastern Europe, Moscow has used the domino theory to justify its military coercion of Lithuania. The Soviet leadership argues that abrupt secession by the Baltic republics would set an intolerable precedent encouraging other regions to do the same. So far, however, such domino ideas have not affected the views of Soviet new thinkers about intervention outside Soviet borders. This may in part be due to their belief that the West does not intend to exploit their setbacks. It is worth considering what Western policies might reverse this benign perception, exacerbating Soviet domino fears.

The answers to these questions must lie in the future. But we can begin to analyze them through an appreciation of the relevant theories and the historical evidence that we address here. The contributors assess what statesmen in the United States and other great powers have believed about falling dominoes, whether their fears had any foundation, and the psychological and domestic political factors that may have contributed to these ideas. Essays on the Soviet Union test for the first time whether the Soviets actually drew the inferences about American credibility that American domino thinkers anticipated. Historical essays examine whether only bipolar international settings give rise to domino thinking, and what kinds of strategic concepts are prevalent in systems of the multipolar variety, like the one which may now be emerging.

We would like to express our appreciation to Howard Wriggins, who helped us conceive the project and offered many helpful suggestions along the way. The book was made possible by a grant from the Ford Foundation to the Institute of War and Peace Studies at Columbia University for the study of regional security in an era of strategic parity. Teresa Pelton Johnson edited several of the chapters, providing tutorial services above and beyond the call of duty in addition to the usual red-pencil work. We are grateful to MIT Press for permission to reprint parts of Stephen Walt's "Testing Theories of Alliance Formation: The Case of Southwest Asia" (*International Organization*, Vol. 42, No. 1 [Spring 1987]), and to Cornell University Press for permission to reprint figure 1 from Walt's *The Origins of Alliance* (Ithaca: Cornell University Press, 1987). The many kind people who commented on parts of the manuscript are thanked in the individual chapters. Kathleen McNamara provided the index.

New York R.J.
August 1990 J.S.

Contents

Contributors

Douglas Blum is assistant professor of political science at Providence College.

Milan Hauner is a visiting scholar in the History Department at the University of California, Berkeley.

Richard Herrmann is associate professor of political science at Ohio State University.

Ted Hopf is assistant professor of political science at the University of Michigan.

Robert Jervis is Adlai E. Stevenson Professor of International Relations at Columbia University.

Deborah Welch Larson is associate professor of political science at the University of California, Los Angeles.

Douglas Macdonald is assistant professor of political science at Colgate University.

Jack Snyder is associate professor of political science at Columbia University.

Stephen Walt is associate professor of political science at the University of Chicago.

DOMINOES AND BANDWAGONS

1

Introduction

JACK SNYDER

The domino theory, in one form or another, has been the central organizing concept behind American containment strategy. America's two major wars since 1945 have been fought under the banner of the domino theory. Neither Korea nor Vietnam was thought to have great economic, military, or cultural value to the United States. Rather, they were thought to be worth fighting for primarily because defeats there might create precedents for areas of greater intrinsic value. Insufficient resistance would embolden aggressors to hunt for bigger game, shake major allies' faith in American backing, and cause smaller states and popular movements to jump on the aggressors' bandwagon.[1]

Debates about containment strategy have revolved around different evaluations of the domino theory. The more a statesman or strategist saw dominoes as poised to cascade, the more likely he was to favor military intervention to prevent communist victories, even at high cost and in peripheral areas.[2] Even in the 1980s, the domino theory and its variants remained central to arguments about American global strategy. Aid to the Nicaraguan contras was seen as forestalling dangers to Mexico, the "ultimate domino."[3] American willingness to maintain its military commitments in Lebanon and the Persian Gulf reflected on its more general reputation as a resolute world power, according to Reagan Administration spokesmen.

This tendency to see tight connections between threats to the periphery and to the core of an empire is not a peculiarly American obsession. Most imperial strategists defending far-flung commitments have feared falling dominoes, and most rising challengers have anticipated bandwagon effects.[4] Even such an astute, skeptical statesman as Lord Salisbury believed that France might somehow build a dam at the inaccessible headwaters of the Nile, cutting off Egypt's water, provoking revolutionary upheaval in Egypt, threatening British control of the Suez Canal, severing sea communications to India, inviting a revolt or outside interference there, and thus wrecking the British imperial economy. Since the French believed this too, they sought to exploit whatever leverage they might gain from an expedition to claim the town of Fashoda on the Upper Nile, producing history's only war-threatening crisis between two democracies.[5]

This widespread belief in domino and bandwagon dynamics is one of the major forces impelling the overextension that afflicts almost all mature imperial powers. Trying to head off threats to would-be dominoes on the "turbulent frontier," they get dragged into quagmires and commitments that divert resources from productive investment.[6] Thus, the question of the domino theory—its causes and consequences—is more than a bone of contention in recent American policy debates. It is a central issue in many of the key puzzles of international politics: why states often fight for stakes that seem meager in comparison to the costs of the struggle, why even status quo states behave aggressively, and why empires almost always make the same mistakes.[7]

Thus, the waning of the cold war does not eliminate the relevance of the domino problem. Dominoes have been falling rapidly in Eastern Europe, and threaten to extend their cascade into the peripheral regions of the Soviet Union itself. Will the perceived need to use military force to forestall falling dominoes undermine the "new thinking" in Gorbachev's political strategy? And in the United States, the belief in falling dominoes, the image of an aggressive Soviet Union, and the justification of America's global role have always been interconnected. Now that the Soviet Union is seen as less threatening, will America still see its security as tightly bound up with developments in the periphery?

Given the importance of the domino theory to questions of theory and policy, it is surprising how little study this question has attracted.[8] What scholarship exists, however, is often of high quality. A number of monographs describe the decisive effect of domino fears, especially concern for the credibility of American commitments, on American containment strategy in Korea, Vietnam, and elsewhere on the Eurasian perimeter.[9] A few theoretical works have explored the logic of "the interdependence of commitments," which holds that a failure to make good on less important threats and promises may call into question the credibility of more important commitments.[10] By contrast, almost nothing substantial has been written on whether the Soviets actually do infer a generalized lack of resolve from American retreats.[11] A very small number of historical works have examined the prevalence before 1945 of the belief that victories tend to snowball or that disparate parts of the globe are strategically interconnected.[12]

Very little has been written on the causes of these beliefs, apart from the role of the Munich analogy in the American case.[13] A handful of works have tried to evaluate the truth of domino beliefs, generally concluding that victories rarely cumulate in this manner. As Kenneth Waltz has put it, "in international politics, winning leads to losing," because states usually throw their weight into the balance against aggressive, rising powers.[14]

The present volume seeks to build on this small, but insightful literature, addressing five questions about the strategic beliefs that have shaped the superpowers' competition in the Eurasian rimland.

First, to what extent have the two superpowers seen the Eurasian rimland as an arena of competition in which dominoes tend to fall, victories create a bandwagon effect, and setbacks tarnish the reputation of the loser in a deep and generalized way? Do these beliefs hinge on evaluations of the character of the superpower opponent, on assessments of the nature of the regional targets, or on both? Were other great powers in multipolar eras prone to the same perceptions?

Second, to what extent have such beliefs been accurate? When do victories cumulate, when not?

Third, what have been the consequences of such beliefs for the intensity of superpower conflict, for superpower military intervention in rimland Asia, and for the credibility of deterrence?

Fourth, in the cases where statesmen's domino and bandwagon beliefs seem unwarranted by a reasonable reading of the evidence available to them, what accounts for those beliefs?

Fifth, what policy prescriptions flow from these findings? What is likely to become of domino thinking as a result of the waning of the cold war and the possible emergence of an increasingly multipolar international system? What will be the consequences for the reassessment of American containment strategy and America's global role?

Most of the contributors to this volume did not tackle all of these questions. Rather, they discussed diverse questions about superpower strategic beliefs, reflecting a variety of theoretical perspectives and drawing on a variety of historical cases. Together, however, their findings suggest some answers to each of the five questions. Equally important, the essays open up a number of new debates and questions for further research.

In the first essay, Robert Jervis provides an overview of domino thinking, especially by American cold war statesmen, analyzing what they believed, whether it made sense, why they believed it, and what consequences the beliefs had. Under some conditions victories may snowball, he suggests, but cognitive or other biases have led American policymakers to exaggerate this tendency.

The next two contributors, Stephen Walt and Deborah Larson, debate the prevalence of bandwagoning in alliance choices. Walt, analyzing the behavior of Southwest Asian states, contends that states almost always choose to balance against rising expansionists, given even modest prospects for success and outside assistance. Larson, in contrast, points to the domestic political weaknesses that led states to bandwagon with Nazi Germany in the 1930s. She argues that American decisions to defend Asian dominoes after 1945 reflected a not entirely unfounded fear that domestically fragile West European states would bandwagon with Soviet Russia, if communism's victories made it seem to be the wave of the future. She adds, however, that Americans overlearned the lessons of the 1930s, and for reasons explained largely by cognitive psychology, occasionally applied them with insufficient discrimination.[15]

In the next chapter, Douglas Macdonald traces the origins of the "falling domino principle" in the Truman years, noting its close correlation with the rise in the U.S.S.R.'s perceived power and aggressiveness. Macdonald's argument may have contemporary relevance, since the process he described may now be reversing itself. The Bush administration did *not* invoke the domino theory to justify its military intervention in Panama, which occurred after the perceived waning of the Soviet threat. Macdonald also stresses the overselling of the domino theory during the political process of gaining support for containment.

The four final contributions examine Soviet and Russian perceptions. Ted Hopf, studying the lessons that the Soviets drew from American setbacks in Vietnam, Angola, and Ethiopia, concludes that the Soviets do not draw the generalized inferences of lack of American resolve and bandwagon opportunities that American domino theorists have traditionally feared. Rather, the Soviets drew only limited inferences about opportunities for cumulative victories, never seeing wins in the periphery as directly increasing their prospects in more central areas. Even at the height of their brief period of optimism after the American exit from Vietnam, the Soviets never saw bandwagoning tendencies as outweighing America's innate disposition to balance against Soviet gains. By the end of the Angola affair, the Soviets saw no favorable bandwagon at all, only resistance.

Douglas Blum, analyzing Soviet perceptions of American responses to the invasion of Afghanistan, likewise finds that most Soviet commentators saw an America innately driven to hostile resistance to Soviet actions. This view should reassure domino theorists who worry about American credibility. Blum, however, also finds that Soviets who see America as unconditionally resistant tend to favor militant strategies toward the West, whereas those who see America as responding flexibly to its environment tend to favor a more restrained, cooperative approach.

Richard Herrmann identifies typical enemy images that the superpowers hold of each other and imperial images that shape their view of the regions in which they compete. Biases in the logic of these images lead the superpowers to overrate each others' hostility and to overrate the superpowers' ability to control events in the periphery. Herrmann shows, however, that Soviet paper-tiger images of the opponent and imperial images of the region are changing, thereby explaining the withdrawal of Soviet troops from Afghanistan.

Milan Hauner examines whether domino and bandwagon thinking are new phenomena, tracing Russian and Soviet conceptions of the Great Game in Asia during the century before World War II. He argues that domino ideas have historically been associated with bipolarity, and that multipolar conditions called forth different strategic conceptions. Insofar as the world may be becoming more multipolar, a decline in domino thinking would seem to follow from Hauner's argument.

For readers who want to consider the essays with the five questions listed above in mind, I offer here some hypothetical answers to them. I will return to these hypotheses in a concluding chapter, judging them in light of the evidence presented in this volume as well as evidence drawn from other historical cases.

1. What Have Statesmen Believed?

There is little question that American statesmen and strategists have very frequently argued in public and in private that failures to prevent, or at least to resist, communist expansion in the periphery would make it harder to contain further expansion. Their reasons vary: local victories would embolden the U.S.S.R. or China, boost the morale of local radical movements, add resources to the communist camp, and dishearten American allies. Usually they have argued that states near a fallen domino would suffer direct and strong effects, but they have even portrayed European allies as directly endangered by peripheral defeats.[16] After a domino has fallen, however, they have always argued that redoubled efforts to show resolve and shore up threatened positions could prevent further dominoes from falling.[17]

Other questions are more contentious. Have the Soviets anticipated that American setbacks will be cumulative? Have they worried about their own dominoes? Do aggressor states in general anticipate a favorable bandwagon as much as status quo states fear an unfavorable one?

Among the various domino mechanisms, which do statesmen focus on the most: the susceptibility of the target, their own credibility as allies, the accumulation of resources by the successful expansionist, or the intensity of expansionist's desire to push hard on the dominoes? Though there is evidence that all of these factors are considered, the essays in this volume suggest that the view of the opponent's intentions is crucial. Whether it is logical or not, defenders readily conjure up nightmares of falling dominoes whenever they perceive an opponent who is strongly inclined to push.[18] Consequently, several of the chapters in this volume are at least as much about images of the enemy as they are about domino beliefs *per se*.

Finally, to what extent have statesmen really believed their own domino arguments? Our contributors see domino perceptions as sincerely rooted, to some degree, in the policymakers' belief system or other cognitive propensities. However, some of the essays also note that policymakers consciously exaggerate domino dangers as a way of selling alliance commitments to a reluctant public and Congress, turn the domino theory on and off depending on their tactical needs of the moment, and sometimes get trapped by their own domino rhetoric.[19]

2. Do Dominoes Really Fall?

The domino theory is neither wholly true nor wholly false. On the one hand, it would be a gross exaggeration to contend that domino dynamics operate so strongly that any peripheral defeat is very likely to touch off a chain of setbacks jeopardizing core positions. On the other hand, it is also untenable to argue that more limited chain reactions never occur, that small powers always balance fiercely against expansionists, or that the balance of power operates so automatically that an insular great power like the United States can ride scot free on the balancing efforts of others.

Consequently, it is important not only to study whether balancing or bandwagoning is more common, but also to test hypotheses about *when* domino effects are more and less likely. Our contributors suggest that defeats are most likely to cumulate when (1) target states are weak domestically,[20] small in size, geographically contiguous, or bereft of strong allies;[21] (2) the initial fallen domino is similar in its main characteristics to a number of subsequent targets; (3) the initial domino is a major country, whose fall adds greatly to the expansionists' resources or raises questions about the status quo power's willingness to fight even for vital interests; and (4) military technology facilitates the offensive.[22] Conditional hypotheses of this type can guide judgments about the need to resist in particular cases. They can also guide estimates of how vulnerable to domino effects the defender's position as a whole is likely to be. In the conclusion, I will argue, based on these hypotheses, that America's current strategic position is highly domino-resistant.

3. What Are the Consequences of Domino Beliefs?

The most direct and obvious consequence of domino beliefs is to encourage intervention, often military, in the geopolitical periphery. The universal corollary to the belief that defeats cumulate is the deduction that it is worth paying high costs in the short run to prevent adverse momentum, which would be even more costly to reverse later. Beyond this, the consequences of domino beliefs are more disputable, hinging largely on whether they are true or not.

If dominoes really do fall and if an expansionist opponent is really pushing hard on them, then domino beliefs held by the defender encourage an appropriate, interventionist response. This minimizes the defender's costs and risks, at least in the long run. It may also head off a deepening of the antagonism between the defender and the expansionist, by using a small issue to send a clear signal that aggression doesn't pay, rather than waiting for a costlier, more dangerous showdown over some vital issue. If the opponent really is a paper tiger—aggressive, but easily deterred by a sharp rebuke—acting on the domino theory will keep him well behaved. Thus, fighting now for Korea is better than fighting in a few years for Europe, evaluated in terms of both likelihood of success and costs of the conflict.

But if dominoes don't tend to fall, then interventions in the far-flung periphery simply sap the strength of the defender, making him more vulnerable to assaults on more vital positions.[23] As for reputational consequences, it may harm the defender's credibility more to fight and lose an untenable outpost rather than simply defining it as outside his "defense perimeter." Thus erroneous belief in the domino theory may actually undermine the credibility of the defender's deterrent posture by leading him to intervene in quagmires that sap his strength, dismay his allies, and undermine domestic support for the maintenance of international commitments. Moreover, if the opponent is motivated not by a desire to roll up a string of victories, but by a strategy of forward defense of his own dominoes, then interventionism will simply fuel a conflict spiral. That is, if the opponent is not a paper tiger, but a prickly hedgehog—unaggressive, but fierce in self-defense—then acting on domino beliefs will cause an unneeded conflict.[24]

4. Causes of Domino Beliefs

Though defeats do sometimes snowball, American statesmen have tended to overrate this possibility, according to several of the contributors to this volume. They have feared domino processes where there were none and exaggerated their consequences when they did exist. As I will argue in the conclusion, history records many instances of this typical bias in other times and countries as well. On the other hand, the strength of domino imagery has varied across states, across individuals, and over time. Any explanation of domino thinking, therefore, must explain both its general prevalence and these variations.

Our contributors and other writers have found three general kinds of explanations for domino thinking: rational hedging, cognitive psychological, and domestic political. The latter two explanations come in numerous variants.

Rational Hedging

In the rough-and-tumble anarchy of international life, it makes sense to worry about the worst thing that can happen. Status quo states, in particular, are likely to play the game in a way that minimizes their maximum loss. Dominoes may not fall, but then again they may. Under uncertainty, a "minimax" strategist might proceed under the assumption that falling dominoes were likely, since underestimating this probability would threaten his very survival, whereas overestimating it would merely incur unnecessary, but finite costs.[25]

Of course, for this to be a rational gamble, the risk-averse defender would have to know somehow that his opponent was more likely to be a paper-tiger expansionist than a prickly hedgehog. Otherwise, his minimax strategy might bring on precisely the disaster that he hoped to avoid. For example, Imperial Japan and Imperial Germany fought for defensible security perimeters against largely imagined enemies, and thereby unnecessarily created an encircling alliance of real, mortal enemies. This is consistent with our contributors' findings that domino beliefs correlate highly with perceptions of an extremely aggressive enemy. The more aggressive the opponent seems, the more it makes sense to hedge against falling dominoes rather than against unnecessary conflict spirals.

The hypotheses of rational hedging suggests several other tests. Being basically rational, this kind of domino theorist should be sensitive to the conditions, enumerated above, that make domino dynamics more or less likely. For example, he should expect reputational consequences of forsaking Quemoy in Taiwan, not in Japan; he should expect reputational consequences of losing Vietnam in Thailand, not in Europe. Moreover, though inclined to worst-case analysis, the rational hedger should reason logically and search for information in appropriate ways.

Cognitive Psychological Explanations

Many of the contributors explain exaggerated expectations of falling dominoes as the result of one or more principles of cognitive psychology. In the American case, in particular, they note that the *lessons of the past*, in particular the Munich analogy and the experience of falling dominoes in Eastern Europe, predisposed American decision makers to see falling dominoes in Asia as well. In the jargon of the psychologists, the domino theory was a highly available schema in the

American internationalists' belief system, firmly implanted in the formative late 1930s and readily applied to any situation that offered even a superficial resemblance.[26]

Skeptics, however, argue that lessons are picked to fit whatever argument the politician wants to make at the moment. This suggests some possible tests. When American statesmen chose not to intervene in force, as in Indochina in 1954 or Angola in late 1975, is this to be explained by the salience of different lessons, or by other factors? Did other great powers that feared falling dominoes also have formative Munich-like experiences?

If not, it may be worthwhile to look for explanations for domino thinking that go beyond salient, formative lessons. Several other cognitive hypotheses, relying on typical biases in the way people process and organize information, offer alternative explanations of greater or lesser plausibility. Here I will list a few possibilities, some of which receive some support from the essays in this volume.

Simple extrapolation. A very simple way to gauge future trends is to extrapolate current trends indefinitely. Thus, if one domino falls, the expansionist gains momentum and is expected to keep gaining more. But do people actually reason this way? One study contends that people exaggerate the phenomenon of the "hot hand" in basketball, but other studies show that most people are biased in the opposite direction. They erroneously think, for example, that a coin is more likely to come up tails on the next trial if it has landed on heads in the last one.[27] There is no reason to think that bandwagoning schemas are simpler or more natural than balancing schemas.

Misjudging cumulative probability. Cognitive psychologists have found that people overestimate the likelihood of outcomes that will occur only if a number of independent causes are all present. For example, let's say that the chances of the French building a dam at Fashoda were 0.8, the independent chance that this would ruin Egyptian agriculture was 0.8, the independent chance that this in turn would lead to the British loss of Suez was 0.8, and so on. In such circumstances, people tend to estimate the cumulative probability of the whole chain of events as close to 0.8, whereas in fact the probability is about 0.5 that all three events will occur, and it is even less for chains with more independent parts.[28]

Of course, this may not be the proper model for the domino theory, which assumes that the sequential probabilities are not entirely independent. Even if it is a partially valid model, however, there remains the problem of the double standard by which policymakers calculate cumulative probabilities. As Jervis's essay notes, policymakers often fear that a failure to carry out a threat will harm their credibility in future showdowns, but they worry more rarely that reneging on a promise will have adverse reputational consequences.[29] Similarly, most statesmen seem to worry more about the cascading of fallen dominoes than they do about the spiraling of conflict as the result of intense regional competition.

Attribution errors and actor/observer differences. Psychologists have found that people explain their own behavior differently than they explain the behavior of others.[30] People tend to say that others' behavior is determined by their innate dispositions, whereas their own behavior is shaped by the force of circumstances. In conflict relationships, this leads to the inference that the other is innately aggressive, whereas the self is primarily reactive and defensive. Coupled with the minimax hedging hypothesized above, this would explain why statesmen worry a lot about aggressive opponents pushing on potential dominoes, while they worry less about reactive opponents getting trapped in a conflict spiral. This explanation fits our contributors' finding that domino beliefs are closely correlated to images of a very aggressive opponent. It does not explain, however, why statesmen who perceive aggressive opponents do not worry more about getting lured into costly struggles in peripheral arenas of competition.

Observers not only have difficulty imagining the threats to which others are reacting, they also find it hard to think about the difficulties blocking the other's path. People are always worrying about their own problems, thinking about how to overcome them, not about the problems of others. Thus, unable to easily imagine barriers to the opponent's success, domino scenarios seem plausible.

A related cognitive bias may reinforce these effects. According to some studies, people tend to offer dispositional explanations for aggressive behavior, but situational explanations for cooperative behavior. That is, "he attacked my ally because he is innately aggressive," but "he accepted my arms control proposal because my military build-up gave him no alternative." This bias, say the psychologists, is rooted in people's expectations that the policies they adopt toward the opponent will work. Thus, when the opponent cooperates, they think "my policy caused it," but when he is aggressive, they say "that proves not that my policy was wrong but that he is inherently aggressive." A pattern of such biased inferences could easily convince the policymaker that his opponent is a paper tiger, inherently aggressive yet deterrable by firm resistance. Like the domino theory, the paper-tiger image of the adversary counsels early and active opposition to keep the paper tiger on a short leash.[31]

These perceptual biases occur, say some psychologists, because of the different focus of attention of actors and observers and differences in the availability of information to them. Observers naturally see the other as salient, and so offer explanations in which his personal characteristics are prominent. In contrast, actors see not themselves, but the environmental forces constraining them. Often, observers have little information about the other's view of how external forces are threatening or constraining him.

This suggests some tests. If these hypotheses are true, then attribution biases promoting domino worries should decline when observers have more information about how the other really makes his calculations. They should also be less prevalent among people with greater knowledge of the opposing country. Area specialists, whose task is to reconstruct the opponent's calculations, should be less prone to dispositional explanations and domino thinking. Conversely, the military and other national security specialists, whose task is to parry the opponent's possible machinations, should be more prone to both.

Finally, if actor/observer differences are a cause of domino and paper-tiger images, then defenders should fear falling dominoes, but self-conscious expansionists should not expect a favorable bandwagon, since attribution biases will make them see potential targets and their backers as innately hostile and resistant. Hopf's chapter suggests that this may be the case, but as I will argue in the conclusions, most past expansionist have counted on the illusory bubble of bandwagon hopes.

Domestic Political Explanations

Domestic explanations for the domino theory see it as an argument used by proponents of increased international commitments. Because of their political roles or institutional or economic interests, some people and groups are especially favorable toward high levels of military and economic aid, military interventions abroad, high defense spending, and widespread alliances. When other arguments are insufficient to convince the rest of the body politic to bear the costs of these commitments, internationalists invoke the domino theory, which purports to show that it is cheaper to incur the moderate costs of an active policy now in order to avoid still greater costs of stopping the juggernaut once it has begun to gain momentum.[32] In this view, purveyors of domino thinking may be cynical manipulators of public or elite opinion, or they may actually believe the domino theory, in the sense that most proponents of self-serving ideologies sincerely believe that their own interests coincide with the interests of the broader group.

Three groups are most likely to use the domino theory to help sell a policy of extensive international commitments: certain economic or military interest groups, the state, and politicians trying to put together a ruling coalition. Domino thinking is widespread because people and groups with a motive to sell it are present in almost every historical context. Domino thinking varies in its intensity, however, because its proponents may vary in their power, persuasiveness, or the strength of their internationalist motivations.

Economic or military interest groups. A wide variety of groups and interests have invoked domino or bandwagon theories in order to "sell their product" to the government or the public at large.[33] Admiral Tirpitz invented his famous "risk fleet" theory to explain why Britain would jump on the German bandwagon if Germany built a fleet that threatened her. The "man on the spot" along the turbulent frontier of the British Empire was always informing Whitehall that a small increase in London-financed troops in his region would shore up a vulnerable domino and greatly diminish security costs in the long run. As Salisbury observed, "it is always open to the military authorities to discover in the immediate vicinity of the area to which your orders confine them, some danger against which it is absolutely necessary to guard, some strategic position whose invaluable qualities will repay ten times any risk or cost that its occupation may involve."[34] Wall Street bankers with extensive European economic interests founded the Council on Foreign Relations after World War I for the express purpose of convincing American public and elite opinion of the risks of isolationism.[35]

Apart from the question of whether strategic beliefs do in fact correlate with economic or bureaucratic interests, there is also the question of how these ideas and interests gain success in the political arena. Hypotheses might stress propaganda resources (e.g., Krupp steel's financial support for the German Navy League), information monopolies (e.g., French colonial officers selling the expedition to Fashoda), or penetration of the state (e.g., Wall Street domination of key State Department posts after World War II).

The state. Domino and bandwagon theories are often propounded not by narrowly self-interested bureaucracies or economic groups but by people at the pinnacle of the state—presidents, secretaries of state, and the like. Eisenhower, for example, coined the domino metaphor. Truman sold aid to Greece and Turkey in terms of the bandwagon psychology that their fall would spur in Western Europe. A century earlier, Palmerston had popularized a domino theory about Russian threats to India and the Mediterranean. While all three believed these arguments to some degree, they also consciously exaggerated them when necessary to sell internationalist policies.

Why would the state try to sell internationalism to a reluctant society? The most straightforward explanation is that the state is the principal institution whose task is to maintain the security and competitive position of the state in the international arena. Those who occupy the key roles in the state organization must, therefore, continually remind social groups and citizens of the need to sacrifice their immediate, parochial aims toward this common good. To put it in a less benign light, we should remember that "states are war-makers, and war is a state-maker."[36] Demanding international tasks allow the state to extract resources from society and enhance its control over autonomous social actors. In short, the domino theory helps the state sell *its* product.

Coalition politics. Top government leaders are not only caretakers of a state apparatus. They are also leaders of a ruling coalition. Their strategic concepts may reflect the need to keep a heterogeneous, even centripetal coalition from flying apart. For example, Brezhnev consolidated his personal rule by putting forth the "correlation of forces" theory of detente, a bandwagon theory purporting to explain how a Soviet military build-up and Third World expansion would be consistent with—indeed would cause—detente and an expansion of sorely needed economic ties with the West. Brezhnev presumably believed this, but it also served as a convenient formula for reconciling idealogues and the military to a detente policy that was needed to head off Kosygin's calls for domestic economic reform. Bandwagon mythology helped to paper over the cracks in an internally inconsistent coalition.[37]

Similarly, American statesmen have sometimes used the domino theory to rationalize international commitments that were forced on them by the logic of domestic politics. Truman and Acheson initially used the domino specter to win support for commitments they *did* want in Europe and the Near East. But then the China lobby and Republicans who were less keen on European commitments began to ask why the same domino logic did not apply to Asia.[38] Acheson's preferred defense perimeter in Asia, which excluded Taiwan and Korea, became untenable after the rise of McCarthyism and the attack on South Korea. Political necessity increasingly thrust forward figures like John Foster Dulles and Dean Rusk, whose pro-Taiwan policies kept the bipartisan internationalist coalition buffered from what the more unyielding Acheson called "the attack of the primitives."[39] While older research tended to portray Dulles as a thorough going true believer in global militancy, newer research is more inclined to stress his political expediency and opportunistic use of public strategic arguments that he privately rejected.[40] Daniel Ellsberg's theory of the "stalemate machine" attempts to explain the Vietnam quagmire, and its rationalization via the domino theory, in a similar way.[41]

Tests

Testing rational, cognitive, and political explanations for domino thinking against each other is an elusive task. Stephen Walt reminds us, for example, that small allies' bandwagoning threats might prove not that the bandwagon fears of the protector were well founded, but simply that the small ally was bluffing in order to extract greater assistance. Likewise, the frequent invocation of a lesson of history may not prove that formative cognitive processes are at work, but simply that a convenient analogy has been selected to rationalize a policy chosen on other grounds.

It may be helpful to ask what would constitute strong evidence against each of the possible explanations. The rational hedging theory would suffer if actions to shore up dominoes consistently led to overcommitments that strategically weakened the state, and if its statesmen failed to learn from this. The formative lessons theory would suffer if lessons were applied inconsistently, or if individuals or states might just as easily have learned the opposite lesson from their experiences. For example, why were the architects of the Vietnam War more impressed by the Munich analogy and the "who lost China" lesson than by the "no more land wars in Asia" lesson?

The actor/observer theory would suffer if people urged the same policy no matter what attributions they made. Hopf shows, for example, that the Brezhnev leadership pursued the same interventionist policy when they thought America was an unremittingly resistant foe as when they perceived a comparatively inert post-Vietnam America. Similarly, William Taubman has noted a "double whammy" in Stalin's thinking on U.S.-Soviet relations: a cooperative America convinced Stalin he could exploit its weakness with impunity, whereas a resistant America convinced him that aggressive measures were needed to forestall blows from the hostile foe.[42] In such circumstances, we should conclude that attributions about the disposition of the opponent and the causes of his actions are merely incidental to a policy that has been chosen for some other reason.

The political theory would suffer if the preferences of foreign policy factions were rooted in purely intellectual differences, rather than economic or organizational interests. The theory would also suffer if factions won not because of their greater power or propaganda tools, but because international events discredited their opponents' arguments. In that case, international pressure would be the underlying cause, and domestic political pressure would only be a superficial cause, with little if any independent influence on the outcome.

Finally, testing might show not that one theory was always right or wrong, but that a variety of these factors may combine to promote or hinder domino thinking in any given case. For example, as Macdonald shows, American domino beliefs were rooted in the apparent lessons of Munich and the early postwar period, but then were exaggerated and ossified due to the overselling of containment and the politics of building the cold war consensus. In another illustration, it may be that actor/observer biases operate more strongly to produce domino perceptions in bipolar settings, when attention is focused on a single major adversary, than in multipolar conditions.[43]

5. Policy Implications

The essays in this volume speak to two kinds of policy question: (1) What kind of containment strategy should America pursue? and (2) How can America's policymakers and public be persuaded to pursue the appropriate strategy?

On the former question, our contributors generally hold that costly interventions in the geopolitical periphery, justified by domino or bandwagon arguments, are warranted only under certain limited conditions. The Korean War, in the view of some, might be a good prototype for the kind of conditions that could give rise to justifiable domino fears: major allies uncertain of their protector's resolve and plagued with domestic weaknesses, a blatant military challenge to one of the protector's existing commitments, and the existence of analogous cases for which inaction might serve as a precedent (e.g., divided Korea as similar to divided Germany; Indochina, Taiwan, and even Japan as logical dominoes falling before the wave of Asian communism).

Indeed, such conditions, apart from the external military threat, help explain the collapse of the East European dominoes in 1989. Perhaps the most interesting aspect of the domino-like collapse of communist governments in Eastern Europe is that it did not immediately give rise to an interventionist backlash on the part of the Soviet Union, despite its implications for additional dominoes among the Soviet peripheral republics. Extrapolating from the arguments advanced by contributors' to this volume, the Soviet new thinker's equanimity must have been due in part to their belief that the West did not intend to exploit this collapse militarily. The clear implication for Western policy is to continue to reassure the Soviet Union along these lines, in order to forestall a Soviet interventionist backlash fueled by domino fears.

But how can America's policymakers and public be persuaded to adopt and maintain a realistic grand strategy, which is neither untainted by excessive domino fears nor provocative of such fears among other great powers? The essays in this volume provide less guidance on this point, because they are equivocal about the causes of domino mythology. To the extent that formative lessons are crucial, the countervailing lessons of the Vietnam War may have already canceled out or even overcompensated for the lessons of Munich. If actor/observer misperceptions are the problem, however, Raymond Garthoff's reconstruction of the demise of detente in the 1970s suggests that attributional double standards were still at work, even in the period of the post-Vietnam syndrome.[44] If so, one solution is for American foreign policy elites to pay attention to works like those of Hopf and Blum, who replace a priori perceptual instincts with hard evidence in reconstructing Soviet views of American motives and resolve.[45]

If domestic politics is the problem, however, different remedies must be considered. Joseph Nye and his co-contributors to a volume on *The Making of America's Soviet Policy* worry that the problems of overselling and oscillation in American containment strategy are actually getting worse due to the post-Vietnam break-up of the elite cold war consensus, which eliminated the moderate "establishment" as an effective buffer between mass whims and foreign policy.[46] They counsel reforging a new elite consensus to recreate the buffer. However, elite consensus-building may be part of the problem, not part of the solution. The creators of the cold war consensus—people like Acheson, Dulles, Nitze, and Rusk—had to oversell the domino theory in order to promote and protect the moderate internationalist policy agenda of the East Coast establishment and the internationalist American state. Rather than resurrecting a unified foreign policy establishment, an alternative solution would be to break down even further the information monopolies, propaganda advantages, and operational secrecy exploited by national security elites and bureaucrats.[47]

The following essays will not definitively answer my five questions about the nature, validity, consequences, causes, and antidotes for domino and bandwagon beliefs. They do, however, offer a diverse body of evidence that suggests some preliminary answers. More important, they provide a conceptually sophisticated window onto the problem, which we hope will open new avenues for research.

Notes

1. See, for example, John Lewis Gaddis, "The Strategic Perspective: The Rise and Fall of the Defense Perimeter Concept, 1947–1951," in *Uncertain Years,* ed. Dorothy Borg and Waldo Heinrichs (New York: Columbia University Press, 1980), 61–118; William Stueck, *The Road to Confrontation: American Policy toward China and Korea, 1947–1950* (Chapel Hill: University of North Carolina Press, 1981); Larry Berman, *Planning a Tragedy: The Americanization of the War in Vietnam* (New York: Norton, 1984).

2. See John Lewis Gaddis, *Strategies of Containment* (New York: Oxford University Press, 1982).

3. Robert H. Johnson, "Exaggerating America's Stakes in Third World Conflicts," *International Security* 10:3 (Winter 1985–1986): 66; Jerome Slater, "Dominoes in Central America: Will They Fall? Does It Matter?" *International Security* 12:2 (Fall 1987): 105–34. In a recent reassertion of the domino concept, Senator Robert Dole has said that "each of the dominoes that the [Democrats'] attitude of apology [to America's foes] helps to topple into the pocket of Communism is also a building block for further Communist power." *New York Times*, Mar. 24, 1988.

4. Paul Kennedy, *The Rise and Fall of the Great Powers* (New York: Random House, 1987), 51, notes that sixteenth-century Spain was led by a domino theory into a debilitating war in the Low Countries. See the concluding chapter of the present volume for more examples.

5. R. E. Robinson and J. A. Gallagher, *Africa and the Victorians* (London: Macmillan, 1961); G. N. Sanderson, *England, Europe and the Upper Nile, 1882–1899* (Edinburgh: Edinburgh University Press, 1965).

6. John Galbraith, "The Turbulent Frontier," in *International Politics*, ed. Robert Art and Robert Jervis (Boston: Little, Brown, 1973).

7. See Kennedy, *Rise and Fall*; Robert Gilpin, *War and Change in International Politics* (Princeton, N. J.: Princeton University Press, 1981); Robert Jervis, "Cooperation under the Security Dilemma," *World Politics* 30:2 (January 1978): 167–214.

8. This paucity is noted by Slater, "Dominoes," 105 n.1.

9. In addition to the works cited by Berman, Stueck, and Gaddis, see also Leslie Gelb with Richard Betts, *The Irony of Vietnam: The System Worked* (Washington, D. C.: Brookings Institution, 1979).

10. Thomas Schelling, *Arms and Influence* (New Haven, Conn.: Yale University Press, 1966), esp. chap. 2; with qualifications discussed by Robert Jervis, "Deterrence Theory Revisited," *World Politics* 31:2 (January 1979); and Jervis, *Perception and Misperception in International Politics* (Princeton, N. J.: Princeton University Press, 1976), chap. 3.

11. Apart from Hopf's essay in the present volume, the only systematic piece is William Zimmerman and Robert Axelrod, "The 'Lessons' of Vietnam and Soviet Foreign Policy," *World Politics* 34:1 (October 1981): 1–24, which surveys the Soviet press for less than three months in the winter of 1972–1973.

12. Stephen Van Evera, "Causes of War" (Ph. D. diss., University of California, Berkeley, 1984); Robert Jervis, "Systems Theories and Diplomatic History," in *Diplomacy,* ed. Paul Gordon Lauren (New York: Free Press, 1979).

13. The chief exception is Van Evera. See Ernest May, *"Lessons" of the Past* (New York: Oxford University Press, 1973), on the Munich analogy.

14. Kenneth Waltz, "Another Gap?" in *Containment, Soviet Behavior, and Grand Strategy*, ed. Robert Osgood (Berkeley, Calif.: Institute of International Studies Policy Papers in International Affairs #16, 1981): 81. For the full development of this argument, see Kenneth Waltz, *Theory of International Politics* (Reading, Mass.: Addison-Wesley, 1979); and Stephen Walt, *The Origins of Alliances* (Ithaca, N. Y.: Cornell University Press, 1987). Johnson and Slater offer less theoretical critiques of the domino theory. See also the articles by Walt, Michael Desch, and Steven David in *International Security* 14:1 (Summer 1989).

15. On the latter point, see esp. 98–101.

16. On the latter point, see Larson, chap. 4.

17. Jervis in this volume, chap. 2.

18. This point is especially prevalent in Macdonald, chap. 5, and also in Jervis's chapter 2, pp. 35–36. In the conclusions, I raise questions about this finding.

19. See Macdonald in this volume, chap. 5; Robert Pollard, *Economic Security and the Origins of the Cold War, 1949–1950* (New York: Columbia University Press, 1985), on the selling of the Marshall Plan; Nancy Bernkopf Tucker, *Patterns in the Dust: Chinese-American Relations and the Recognition Controversy, 1949–1950* (New York: Columbia University Press, 1983), 11, on rhetorical entrapment.

20. Larson in this volume, chap. 4.

21. Walt, *Origins of Alliance*.

22. Jervis in this volume, chap. 2, and in *Perception and Misperception*, chap. 3.

23. In the years before the Korean War, this was probably the predominant view among American decision makers. See Gaddis, "Defense Perimeter"; and Gaddis, *Strategies of Containment*.

24. Analysis supporting these points may be found in Jervis, *Perception and Misperception*, chap. 3, or in Jervis in this volume, chap. 2.

25. Macdonald makes this argument on p. 134 in this volume.

26. For a discussion of schema theory, see Deborah Welch Larson, *Origins of Containment* (Princeton, N. J.: Princeton University Press, 1985), 50–57.

27. Amos Tversky and Daniel Kahneman, "Judgment under Uncertainty: Heuristics and Biases," in *Judgment under Uncertainty: Heuristics and Biases*, ed. Kahneman, Paul Slovic, and Tversky (Cambridge: Cambridge University Press, 1982), 7–8.

28. Amos Tversky and Daniel Kahneman, "Judgments of and by Representativeness," in Kahneman, Slovic, and Tversky, *Judgment under Uncertainty*, 90–98. See also Nancy Kanwisher, "Cognitive Heuristics and American Security Policy," *Journal of Conflict Resolution* 33:4 (December 1989): 663–65.

29. Jervis in this volume, p. 25.

30. The following hypotheses are derived from literature summarized in Harold Kelley and John Michaela, "Attribution Theory and Research," *Annual Review of Psychology* 31 (1980): 457–501; and Lee Ross, "The Intuitive Psychologist and His Shortcomings: Distortions in the Attribution Process," in *Advances in Experimental Social Psychology,* ed. Leonard Berkowitz, vol. 10 (New York: Academic Press, 1977), 184–87.

31. A similar argument may be found in Jervis, *Perception and Misperception*, chap. 9.

32. I will develop this argument in a forthcoming book, *Myths of Empire: Domestic Politics and Strategic Ideology* (Ithaca, N. Y.: Cornell University Press, forthcoming in 1991), and more briefly in the conclusions to the present volume. Van Evera, "Causes of War," makes a similar argument.

33. Van Evera, "Causes of War."

34. Malcolm E. Yapp, *Strategies of British India: Britain, Iran, and Afghanistan, 1798–1850* (Oxford: Clarendon Press, 1980), 589.

35. Frank Costigliola, *Awkward Dominion* (Ithaca, N. Y.: Cornell University Press, 1984), 69–75.

36. Charles Tilly, "Does Modernization Breed Revolution?" in *Revolution,* ed. Jack Goldstone (New York: Harcourt, Brace, Jovanovich, 1986), 56.

37. Drawing on the arguments of several Sovietologists, I develop this argument in "The Gorbachev Revolution: A Waning of Soviet Expansionism?" *International Security* 12:3 (Winter 1987–1988): esp. 106–107. The prototype for this sort of analysis is Eckart Kehr, *Economic Interest, Militarism, and Foreign Policy* (Berkeley: University of California, 1977).

38. Thomas Paterson, "If Europe, Why Not China?" *Prologue* 13:1 (Spring 1981): 19–38.

39. For background, see Warren I. Cohen, "Acheson, His Advisers, and China, 1949–1950"; and Gaddis, "Defense Perimeter," both in Borg and Heinrichs, *Uncertain Years*, 13–118. These works, unlike some earlier books on the domestic politics of the Korean War, show the important role of the domestic context, especially for China policy, while also giving significant weight to our factors.

40. See especially Ronald Pruessen, *John Foster Dulles: The Road to Power* (New York: Free Press, 1982); but also John Lewis Gaddis, *The Long Peace* (New York: Oxford University Press, 1987), esp. chap. 6; H. W. Brands, Jr., *Cold Warriors* (New York: Columbia University Press, 1988); and David Allan Mayers, *Cracking the Monolith: Sino-Soviet Alliance, 1949–1955* (Baton Rouge: Louisiana State University Press, 1986). Note also Morton Halperin and Tang Tsou, "United States Policy toward the

Offshore Islands," *Public Policy* 15 (1966): 119–38, regarding the calculated bureaucratic and political use of the domino argument in Taiwan Straits crises.

41. Ellsberg, "The Quagmire Myth and the Stalemate Machine," in Ellsberg, *Papers on the War* (New York: Simon and Schuster, 1972), 42–135. Note the related evidence in Gaddis, *Strategies of Containment*, 242; Berman, *Planning a Tragedy*, 22–23, 110, 150–51.

42. Taubman, *Stalin's American Policy* (New York: Norton, 1982), 10 and passim.

43. See Jervis in this volume, p. 42, for a related discussion.

44. Raymond Garthoff, *Detente and Confrontation* (Washington, D. C.: Brookings Institution, 1985).

45. An exceptionally useful work of this genre is Franklyn Griffiths, "The Sources of American Conduct: Soviet Perspectives and Their Policy Implications," *International Security* 9:2 (Fall 1984): 3–50.

46. Joseph S. Nye, ed., *The Making of America's Soviet Policy* (New Haven, Conn.: Yale University Press, 1984).

47. I will elaborate on this point in chap. 10.

2

Domino Beliefs and Strategic Behavior

ROBERT JERVIS

We have had a very careful study of the situation made by our intelligence community, by the State Department officials, by the Joint Chiefs of Staff, and they are unanimous to the effect that if Quemoy were lost either through assault or surrender . . . this would probably bring about a government [on Formosa] which would eventually advocate union with Communist China; that if this occurred it would seriously jeopardize the anti-Communist barrier, including Japan, the Republic of Korea, the Republic of China, the Republic of the Philippines, Thailand, and Vietnam; that other governments in Southeast Asia such as those of Indonesia, Malaya, Cambodia, Laos, and Burma would probably come fully under communist influence; that Japan . . . would probably fall within the Sino-Soviet orbit, and Australia and New Zealand would become strategically isolated. (Letter from President Dwight D. Eisenhower to Prime Minister Harold Macmillan, September 4, 1958.)

The first and greatest dangers [to Spain in 1635] are those that threaten Lombardy, the Netherlands and Germany. A defeat in any of these three is fatal for this Monarchy, so much so that if the defeat in those parts is a great one, the rest of the monarchy will collapse; for Germany will be followed by Italy and the Netherlands, and the Netherlands will be followed by America; and Lombardy will be followed by Naples and Sicily, without the possibility of being able to defend either. (Adviser to King Philip IV, quoted in Paul Kennedy, *The Rise and Fall of the Great Powers* [New York: Random House, 1988], 51.)

Our retreat from Berlin would be tantamount to an acknowledgment of lack of courage to resist Soviet pressure short of war and would amount to a public confession of weakness under pressure. It would be the Munich of 1948 . . . [and] would raise justifiable doubts in the minds of Europeans as to the firmness of our European policy and our ability to resist the spread of communism. (Robert Murphy, American Political Advisor to Germany, in U.S. Department of State, *Foreign Relations of the U.S., 1948,* vol. 2, *Germany and Austria* [Washington, D.C.: U.S. Government Printing Office, 1973], 920.)

If we let Korea down, the Soviets will keep right on going and swallow up one piece of Asia after another . . . if we were to let Asia go, the Near East would collapse [there is] no telling what would happen in Europe. (President

Harry S. Truman briefing members of Congress, June 27, 1950, quoted in Lloyd Gardner, "Truman Era Foreign Policy: Recent Historical Trends," in Richard Kirkendall, ed., *The Truman Period as a Research Field, a Reappraisal, 1972* [Columbia: University of Missouri Press, 1974], 63.)

If America's efforts for peaceful solutions [in Lebanon] are overwhelmed by brute force, our role in the world is that much weakened everywhere. If we are driven out of Lebanon, . . . the message is sent that relying on the Soviet Union pays off and that relying on the United States is a fatal mistake. (Secretary of State George Schultz, in *Department of State Bulletin,* vol. 83, December 1983, 44.)

We begin to see light. Germany is playing for the highest stakes. If her demands are acceded to either on the Congo or in Morocco, . . . it will mean definitely the subjection of France. The conditions demanded are not such as a country having an independent foreign policy can possibly accept. The details of the terms are not so very important now. This is a trial of strength, if anything. Concession means not loss of interests or loss of prestige. It means defeat, with all its inevitable consequences. (Sir Eyre Crowe, July 18, 1911, in G. P. Gooch and Harold Temperley, eds., *British Documents on the Origins of the War,* vol. VII [London: His Majesty's Stationery Office, 1932], 372.)

If Germany were to allow France to create "a new, great, and valuable colonial territory [in Morocco] . . . , our credit in the world, not only for the moment, but also for all future international actions, suffers an intolerable blow." (Alfred Kiderlen, German Foreign Minister during the Second Moroccan Crisis, quoted in Ima Barlow, *The Agadir Crisis* [Chapel Hill: University of North Carolina Press, 1940], 266.)

It is a most critical moment in European politics. If Russia is not checked [in her demands against Turkey], the Holy Alliance will be revived in aggravated form and force. Germany will have Holland: and France, Belgium and England will be in a position I trust I shall never live to witness. If we act in the manner I have generally indicated, we shall probably in conclusion obtain some commanding stronghold in Turkey from which we need never recede. (Prime Minister Disraeli during the Eastern Crisis of 1877–1878, quoted in R. W. Seton-Watson, *Disraeli, Gladstone, and the Eastern Question* [New York: Norton, 1972], 109.)

Lord Salisbury said that a friend told him "that Russia was in Armenia, that Armenia is the key to Syria, that Syria is the key to Egypt, and that anyone advancing into Egypt has the key to Africa." That is characteristic of the apprehensions I hear around me. It has generally been acknowledged to be madness to go to war for an idea, but if anything is more unsatisfactory, it is to go to war against a nightmare. (Lord Salisbury on the Eastern Crisis of 1877–1878, quoted in Seton-Watson, 222.)

Is this the end of an old adventure or is it the beginning of a new? Is this the last attack upon a small State, or is it to be followed by others? Is this, in fact, a step in the direction of an attempt to dominate the world by force?

(Prime Minister Neville Chamberlain, speech in Birmingham after the German takeover of Czechoslovakia, printed in Chamberlain, *The Struggle for Peace* (London: Hutchinson, 1940), 418.)

Many foreign policy disagreements turn on different evaluations of the consequences of concessions and limited defeats.[1] States often stand firm in a confrontation, not because the issue is important when taken in isolation, but because they believe that how it is resolved will strongly influence the course of other events, often far removed in time, substance, and geography. Although President Eisenhower is credited with inventing the metaphor of falling dominoes, the phenomena and beliefs are ancient. Here we will examine the internal structures, logics, and implications of these beliefs and then briefly analyze their validity.

By domino beliefs I mean the expectation that a defeat or retreat on one issue or in one area of the world is likely to produce, through a variety of mechanisms discussed later, further demands on the state by its adversaries and defections from its allies. Two aspects of these beliefs are unusual. First, we often expect that decision makers will focus on the short run. But here they are looking well into the future. In criticizing the British attempt to overthrow Nasser in 1956 because of their concerns about what might happen years later if they did not, Eisenhower said that he had "insisted long and earnestly that you cannot resort to force in international relationships because of your fear of what might happen in the future."[2] The British policy certainly was unwise, but few statesmen, even Eisenhower himself, would be willing to adopt his standard.

That the immediate issue is not a vital one is beside the point. As Palmerston noted, "any nation which were to act upon the principle of yielding to every demand made upon it, if each separate demand could be shown not to involve directly and immediately a vital interest, would at no distant period find itself progressively stripped of the means of defending its vital interests, when those interests came at last to be attacked."[3] Social scientists discovered this principle—Reinhard Selten's "chain store paradox"[4]—almost a century and half later. A large department store which has a monopoly in a small town is faced by the opening of a smaller store which is providing effective competition. It would be less costly to accommodate the newcomer at the sacrifice of some profit than to engage in a price war. But to follow this course of action might be to encourage others to open additional stores, further eating into the department store's profits and power. If the store can succeed not only in driving its competitor out of business, but convincing would-be entrants into the market that they will suffer the same fate, then the cost of a price war is a good investment.

The second point is more familiar but easy to forget when we focus on domino dynamics: as Kenneth Waltz and Stephen Walt have stressed, states usually oppose rather than join the most menacing state in the system. Power balancing is the rule, bandwagoning the exception.[5] This dichotomy goes under other terms as well—negative versus positive feedback, instability versus stability. The question is whether the change of a variable will call up forces that tend to return that variable to its previous value or whether the changes will lead to further movement in the same direction, thus leading to a reinforcing cycle of change. As we will discuss later, domino dynamics can operate through a number of quite different mechanisms. But those who hold the domino beliefs rarely acknowledge that their expectations run contrary to the most widely accepted generalization held by both theorists and practitioners of international politics alike. Instead, they usually imply that positive feedback is the "natural order" in international politics.[6]

What Is at Stake

As long as the particular issue is relatively unimportant, the costs of resisting a strongly motivated adversary are likely to be greater than the costs of conceding. But a decision maker who believes that the failure to resist will undercut his state's general position may conclude that he must stand firm. Those who seek to persuade the state to follow a conciliatory path argue that, on the contrary, the issue is in fact isolated from others. "No war for Danzig" makes sense when the issue is put that way. As Chamberlain said in his speech during the Munich crisis the year before: "However much we may sympathize with a small nation confronted by a big and powerful neighbor, we cannot in all circumstances undertake to involve the whole British Empire in a war simply on her account. If we have to fight it must be on larger issues than that."[7] The classic generic counterargument was made by Pericles in the crucial debate at the start of the Peloponnesian War:

> Let none of you think . . . that we should be going to war for a trifle if we refuse to revoke the Megarian decree. It is a point they make much of, and say that war need not take place if we revoke this decree; but if we do go to war, let there be no kind suspicion in your hearts that the war was over a small matter. For you this trifle is both the assurance and the proof of your determination.[8]

Similar beliefs underpinned the American resistance to Soviet demands in Berlin. During the 1948 Berlin blockade, the American military governor in Germany, General Lucius Clay, stressed to his superiors: "Please remember, emphasize and never stop repeating that currency in Berlin is not the issue—the issue is our position in Europe and plans for western Germany."[9] In the crisis over the access routes thirteen years later, most American statesmen agreed with Dean Acheson that, in Arthur Schlesinger's paraphrase, "West Berlin was not a problem but a pretext. Khrushchev's . . . object . . . was not to rectify a local situation but to test the general American will to resist. . . . Since there was nothing to negotiate, willingness on our part to go to the conference table would be taken in Moscow as evidence of weakness and make the crisis so much the worse." Those who disagreed did so because they did not see the issue in such general terms. "Some who knew the Soviet Union best, like Ambassadors Thompson and Harriman, believed that, on the contrary, Khrushchev's objectives might well be limited. Thompson argued . . . that the predominant Soviet motive was the desire to improve the communist position in Eastern Europe rather than to achieve the world-wide political humiliation of the United

States."[10] Khrushchev himself described the issue in terms that mirrored Acheson's:

> The question of access to West Berlin and the whole question of the peace treaty is for [the Western Powers] only a pretext. If we abandoned our intention of concluding a peace treaty, they would take this as a strategic breakthrough and would in no time broaden the range of their demands. They would demand the abolition of the socialist system in the German Democratic Republic. If they achieved this too, they would, of course, undertake to wrest from Poland and Czechoslovakia the lands that were restored to them under the Potsdam Agreement—and these are Polish and Czechoslovak lands. And if the Western powers achieved all this, they would come forward with their principal demand—that the socialist system be abolished in all the countries of the socialist camp.[11]

In none of the conflicts of cold war in which the United States fought was the country being defended important enough to justify heavy loss of American life. Thus in the words of one presidential adviser: "The real basis of the Korean decision had almost nothing to do with Korea. It had to do with aggression."[12] The central justification for fighting in Vietnam was identical, and in Angola Kissinger argued that "the question is whether America still maintains the resolve to act responsibly as a great power—prepared to face a challenge when it arises."[13] In other words, it is the expectation of future interactions that creates, or at least magnifies, the conflict. Contrary to the well-known cases in which states cooperate in one instance because they think that doing so will encourage cooperation over the long run, when competitiveness is higher, the knowledge that the game will continue makes actors less willing to be conciliatory.

Taken to its limit, this way of looking at the future not only expands but homogenizes the state's interests. Thus Secretary of Defense Weinberger could argue: "In every corner of the globe, America's vital interests are threatened by an ever-growing Soviet military threat."[14] Without a belief in domino dynamics, it is hard to see how even the most important country in the world could have literally vital interests in all parts of the globe. As Douglas Macdonald has noted in his contribution to this volume, this perspective makes it impossible to separate central from peripheral interests: President Kennedy admitted, "I don't know where the non-essential areas are."[15] Indeed, often what makes an interest or a geographical area essential is the fact that it is threatened by the adversary. Because the two states are in a struggle for influence, each must take the opposite side from the other. It would otherwise be hard to explain why the United States is supporting Jonas Savimbi in Angola. The French prime minister reasoned similarly about the rivalry with Britain in the mid–nineteenth century: his country had to weigh in strongly on behalf of one faction in the dispute over royal marriages in Spain because "Palmerston wishes to deny the Duchess her natural rights, we must therefore support them."[16]

Four consequences follow from the inflation of the importance of local disputes caused by the expectation of domino dynamics. First, the adversary can create a crisis at the time and place of its choosing. This is unfortunate, but inevitable: "Unlike those sociable games it takes two to play, with chicken it takes two *not* to play. If you are publicly invited to play chicken and say you would rather not, you have just played."[17] Second, cooperative adjustments of local disputes will be difficult because one obvious mechanism for conflict resolution is nullified. States are often willing to make concessions when they believe that the other's interests are more deeply involved than their own. But if what is at stake is a reputation that will strongly influence future disputes, conflicts have a zero-sum cast.[18] Third, there is at least an element of self-fulfilling prophecy here. The small issue really is vital because it is treated as such. The logic of the defender rests at least in part on the belief that the challenger believes that the defender believes that what is at stake is the future relationship between them. Fourth, as Walt argues, to the extent that the state expects domino dynamics, it cedes great power to its local allies. The threat to abandon them will lack credibility if the client state realizes that the patron believes that a local defeat will endanger its own vital interests.[19]

Threats, Promises, and Credibility

While scholars and decision makers have stressed that failing to live up to threats undermines the state's position, almost nothing has been said about the value of a reputation for living up to promises.[20] Reneging on one promise would seem to produce a sort of domino effect in that other promises, at least of a similar nature, would not be believed. But most current discussions apply this argument only in cases where the promise is the obverse side of a threat, such as the American promise to protect a country against communist predation.[21] Only occasionally is the issue raised in other contexts. For example, during World War II President Roosevelt argued that "the only reason we stand so well with the Russians is that up to date we have kept our promises."[22] Similarly, in 1962 the Russians resisted Chinese pressures to violate their commitment to the United States and supply arms to the Pathet Lao by saying that to do so "would put in the hands of our enemies a great political trump; enabling them to say in their propaganda that socialist countries do not meet their obligations. For example, how would socialist proposals to guarantee a free city status for West Berlin look if socialist countries began to violate the only recently signed Geneva agreement?"[23] But such concerns seem to be exceptional. More typically, few people have raised the question of whether the American reinterpretation of the ABM treaty and apparent desire to abrogate the agreement if strategic defense appears feasible would reduce the value of its other commitments.

Although states seem preoccupied with the credibility of their threats and uninterested in the credibility of their promises, the reverse appears to be the case when they examine others' past behavior. If another state—especially an adversary—fails to live up to a promise, this is sharply noted and taken as evidence that other pledges are worth little. Thus those who claim that the Soviet Union has violated its arms control agreements argue that this behavior shows that future treaties are not likely to restrain a Soviet arms build-up. The belief that the Soviets broke the Basic Principles Agreement when it failed to notify the United States that Egypt and Syria were about to attack Israel in October 1973 led many to conclude that the Soviets would not abide by other promises to respect the "rules of the game." Similarly, when in late 1988 it seemed that the Soviets might not withdraw from Afghanistan by the promised date, a Western diplomat said: "If they're not out by February 15, the cost would be tremendous."[24]

But while states seize on occasions when the adversary appears not to live up to its promises, they seem to pay little attention when others fail to carry out their threats to harm them. The evidence here is particularly impressionistic, but the point is very important because it contradicts one of the central premises of the domino theory. Thus for example, it is not clear that Soviet credibility has greatly suffered from the fact that it failed to respond vigorously to the NATO deployment of INF, returned to the bargaining table after saying it would not do so, and eventually made major concessions. Similarly, the failure of the U.S.S.R. to carry out its threats over Berlin in the first decades of the cold war did not seem to have convinced the United States that Russia was prone to bluff. Neither did the Soviet retreat from Afghanistan lead the United States to draw inferences parallel to those it thought others would draw after it withdrew from Vietnam.

Interconnections

Seemingly small issues are seen as highly consequential because the world is believed to be tightly interconnected.[25] It is one world; behavior cannot be separated into rigid compartments; "we cannot abandon friends in one part of the world without jeopardizing the security of friends everywhere."[26] Thus Oliver Harvey, principal private secretary to the British foreign secretary in the late 1930s, reminded Lord Halifax that "foreign policy must be regarded as a whole. It is not possible to take a strong line in one quarter and an apparently weak one in another indefinitely." As he put it in his diary, "We were weak with Franco, and as a direct consequence Japan is now bullying us. If we are weak again with Japan, we shall have Hitler and Mussolini beating us up. And, above all, if we are weak in helping China, who is fighting our battle, we shall find our own little allies ratting on us. Why shouldn't they?"[27] So it is not surprising that one common axis of disagreement on American policy is between those who focus on the specific situation and the particular nations involved (often State Department officials or area experts), and those who take a global geopolitical perspective (often in the White House or outside foreign policy generalists). The former usually believe that states in a region are strongly driven by domestic concerns and local rivalries; the latter are predisposed to think that these states look to the major powers for their cues and have only little control over their own fates.[28]

Kind of interests. In many cases, the interconnections of domino dynamics work through the kind of national interest that is believed to be involved.[29] We can distinguish between intrinsic interest and what can be called image or reputational interest.

> Intrinsic values are "end values"; they are valued for their own sake rather than for what they contribute to the power relations between the protagonists. They

> include such things as the value we place upon our own independence . . . , the value we attach to the independence (or nonCommunization) of other countries with which we feel a cultural or psychic affinity (apart from what their independence contributes to our own security), the economic values which we find in trading with other free countries (to the extent that these values would be lost should these countries fall under Communist control), and moral values such as self-respect [and] honor.[30]

If the world is not tightly interconnected, behavior will be driven by the intrinsic value of the issue. But if statesmen believe that others are drawing important inferences from their behavior, reputational interest will be crucial. The latter represents the influence the state's behavior will have on other events because of the changes in the expectations about how the state will behave in the future. When others think that the state has defaulted on a pledge, they may be less likely to believe its other promises and threats; when the state has displayed boldness or weakness in one case, they may expect similar behavior in other cases.

When observers believe intrinsic interests to be primary, they will expect the state's behavior to vary greatly depending on the situation. But if reputational interests dominate, similar behavior will be expected over a wide range of situations because observers will attribute the state's behavior to its relatively unchanging characteristics. Thus the argument for why Britain had to suppress the Irish rebellion in 1917 even though doing so detracted from the war effort (more troops were required to maintain order there than could be raised for service in the army): "If you tell your empire in India, in Egypt and all over the world that you have not got the men, the money, the pluck, the inclination, and the backing to restore order in a country within twenty miles of your own shore, you may as well begin to abandon the attempt to make British rule prevail throughout the empire at all."[31]

At first glance arguments like these make perfect sense, and indeed are often correct. But the alternative should be explicated. If a country retreats rather than pay an enormous price for an object of little intrinsic value, it is not clear that others should or will expect it to back down on issues that matter more to it. Thus at the start of the Korean War the State Department intelligence office made a statement that seems self-evident, but in fact is not: "Japanese reactions to the invasion will depend almost entirely upon the course of action pursued by the United States since they will regard the position taken by the United States as presaging U.S. action should Japan be threatened with invasion."[32] But if the Japanese reasoned that their country was much more important to the United States than was South Korea, they would have no reason to expect that an unwillingness to fight for the latter meant that they would not be protected.

What is largely at issue, then, is how others see the world and the kind of interest they believe predicts the state's behavior. This was explicitly recognized by Henry Kissinger in a response to a reporter's question a month before Saigon fell: "With respect to Indo-China, we are not equating the intrinsic importance of each part of the world, and we are not saying that every part of the world is strategically as important to the United States as any other part of the world. . . . [Whether or not we give economic and military aid to Vietnam] is a fundamental question of how we are viewed by all other people."[33] Kissinger's prediction of the dire consequences of not opposing the Soviet Union in Angola ten months later rested on a similar analysis of others' beliefs:

> When one great power tips the balance of forces decisively in a conflict through its military intervention—and meets no resistance—an ominous precedent is set, of grave consequences even if the intervention occurs in a seemingly remote area. . . . To claim that Angola is not an important country, or that the United States has no important interests there, begs the principal question. If the United States is seen to waver in the face of massive Soviet and Cuban intervention, what will be the perception of leaders around the world as they make decisions concerning their future security? And what conclusions will an unopposed superpower draw when the next opportunity for intervention beckons?[34]

George Kennan's argument reveals both the obvious line of rebuttal and its difficulty: "It is important to recognize that not all places . . . are of equal importance. . . . There are some, such as Korea and Cuba, that are of high strategic importance in the sense that they affect the interest of this country and other great powers in an intimate and sensitive way. There are others . . . [that] are of minor significance from the standpoint of the world balance of power. The two must not be equated."[35] But the criteria by which Cuba has "high strategic importance" are far from clear. Indeed, Walter Lippmann's central criticism of Kennan's original article on containment was that this doctrine did not permit discrimination between vital and less central interests.[36] For, as Kennan himself sometimes recognized, defeats in the periphery could demoralize elites and the publics in areas of high intrinsic importance. Psychological connections must either be altered or accommodated.[37]

The belief in the centrality of reputational interests makes extended deterrence (i.e., the deterrence of attacks on allies) both possible and necessary. Extended deterrence is possible because if potential aggressors believe that the defenders see events as interconnected they will conclude that the latter will be willing to pay more to resist than the area's intrinsic value would merit.[38] For the same reason, extended deterrence is necessary because a failure to act at the periphery menaces areas of greater intrinsic value. To put this another way, much of the discussion of the importance of enforcing certain "rules of conduct," especially the prohibition against either superpower using force to change the status quo, rests on the importance of reputational interests. If the Soviets are allowed to use force in Afghanistan, they and others will believe that the Soviets—and perhaps other countries as well—will be permitted to use force elsewhere. Because people expect a high degree of consistency, undesired behavior on one issue or in one area of the world must be resisted in order to prevent it from becoming accepted as normal.

It is often argued that the United States (and presumably the U.S.S.R.) must display high resolve in limited conflicts in order to deter the other superpower from challenging it in places and ways that could produce an all-out war. But "scaling up" from small issues and wars to nuclear confrontations is problematical because the costs and the stakes of the latter are incomparably greater than those of the former. It seems unreasonable that anyone should draw inferences about how the United States might behave at the brink of nuclear war from how it behaved in Vietnam. Indeed, if fighting a small war would markedly increase the American ability to deter the Soviets from menacing its vital interests, then the war in Vietnam would have been a cheap way to protect the United States. This example shows that inferences about resolve can undermine rather than support themselves: if the United States felt that fighting a small war for a country of little intrinsic value would lead others to conclude that it would display high resolve in a dangerous confrontation, then this action actually would not provide reliable evidence because the United States would fight this war in order to create a favorable impression irrespective of whether or not it would run high risks in a nuclear challenge. In many instances, then, for a state to admit that it is behaving as it is in order to bolster its reputation should be self-defeating: there would be no reason for others to see the behavior as typical of what the state will do in the future.

Early Resistance Can Be Effective

If small gains and losses lead to larger ones, it is obviously important to stop the bandwagon before it gathers momentum. Thus in the spring of 1985, the U.S. National Intelligence Officer for the Near East argued that both the United States and the Soviet Union "lack . . . preferred access to Iran. Whoever gets there first is in a strong position to work towards the exclusion of the other."[39] But claims like this imply that the target state will remain passive or that the dynamics of its internal politics will work to the advantage of whichever outside state first recruits important political allies. In faction-ridden countries, this is quite questionable. Shifting the focus to international struggles, proponents of the domino theory often also believe what Jack Snyder has called the Thermopylae Corollary—the claim that it is easier to resist the adversary at the point of the initial challenge than the fend off later attacks on more central values.[40] Thus in 1950, the State Department working group advocating military aid for the French in Indochina argued: "The choice confronting the United States is to support the French in Indochina or face the extension of Communism over the remainder of the continental area of the Southeast Asia and, possibly, farther westward. We then would be obliged to make staggering investments in those areas. . . . It would seem a case of 'Penny wise, Pound foolish' to deny support to the French in Indochina."[41] When the other side is seen as currently weak, the resulting paper-tiger image strongly supports immediate resistance.[42] This kind of claim is implicit in Kissinger's arguments about Angola quoted earlier. A firm American response to the Soviet and Cuban intervention would have been met not by matching escalation but by a retreat because the other side lacked the physical capability and the resolve to carry the struggle to a higher level of violence.

Why can it be believed—or rationalized—that resistance is cheaper and safer when it comes early? First, and most obviously, conquests can add to the aggressor's physical strength. Thus Hitler found it easier to wage World War II once he had absorbed Czechoslovakia's resources. A second reason is that the adversary's initial probes may be tentative because of uncertainty about the defender's reactions. But if the latter retreats once or twice, the former, expecting similar behavior in the future, will become bolder and can be stopped only by stronger resistance. The belief that the other's move is a probe implies both that it must be and that it can be resisted. One reason why the United States thought it was relatively safe to fight in Korea was the belief that if the Russians had been willing to engage in all-out war, they would have launched a full attack rather than move in the periphery.[43] Furthermore, probes can be turned to the defender's advantage, as the Moscow embassy cabled to Washington the day after the outbreak of the Korean War: "Kremlin's Korean adventure . . . offers us opportunity to show that we mean what we say by talking of firmness, and at the same time, to unmask present important Soviet weaknesses before eyes world and particularly Asia where popular concept Soviet power grossly exaggerated as result recent Soviet political and propaganda successes."[44]

Munich

Thermopylae and paper-tiger beliefs, like the domino theory itself, were made more salient by the experience of the 1930s. Thus during the Munich crisis French Prime Minister Edouard Daladier argued to Chamberlain that:

> Germany's real aim was the disintegration of Czechoslovakia [rather than the incorporation of the Sudeten Germans] and the realization of pan-German ideals through a march to the East. . . . The result would be that in a very short time Germany would be master of Europe, and, in particular, of the wheat and petrol of South-Eastern Europe. Within one year we might expect her to turn back against France and Great Britain, who would then have to meet her in much more difficult circumstances than those existing today.[45]

The British analysis differed: "Chamberlain did not accept this view and mentioned that the absorption of Austria had not proved easy and had in any event stirred world opinion."[46] A parallel difference emerged a bit later in a conversation between the British foreign secretary and the French ambassador. According to the former, the latter

> said that if it was only a question of Czechoslovakia, it might be possible to judge the issue differently. The French Government, however, felt that if this contemplated aggression were allowed to pass unresisted, their turn would come next. I said that this really was an argument in favor of a certain war now, against the possibility of war, perhaps in more unfavorable conditions, later. With that argument I had never been able to feel any sympathy: nor did I think that the conclusion of it could be justified.[47]

Although the experience of the 1930s has provided the matrix for later arguments for the need to stop aggressors early, in fact there was no way to deter Hitler—some sort of war was unavoidable. (The only plausible line of rebuttal is to argue that if the Allies had stood firm at Munich, the German generals would have overthrown Hitler. Obviously, a definitive conclusion is hard to draw, but I remain skeptical.) Indeed, Hitler's appetite did not grow with the eating—it was enormous from the beginning. This is not to deny that British and French weakness produced significant bandwagoning—Belgium returned to neutrality; Hungary, Bulgaria, and Rumania supported Germany, and even as major a power as the Soviet Union finally did so, although whether or not in response to Western policy is hotly debated.[48] Furthermore, forcibly resisting Hitler in the first years would have been easier than fighting in 1939. But we should not lose sight of three points. First, even a war fought as early as the 1936 Rhineland crisis would not have been quick or easy.[49] Second, it is not clear whether the year that intervened between Munich and the start of World War II benefited the Germans or the Allies.[50] Third, an early war would have left large segments of the allied countries—let alone Germany—unconvinced that the war was necessary, thereby creating an uneasy postwar world.

Domino Mechanisms

Critics of the domino theory note that it is vague on how a local defeat will be transformed into a far-reaching one. Part of the reason for this is that there are many channels by which these effects can be produced. Indeed, the validity of domino arguments may vary not only according to the circumstances, but also according to the particular mechanism that is supposed to be at work.

The most obvious possibility was mentioned earlier: the conquest or dominance of one area of the world can significantly increase the state's physical resources. Thus in reply to Treasury Secretary Humphrey's claim that the United States did not have a major stake in areas of the Third World outside of the Western Hemisphere, President Eisenhower "pointed out that India contained a population of 350 million, among which was a lot of very good military material."[51] At Munich and in the first years of World War II the Allies failed to appreciate the magnitude of this effect. In other cases, what can be more important is the increased vulnerability of the status quo power, rather than a positive accretion to the resources of the expansionist state. Thus if the Soviet Union could deny the West access to oil from the Persian Gulf, the West would be greatly weakened.

Geography provides a related form of domino dynamics: the fall of one area of the world can give an aggressor access to surrounding areas. In the nineteenth century, British statesmen argued that Russian influence had to be kept out of Afghanistan lest neighboring India be menaced. President Reagan made a similar claim about Central America: "Using Nicaragua as a base, the Soviets and Cubans can become the dominant power in the crucial corridor between North and South America. Established there, they will be in a position to threaten the Panama Canal, interdict our vital Caribbean sea lanes, and ultimately move against Mexico."[52] Indeed, the United States has so many interests that it is easy to argue for the geographical importance of any country, especially if the effects of its falling to communism are seen as spreading from one neighbor to the next. Thus although Henry Kissinger initially rebuffed those who were alarmed by the Allende regime by the quip that "Chile is a dagger pointed at the heart of Antarctica," he soon came around to arguing that its geography did indeed endow it with special importance.

More often, especially in the postwar era, the mechanisms are less direct and more psychological, being mediated by the predictions about the inferences actors will draw from the state's behavior, as I have discussed in earlier sections of this chapter. The state will be especially likely to expect others to draw wide-ranging inferences if it believes that the local conflict is a probe designed to determine the resolve and character of the defender.

The state is also likely to be especially concerned if it thinks that the instruments being used in the local conflict are under the aggressor's control. In addition to the direct use of threats or force, revolutions stimulated from abroad fit this category. Thus one difference between those who accept and those who reject domino theories in recent years is that the former tend to see conflicts and insurgencies as sponsored by the Soviet Union, whereas the latter argue that indigenous actors play the dominant role.[53] Similarly, one reason why Kissinger was adamant that the United States support Pakistan in the 1971 crisis was his belief that "the Soviets encouraged India to exploit Pakistan's travail in part to deliver a blow to our system of alliances, in even greater measure to demonstrate Chinese impotence."[54] This is not to say that the belief that the adversary is responsible for the conflict is a necessary condition for believing that it will draw wide-ranging inferences from the state's behavior. Some argued that it was important for the United States to protect Kuwaiti shipping against Iranian attacks in order to impress the Soviet Union even though that country was not behind the conflict and indeed may have had as much to lose from an Iranian victory as the United States did. But if the adversary is seen as directly involved, the conclusion that it will expect any weakness to be repeated almost always follows.

States need to impress allies as well as adversaries. American statesmen often say they need to stand firm in a conflict in the Third World in order to show the NATO countries that we will protect them. But the expected inferences can be less direct. Thus Nixon's explanations of the "tilt" toward Pakistan in the 1971 contest with India: "If we failed to help Pakistan, then Iran or any other country within the reach of Soviet influence might begin to question the dependability of American support."[55] Particularly important was the fact that this conflict occurred just as the United States was developing its opening to China, an effort in which Pakistan played an important role. One of Kissinger's assistants argued that "we had to show China that we respect a mutual friend and opposed the crossing of international borders. So it was not so much a 'thanks, Yahya, for helping us with China' as demonstrating to China we were a reliable country to deal with."[56]

A country that fails to stand up for one ally is presumed to be unwilling to stand by others as well. This was one reason why Kissinger was so vexed at Congress for cutting off aid to South Vietnam in the dying moments of that country: just as this was happening, the United States was in the midst of trying to broker peace between Egypt and Israel. Later Kissinger attributed the breakdown of these negotiations in part to the congressional limits in Vietnam because "one of our problems was to substitute American assurances for some physical terrain features."[57]

In other cases, the third countries of concern may be neutrals, or at least countries without formal alliances to the status quo power. Since World War II, these states are more likely to fear internal unrest than direct Soviet pressure, let alone invasion. What may lead them to join the Soviet bandwagon is not the belief that an American army will not be coming, but rather the vaguer feeling that communism represents "the wave of the future."[58] For this reason, the views of political elites and mobilizable masses may be as important as the inferences of the top decision makers. This was the dynamic that most worried George Kennan in 1947:

> One of the vital facts to be borne in mind about the international communist movement in the parts of Europe which are not yet under Soviet military and police control is the pronounced "bandwagon" character which that movement bears. By that I mean the fact that a given proportion of the adherents to the movement are drawn to it by no ideological enthusiasm . . . but primarily by the belief that it is the coming thing, the movement of the future . . . and that those who hope to survive—let alone to thrive—in the coming days will be those who had the foresight to climb on the bandwagon when it was still the movement of the future.[59]

Prestige, Credibility, and Inferences

When an earlier contest affects either side's physical power, the arguments for why dominoes should fall are obvious, although not uncontroversial. But when the claim is that the contest has undermined the defender's prestige or credibility, the reasoning needs to be explicated. In many cases, statesmen and analysts stress the importance of precedent, as Kissinger did when he argued that Soviet intervention in Angola was dangerous because it set "an ominous precedent."[60] Similarly, the reason that the United States strongly resisted New Zealand's demand that the United States declare that American warships entering New Zealand's harbors were not carrying nuclear weapons was the fear that Australia, Japan, and other countries would be primed to make the same demand.[61] The way in which precedent is supposed to influence future behavior is not entirely clear, however. It can be argued that behavior sets expectations, if not rules, that will guide how it and others can act later. Thus Abram Chayes notes that the American justification for quarantining Cuba in October 1962 was carefully crafted to avoid legitimating justifications that could be used against the West.[62] While these claims make sense within a framework of shared norms and international law, most of the proponents of this view are Realists who ordinarily stress power and narrow national interests. Doing less violence to the framework they ordinarily use, Realists can employ a second argument—precedents are important because statesmen expect consistency in national behavior. Indeed—though more questionably—not only is the behavior expected to be consistent with previous actions, it is thought to be a simple linear projection of it. Thus if the United States permits Soviet and Cuban intervention in Angola, the Soviet Union and other countries will expect the United States to permit similar behavior in later situations.

A third line of reasoning is a bit more complex. Rather than simply projecting behavior forward in time, observers draw inferences according to their explanations of the state's behavior. Other actors try to determine not only *what* a state did, but also *why* it did it. The underlying assumption is that state motivation is fairly stable and so the reasons why a state took certain actions will be reflected in later behavior. For example, in his speech announcing the American incursion into Cambodia in April 1970, Richard Nixon argued that it is "our will and character that is being tested," and that "if we fail to meet this challenge, all other nations will be on notice that despite its overwhelming power the United States, when a real crisis comes, will be found wanting."[63] To act under duress therefore is likely to produce domino effects. This is one reason why states resist accepting unequal bargains even if the issue at stake is unimportant. It also explains why during the Cuban missile crisis the United States was willing to inform the Soviet Union that it would soon carry out its decision to withdraw IRBMs from Turkey, but resisted openly trading them for the Soviet missiles in Cuba.

If cooperation is viewed not as the product of a laudatory impulse to reach a reasonable solution, but rather as the course of action forced on the state by its inability to protect its interests, the result is likely to be increased pressure for further concessions. Russian statesmen believed that they had inadvertently set this process in motion in the decade before World War I. According to the Russian foreign minister, "Germany had looked upon our concessions as so many proofs of our weakness and far from having prevented our neighbors from using aggressive methods, we had encouraged them."[64] As is so often the case, the basic point can be found in Thucydides. Pericles argues against acceding to the demand to withdraw the Megarian decree in terms that were probably familiar even then: "If you give in, you will immediately be confronted with some greater demand, since they will think that you only gave way on this point through fear."[65] Similarly, if the state refrains from opposing the adversary when it has both an interest in doing so and the necessary capabilities, others will see fear as the explanation. Thus the argument by John Foster Dulles and Dean Rusk in the spring of 1950 that the United States had to protect Formosa:

> If the United States were to announce that it would neutralize Formosa, not permitting it either to be taken by Communists or to be used as a base of military operations against the mainland, that is a decision which we could certainly maintain, short of open war by the Soviet Union. Everyone knows that is the case. If we do not act, it will be everywhere interpreted that we are making another retreat because we do not dare risk war.[66]

This reasoning can be carried a step further. There is no reason why only international actions should be used to infer the character of the state and its leaders. That is, if observers are interested in the state's—and the decision maker's[67]—willingness to pay a significant price to reach valued objectives, then domestic behavior can also be highly diagnostic. Jonathan Schell may be correct to argue that one reason why Nixon was so disturbed by the domestic protests against the Vietnam war was that he believed that foreign adversaries would infer that an unwillingness to suppress them indicated "softness" that would also be reflected in foreign policy.[68] In the same way, it is possible that Ronald Reagan's firing of the air controllers did more to impress the Russians than did his increases in the defense budget or the liberation of Grenada.[69]

Effect or effort? The reasoning processes described in the previous section help explain the puzzling fact that statesmen often argue that the damage to their state's reputation comes, not from being unable to prevent a local defeat, but from refusing to make a major effort to do so. This leads to what Assistant Secretary of Defense John McNaughton called the "good doctor" approach to Vietnam. In order to impress "other nations regarding U.S. . . . resolve and competence," the United States had to "be tough, take risks, get bloodied, and hurt the enemy badly" even if it did not win.[70] Perhaps the strongest version of this argument was made by a White House assistant who justified continued American support for what was clearly a losing cause in Iran in these terms: "The goal now is to bend over backward to reassure a lot of jittery allies that we are prepared, if necessary, to go up in flames with the Shah."[71] In the same vein, at the outbreak of the Korean War, Secretary of State Acheson argued that "it was important for us to do something even if the effort were not successful." Secretary of Defense Johnson agreed: "Even if we lose Korea [providing aid] would save the situation."[72] A few years later President Eisenhower put a positive cast on a similar argument for the importance of strong resistance if the Chinese Communists were to attack the offshore islands of Quemoy and Matsu:

> While it is true under this system one or more of the forward positions might eventually be lost, such loss would occur only after the defending forces had exacted a fearful toll from the attackers, and Chiang's prestige and standing in Southeast Asia would be increased rather than decreased as a result of a gallant, prolonged and bitter defense conducted under these circumstances.[73]

This line of thought is not unique to the postwar era or to the United States. After Pearl Harbor, Eisenhower argued that even though the Unites States was outnumbered, it had to defend the Philippines because the people of Asia "may excuse failure but they will not excuse abandonment."[74] Earlier that year, British Foreign Minister Anthony Eden urged support for Greece against the overwhelming German attack on similar grounds: "No doubt our prestige will suffer if we are ignominiously ejected, but in any event to have fought and suffered in Greece would be less damaging to us than to have left Greece to her fate."[75]

The claim is not that audiences will be impressed by empty gestures. It is rather that the effort indicates that the state will incur high costs to help its allies. Thus in early 1975 Secretary of Defense Schlesinger urged continued American aid to South Vietnam because it was crucial that the fall of Indochina "should clearly be marked as the result of the ineptitude of the [Cambodian and South Vietnamese] governments rather than due to a cut-off of American aid."[76] The skill, dedication, and capabilities of regimes under communist pressures would vary from one instance to another. American aid might not always be able to prevent defeat. But if countries believed that the United States would stand behind them, the fall of Vietnam would not convince them that resistance was hopeless.

This line of argument must be qualified, however, and several implicit assumptions brought to the surface. First, sometimes it is the effect rather than the effort that is believed to be primary. If others believe that even though their patron will support them, this support will not be sufficient to deter or defeat the adversary, they may bandwagon. Thus at the outbreak of the Korean War the State Department Office of Intelligence Research disagreed with the claims of Acheson and Johnson quoted above, and argued: "If the United States abandons South Korea, whether or not token military assistance has been provided, the Southeast Asian leaders will lose whatever confidence they may have had in the effectiveness of U.S. aid to combat communism." The reasoning is not obscure: "Should U.S. support prove insufficient to prevent defeat of [South Korea], the question of the value to Japan of similar support . . . will inevitably be raised."[77] Second, the effort to help an ally—whether successful or not—will not make the desired impression if others believe that it has so drained the defender's power or resolve that it will not repeat the exercise. Thus even had North Vietnam conceded defeat in the early 1970s, it is far from clear that anyone would have expected the United States to send troops abroad under similar circumstances in the near future. Third, results, not the level of effort, will be primary if the country under attack owes its importance to its resources or geographical location.

Finally, the obvious drawback of making a major effort, aside from the direct costs involved, is that if the effort does not succeed, the price the state will pay in terms of its reputation will be greater. That is, after all, the way in which the tactic of commitment works. Thus Vance was unpersuaded by Brzenzinski's argument that the United States should move an aircraft carrier task force off the coast of Ethiopia to deter that country from following its defeat of the Somalian forces in the Ogaden with an invasion of its neighbor. If Brzezinski's advice were taken but Somalia was nonetheless invaded, "it would be viewed as a failure of the U.S. task force to do its job, and that failure would impair the credibility of such task forces in future crises elsewhere."[78]

Two Paradoxes

Arguments about domino dynamics are set within systems of interactions and unintended consequences. But, unlike systems in nature, international systems are composed of calculating actors who try to understand and manipulate the forces at work. One result is that the actors' beliefs about domino effects may lead them to behave in ways that counteract these effects. Although domino beliefs can be self-fulfilling when states accommodate to a powerful actor in the expectation that everyone else will do so, in other circumstances they can be a self-defeating prophecy. An actor who has had to back down once will feel especially strong incentives to prevail the next time in order to show that the domino theory is not correct, or at least does not apply to him. In other words, an actor who believes the domino theory—or who believes that others accept it—will have incentives to act contrary to it. Indeed, statesmen sometimes respond to a defeat by warning others that this history will make them extremely resistent to retreating again.[79] Furthermore, if others foresee this, they will expect a defeated actor to be particularly unyielding in the next confrontation. And if this is true, then the others are not expecting domino dynamics to operate and so defeated actors should not have any special incentives in that confrontation.[80]

This paradox is not hypothetical. Shortly after President Eisenhower propounded the domino theory, he also acted to confound it. The records of a National Security Council meeting preceding the Geneva Conference indicate that he "expressed his hostility to the notion that because we might lose Indochina we would necessarily have to lose all the rest of Southeast Asia. This had not been the view of the Council at an earlier time. Indeed, the Council had set up a Special Committee to recommend measures for saving the rest of Southeast Asia in the event that Indochina were lost."[81] The most important of these measures was the formation of SEATO, whose purpose was to prevent the occurrence of the consequences that American leaders had previously predicted would flow from a Viet Minh victory. Indeed, when explaining the purposes of such efforts, Eisenhower used the domino metaphor in a very different way: "When, each [domino is] standing alone, one falls, it has the effect on the next, and finally the whole row is down. You are trying, through a unifying influence, to build that row of dominoes so they can stand the fall of one, if necessary."[82] Secretary of State Dulles explained the goals of American policy in similar terms: "What we are trying to do is create a situation in Southeast Asia where the domino situation will not apply."[83] Indeed, Ted Hopf found that in the 1970s the Soviets, anticipating these effects, thought that American allies, although not the United States itself, would "increase their commitments and energies to resist further Soviet expansion after a Soviet victory."[84] By 1976, Brezhnev had to report: "The fact is that to these defeats . . . aggressive circles of the capitalist world react by furiously unleashing military preparations. They inflate their defense budgets, . . . build military bases and undertake military demonstrations."[85]

Like the domino effect itself, these counterbalancing efforts can take a number of forms. Most obviously, statesmen are likely to react to defeats by displaying their resolve and strength. In 1971, Kissinger justified his policy in the clash between India and Pakistan in these terms: "I told Nixon that precisely because we were retreating from Vietnam we could not permit the impression to be created that all issues could be settled by naked force."[86] Shortly after the fall of Saigon, he said that "the United States must carry out some act somewhere in the world which shows its determination to continue to be a world power."[87] This may help explain why the United States acted so quickly and sharply when the Cambodians seized the *Mayaguez*.

A statesman's willingness to resist retreat thus may be inversely related to how well he has done in the recent past. As John Kennedy explained his increasing commitment to South Vietnam in the fall of 1961: "There are limits to the number of defeats I can defend in one twelve-month period. I've had the Bay of Pigs and pulling out of Laos, and I can't accept a third."[88] The same imperative was put more crudely by Germany's foreign minister in the second Moroccan crisis: "When our prestige in foreign lands is lowered we must fight."[89] This course of action is not without its dangers, as proponents of the domino theory warn and as the miscalculations in July 1914 illustrates. Part of the reason why Germany and Austria believed that the Triple Entente might accept a diplomatic defeat was that they had done so in previous confrontations; part of the reason why Russia felt she had to stand firm and why France and Britain felt they had to support her was that previous defeats had led Russia to feel that she had to restore her credibility and her allies to fear that if they repeated their attempts to restrain her, Russia would make her own accommodation with Germany.

Occasionally statesmen anticipate that their adversary is particularly likely to move decisively in order to mitigate the consequences of the losses it has just suffered. Thus in the wake of the communist defeat in the Italian elections of 1948, the State Department worried that the Soviet leaders "may come to the conclusion that to accept without counteraction this blow to the prestige of the Communist movement would place the Soviet Union so clearly on the defensive as to set in motion a train of events which would eventually jeopardize the security of its power in East Europe and at home. In [this] case, the tendency might be to undertake some spectacular further move designed to recoup the loss of prestige inherent in recent developments."[90] But such analyses seem to be rare. More often, however, states do react to a loss by taking strong counteractions.

Such responses, even though paradoxical in light of the domino theory, are not really surprising. They represent states' abilities to influence as well as understand the system of which they are a part. In many areas of social life we find people altering their behavior in order to neutralize or prevent the operation of what are seen as natural dynamics—that is, those that would hold if they did not intervene. Thus Arend Lijphart and others have argued that some ethnically divided states are stable because the leaders of the various communities realize how dangerous the situation is and restrain their constituencies in order to maintain the peace.[91] Less dramatically, one reason for the success of the cooperation between the United States and the United Kingdom on nuclear issues in 1957 and 1958 was that the leaders of both countries wanted to reduce the bitterness caused by the Suez crisis.[92]

The second paradox can be outlined more quickly. A successful effort to prevent a local defeat can be so costly that it undermines support for the policy, thus leading others to doubt that the state will undertake similar actions in the future. Vietnam is the obvious example. Hopf shows that much of the reason why the Soviets expected domino dynamics to follow this episode was their analysis of the impact of the war on American public and elite opinion. No such effects were expected after Angola because the American defeat—if it really should be so labeled—did not alienate the public. Many American leaders have blamed American reverses since the mid-1970s on the public's reaction to Vietnam, but have failed to note that it was American policies that were the cause of this reaction. Thus it is ironic that Ronald Reagan bolstered his call for congressional support for the rebels in Nicaragua and Angola as well as to fund SDI by noting that he would soon be conferring with the Soviet First Secretary. "Make no mistake about it . . . , the ability to succeed in that meeting will be directly affected by Gorbachev's perception of our global position *and internal solidarity*."[93]

Validity of the Theory

It is easier to describe the variety of domino beliefs than to judge their validity. While unfortunate, this is not surprising. If scholars understood the world much better than decision makers—and if the beliefs of the latter are not rationalizations for policies derived on other grounds[94]—then statesmen should soon learn from the scholars' superior knowledge and systematic errors would not persist. Nevertheless, some tentative generalizations about domino effects are possible.

Conditions Under Which Domino Effects Are Most Likely

The question of whether or not domino effects will occur is not likely to receive a single answer; the effects are more likely under some conditions than others. Three categories of conditions can be isolated, each with several subcomponents. One set deals with the structure of the international system,[95] a second with the nature of the specific situation, and a third with beliefs and behavior.

Three aspects of the international system enter in. The first is whether military technology and political strategy give the offense or the defense an advantage.[96] Domino effects will operate most strongly in the former circumstance: when attacking is easier than defending, initial gains multiply and it is hard for states that seek to maintain the status quo to do so without threatening others. The belief that the offense has an advantage often underlies Snyder's Thermopylae Corollary as it leads to the conclusion that it is easier to stop the adversary in the initial stages of his advances.

There is more room for argument about the impact of nuclear weapons. Their existence—or, to be more precise, both superpowers' possession of second strike capability—increases domino effects by making credibility more central.[97] To the extent that each superpower judges the other's willingness to run risks of nuclear war by its behavior in confrontations through the world, defeats anywhere undercut the state's reputation for protecting its allies and vital interests. On the other hand, the physical importance of the potential dominoes has decreased because mutual second strike capability enables the superpowers to protect themselves without assistance.

There is also room for argument about the effects of bipolarity. At issue is a variant of the familiar argument over whether a bipolar world is more or less stable than a multipolar one.[98] On the one hand, the fact that power is concentrated in the hands of two superpowers means that their security is not directly determined by the fates of third actors. But the fact that disparate issues are likely to become linked to superpower rivalry means that what each side does anywhere can readily be seen as predicting its behavior in other cases. In multipolar eras, retreating in the face of one adversary might not affect the image held by others; now attention is more focused.

Domino dynamics are also influenced by aspects of the specific situation. First, domino effects are more likely if the state that falls is a large and important one because of the resulting change in the distribution of power between the state and its adversary. Second, the effect of a defeat on one issue or in one area will be greatest on other issues and in other areas that most resemble the first. If a state faces a series of very similar issues, it is hard for it to retreat on one without endangering its position on the others. Third, concessions and defeats are more likely to produce domino effects when the state retreats from a position that is generally agreed to be legitimate and in which its intrinsic interest is higher than that of the other side. Since these circumstances are conducive to the state's standing firm, others are likely to draw far-reaching conclusions from such retreats.

The fourth factor deals not with the superpowers, but with the smaller states. They will be most likely to bandwagon when each of them is small and believes that it cannot stand up to great pressure. In an application of the familiar collective goods problem, when their unassisted resistance is likely to be futile, local actors will make few efforts to defend themselves and instead will look to the strongest state. Thus Prince Sihanouk's plea in 1964: "To understand what I'm trying to achieve, just remember this: All of Southeast Asia is destined to become Communist. . . . When it happens in Cambodia, I want it to happen without breakage."[99] On the other hand, third parties will be likely to follow balance of power prescriptions when they believe that it is possible for them to meet the adversary's increased strength with increases in their own resistance. Indeed, under these circumstances they will increase rather than decrease their efforts if their superpower patron seems to weaken.

The smaller states' domestic politics also influence the likelihood of domino effects. If they are unstable internally, they are more likely to bandwagon. Factional conflicts or a widely shared sense of uncertainty can lead politicians to try to join the "wave of the future." Thus, as Macdonald and Larson note,[100] postwar Europe probably was unusually at risk from domino effects. This is not to say that any communist victory automatically led to others—the coup in Czechoslovakia increased rather than decreased the Western democracies' willingness to resist Soviet blandishments and threats—but only that the danger was real.

Finally, decision makers beliefs affect domino dynamics. As we discussed earlier, both self-fulfilling and self-denying prophecies are possible, but in either case it will not be possible to infer outcomes from the objective situation without considering the decision makers' analyses and expectations. People who believe that domino dynamics are common and powerful may be more likely to join what they see as the strongest side; those who believe that such dynamics are "natural" but can be overcome may try to counteract them; those who doubt the existence of strong interconnections are more likely to set policy on the basis of the intrinsic interests involved.

General Validity

It is impossible to render a general judgment on the validity of the domino theory, not only because judgments must be conditional, but also because there have been few empirical studies of the consequences of limited retreats and losses on the periphery. One point is obvious, however; in the modern world,[101] balancing dynamics have always come into operation at some point—the international system has never seen sufficient bandwagoning to permit one power to dominate.

Clearly, the more extreme domino predictions have not been fulfilled. The establishment of Castro's regime did not lead to the communization of Latin America; even though the success of the Chinese revolution made possible Ho Chi Minh's victory in North Vietnam, the effect stopped there; although Cambodia and Laos followed South Vietnam into communism, Burma, Thailand, Malaysia, and Indonesia did not move into the Soviet or Chinese orbit. The American defeat may have encouraged Soviet and Cuban intervention in Angola and even—although more arguably—in Ethiopia, but, as noted earlier, the crucial factor here was American public opinion, not the defeat itself. Furthermore, it is hard to believe that if the United States had prevailed in Vietnam, Russia would have behaved differently in Afghanistan.[102] To take a more recent case, the American defeats in Lebanon did not reduce the extent to which others in the Mideast looked to the United States for support and assistance. Walt's analysis of the Middle East shows that almost 90 percent of the alliances traceable to external threats were aimed at blocking, not accommodating, the menacing power.[103] Daniel Baugh similarly finds that "the historical facts of the period 1689–1815 tend to favor the self-adjustment [or balance of power] theory over the domino theory."[104]

The other side of this coin is that strongly motivated challengers will seek to change the status quo even if previous attempts have failed. In examining a series of cases in which the United States sought to provide extended deterrence in the Middle East, Janice Stein finds that "the demonstration [of resolve] in one case had no appreciable impact on the outcome of the next."[105] The case of Hitler is again instructive. Although it is true that many of the smaller European states (and, to some extent, the U.S.S.R.) moved toward Germany as it grew stronger, it probably is not true that had Hitler been thwarted in his first years in power he would have given up his ambitions. Indeed, the rebuff he suffered when he tried to move against Austria in 1934 did not curb his ambitions. This is not to argue that the previous history of interaction between two states is irrelevant,[106] or to deny that even a dedicated aggressor may eventually reform or conform, but only to point out that maintaining the status quo in one case does not automatically make it easy to do so in others.

Statesmen are prone to exaggerate the likelihood and magnitude of domino effects. Judgments of general characteristics such as resolve are less important than is often asserted; intrinsic interest in the issue at stake often plays a very large role; major actors try to prevent domino effects; and local actors play a larger role than is frequently believed. Each of these points calls for elaboration. First, in Snyder and Diesing's examination of a large number of confrontations from the early twentieth century to the present "what stands out is the discrepancy between the little evidence statesmen *do* infer an opponent's resolve from his behavior in previous cases and the massive evidence that decision makers *think* such inferences are made." Just before he invaded Poland, Hitler rebutted his resisting military advisors by saying, "Our enemies are little worms. I saw them at Munich."[107] But this was the only such remark Snyder and Diesing could find. One other is Eisenhower's report to congressional leaders that his confidence in taking a strong stand in Berlin was rooted in part in his knowledge of other cases in which the Soviets had bluffed.[108]

This is not to claim that decision makers make no general judgments about others' willingness to pay costs and run risks, or that they think that all countries will behave the same way in the same situation. But it does seem that these judgments do not dominate and that more attention is given to the specific situation the other side is believed to face. Quite contrary to the expectations American decision makers had about the inferences others would draw from the American withdrawal from Vietnam, the former did not infer from the Soviet withdrawal from Afghanistan that other Soviet retreats were likely (even though in retrospect we can trace some linkages).

Second, and related to this, it appears that the domino theory exaggerates the role of reputational interests in determining the outcomes of confrontations and the inferences observers draw and commensurately underestimates the importance of intrinsic interest. This topic is large and difficult; only tentative conclusions are possible.[109] Quantitative studies tap these dimensions only approximately and have yielded ambiguous results.[110] Although Snyder and Diesing did not find "more than one or two explicit estimates of the adversary's intensity of interest," they also note that "the lack of direct interest comparisons may be only an artifact of the record—the intensity of the opponent's interests may be 'felt,' perhaps subconsciously, but just not articulated."[111] Examinations of a series of cases in the Middle East and of naval demonstrations concluded that intrinsic interests are an important determinant of the outcomes.[112] Furthermore, other studies have found that the balance of interests plays a large role and that statesmen even sometimes make explicit references to it.[113] Of course in many cases the balance of interest is ambiguous and, even worse, each side may think it to be in its favor, thus leading it to expect that the other side will back down.[114] But at minimum, states seem able to separate peripheral from vital interests.

A third reason why predictions of extreme domino effects usually are falsified is that the defender purposely acts to falsify them. Great powers generally have the resolve and capability to shore up their positions in the wake of limited defeats. Major states are able to act in accord with the balance of power theory and prevent a potential hegemon from accumulating sufficient victories to dominate the system.

Finally, claims for the prevalence of domino dynamics tend to underestimate the strength and vitality of local actors. The states of the Third World are not mere pawns in a superpower struggle. Instead, they usually are aware of the danger of dominance by either superpower and believe that they can effectively protect themselves. Thus, India has not become more pro-Soviet because of the events in Afghanistan and, contrary to numerous predictions, the states of Southeast Asia did not accommodate to the communist victory in Indochina. Regional rivalries, so troublesome in other contexts, are helpful here. An increase in Soviet influence in one country—such as Ethiopia—is likely to lead others in the region—such as Somalia—to turn to the United States for support.

The diversity of local interests and actors often is not appreciated by the superpowers' decision makers, in part because they cannot know in detail countries and situations all over the world and in part because their focus has been concentrated on the superpower rivalry.[115] In declassified documents, little is said about the strength of nationalism; rarely are there analyses of which countries and individuals are strong and self-confident; rarely is it recognized that countries in the Third World can protect their interests and limit Soviet influence.

Summary

Although we live in one world, not all events and states in it are tightly coupled together. Furthermore, many of the interconnections that operate produce stability, not instability. The image of falling dominoes neglects the power of the local states and the actions of the great powers whose resistance is likely to increase, rather than decrease, as the result of a local defeat. "Resolve" is not a constant characteristic of the actor, but is sensitive to time and context. Limited defeats do not have unlimited ramifications; preventing aggression in one area will not greatly ease the burden of having to do so in other areas. Ironically, the recent revolution in Soviet foreign and domestic policy was facilitated by the Soviet disenchantment with the Third World stemming from the frustrations and costs of the apparent Soviet victories there, which yielded unexpected costs and responsibilities. Far from other dominoes falling along the periphery, the center discovered that some gains are hard to distinguish from losses.

Notes

1. See, for example, the alternative predictions of the effect of the fall of Vietnam made by members of the NSC staff and representatives of the Joint Chiefs of Staff in *The Pentagon Papers* (Senator Gravel edition), vol. 3 (Boston: Beacon Press, 1972), 625–28.

2. Quoted in Stephen Ambrose, *Eisenhower,* vol. 2, *The President* (New York: Simon & Schuster, 1984), 365. Similarly, when Konrad Adenauer told Eisenhower that the communists were responsible for the Algerian rebellion and that if it succeeded, Morocco, Tunisia, and the Middle East would also fall to communism Eisenhower responded that he could not "foresee such a chain of disaster." Ibid., 538.

3. Quoted in Roger Bullen, *Palmerston, Guizot and the Collapse of the Entente Cordiale* (London: Athlone Press, 1974), 56.

4. Reinhart Selten, "The Chain Store Paradox," *Theory and Decision* 9 (1978): 127–59.

5. Kenneth Waltz, *Theory of International Politics* (Reading, Mass.: Addison Wesley, 1979); Stephen Walt, "Alliance Formation and the Balance of World Power," *International Security* 9 (1985): 3–43; Walt, *The Origins of Alliances* (Ithaca, N.Y.: Cornell University Press, 1987). Also see Arnold Wolfers, "The Balance of Power in Theory and Practice," in Wolfers, *Discord and Collaboration* (Baltimore: Johns Hopkins University Press, 1962), 122–24. For other analyses of domino effects, see Jerome Slater, "Dominos in Central America: Will They Fall? Does It Matter?" *International Security* 12 (1987): 105–34; Betty Glad and Charles Taber, "The Domino Theory," in *War: The Psychological Dimension,* ed. Betty Glad (Syracuse: Syracuse University Press, 1988); Ross Gregory, "The Domino Theory," in *Encyclopedia of American Foreign Policy,* ed. Alexander DeConde, vol. 1 (New York: Scribner's, 1978), 275–80; and Lars Schoultz, *National Security and United States Policy toward Latin America* (Princeton, N.J.: Princeton University Press, 1987). For the analogy, not to dominoes, but to ten-pins, see Stewart Alsop quoted in Paul Kennedy, *The Rise and Fall of the Great Powers* (New York: Random House, 1988), 382.

6. For the concept of natural order see Stephen Toulmin, *Foresight and Understanding* (New York: Harper & Row, 1963).

7. Quoted in Telford Taylor, *Munich* (Garden City, N.Y.: Doubleday, 1979), 885. Some in the cabinet endorsed the appeasement on the quite different grounds that Hitler already dominated the continent and so what happened to Czechoslovakia did not matter. Ibid., 750–51.

8. Thucydides, *The Peloponnesian War,* trans. Rex Warner (Harmondsworth, Middlesex: Penguin, 1954), 92.

9. Quoted Avi Shlaim, *The United States and the Berlin Blockade, 1948–1949* (Berkeley: University of California Press, 1983), 188. The Russians clearly agreed. For them, the major objective in all the Berlin crises has been to influence Western policy on wider German issues. Berlin was a pressure point, not an issue of great intrinsic importance.

10. Arthur Schlesinger, Jr., *A Thousand Days* (Boston: Houghton Mifflin, 1965), 381, 383.

11. Quoted in Robert Slusser, *The Berlin Crisis of 1961* (Baltimore: Johns Hopkins University Press, 1973), 112.

12. Quoted in Glenn Paige, *The Korean Decision* (New York: Free Press, 1968), 298.

13. *Department of State Bulletin* 74 (February 16, 1976): 175.

14. *Annual Report to the Congress for Fiscal Year 1988* (Washington, D.C.: U.S. Government Printing Office, 1987), 4.

15. Douglas Macdonald, this volume, chap. 5; the quotation from Kennedy can be found on page 133 and comes from Herbert Parmet, *JFK: The Presidency of John F. Kennedy* (New York: Dial Press, 1983), 328.

16. Bullen, *Collapse of the Entente Cordial,* 268.

17. Thomas Schelling, *Arms and Influence,* (New Haven, Conn.: Yale University Press, 1966), 118, emphasis in the original.

18. This raises the question, discussed below, of why the state should think it can make the adversary retreat. As Richard Herrmann notes in this volume, the belief that the adversary will back down even though winning would undermine the state's influence throughout the world is hard to reconcile with the image of it as highly aggressive, chap. 8. Also see his "Soviet Foreign Policy: Reconsidering Three Competing Perspectives," *Political Psychology* 6 (1985): 377–80.

19. Walt, *Origins of Alliances,* 21, 45.

20. This error was not made by Schelling. See Thomas Schelling, *The Strategy of Conflict* (Cambridge: Harvard University Press, 1960), 43–46, 131–37.

21. Kissinger's claim for the importance of living up to our promises to Pakistan in the 1971 war was partly based on this consideration. *White House Years* (Boston: Little, Brown, 1979), 895–913.

22. Quoted in Deborah Larson, "The Non-strategy of Containment," unpublished MS (Columbia University), 7. See Churchill's similar statement of the importance of convincing the Russians that the West would respect its promises in Martin Gilbert, *Churchill,* vol. 7, *Road to Victory* (Boston: Houghton Mifflin, 1986), 639.

23. Quoted in David Hall, "The Laos Neutralization Agreement, 1962," in *U.S.-Soviet Security Cooperation,* ed. Alexander George, Philip Farley, and Alexander Dallin (New York: Oxford University Press, 1988), 457. For another example, see Glen Seaborg with Benjamin Loeb, *Stemming the Tide: Arms Control in the Johnson Years* (Lexington, Mass.: Lexington Books, 1987), 328.

24. Philip Taubman, "Moscow Suspends Pullout of Its Afghan Forces; Charges Violations of Pact," *New York Times,* Nov. 5, 1988.

25. For a discussion in these terms of American decision makers' belief systems during the Berlin blockade, see Alexander George and Richard Smoke, *Deterrence in American Foreign Policy* (New York: Columbia University Press, 1974), 109–17; and Shlaim, *The U.S. and the Berlin Blockade,* 68–69. For arguments that American statesmen have generally overestimated the extent to which events all over the world are tightly coupled, see Max Singer and Aaron Wildavsky, "A Third World Averaging Strategy," in *US Foreign Policy: Perspectives and Proposals for the 1970s,* ed. Paul Seabury and Aaron Wildavsky (New York: McGraw-Hill, 1969), 13–35; Robert Johnson, "Exaggerating America's Stakes in Third World Conflicts," *International Security* 10 (1985/86): 32–68; Patrick Morgan, "Saving Face for the Sake of Deterrence," in *Psychology and Deterrence,* ed. Robert Jervis, Richard Ned Lebow, and Janice Stein (Baltimore: Johns Hopkins Press, 1985), 125–52; Charles Kupchan "American Globalism and the Middle East," *Political Science Quarterly* 103 (1988–1989): 585–611.

26. Henry Kissinger, in *Department of State Bulletin* 72 (April 14, 1975): 461–62. Secretary of State Cordell Hull made a similar point in 1937 when he told the Japanese ambassador: "There can be no serious hostilities anywhere in the world which will not one way or another affect interests or rights or obligations of this country." Quoted in Jonathan Utley, *Going to War With Japan, 1937–1941* (Knoxville: University of Tennessee Press, 1985), 5.

27. John Harvey, ed., *The Diplomatic Diaries of Oliver Harvey, 1937–1940* (New York: St. Martin's, 1970), 299, 425.

28. Of course there are many exceptions. Thus Susan Purcell, a Latin America expert, attributes Central American countries' willingness to sign the Arias plan even though they had previously objected to some of its key provisions to "the decline in the power and prestige of the United States in general and of President Reagan in particular in the wake of the Iran–contra affair." "The Choice in Central America," *Foreign Affairs* 66 (1987): 117.

29. Of course domino dynamics are not the only ways in which events can be tightly coupled. For example, military leaders often are preoccupied by the danger that increasing military forces in one area will make it harder for the state to live up to other obligations elsewhere by decreasing the resources that remain available. This perspective characterized the American military establishment from the onset of the cold war to the vast increases in the military budget that occurred in the wake of the Korean conflict. For an example of similar thinking on the part of British military officials in the earlier

twentieth century, see Keith Jeffery, "The Eastern Arc of Empire: A Strategic View, 1850–1950," *Journal of Strategic Studies* 5 (1982): 531–45.

30. Glenn Snyder, *Deterrence and Defense* (Princeton, N.J.: Princeton University Press, 1961), 31. Also see Franklin Weinstein, "The Concept of Commitment in International Relations," *International Studies Quarterly* 12 (1969): 39–56; George and Smoke, *Deterrence in American Foreign Policy,* 552–61; Schelling's distinction between threats and warnings in *Strategy of Conflict,* 123–24; and Samuel Huntington, "Patterns of Intervention," *National Interest* 7 (1987): 39.

31. Quoted in Brian Bond, *British Military Policy Between the Two World Wars* (Oxford: Clarendon Press, 1980), 18.

32. Department of State, *Foreign Relations of the United States 1950,* vol. VII, *Korea* (Washington, D.C.: U.S. Government Printing Office, 1976) [hereafter abbreviated as *FRUS,* followed by appropriate year and volume], 151.

33. *Department of State Bulletin* 72 (April 14, 1975): 462.

34. Henry Kissinger, "Containment of the Kremlin," *Washington Post,* Feb. 16, 1976, A 15.

35. George Kennan, "Containment of the Kremlin," *Washington Post,* Feb. 16, 1976, A 15.

36. *The Cold War* (New York: Harper & Brothers, 1947).

37. See John Lewis Gaddis, "Introduction: The Evolution of Containment," in *Containment: Concept and Policy,* ed. Jerry Deibel and Gaddis, vol. 1 (Washington, D.C.: National Defense University Press, 1986), 5–7; Gaddis, *Strategies of Containment* (New York: Oxford University Press, 1982), 85, 88.

38. Sometimes even the core values being protected do not seem to justify the effort at resisting the initial predation period. This possibility is raised by Margaret Thatcher's justification of using force to reclaim the Falklands: "We can't let this go. Otherwise, what would happen to Gibraltar, Belize and to other similar places?" Quoted in William Borders, "'Iron Lady' Displays Grit at Reception," *New York Times,* Apr. 22, 1982.

39. Quoted in *Report of the President's Special Review Board* (Tower Commission) (Washington, D.C.: U.S. Government Printing Office, 1987), B-6.

40. See Jack Snyder, *Myths of Empire: Domestic Politics and Strategic Ideology* (Ithaca, N.Y.: Cornell University Press, forthcoming).

41. *FRUS 1950* VI, *East Asia and the Pacific* (1976), 714.

42. Snyder, *Myths of Empire.*

43. For an analysis of the American interpretations, see Alexander George, "American Policy-Making and the North Korean Aggression," *World Politics* 7 (1955): 209–32.

44. *FRUS 1950* VII, 139.

45. E. L. Woodward, Rohan Butler, and Margaret Lambert, eds., *Document on British Foreign Policy—1939,* Third Series, vol. II, *European Affairs, July–September 1938* (London: His Majesty's Stationery Office, 1949), 384.

46. Ibid., 213. Although this remark was made two weeks before Daladier's and not in direct response to it, the nature of the dialogue remains clear.

47. Ibid., 277. As noted above, Chamberlain implicitly gave a different answer to this question six months later when Germany invaded the non-German portions of Czechoslovakia.

48. On Belgium, see David Kieft, *Belgium's Return to Neutrality* (Oxford: Clarendon Press, 1972); on Russia compare, for example, Jiri Hochman, *The Soviet Union and the Failure of Collective Security, 1934–38* (Ithaca, N.Y.: Cornell University Press, 1984); and Jonathan Halsam, *The Soviet Union and the Search for Collective Security* (New York: St. Martin's, 1984).

49. See Stephen Schuker, "France and the Remilitarization of the Rhineland, 1936," *French Historical Studies* 14 (1986): 299–338.

50. See Williamson Murray, *The Change in the European Balance of Power, 1938–1939* (Princeton, N.J.: Princeton University Press, 1984), chaps. 7–8, including the literature cited there; and Milan Hauner, "Czechoslovakia as a Military Factor in British Considerations of 1938," *Journal of Strategic Studies* I (1978): 194–222.

51. *FRUS 1952–1954* II, *National Security Affairs,* Part 1 (1984), 838.

52. Bernard Weinraub, "Reagan Condemns Nicaragua in Plea for Aid to Rebels," *New York Times,* Mar. 17, 1986.

53. Note Adenauer's view of the Algerian rebellion cited above in note 2, and also Prime Minister Disraeli's description of the Balkan unrest in the late 1870s: "The so-called insurgents are not natives of any Turkish province, but are simply an invasion of revolutionary bands, whose strength lay in the support afforded to them by Serbia and Montenegro, acting on the instigation of foreign agents and foreign committees" Quoted in R. W. Seton-Watson, *Disraeli, Gladstone, and the Eastern Question* (New York: Norton, 1972), 44.

54. Kissinger, *White House Years,* 886; also see 767, 913.

55. Richard Nixon, *RN: The Memoirs of Richard Nixon* (New York: Grosset & Dunlap, 1978), 527.

56. Quoted in Seymour Hersh, *The Price of Power: Kissinger in the Nixon White House* (New York: Summit Books, 1983), 458.

57. "Secretary Kissinger's news conference of March 26," *Department of State Bulletin* 72 (April 14, 1975): 463. It should be noted, however, that Kissinger went on to say that "the major reason for the breakdown of the negotiations was intrinsic to the negotiations themselves."

58. Larson reserves the term "bandwagoning" for these dynamics: see chap. 4 in this volume, p. 88.

59. Quoted in Larson, "The Non-strategy of Containment," 33–34.

60. Kissinger, "Containment of the Kremlin," 15. Kissinger referred to "the unacceptable precedent of massive Soviet and Cuban military intervention in a conflict thousands of miles from their shores [which had] broad implications for the rest of Africa and, indeed, many other regions of the world." Also see Henry Kissinger, "Foreign Policy and National Security," *International Security* 1 (1976): 189; and Kissinger, *American Foreign Policy,* 3d ed. (New York: Norton, 1977), 317–21.

61. For similar American fears about the effects of renegotiating American military rights in Spain, see Paul Delaney, "U.S. and Spain Still Far Apart in Talks on Bases," *New York Times,* Oct. 4. 1987.

62. Abram Chayes, *The Cuban Missile Crisis* (New York: Oxford University Press, 1974).

63. *New York Times,* May 1, 1970. Some of the rationale for building the MX was similar—the United States had to go ahead in part because the Russians opposed it and American domestic resistance had led many at home and abroad to conclude that deployment was beyond the country's abilities.

64. Quoted in D. C. B. Lieven, *Russia and the Origins of the First World War* (London: Macmillan, 1983), 141–42.

65. Thucydides, *The Peloponnesian War,* 92.

66. Identical memoranda were submitted by Dulles and Rusk and can be found in *FRUS 1950* I, *National Security Affairs, Foreign Economic Policy* (1977), 314–16 (Dulles) and *FRUS 1950* VI (1976), 349–51 (Rusk).

67. The question of whether the characteristics of interest are believed to reside in the

individual leader, the state, or the type of state is explored in Robert Jervis, "Deterrence and Perception," *International Security* 7 (1982/1983):8–10.

68. Jonathon Schell, *The Time of Illusion* (New York: Vintage, 1976), 132–34.

69. I am grateful to George Quester for this point. Similar calculations may have influenced President Bush's behavior during the Eastern Airline strike. Bernard Weinraub, "Airline Dispute: Rite of Passage for Bush," *New York Times,* Mar. 3, 1989.

70. *Pentagon Papers,* vol. 3, 604; also see William Gibbons, *U.S. Government and the Vietnam War,* pt. II (Princeton, N.J.: Princeton University Press, 1986), 367.

71. Quoted in Richard Burt, "U.S. Reappraises Persian Gulf Policies," *New York Times,* Jan. 1, 1979. Also see Scott Armstrong, "Vance Was Preoccupied With SALT as Shah's Rule Disintegrated," *International Herald Tribune,* Oct. 31, 1980.

72. *FRUS 1950* VII, 182. The quotations are from detailed minutes of the meetings and may not be the actual words that were used.

73. Dwight D. Eisenhower, "Memorandum for the Secretary of State," April 5, 1955, 9, *FRUS 1954–1956* II, *China* (1986), 450. For other examples, see Kissinger, *White House Years,* 898–99; Zbigniew Brzezinski, *Power and Principle* (New York: Farrar, Straus & Giroux, 1983), 182–83.

74. Quoted in Stephen Ambrose, *The Supreme Commander: The War Years of General Dwight D. Eisenhower* (Garden City, N.Y.: Doubleday, 1970), 6.

75. Quoted in Martin Gilbert, *Winston S. Churchill,* vol. 6, *Finest Hour, 1939–41* (London: Heinemann, 1983), 1029.

76. Quoted in John Finney, "Schlesinger Terms Cambodian Situation Grim, Not Hopeless," *New York Times,* Feb. 28, 1975. Also see Leslie Gelb, "Pentagon Fears Cambodia's Fall," *New York Times,* Feb. 24, 1975. When the NSC working group considered "fall-back objectives" for Vietnam in 1964, it stressed the importance of making "clear to the world . . . that failure in South Viet Nam, if it comes, was due to special local factors that do not apply to other nations we are committed to defend—that, in short, our will and ability to help those nations defend themselves is not impaired." The representatives of the Joint Chiefs of Staff were not impressed, calling this plan "a slight paraphrase of Aesop's fox and grapes story. No matter how we talk amongst ourselves, [defeat] could only be completely transparent to intelligent outside observers." *Pentagon Papers,* vol. 3, 624; also see 657.

77. *FRUS 1950* VII, 151, 153–54.

78. Brzezinski, *Power and Principle,* 183.

79. See, for example, Kissinger's statement on Angola in *Department of State Bulletin* 74 (February 1976), 182.

80. For an interesting attempt to resolve this paradox, see Barry Nalebuff, "Rational Deterrence in an Imperfect World," unpublished MS (Princeton University).

81. *FRUS 1952–1954* XIII, *Indochina* (1982), 1257.

82. This was in response to a question at a press conference on May 12, 1954, and is printed in *Public Papers of the Presidents of the United States, Dwight D. Eisenhower, 1954* (Washington, D.C.: U.S. Government Printing Office, 1960), 473. In 1961, Dean Acheson predicted that, assuming the West resisted, the effect of a defeat in Berlin would be not falling dominoes but renewed Western strength and unity. Marc Trachtenberg, "The Berlin Crisis, 1958–1962," unpublished MS, 27–28.

83. Quoted in Melvin Gurtov, *The First Vietnam Crisis* (New York: Columbia University Press, 1967), 121.

84. Theodore Hopf, this volume, chap. 6, p. 178.

85. *Pravda,* Oct. 16, 1976, 2–3. I am grateful to Theodore Hopf for the citation and translation.

86. Kissinger, *White House Years,* 886.

87. Quoted in Tom Braden, "Why Are We Looking for Problems?" *Washington Post,* Apr. 14, 1975.

88. Quoted in Arthur Schlesinger, Jr., *Robert Kennedy and His Times* (Boston: Houghton Mifflin, 1978), 761. Also see Gibbons, *U.S. Government and the Vietnam War,* 23–25, 32. As William Bundy, then Assistant Secretary of State for Southeast Asia, recalls: "The decision to compromise in Laos made it essential to convey by word and deed that the United States would stand firm in South Vietnam and in the rest of Southeast Asia." (Quoted on p. 41.) For a similar but less extreme example, see Weinraub, "Airline Dispute."

89. Quoted in Ima Barlow, *The Agadir Crisis* (New York: Archon, 1971), 327. A high CIA official similarly said of the Reagan Administration that it "came to power with the intention of punching someone in the nose," thus partly explaining the Grenada operation. Quoted in Richard Gabriel, *Military Incompetence* (New York: Hill and Wang, 1985), 150.

90. *FRUS 1948* IV, *East Europe, The Soviet Union* (1974), 834.

91. Arend Lijphart, *Democracy in Plural Societies* (New Haven, Conn.: Yale University Press, 1977).

92. McGeorge Bundy, *Danger and Survival* (New York: Random House, 1988), 471.

93. Quoted in Bernard Weinraub, "Reagan Will Seek $100,000,000 in Aid for the Contras," *New York Times,* Jan. 22, 1986, emphasis added.

94. For a discussion of when they are, see Jack Snyder's chapters in this book and his *Myths of Empire*.

95. I am using the terms structure and system in quite loose senses—strict followers of Kenneth Waltz would object.

96. See Robert Jervis, "Cooperation Under the Security Dilemma," *World Politics* 30 (1978): 167–214; George Quester, *Offense and Defense in the International System* (New York: Wiley, 1977); Jack Levy, "The Offensive/Defensive Balance of Military Technology: A Theoretical and Historical Analysis," *International Studies Quarterly* 28 (1984): 219–38; Barry Posen, *The Sources of Military Doctrine* (Ithaca, N.Y.: Cornell University Press, 1984); Stephen Van Evera, "Why Cooperation Failed in 1914," *World Politics* 38 (1985): 80–117; Van Evera, "The Cult of the Offensive and the Origins of the First World War," *International Security* 9 (1984): 58–107; Jack Snyder, "Civil-Military Relations and the Cult of the Offensive, 1914 and 1984," ibid., 108–46; Snyder, *The Ideology of the Offensive: Military Decision Making and the Disasters of 1914* (Ithaca, N.Y.: Cornell University Press, 1984).

97. See Robert Jervis, *The Meaning of the Nuclear Revolution* (Ithaca, N.Y.: Cornell University Press, 1989), chap. 1.

98. See Waltz, *Theory of International Politics;* Karl Deutsch and J. David Singer, "Multi-polar Power Systems and International Stability," *World Politics* 16 (1964): 390–406; Richard Rosecrance, "Bipolarity, Multipolarity, and the Future," *Journal of Conflict Resolution* 10 (1966): 314–27. For an early claim for the stability of a bipolar world, William Liscum Borden, *There Will Be No Time* (New York: Macmillan, 1946), 160–65.

99. Quoted in Henry Kamm, "A Broken Country," *New York Times Magazine,* Sept. 19, 1987, 96.

100. See their chapters in this book, chaps. 5 and 4, respectively.

101. In the third century B.C., China formed out of the failure of the balance of power.

102. But there is room for disagreement: thus Brzezinski's famous claim that through a chain of underreactions and overreactions, "SALT lies buried in the sands of the Ogaden." *Power and Principle,* 189.

103. Walt, *Origins of Alliances,* 149. Such alliances also lasted longer than did those reflecting bandwagoning; see p. 152.

104. Daniel Baugh, "Great Britain's 'Blue-Water' Policy, 1689–1815," *International History Review* 10 (1988): 48.

105. Janice Stein, "Extended Deterrence in the Middle East: American Strategy Reconsidered," *World Politics* 39 (1987): 351.

106. Thus quantitative analysis reveals surprisingly little connection between how a state behaves in one conflict and how it will behave in conflicts with the same adversary. See Robert Mandel, "The Effectiveness of Gunboat Diplomacy," *International Studies Quarterly* 30 (1986): 68–69; Paul Huth and Bruce Russett, "After Deterrence Fails: Escalation to War?" paper presented to the Conference on the Risk of Accidental Nuclear War, University of British Columbia, Vancouver, B.C., May 1986; and Huth, *Deterrence and War* (New Haven, Conn.: Yale University Press, 1988), 80–82.

107. Glenn Snyder and Paul Diesing, *Conflict Among Nations* (Princeton, N.J.: Princeton University Press, 1977), 187, emphasis in the original. One reason for this expectation is that statesmen tend to exaggerate the extent to which their countries are at the center of others' focuses and concerns.

108. Trachtenberg, "Berlin Crisis," 30.

109. For further discussion, see Stephen Maxwell, *Rationality in Deterrence* (London: Institute for Strategic Studies, 1968), Adelphi Paper No. 50; George and Smoke, *Deterrence in American Foreign Policy,* 552–61; Robert Jervis, "Deterrence Theory Revisited," *World Politics* 31 (1979): 317–22. It should also be noted that statesmen could be strongly influenced by commitment or strategic interest but expect others to be more driven by intrinsic interest; the reverse is also possible but seems to me less likely. For a parallel argument that states estimate their own and their adversary's resolve on different bases, see Snyder and Diesing, *Conflict Among Nations,* 496–97.

110. Two studies found that economic and military ties between the major power and its local client made a significant contribution to a successful deterrence, but a third did not. See Bruce Russett, "The Calculus of Deterrence," *Journal of Conflict Resolution* 7 (1963): 97–109; Huth and Russett, "What Makes Deterrence Work?"; Huth, *Deterrence and War.*

111. Snyder and Diesing, *Conflict Among Nations,* 496.

112. Janice Stein, "Extended Deterrence in the Middle East"; and James McConnell, "The 'Rules of the Game': A Theory on the Practice of Superpower Naval Diplomacy," in *Soviet Naval Diplomacy,* ed. Bradford Dismukes and James McConnell (New York: Pergamon, 1979), 240–80.

113. Phil Williams, *Crisis Management* (New York: Wiley, 1976), 155–64; Jervis, "Deterrence Theory Revisited," 314–22.

114. Richard Betts, *Nuclear Blackmail* (Washington, D.C.: Brookings Institution, 1987), chap. 4.

115. The importance of local politics and regional dynamics is brought out in the companion volume to this one: Howard Wriggins, ed., *The Dynamics of Regional Politics: Four Cases From Rimland Asia.*

3

Alliance Formation in Southwest Asia: Balancing and Bandwagoning in Cold War Competition

STEPHEN M. WALT

When will states form alliances, and what determines their choice of allies? This question is important for at least two reasons. First, from a policy perspective, competing hypotheses about the causes of alignment lie at the heart of many recurring debates in U.S. foreign policy. As Deborah Larson (Chapter 4) reveals in this volume, the belief that states tend to bandwagon (i.e., to ally with the strongest or most threatening power) was an important motive behind the "globalization" of containment in the early years of the cold war. In particular, bandwagoning logic heightened concern for the credibility of U.S. commitments and is still used to justify U.S. involvement in Third World conflicts.[1] In the same way, concern over the "Finlandization" of Europe rests on the assumption that U.S. allies will tilt toward the Soviet Union should the United States decrease its commitment to NATO.[2] Contrary to these views, some analysts have argued that U.S. allies would do more for themselves if the United States did less.[3] In short, the question of whether balancing or bandwagoning is more likely still occupies a central place in key foreign policy debates.

Second, examining the causes of alliances is also an ideal way to test balance-of-power theory. Common to the various versions of this theory is the prediction that weaker states will form alliances to oppose stronger powers. According to Kenneth Waltz, whose *Theory of International Politics* contains the most rigorous presentation of this view, this tendency contributes to "the recurrent formation of balances of power."[4] But is this really the case? Although Waltz's book sparked a heated debate, most of the criticism has focused on its epistemological foundations or (alleged) normative biases.[5] For the most part, neither Waltz nor his critics have sought to *test* specific hypotheses derived from balance-of-power theory, to either refine it or reject it on empirical grounds.[6] This omission is unfortunate, because balance-of-power theory remains a rich source of insights about international politics. At the same time, its limitations suggest that certain modifications are in order. Because predictions about alliances are a central part of the theory, and because alliances play an especially important role in international politics, examining alliance formation is an obvious place to start.[7]

In an earlier work, I elaborated and tested these hypotheses by drawing upon traditional diplomatic history and a detailed examination of postwar alliances in the Middle East.[8] This study revealed that states form alliances primarily to *balance* against other states, and that "bandwagoning" behavior—alignment *with* the dominant state or coalition—was relatively rare. Contrary to balance-of-power theory, however, this research also showed that states balanced against several different kinds of threats, and not just against power alone. In this chapter, I refine these ideas further and present additional evidence to support these conclusions.

I do this by examining alliance formation in Southwest Asia since World War II, focusing on the alliance commitments of Iran, Turkey, India, and Pakistan. As discussed at greater length below, these cases are especially useful because they provide strong tests of several especially important propositions. The Section "Definitions and Hypotheses" outlines the logic of the different hypotheses and examines several important issues of interpretation. "Alliances and Alignments in Southwest Asia" describes the postwar alliance policies of these four states and identifies why each chose the allies that it did. The last section analyzes the different hypotheses in light of these decisions and explores the implications of these results.

Definitions and Hypotheses[9]

Balancing and Bandwagoning

When facing a significant external threat, states may either *balance* or *bandwagon*. Balancing is alignment *against* the threatening power, to deter it from attacking or to defeat it if it does. Bandwagoning, by contrast, refers to alignment *with* the dominant power, either to appease it or to profit from its victory. The question is: which tendency is more common?

As suggested above, the answer to this question has far-reaching implications. If states tend to balance, then great powers can take a relaxed view of most international events. Aggressors will face numerous opponents, and sustained efforts to expand are likely to fail. Statesmen should avoid bellicose behavior, because it will encourage others to align against them. But if bandwagoning is the dominant tendency, then security is scarce because allies will be prone to defect.[10] The danger of "falling dominoes" will increase, because the loss of one or two allies may signal others that it is time to switch to the ascending side.[11] In a bandwagoning world, great powers should work harder to preserve their credibility, so that fear does not lead their allies to realign.

Ironically, although balance-of-power notions pervade the scholarly literature on international politics, the United States (and to a lesser extent the Soviet Union) has often acted as if bandwagoning were the dominant tendency. United States leaders have been preoccupied with preserving credibility and have feared that setbacks in one area could lead to widespread defections elsewhere. As John F. Kennedy once put it, "If the United States were to falter, the whole world would inevitably move towards the Communist bloc."[12] The fear that allies will bandwagon has been used to justify intervention abroad and military spending at home, to convince allies that the United States is still a reliable partner. Yet despite the importance of this hypothesis as a justification for policy, it has rarely been challenged or tested.

In general, calculations of intent should encourage states to balance. Bandwagoning is risky because it requires trust; one assists a dominant power in the hope that it will remain benevolent. It is safer to balance, in case the dominant power turns out to be aggressive. Furthermore, alignment with the weaker side enhances one's influence within the resulting coalition, because the weaker side has greater need of assistance.[13]

Bandwagoning may be chosen under some conditions, however. Extremely weak states may be more inclined to bandwagon; because they have little deterrent or defensive strength to contribute, they must seek the winning side at all costs.[14] And when allies are unavailable, weak states may be forced to bandwagon even if this is not their first choice. Bandwagoning is also more likely when the dominant power appears to be appeasable, that is, when its ambitions can be satisfied or deflected should the threatened power opt for alignment with it. Because perceptions are unreliable and intentions can change, however, bandwagoning should be relatively rare.

Balance of Power or Balance of Threat?

In structural balance-of-power theory, balancing and bandwagoning are defined solely in terms of capabilities. Balancing is alignment with the weaker side, bandwagoning means to choose the stronger. Although this conception is elegant and parsimonious—the distribution of power (defined as aggregate capabilities) is the only important variable—it has serious limitations as well. In particular, states may balance by aligning with the stronger side, if a weaker power is more dangerous for other reasons (e.g., if its intentions are especially malign). By focusing solely on the distribution of capabilities, structural balance-of-power theory ignores the other factors that statesmen will consider when making alliance choices. As a result, the theory cannot explain why balances often fail to form.

For example, the coalitions that formed against Germany and its allies in World Wars I and II possessed far greater overall capabilities, and the disparity grew steadily until Germany was totally defeated.[15] Although balance-of-power theory helps explain why these alliances eventually dissolved (German power was nullified by its defeat), it cannot explain why Germany attracted such widespread opposition, given that it was ultimately weaker than the coalition it fought.[16]

Similarly, if states were concerned solely with balancing *power,* America's predominant position after World War II should have led the nations of Western Europe to align with the Soviet Union against the United States.[17] Instead, they chose to *balance* the Soviet Union by aligning with the United States, because the proximity of the Soviet Union, its impressive military power, and its apparently aggressive aims made it appear more threatening. As a result, the U.S. alliance network dwarfs the Soviet Union and its allies on most measures of national power, and this imbalance of power has remained relatively constant for nearly four decades.[18] At a minimum, therefore, structural balance-of-power theory often leads to inaccurate predictions.[19]

These deficiencies can be overcome by recognizing that states seek allies in order to balance *threats,* and that power is merely one element in their calculations—albeit an important one. In addition to its overall capabilities, the degree to which a state threatens others is also affected by its geographic proximity, offensive capabilities, and perceived intentions. Other things being equal, states that are nearby are more dangerous than those that are far away. States with large offensive capabilities—defined as the capacity to threaten the sovereignty of other states—pose a greater threat than states whose capabilities are more suitable for defense. Lastly, states with aggressive intentions are more threatening than those who are primarily interested in preserving the status quo. If balancing behavior is the norm, therefore, an increase in any of these factors—power, proximity, offensive capabilities, or aggressive intentions—should encourage other states to ally against the most threatening power.

"Balance-of-threat" theory should be viewd as a refinement of balance-of-power theory. Where balance-of-power theory predicts that states ally in response to imbalances of power, balance-of-threat theory predicts that states seek allies when there is an imbalance of threat (i.e., when one state or coalition is especially dangerous). The two theories are equally parsimonious, but balance-of-threat theory is more general and abstract. As shown in Figure 3-1, the main concept informing balance-of-power theory is the distribution of capabilities, which is based on population, economic capacity, military power, resource endowments, and so forth. The central concept of balance-of-threat theory is the distribution of threats, which consists of capabilities, proximity, offensive power, and intentions. Thus both theories are based on a single general concept

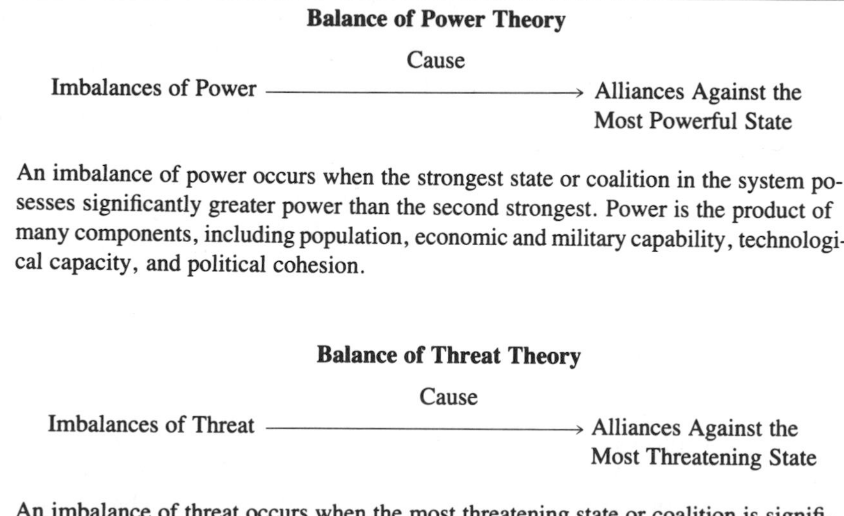

Fig. 3.1. Balance-of-power versus balance-of-threat theory.
(Reprinted from Stephen M. Walt: *The Origins of Alliances*. Copyright © 1987 by Cornell University. Used by permission of the publisher, Cornell University Press.)

incorporating a number of components, although balance-of-threat theory *subsumes* balance-of-power theory by incorporating capabilities, geography, and intentions. As we shall see, it offers a more compelling explanation of alliance choices than an exclusive focus on the distribution of capabilities does.

Problems of Interpretation

Before turning to the historical record, several issues of interpretation should be clarified. First, balancing and bandwagoning are ideal types, and actual behavior will only approximate either model. States that choose to bandwagon will not leave themselves completely vulnerable, and they may offer only modest support to the dominant power. Conversely, states that choose to balance may also seek cordial relations with their opponents, while simultaneously obtaining protection against them. Accordingly, testing these hypotheses requires careful historical interpretation.

A second issue concerns the definition of bandwagoning itself. Whenever one state seeks better relations with an opponent, its allies may view this as a form of bandwagoning. If they believe that this behavior is due to a decline in their own position(s), they will fear that additional defections are likely. Yet an ally's decision to seek better relations with the adversary may actually reflect the belief that the adversary is no longer as dangerous. If the adversary appears less aggressive or if one's own capabilities have grown, then a detente may be feasible. Far from reflecting fear or vulnerability, a successful detente may indicate that the effort to balance had worked quite well.

Several criteria can help distinguish between bandwagoning and detente. Bandwagoning involves *unequal exchange;* the vulnerable state makes asymmetrical concessions to the dominant power and accepts a subordinate role. Detente, by contrast, involves roughly equal concessions in which both sides benefit. Bandwagoning is an accomodation to pressure (either latent or manifest), while detente implies a mutual recognition of legitimate interests. Most important of all, bandwagoning suggests a willingness to support or tolerate illegitimate actions by the dominant ally. By contrast, detente carries no such implication; indeed, a detente will probably collapse if an opponent seeks to exploit it.[20]

Third, when examining the historical record, we should focus not only on what states did, but even more important, on what they preferred to do. As noted above, some states may be forced to bandwagon if they cannot obtain external support. If the United States returned to an isolationist policy, for example, some of its present allies might be inclined to move closer to the Soviet Union. But the real question is the *relative propensity* for states to balance or bandwagon: how much support is needed to persuade others to balance a threat? If bandwagoning is the dominant tendency, then patrons must work hard to prevent defections. But if balancing is the preferred choice, then rather modest support should convince others to oppose an aggressor.

Fourth, testing these hypotheses may be complicated by the tendency for client states to exaggerate their propensity to bandwagon, in order to extract greater support from their patrons. During the War of Attrition, for example,

President Nasser of Egypt convinced the Soviet Union to increase its aid by threatening to resign in favor of a pro-U.S. president.[21] Because the propensity for states to bandwagon will be exaggerated if we look only at what elites say and ignore what they do, careful interpretation is necessary.

Finally, testing these hypotheses can be undermined by tautological reasoning. In particular, we cannot use the existence of an alliance as evidence that national leaders perceived a threat, and then use that same alliance as evidence that external threats cause states to seek allies. Instead, we should collect independent evidence about the distribution of threats (such as shifts in relative power, bellicose behavior by one state, or the testimony of regional experts) and compare it with each state's response (did it balance against the main threat or bandwagon with it?). And because conclusive evidence may be elusive, we should consider a wide range of cases and seek strong tests of the different hypotheses, rather than relying solely upon cases where one theory's predictions are likely to be confirmed.

For these reasons, examining alliance formation in Southwest Asia is especially revealing. Because earlier studies have focused on other areas, these cases add new evidence from an increasingly important yet often neglected region. Even more important, the history of this area provides a strong test of the hypotheses on balancing and bandwagoning. Each of these states has faced a variety of internal and external pressures. All are close to the Soviet Union and far from the United States, which increased their vulnerability to Soviet pressure. Because U.S. involvement in this region was minimal prior to World War II, the United States could not invoke a traditional commitment there in order to bolster its credibility. With respect to the Soviet Union, therefore, these states were likely candidates for bandwagoning. If they chose to balance instead, that would be powerful evidence that balancing is the preferred response. Similarly, if these states sought allies primarily to counter the most powerful state in the system, or if their commitments shifted with changes in the distribution of capabilities, that would tend to support balance-of-power theory. But if they sought allies in order to oppose other regional powers, or if changes in intentions were more important than shifts in relative power, we should conclude that it is the balance of threats, not the balance of power, that plays the principal role in determining alliance choices. With these predictions in mind, let us now turn to the historical record.

Alliances and Alignments in Southwest Asia

Iran

The United States-Iranian relationship was forged in 1946, and these events provide an especially instructive example of balancing behavior.[22] Having occupied northern Iran during the war, the Soviets established independent republics in Azerbaijan and Kurdistan, which sought independence from the central government. During the first phase of the crisis (February–April 1946), Iranian Premier Ahmad Qavam resisted "tremendous pressure" from Stalin, who demanded a continued Soviet presence in the north.[23] When additional Soviet troops entered Iran in March, Iran brought the matter before the UN Security Council. The Soviets agreed to withdraw in April and acknowledged that the status of Azerbaijan and Kurdistan was an internal affair of Iran. In exchange, Qavam agreed to establish a joint Soviet-Iranian company to conduct oil explorations in Northern Iran, subject to ratification by the Iranian *Majlis* (Parliament).

The second phase of the crisis focused on internal matters. Although Soviet forces had withdrawn, Qavam and the shah still faced challenges from the communist Tudeh party, several rebellious tribes, and the two dissident republics. Qavam's efforts to appease these groups led U.S. officials to fear that he was unwittingly delivering Iran into communist hands.[24] By October, both Qavam and the shah shared these concerns, and with U.S. encouragement, they abandoned their conciliatory approach.[25] The Tudeh ministers were ousted and the Iranian Army reoccupied the rebellious republics in December. The *Majlis* then rejected the oil agreement in 1947, leaving the Soviets empty-handed.

Iran's behavior during the crisis is revealing. Despite its extreme vulnerability to Soviet pressure, Iran made only minor concessions to its more powerful neighbor. Qavam displayed great resolution in his dealings with Stalin, and his domestic compromises were largely tactical. For example, although U.S. officials were alarmed by the oil agreement in April, it was not an especially significant concession.[26] The Iranians clearly wanted to avoid antagonizing the Soviet Union, but they clearly *preferred* to balance the Soviets through an alignment with the United States. Indeed, the shah had tried to obtain a U.S. guarantee as early as 1943, and Iranian officials made repeated requests for U.S. support during 1945.[27]

Yet the United States did not make a clear commitment to Iran until October 1946. Despite the shah's requests, the United States did not adhere to the 1942 Anglo-Russian-Iranian treaty guaranteeing Iranian sovereignty. In his talks with Qavam in March 1946, U.S. Ambassador Wallace Murray refused to offer tangible support because "he could not be sure that the U.S. Government or the U.N.O. could save Iran [if the Soviets attacked]."[28] In August, Qavam's requests for U.S. help received only the "*suggestion* of American support . . . less than a forthright promise," and by September, the Iranians had concluded that concrete aid was unlikely.[29] This conclusion was not surprising; when the Iranians requested a $250 million credit, they were informed that $10 million was a more realistic possibility.[30]

It is true that George V. Allen, who became U.S. Ambassador to Iran in May 1946, worked hard to bolster Qavam's resolve.[31] Yet it is also striking how small the U.S. commitment was and how long the Iranians waited for it.[32] First, the United States did not pledge its support until *after* Qavam expelled the Tudeh representatives from the cabinet on October 18.[33] Allen himself believed that U.S. backing for Iran had been paltry, and he was convinced that Qavam preferred to resist Soviet pressure.[34] As he wrote several weeks later: "many people wanted the [removal of the Tudeh], *not least of whom was Qavam himself.*"[35] Finally, Qavam and the shah chose to subdue the rebellious province of Azerbaijan (thereby risking direct Soviet intervention) despite their awareness that direct U.S. assistance was unlikely.[36] They courted Soviet displeasure again several months later by reneging on the oil agreement. The United States supported each of these actions, but still refused to provide Tehran with significant economic or military aid.[37]

In sum, the crisis of 1946 suggests that it takes relatively little effort to persuade states to balance. Despite its own weakness, repeated Soviet threats, and very limited American support, Iran's leaders clearly preferred to balance rather than bandwagon. Qavam and the shah were challenged by the Tudeh party, by autonomy movements in Azerbaijan and Kurdistan, by several rebellious tribes, and by British efforts to preserve their access to Iranian oil. Alignment with the United States helped meet these various threats. Indeed, using a less threatening third power to counter external interference was a familiar Iranian tactic.[38]

Until the mid-1950s, Iran's repeated efforts to obtain a greater U.S. commitment met with little success. The principal link was a small U.S. military training mission, and the United States provided a mere $16 million worth of military credits (and no economic aid) from 1946 to 1951.[39] Taking Iran for granted was easy: although he was perennially dissatisfied with the level of U.S. aid, the shah made no attempt to obtain support elsewhere.[40]

The "globalization" of containment in the 1950s breathed new life into the U.S.-Iranian relationship. The United States and Great Britain staged a successful covert operation to restore the shah to the throne in 1953, after Prime Minister Mossadegh's efforts to nationalize the Anglo-Iranian Oil Company led to prolonged internal turmoil and U.S. fears of a communist takeover.[41] Subsequent efforts to establish an anti-Soviet alliance in the Near East brought an enthusiastic response from Tehran, and Iran joined the so-called Baghdad Pact despite U.S. reservations.[42] Iran began receiving substantial U.S. assistance, the shah endorsed the anticommunist "Eisenhower Doctrine," and relations grew even closer following the Iraqi revolution in July 1958. The shah continued to resist Soviet pressure to adopt a more neutral policy, U.S. military aid increased even further, and the United States and Iran signed a bilateral security agreement in March 1959.[43]

In the 1960s, however, Iran initiated a significant detente with the Soviet Union, under the guise of the shah's "Independent National Policy." In response to Soviet requests, Iran announced that it would not permit foreign missile bases on its territory. This decision paved the way for a series of agreements on trade, transit, and economic assistance. The shah visited Moscow in June 1965 and agreed to purchase roughly $100 million worth of Soviet arms in 1967.[44]

This shift was the result of several factors. First, the shah resented U.S. pressure for internal reforms and the limits the United States placed on Iranian military expenditures. Second, the development of intercontinental-range ballistic missiles made his statement on missile bases meaningless, as the United States had no need for missile bases in Iran at this point. Finally, Iranian perceptions of a Soviet threat had declined substantially by this time, both because the Tudeh party was no longer a powerful force and because the Soviet Union no longer insisted that Iran abandon its security ties with the West. And given the United States had begun its own detente with the Soviet Union after the Cuban missile crisis, Iran's desire to do so is understandable.[45]

Iran's Independent National Policy was not an example of bandwagoning, therefore. Security cooperation between the United States and Iran continued, including joint military exercises in 1964. Although the shah questioned U.S. credibility when the United States cut off arms to Pakistan in 1965, this did not end his efforts to obtain greater U.S. assistance.[46] Indeed, his flirtation with Moscow (e.g., the arms deal) was partly intended to persuade the United States to increase its own support for Iran.[47] Moreover, although the U.S.S.R. had been the major threat in the 1940s and 1950s, the shah now viewed revolutionary forces in the Middle East (and especially Nasser's Egypt) as Iran's main security threat. Obtaining arms from Moscow increased Iran's military capabilities and helped persuade the United States to do more as well. Iran also established tacit alliances with Jordan, Saudi Arabia, and Israel in response to these concerns.[48] Although the United States remained Iran's principal ally, the shah had learned that a degree of independence was more profitable than unswerving loyalty.[49]

Iran's freedom of action increased even more in the 1970s. This was due to three main developments: the British withdrawal east of Suez in 1967, the prolonged U.S. involvement in the Vietnam War, and the oil boom. Security ties with the United States expanded even more (primarily through arms sales) despite the shah's complaints about the U.S. failure to support Pakistan in 1965 and 1971. In particular, his desire to incresae Iran's military capabilities fit in well with the Nixon Doctrine, which called for the United States to rely less on its own troops and more on regional allies.[50]

As a result, Nixon endorsed the shah's imperial ambitions at his visit to Tehran in 1972.[51] Iran now enjoyed unrestricted access to U.S. weaponry, and the shah began taking direct action against the radical forces that he saw as the main threat to his rule. Iranian troops helped defeat the Dhofar rebellion in Oman, and the shah joined with Israel and the Central Intelligence Agency to support the Kurdish insurgency in Iraq. Iran occupied several disputed islands in the Persian Gulf, and the shah began a campaign to establish a collective security organization in the region. Iran also increased its support for Pakistan after its defeat by India in 1971, in order to discourage separatist movements that might endanger both countries.[52]

Predictably, relations with Moscow were guarded. The Soviets opposed the shah's role as a defender of U.S. interests, his hostility toward Iraq (which signed a treaty of friendship with the U.S.S.R. in 1972), and his recognition of the People's Republic of China in 1971. Although economic exchanges continued, Soviet-Iranian relations grew more distant after 1973. This reveals the shah's preferences clearly; although he still sought cordial relations with the U.S.S.R., his overriding interest lay in a continued alignment with the United States.

The revolution that overthrew the shah in 1979 brought the United States-Iranian alliance to an abrupt end. Iran's new rulers were understandably suspicious of the shah's principal patron, and this attitude was intensified by an ideological antipathy toward the West in general and the United States in particular.[53] Among other things, these events reveal that balance-of-threat theory cannot explain everything; Iran's realignment was due to a domestic upheaval rather than a change in the distribution of external threats. Because Khomeini and his followers defined Iran's interests in a radically different way—for both ideological and historical reasons—they abandoned the shah's traditional allies (the United States and Israel) in favor of alignment with Syria, Libya, and various Islamic fundamentalists in Lebanon and elsewhere.

Although domestic factors have largely determined Iran's international behavior since the revolution, its tendency to balance threats remained. The revolution did not lead Iran to move toward the U.S.S.R.; indeed, Soviet-Iranian relations have been worse under Khomeini than they were under the shah.[54] Iran forged close ties with Syria in order to balance Iraq (a traditional enemy for both states), and the war with Iraq forced the Islamic Republic to obtain assistance from a diverse array of otherwise unlikely supporters.[55] It is also worth noting that Iran's bellicosity has encouraged balancing behavior by its various neighbors, as the formation of the Gulf Cooperation Council, the tacit alignment between Saudi Arabia and Iraq, and the various naval deployments by the United States, Great Britain, and France all reveal.

Summary. Iran's behavior throughout the cold war supports the balancing hypothesis. Despite lukewarm U.S. support, Iran chose to resist Soviet pressure after World War II. The shah sought an active U.S. commitment during the 1950s, but shifted to a more independent posture as the Soviet threat declined and Iran's own capabilities improved. At the same time, he balanced against emerging regional threats by forging cooperative ties with Israel, Saudi Arabia, Pakistan, and Oman. In the 1970s, Iran took a more active role in the Persian Gulf, relying on its own capabilities and indirect support from the United States. Although the fall of the shah altered Iran's aims and interests considerably, it did not alter its tendency to balance threats. Iran's alliance policy, in short, provides little evidence of bandwagoning.

Turkey

Turkey's alliance policy presents an even clearer example of balancing behavior. During World War II, Turkey maintained a neutral position between Nazi Germany and its traditional Russian rival. Turkey swung toward the Allies as Germany's defeat approached, in order to ensure Western support against any future threat from the Soviet Union.[56] Soviet pressure on Turkey increased steadily, and the Soviets denounced the Soviet-Turkish Non-Aggression Treaty in March 1945. In June, they informed the Turks that renewal of the treaty was contingent on revision of the Montreux Agreement governing the Turkish Straits and upon territorial concessions in Eastern Turkey.[57]

Turkey refused to budge. Although the United States and Great Britain were initially willing to discuss the Soviet demands, the Turks rejected them outright and began an active campaign for U.S. support.[58] Stalin's continued threats and the simultaneous crisis in Iran encouraged a favorable U.S. response: Truman sent the battleship *Missouri* to Turkey in April 1946, and additional Soviet pressure in August led Truman to decide to "resist with all means at our disposal . . . any Soviet aggression against Turkey."[59] The United States rejected several Turkish requests for economic and military aid, but Turkey did receive credits worth between $25 and $50 million in November 1946. Finally, in March 1947, the Truman Doctrine publically committed the United States to defend Turkey against Soviet expansion.[60]

Still fearful of the U.S.S.R., Turkey sought a more substantial Western commitment.[61] After a lengthy campaign, Turkey was admitted to NATO in 1952.[62] United States assistance averaged nearly $100 million per year from 1950 to 1960, the United States enjoyed access to Turkish bases, and Turkey participated actively in NATO's military planning. Turkey agreed to join the Baghdad Pact in February 1955, and concern over Soviet involvement in Syria and Egypt led them to support an ill-conceived Western campaign against Syria in 1957.[63] After the Iraqi Revolution, the Turks agreed to join the Central Treaty Organization (CENTO), the successor to the Baghdad Pact, and a bilateral defense agreement with the United States was signed at this time. Although disturbed by the U.S. refusal to become a full member of CENTO, Turkey's anti-Soviet position remained intact through 1960.[64]

As with Iran, however, Turkey's unquestioning alignment with the West eroded in the 1960s. Relations with the Soviet Union, in turn, improved dramatically. Several factors were at work. Kennedy's decision to withdraw U.S. missiles from Turkey following the Cuban missile crisis alarmed the Turks, primarily because they were not consulted in advance.[65] Even more important, the growing struggle with Greece over Cyprus led to a serious rift between Washington and Ankara. The Turks were especially incensed by President Johnson's warning against the use of U.S. arms in the event of hostilities over Cyprus and his hint that NATO would not support Turkey if its actions on Cyprus led to Soviet intervention.[66] Lastly, the growing burden of the Vietnam War led to a significant reduction in U.S. aid.

In response, Turkey moved to increase its diplomatic options. In addition to attending the Non-Aligned Conference in Cairo in 1964, Turkey and the U.S.S.R. began what Alvin Rubinstein has termed a "wary detente." Soviet Foreign Minister Andrei Gromyko and Turkish Prime Minister Suat Urguplu exchanged visits in 1964, Soviet President Nikolai Podgorny came to Ankara the following year, and Soviet Premier Alexei Kosygin followed suit in 1966. The principal avenue of cooperation was economic: Turkey obtained a $200 million credit for industrial development in 1967, and Soviet-Turkish trade expanded rapidly.[67]

Although this shift was a marked departure from Turkey's previous policy, it was not an accomodation to Soviet pressure. In particular, the Turks repeatedly proclaimed that detente with the U.S.S.R. would not affect their existing commitments. Turkey's new approach was also encouraged by shifts in Soviet policy: Soviet criticisms of Turkey's NATO membership were dropped and Podgorny publically condemned Stalin's earlier claims on Turkish territory.[68] Moreover, the fact that the postwar boundaries had been in place for two decades no doubt decreased fears of Soviet pressure as well. Because Turkey was less vulnerable, the Soviets less threatening, and the United States less forthcoming, detente with the Soviet Union was an appealing strategy.

This situation persisted during the 1970s. Although Turkey remained a full member of NATO, recurring internal crises and the simmering dispute over Cyprus continued to mar relations with the United States. Responding to pressures by Greek-Americans, Congress cut off U.S. military aid to Turkey following the Turkish invasion of Cyprus in 1974. In response, the Turks restricted U.S. access to a number of military facilities. The restrictions were partially lifted in 1978 (after agreement was reached on a new Defense and Economic Cooperation Agreement), but the incident reinforced Turkish reservations about its alliance with the United States.[69]

Meanwhile, cooperation with the U.S.S.R. continued to grow. Podgorny signed an agreement for an additional $288 million worth of economic assistance during his visit in 1972, and a $700 million Soviet credit for industrial development was arranged in 1975. The two countries established a Joint Economic Cooperation Committee at this time, and a ten-year agreement for economic assistance was signed in 1977. By 1980, the Soviet Union had pledged over $3 billion worth of economic aid. Soviet-Turkish trade quadrupled between 1967 and 1977, and Turkey began importing increasing amounts of energy from the Soviet Union as well.[70]

Economic cooperation was matched by improved political ties. The U.S. weapons embargo led the Turks to explore the possibility of Soviet support; Turkish military observers attended Soviet military exercises in 1976 and 1978 and Prime Minister Ecevit told the Turkish Senate that "Turkey can no longer leave its national security only to its cooperation with the U.S. and NATO." Soviet Chief of Staff Ogarkov reportedly offered Turkey military aid that same year, although this offer was declined. The Turks refused Soviet requests for a nonaggression pact, but ultimately agreed to sign the set of "Principles of Good Neighborly and Friendly Cooperation" in June 1978. They also refused a U.S. request to use Turkish territory for monitoring Sovet missile tests following the loss of American intelligence stations in Iran. In short, by 1979 Turkey had established extensive economic ties and cordial political relations with its Soviet neighbor, in a sharp departure from its earlier policies.[71]

As with Iran, however, this was clearly a case of detente rather than bandwagoning. Turkey's improved ties with Moscow followed directly from the belief that the U.S.S.R. was no longer an imminent threat. The new relationship did not involve significant Turkish concessions; on the contrary, Turkey received important economic benefits as a result. Furthermore, detente with Moscow was accompanied by active efforts to expand Turkey's ties with Pakistan, Iran, and several Arab states, thereby reinforcing its diplomatic position.[72]

Finally, the Soviet invasion of Afghanistan helped revive Turkey's status within NATO, both by increasing Western perceptions of Turkey's value and by reminding the Turks that the Soviet Union might not be entirely benevolent. The new Defense and Economic Cooperation Agreement with the United States was signed in 1980, restoring full U.S. access to Turkish bases and providing over $500 million worth of military and economic assistance. In addition, a NATO consortium pledged more than $1 billion in aid in April 1980, underscoring Turkey's continued commitment to NATO.[73]

Summary. Since World War II, Turkey's security from Soviet pressure has been based on a formal alliance with Europe and the United States. Once this objective was achieved, however, establishing cordial relations with Moscow was clearly in Turkey's interest. The Soviet Union has become a valuable economic partner, it no longer poses an imminent threat, and Soviet-Turkish ties make it less likely that Turkey's allies will take it for granted. Thus detente with the Soviet Union has been a reflection of NATO's success in providing for Turkey's security. And after more than thirty-five years, Turkey remains fully integrated in NATO defense planning.[74] All things considered, Turkish foreign policy offers substantial support for the balancing hypothesis.

India

Indian foreign policy is based on an explicit policy of nonalignment. Its size and stature have enabled it to avoid formal attachments, and the legacy of colonial rule has reinforced suspicion of Western security schemes. Despite its public posture, however, India has departed from strict nonalignment whenever serious threats emerged. Given the nature of these threats and India's geographic position, this has usually meant a close relationship with the Soviet Union.[75]

Pakistan has been India's most important rival. The Indo-Pakistani conflict arises from the traditional enmity between Hindus and Moslems on the subcontinent, compounded by the specific disputes that emerged during independence and partition.[76] Given that approximately 500,000 people died in communal violence after independence, triggering the migration of roughly 10 million people, it is hardly surprising that the conflict has dominated both countries' security concerns since then.[77]

China was a potential threat as well, but Nehru actively sought good relations with India's large northern neighbor. India supported China's entry into the United Nations and helped mediate between China and the West during the Korean War. When China's occupation of Tibet in 1950 threatened the Indian border, Nehru made only minor protests and negotiated a conciliatory agreement on the issue. This policy was temporarily successful: Nehru and Chou En-lai announced in 1954 that Sino-Indian relations would henceforth be guided by the principles of *panch sheel* (peaceful coexistence).[78]

The decision to accomodate China was based on several factors. Nehru placed great value on "Asian solidarity" and, because he saw both China and India as victims of imperialist domination, he assumed that Sino-Indian differences could be overcome rather easily. Nehru also saw Sino-Indian cooperation as a way for both countries to protect themselves from great power interference. Finally, he believed that a confrontation with China would require sacrifices India could not afford, given the existing conflict with Pakistan and India's pressing domestic needs.[79]

India's attitude toward both superpowers was more reserved. In contrast to Turkey and Iran, India did not support the U.S. campaign to contain communism. As a result, early contacts between Nehru and the United States were disappointing.[80] Nehru was at least partly sympathetic to socialist ideas (though he occasionally imprisoned communists in India) and he did not view the Soviet Union as a significant threat. India's refusal to sign the Japanese Peace treaty or to condemn China's intervention in the Korean War also undermined its image in the United States.[81] Relations with the Soviet Union were also limited, due to Stalin's belief that the former colonies were still pawns of the imperialist powers.[82] Nonalignment presented little difficulty for India, however; so long as relations with China were good and Pakistan did not become too powerful, India had little need of allies.[83]

The first hint that India would seek Soviet assistance followed Pakistan's decision to join the Baghdad Pact and SEATO in 1955. Convinced that Stalin's successors were more moderate, Nehru countered by inviting Khrushchev and Bulganin to India in 1955. The Soviets backed India's position on Kashmir, and India received a $112 million loan at this time.[84] In return, Nehru paid a highly successful visit to the Soviet Union later in the year. India continued to receive economic aid from the West and remained a member of the British Commonwealth, but these steps demonstrated its diplomatic options.

India's nonaligned status eroded further once relations with China deteriorated. Although Chinese and Indian interests clashed on a number of issues, the dispute centered on several disputed border areas. The Tibetan revolt of 1959 accelerated the decline; Indian public opinion was aroused while the Chinese accused India of supporting the rebels. Talks between Nehru and Chou in 1960 failed to resolve their differences, and public opinion forced Nehru to take an increasingly provocative position.[85]

In response, India increased its security efforts and sought greater foreign support. Defense spending doubled from 1959 to 1962, and India consolidated its influence in the buffer states of Nepal, Bhutan, and Sikkim.[86] India agreed to purchase Soviet arms for the first time in 1959, and negotiations to purchase advanced fighter aircraft began in 1961.[87] India's quarrel with China was especially welcome news in Washington, and the Kennedy administration began a major effort to improve relations with New Delhi, through a combination of diplomacy and increased economic aid.[88]

These trends were reinforced when China inflicted a brief but decisive defeat on the Indian Army in October 1962.[89] Although India was the principal aggressor, the United States, Great Britain, and the Soviet Union all sent military equipment to India during and after the war.[90] India's ability to balance China was enhanced by the U.S.-Soviet competition and by the fact that both superpowers were now hostile to Peking.

The Indian Army's poor showing in 1962 triggered a major campaign to enhance its military capabilities, a decision that China's growing relationship with Pakistan reinforced. The Soviet Union was the most willing supplier, and Soviet-Indian military ties began to expand rapidly after 1962.[91]

The effort paid off in the two subsequent wars with Pakistan. In the first, Pakistan sought to exploit India's weakness and China's support by "leaning on India."[92] Border incidents rose steadily, and Pakistan began infiltrating troops into Kashmir in August 1965. After several minor skirmishes, India attacked

West Pakistan in force on September 5. After several weeks of fighting (in which the Indian forces gradually gained the upper hand), a ceasefire was arranged on September 22.[93]

Unwilling to take sides, the United States imposed a military embargo on both countries and reduced its involvement in South Asian affairs substantially.[94] By contrast, the Soviet Union continued to ship arms to India, began a campaign to improve relations with Pakistan, and initiated a successful effort to mediate the conflict. Meanwhile, India's superiority vis-à-vis Pakistan continued to grow.[95]

India's "nonalignment" was now overwhelmingly pro-Soviet, as a means of balancing against Pakistan and China. This motive was apparent in the Indo-Pakistani war of 1971. When the outbreak of a brutal civil war in East Pakistan triggered a confrontation beween India and Pakistan, Gandhi quickly reinforced India's ties with Moscow. United States military aid to Pakistan had been restored in 1969, and the announcement that President Nixon had been invited to Peking reinforced Indian fears of an incipient Sino-Pakistani-U.S. coalition. In response, India and the U.S.S.R. signed the Treaty of Friendship and Cooperation in August 1971, pledging "mutual consultation" in the event "of either being subjected to an attack or a threat thereof."[96]

After several months of skirmishing, open war broke out in December. Viewing the crisis as the result of Indian aggression (and intent on showing China that the United States was a reliable ally), Nixon and Kissinger "tilted" toward Pakistan.[97] When the Indian forces swept through East Pakistan and inflicted a decisive defeat in the West as well, the Soviet Union aided their efforts by deterring Chinese intervention and by vetoing several UN ceasefire resolutions.

Once again, an external threat had led India to seek allied support. Although Gandhi's motives were not entirely defensive—the war was a golden opportunity for India to establish its hegemony on the subcontinent—its actions were primarily reactive rather than aggressive. Having demonstrated its preeminence, India gradually moved back toward nonalignment. Pakistan was no longer an especially potent threat—a fact signified by the Simla Accord of 1972[98]—and China's rapprochement with the United States was partially neutralized by India's successful nuclear test in 1974. The Indo-Soviet treaty remained in force, and the U.S.S.R. continued to be a major trading partner and India's principal source of arms. After 1971, however, India began to diversify in both areas to avoid excessive reliance on Moscow.[99] Although Indo-Soviet relations survived Gandhi's electoral defeat in 1977 and the invasion of Afghanistan in 1979, disagreements on a number of issues highlighted India's continued freedom of action.[100]

That freedom was also revealed by the recovery of India's relations with the United States, which had reached an all-time low during the 1971 war. Although impeded by India's nuclear test, the U.S. rapprochement with China, and the resumption of U.S. arms sales to Pakistan, a tangible improvement was apparent by the end of the decade. Economic aid returned to pre-1971 levels, and President Carter staged a successful visit to India in 1978. Although Indira Gandhi (who regained power in 1979) was critical of U.S. aid to Pakistan after the invasion of Afghanistan, India's opposition was relatively mild by historical standards. Indeed, Gandhi's visit to Washington in 1982 suggested a growing awareness that U.S. involvement in South Asian security might be a useful hedge against further Soviet encroachments.

Finally, India's enhanced position after 1971 permitted it to seek better relations with Pakistan and China, although they proceeded cautiously on both fronts. Gandhi inaugurated a modest detente with China in 1976, and Sino-Indian relations slowly revived on several fronts.[101] Relations with Pakistan remain erratic and have been exacerbated by India's concerns over Pakistan's nuclear program and the effects of U.S. military aid.[102] In general, however, India's willingness to pursue more cooperative relations reflects the fact that the threat from its traditional adversaries has declined significantly.

Summary. India's foreign policy also suggests that states prefer to balance rather than bandwagon. A partial exception was the attempt to appease China in the 1950s, and this failure was clearly instructive. Although India's size and status made nonalignment feasible (because it could always count on at least one of the superpowers to come to its aid), India's leaders have abandoned strict nonalignment whenever serious threats emerged.[103] Indeed, the tacit alignment between India and the Soviet Union is precisely what the balance-of-threat theory would predict, given that geography and history have placed Pakistan and China at odds with both.

Pakistan

After independence, Pakistan quickly adopted a pro-Western policy. Indeed, its early overtures to the Soviet Union were intended primarily to attract greater U.S. attention.[104] Unlike India, Pakistan supported the peace treaty with Japan and opposed China's intervention in Korea and its admission to the United Nations. Even more important, Pakistani and American officials began exploring the possibility of military cooperation as early as 1951. Pakistan joined the Baghdad Pact in 1954 and later joined SEATO as well.[105]

As with Iran and Turkey, the U.S. alliance with Pakistan was part of its effort to contain the Soviet Union. For Pakistan, the principal motive was a desire to balance India, although domestic factors and pressure from Afghanistan played an important role as well.[106] The United States refused to support Pakistan's efforts to regain Kashmir, but did provide an average of $120 million in economic and military aid from 1953 to 1958.[107]

Pakistan's position as America's "most allied ally" declined dramatically in the 1960s. The Pakistanis were alarmed by the Kennedy administration's efforts to court India, especially when the United States shipped arms to India during the Sino-Indian war of 1962. Pakistan's response was predictable; they balanced by moving closer to China. Border talks began in October 1962, an agreement was announced in March 1963, and Sino-Pakistani cooperation expanded steadily over the next two years.[108] In addition to economic assistance, China supported

Pakistan's claims to Kashmir while Pakistan backed China's efforts to join the United Nations.[109]

These trends accelerated after Pakistan's defeat in 1965. The arms embargo revealed that the U.S. alliance was worthless against India, and President Ayub adopted a policy of "bilateralism" aimed at expanding Pakistan's relations with China *and* the Soviet Union.[110] Pakistan began receiving Chinese weaponry in 1966, and the Soviets pledged $112 million in economic aid. Trade with the Soviet Union began to expand, and the Soviets sent several small arms shipments in 1967. Ayub also announced that Pakistan would not renew the U.S. lease for its intelligence facility at Peshawar, in an attempt to persuade the Soviet Union to reduce its support for India.

These measures were an obvious response to what Pakistan's leaders saw as inadequate U.S. support, but they do not qualify as bandwagoning behavior. Pakistan did not shift to a pro-Soviet or pro-Indian position; for example, Ayub rejected Soviet requests to use Pakistani facilities and opposed the Soviet plan for a collective security system in Asia. And when it became clear that the Soviet Union would not reduce its support for India, Soviet-Pakistani relations cooled quickly. In short, "bilateralism" was not an accomodation to Soviet or Indian power, it was an attempt to balance the main threat—India.[111]

As noted earlier, Pakistan's relations with the United States revived during the Nixon administration. The arms embargo was lifted and Nixon told President Khan that "nobody has occupied the White House who is friendlier to Pakistan than me."[112] Yet neither the United States nor China did much to prevent Pakistan's dismemberment in 1971. Nixon's "tilt" toward Pakistan had little effect, and China carefully limited its commitment to West Pakistan.[113]

Gravely weakened by the 1971 debacle, Pakistan's response was two-fold. First, the new president, Zulfikar Ali Bhutto, began an active effort to appease India, beginning with the Simla Accord in April 1972. A gradual detente began to take shape, although lingering suspicions made extensive cooperation unlikely. Bhutto also sought cordial relations with the Soviet Union, and his visit to Moscow in March 1972 helped overcome the hostility that had arisen the previous year. Finally, Bhutto extended diplomatic recognition to Bangladesh in 1973, both to obtain the release of West Pakistani prisoners and to begin a process of reconciliation between the two countries.[114]

Second, these acts of accommodation were accompanied by an energetic search for additional allied support. China increased its military aid substantially and continued to assist Pakistan's nuclear program.[115] Bhutto also began a campaign to attract support from other Muslim countries. Pakistan hosted the Second Islamic Conference in 1974, and financial assistance from Iran, Saudi Arabia, and others helped reequip the Pakistani armed forces. Thus the desire to balance continued even as detente with India began.[116]

Relations with the United States remained turbulent for most of the decade, however. The United States resumed large-scale economic aid after the war and lifted its ban on military sales in 1975. Yet Pakistan's efforts to obtain direct U.S. military aid failed, due to U.S. opposition to Pakistan's nuclear program, its concerns about human rights under both Bhutto and his successor, General

Zia al-Huq, and the Carter administration's campaign to improve relations with India.[117]

As one would expect, however, the invasion of Afghanistan ended the impasse. After years of "benign neglect," Pakistan's security had once again become a vital concern. The Carter administration reaffirmed the U.S. commitment to Pakistan, offered a $400 million military aid package, and, as Alvin Z. Rubinstein has noted, established the Rapid Deployment Joint Task Force to enhance the U.S. military posture in the region. Yet Pakistan did not rush to welcome American assistance, and its apparent reluctance to stand up to the Soviets was revealed by Zia's statement that "you can't live in the sea and create enmity with whales . . . you have to be friendly with them."[118] Zia dismissed the U.S. aid offer as "peanuts" and pointed out that prior U.S. commitments had been less than reliable. Pakistan now sought a formal treaty of alliance, and Carter's refusal to go beyond the 1959 Defense Agreement reinforced Pakistani concerns about U.S. credibility.[119]

Yet despite these reservations, Pakistan ultimately chose to balance once more. Indeed, Zia's initial reluctance was undoubtedly intended to force the United States to make a more visible and extensive commitment. The tactic worked well: the Reagan administration arranged a $3.2 billion defense package for Pakistan in March 1981, which included forty F-16 aircraft. The administration overlooked earlier concerns about Pakistan's nuclear program and human rights practices and successfully overcame congressional opposition to the aid package. Less visible, but no less important, was Pakistan's cooperation with U.S. and Chinese efforts to support the Afghan resistance. Despite Soviet protests and repeated Soviet violations of Pakistani airspace, Zia now stated that Pakistan "would not yield to the far greater pressure expected from the Soviets in the near future."[120] Pakistan obtained support from the Muslim world as well: an Islamic summit condemned the Soviet invasion in January 1980, and several Arab states provided funding for additional arms purchases.[121]

At the same time, Zia tried to minimize the inevitable tensions with the Soviet Union. He welcomed efforts to negotiate the withdrawal of Soviet forces from Afghanistan and avoided an overtly anti-Soviet posture. On the whole, however, the invasion reinforced Pakistan's familiar policy of countering internal and external challenges by obtaining support from the United States and China. In short, although Pakistan's rulers have sought better relations with their adversaries when this seemed feasible, balancing behavior still dominates Pakistani policy.[122]

Summary. The Pakistani case is especially revealing. Pakistan is much weaker than its principal adversaries, it has faced numerous internal problems, and U.S. and Chinese support have been erratic at best. Yet Pakistan has made only minor concessions to its principal opponents, and then only after major defeats. In particular, Pakistan has not adopted a pro-Indian or pro-Soviet policy, despite its obvious vulnerability to both. Thus this case also provides strong support for the balancing hypothesis.

Analysis

Balancing Versus Bandwagoning

Each of the cases examined in this article supports the balancing hypothesis. When faced with a clear external threat, these states almost always sought to counter the threat through some combination of external alignment and internal effort. Furthermore, when the level of threat increased (i.e., during a crisis or war), efforts to balance intensified. This is true even when the leaders in question preferred a policy of neutrality. Thus Nehru was a leading advocate of nonalignment and tried to foster good relations between India and China, but he welcomed aid from both superpowers when relations with Beijing deteriorated.

Most important of all, these states chose to balance even when allied support was uncertain. Both Turkey and Iran required little encouragement to oppose the Soviet Union after World War II; in fact, they were far more interested in obtaining U.S. backing than the United States was in providing it. Similarly, Pakistan did not bandwagon when the Kennedy administration's courtship of India raised doubts about the U.S. commitment to Pakistan; instead, it balanced by moving closer to China. And although the United States and China had been rather unreliable allies in the past, the Soviet invasion of Afghanistan led the Pakistanis to turn to them once more (although General Zia did extract a higher price). The lesson is clear: balancing is what states prefer to do.

By contrast, examples of bandwagoning were almost nonexistent. None of the alignments examined here resulted from a decision to bandwagon; at most, they are examples of detente. And the fate of these very limited efforts is revealing. India's efforts to appease China during the 1950s were abandoned as soon as "Asian solidarity" and *panch sheel* proved a weak guarantee of amicable relations. Pakistan's willingness to appease India after 1965 and 1971 did not go very far either, and both sides remain sensitive to the other's actions and capabilities. Similarly, although Soviet relations with Turkey and Iran improved dramatically after 1960, neither country abandoned its pro-Western alignment or seemed reluctant to oppose Soviet expansion, as their reactions to the invasion of Afghanistan suggest.[123]

The key issue is whether these limited efforts at accomodation were a response to increases in Soviet power or the erosion of American credibility. If so, then the bandwagoning hypothesis should be given greater weight. Although the evidence is mixed, a careful analysis suggests that this is not the case. On the one hand, the erosion of U.S. commitments in South Asia and the improvement of relations with the Soviet Union coincided with events that revealed the limits of U.S. support. For Turkey, it was the removal of U.S. missiles and the growing dispute over Cyprus. For Pakistan, it was the U.S. courtship of India and the arms embargo in 1965, reinforced by the weak support Pakistan received in 1971. For Iran, it was U.S. opposition to the shah's domestic programs and regional ambitions, as well as its inconsistent commitment to CENTO. Thus there is some evidence that detente with the Soviet Union was encouraged by doubts about U.S. credibility.

On the other hand, such concerns did not lead these states to realign. Instead, they balanced through new defensive arrangements. Pakistan moved closer to China and sought new allies in the Moslem world, and its detente with Moscow in the 1960s was a response to the threat from India rather than an attempt to appease the Soviet Union. Iran's detente with the U.S.S.R. was accompanied by new alliances with several regional powers (Israel, Saudi Arabia, and Oman) *and* a growing relationship with the United States. Turkey joined the Non-Allied Movement and welcomed Soviet support over Cyprus, but remained an active member of NATO. Even if U.S. backing no longer seemed 100 percent reliable, this perception did not trigger widespread defections.

Second, these developments coincided with Soviet efforts to improve its bellicose image. Although Soviet power was growing steadily, an adroit combination of economic aid, cultural exchanges, and conciliatory diplomacy helped reduce the threat that Soviet neighbors perceived. Moreover, these states were all more capable than they had been in the early 1950s. All save India enjoyed formal security ties with the West, and the territorial status quo had acquired considerable legitimacy since 1945. Detente with the Soviet Union was less dangerous, and U.S. efforts to reduce tensions with the Soviets made this approach more legitimate for other states as well. Far from being evidence of bandwagoning tendencies, therefore, these detentes between the Soviet Union and these states supported balance-of-threat theory. As the level of threat declined, the incentive to balance declined as well.[124]

Third, the erosion of the United States's earlier position was due more to the tensions that are part of every alliance than to declining U.S. credibility. The United States did not support Pakistan's ambitions in Kashmir, Turkey's objectives on Cyprus, or the shah's regional pretensions. But these differences did not mean that its commitment to defend them against Soviet aggression had waned. Once the Soviet threat no longer loomed as large, the United States and its allies had less reason to overlook these bilateral disputes. Moreover, U.S. support helped its allies gain the strength necessary to pursue more independent policies. Thus a decline in alliance cohesion was virtually inevitable. Rather than providing evidence of Soviet intimidation, these events suggest that the effort to balance the U.S.S.R. had worked quite well.

Finally, as suggested at the beginning of this chapter, client states are likely to exaggerate their propensity to bandwagon, in order to persuade their patrons to provide more support. The states examined here have clearly recognized the value of this tactic. Iranian officials encouraged U.S. support in 1946 by arguing that a Soviet victory there would undermine international confidence in the United States and the United Nations. The shah claimed that the U.S. failure to aid Pakistan in 1965 and 1971 gravely weakened the credibility of U.S. promises (despite the fact that Pakistan bore greater responsibility for both wars). Marshal Zia of Pakistan used the same arguments when seeking a greater U.S. commitment in 1980, implying that he would be forced to succumb to Soviet pressure if U.S. aid were not increased. Despite these threats, however, each of these leaders ultimately chose not to realign. When listening to allied complaints about U.S. credibility, therefore, we should not forget that client states have a powerful incentive to overstate their propensity to defect.

In short, there is little evidence that declining U.S. power has led others to bandwagon. The extent of accommodation was minimal, and other factors were far more important. Of course, U.S. leaders cannot be indifferent to their allies' concerns, but they should recognize that decisions to bandwagon are made with great reluctance. Accordingly, relatively little effort is required to prevent them from occurring.

Balance of Power Versus Balance of Threat

These cases also illustrate the limitations of structural balance-of-power theory and the greater explanatory power of what I have called "balance-of-threat" theory. The states examined here did not balance against the most powerful state. Instead, they balanced against the state(s) they perceived as most *threatening*. The importance of this distinction can be seen in several ways.

First, the United States was far more powerful that the Soviet Union during the early cold war (e.g., it controlled nearly 40 percent of gross world product and was sole possessor of the atomic bomb). Yet geographic proximity and Soviet ambitions made the U.S.S.R. appear more threatening to Turkey and Iran. And the subsequent improvement in Soviet relations with both of these countries was due primarily to changing perceptions of Soviet intentions rather than changes in Soviet capabilities. By contrast, the United States was an appealing ally because it was powerful but not hostile and because it was far away.[125] In short, focusing on power alone can be very misleading, because it overlooks the other factors that affect the level of threat that national leaders will perceive.

Second, although the superpowers have been primarily concerned with each other, regional powers are more sensitive to regional factors than to the global balance of power. As noted earlier, Soviet proximity and U.S. distance encouraged Turkey and Iran to seek an alliance with the West, a tendency that Soviet actions reinforced. In the 1960s and 1970s, however, Iran's concerns focused on Egypt, Iraq, and South Yemen, and relations with the Soviet Union improved. Similarly, the Cyprus dispute dominated Turkey's security agenda after 1963, to the detriment of its ties with the United States.

The same is true for India and Pakistan. Were power the only significant factor, India and Pakistan might be inclined to join forces against whichever superpower was strongest, either in association with the weaker superpower or with China. Instead, India and Pakistan have relied upon the United States and Soviet Union in order to counter each other. Geography and history make each the other's most significant rival, which explains why neither superpower has been able to enjoy good relations with both India and Pakistan for very long.[126]

Finally, by focusing on power alone, balance-of-power theory overlooks the fact that domestic threats may provide an important motive for alignment. Although external threats were probably more important, domestic concerns also encouraged Pakistan and Iran to seek U.S. support. As Steven David has suggested, regime stability and personal survival rank high on the agendas of many Third World leaders.[127] Balance-of-threat theory can accomodate this possibility—that is, states seek allies to counter both internal or external threats, whichever is most imminent—but balance-of-power theory cannot.

In short, although the distribution of power is hardly irrelevent, it is not the only (or even the most important) factor. Examining the different components of threat (power, proximity, offensive capability, and perceived intentions) provides a more compelling account of how and why states seek alliance partners. Of course, it will not always be clear which threats are most dangerous or which allies will be most valuable. Yet despite these limitations, balance-of-threat theory provides a more powerful explanation of alliance choices than structural balance-of-power theory.

Conclusion

The evidence in favor of balance-of-threat theory is impressive. The cases examined in this chapter confirm the results of earlier studies: balancing is far more common than bandwagoning and states ally in response to *threats* rather than just the balance of power.[128] Despite widespread fears to the contrary, dominoes rarely fall and bandwagons rarely form.

Among other things, these results undermine the justification for much of postwar U.S. foreign policy. Throughout the cold war, the fear of falling dominoes and pro-Soviet bandwagons has been invoked repeatedly to justify increased U.S. defense spending or overseas military intervention. The events examined here suggest that these alleged dangers were greatly exaggerated.

Contrary to several recent proposals, however, the tendency for states to balance does not mean that the United States should return to isolationism, confident that its allies will quickly take up the slack.[129] Although most U.S. allies would probably balance if the United States withdrew, the real question is whether they would do enough to compensate for the loss of U.S. support. United States withdrawal would undermine deterrence, because a Soviet challenge would be more likely if they believed that the United States would not be involved. The U.S. presence in Europe also helps protect its allies from each other; if the United States withdraws, tensions between our present allies would probably increase. Thus, the tendency for states to prefer balancing does not mean that the United States should try to "free-ride" on others.[130]

Balance of threat theory carries several other implications as well. Because states balance against *threats* (rather than power alone), U.S. allies are likely to assess their security interests differently than the United States does. Preoccupied with Soviet power, U.S. leaders often forget that client states will worry more about local threats than they do about the Soviet Union. Accordingly, efforts to fashion a "strategic consensus" against the Soviet Union, as John Foster Dulles and Alexander Haig tired to do, may simply exacerbate U.S. relations with otherwise friendly states and destabilize regional relations unnecessarily.

Furthermore, if U.S. leaders focus solely on power and ignore the impact of changing intentions, they are likely to misinterpret their allies' efforts to improve relations with the Soviet Union. If one looks only at the balance of power, then a detente between the Soviet Union and an important U.S. ally may be seen in

Washington as an example of bandwagoning. United States leaders may worry that U.S. credibility is eroding, even when it is actually quite robust. By focusing on threats—thus incorporating changing estimates of Soviet intentions—U.S. leaders are more likely to recognize that an attempted detente in fact suggests that U.S. efforts to moderate Soviet intentions and to reassure allies are working

These observations are especially pertinent in light of the "Gorbachev revolution." Since World War II, NATO's political cohesion has been enhanced by the fact that the Soviet Union usually appeared to be more dangerous than the United States. Under Gorbachev, however, Sovet foreign policy has focused primarily on reducing Western perceptions of a Soviet threat. To do so, Gorbachev has downplayed the ideological themes of world revolution and class struggle, initiated major domestic reforms, made dramatic concessions on arms control, and taken steps to reduce Soviet military power. And just as balance-of-threat theory would predict, this apparent decline in the Soviet threat has led to increased political tensions within the Western alliance, as the United States and its allies argue over how to respond to these various initiatives.

The cases examined here may offer some useful guidance. First, balance-of-threat theory suggests that the United States must ensure that it does not appear more bellicose than the Soviet Union, or less interested in forging more cordial and stable relations. Thus U.S. reluctance to conduct wide-ranging arms control negotiations is counterproductive, as is U.S. insistence that NATO's short-range nuclear forces be modernized by deploying the LANCE II missile. Given the overkill that both sides possess at all levels of nuclear combat, the deterrent value of a handful of new missiles hardly outweighs the political cost of appearing less interested in peace than the Soviet Union.

Second, the cases examined in this chapter remind us that even acknowledged adversaries can establish better relations without sacrificing existing alliance commitments. Balancing against a threatening state need not entail a relationship of unremitting hostility; indeed, the optimal strategy for most states is to forge a reliable alliance with the least threatening great power while maintaining the best possible relations with the others. That is exactly what Turkey, Pakistan, and Iran tried to do, and India's policy of "nonaligned alignment" reflects a similar awareness.[131] Given that the Soviet Union may now be offering NATO the chance to reduce East–West tensions within the context of existing alliance commitments, NATO's leaders would do well to ponder these lessons carefully.

Notes

I would like to thank Doug Blum, Selig Harrison, Ted Hopf, Robert Jervis, Zalmay Khalilizad, Bruce R. Kuniholm, Deborah Welch Larson, Jack Snyder, Stephen Van Evera, and W. Howard Wriggins for their comments on this paper. I am also grateful to the Carnegie Endowment for International Peace and the Center for International Studies at Princeton University for financial support.

1. As President Reagan stated in a speech advocating support for the *contras:* "If we cannot defend ourselves [in Central America] . . . then we cannot expect to prevail

elsewhere . . . . Our credibility will collapse and our alliances will crumble." See *New York Times,* Apr. 28, 1983, A 12.

2. For example, General Bernard Rogers, former Supreme Allied Commander in Europe, has stated that "if the U.S. withdraws 100,000 troops from Europe, this won't make the Europeans do more . . . [it] is going to send the kind of message that will lead [the European NATO members] to start to accomodate to the East." Quoted in Edgar Ulsamer, "The Potential Checkmate in Europe," *Air Force Magazine* 69 (November 1986): 55–56.

3. See Christopher Layne, "Atlanticism Without NATO," *Foreign Policy* no. 67 (Summer 1987); and Earl Ravenal, "Europe Without America: The Erosion of NATO," *Foreign Affairs* 63:5 (Summer 1985).

4. See Kenneth N. Waltz, *Theory of International Politics* (Reading, Mass.: Addison-Wesley, 1979), chap. 6. Other prominent versions of balance-of-power theory include Hans Morgenthau and Kenneth W. Thompson, *Politics Among Nations: The Struggle for Power and Peace,* 6th ed. (New York: Alfred A. Knopf, 1985); and Morton A. Kaplan, *System and Process in International Politics* (New York: John Wiley, 1957).

5. The best guide to this debate is *Neorealism and Its Critics,* ed. Robert O. Keohane (New York: Columbia University Press, 1986).

6. An exception to this assertion is Barry R. Posen, *The Sources of the Military Doctrine: Britain, France, and Germany Between the World Wars* (Ithaca, N.Y.: Cornell University Press, 1984). John Ruggie addresses the empirical limitations of balance-of-power theory in his own critique of Waltz, but he focuses primarily on the question of systems transformation rather than on predictive failures *within* the context of the existing state system. See his "Continuity and Transformation in the World Polity: Toward a Neorealist Synthesis," in Keohane, *Neorealism and Its Critics.* Richard Rosecrance has also challenged Waltz's analysis on empirical grounds, arguing that Waltz understates the level of international economic interdependence. See his "International Theory Revisited," *International Organization* 35:4 (Autumn 1981), plus Waltz's reply and Rosecrance's rejoinder in *International Organization* 36:3 (Summer 1982): 679–85.

7. The importance of alliances in international politics is widely acknowledged. According to George Modelski, alliance is "one of a dozen or so key terms of international relations." See Modelski, "The Study of Alliances: A Review," *Journal of Conflict Resolution* 7:4 (1963): 773. Ole Holsti describes alliances as "a universal component of relations between political units," and Hans Morgenthau states that "alliances are a necessary function of the balance-of-power operating in a multiple state system." See Ole Holsti, P. Terrence Hopmann, and John D. Sullivan, *Unity and Disintegration in International Alliances* (New York: John Wiley, 1973), 2; and Hans J. Morgenthau, "Alliances in Theory and Practice," in *Alliance Policy in the Cold War,* ed. Arnold Wolfers (Baltimore: Johns Hopkins University Press, 1959), 185.

8. See Stephen M. Walt, *The Origin of Alliances* (Ithaca, N.Y.: Cornell University Press, 1987); and Walt, "Alliance Formation and the Balance of World Power," *International Security* 9:4 (Spring 1985).

9. Portions of this section are based on Walt, *Origins of Alliances,* chaps. 2 and 8.

10. See W. Scott Thompson, "The Communist International System," *Orbis* 20:4 (Winter 1977); Charles Krauthammer, "Isolationism: Left and Right," *The New Republic,* Mar. 4, 1985; and Colin S. Gray, *Maritime Strategy, Geopolitics, and the Defense of the West* (New York: National Strategy Information Center, 1986), 38–40.

11. The domino metaphor describes the fear that an opponent's victory in an area will make further expansion easier or more likely. Dominoes may fall because (1) expansion increases the victor's capabilities; (2) defeat undermines the defender's morale and thus

weakens its ability to resist; (3) victory in one area encourages sympathizers in other countries to increase their efforts to subvert existing regimes; and (4) one side's victories convince other states to shift their alignment to the winning side voluntarily. Strictly speaking, only the last variant should be viewed as bandwagoning.

12. Quoted in Seyom Brown, *The Faces of Power: Constancy and Change in United States Foreign Policy from Truman to Johnson* (New York: Columbia University Press, 1968), 217. For additional evidence on U.S. perceptions, see Walt, *Origins of Alliances,* chaps. 1 and 2; Patrick Morgan, "Saving Face for the Sake of Deterrence," in Robert Jervis, Richard Ned Lebow, and Janice Gross Stein, eds., *Psychology and Deterrence* (Baltimore: Johns Hopkins University Press, 1985); John Lewis Gaddis, *Strategies of Containment: A Critical Analysis of Postwar American National Security Policy* (New York: Oxford University Press, 1981), 91–92, 97, 103, 202, 235–36, 240–41; and Deborah Larson's contribution to this volume, chap. 4. The Soviet belief in bandwagoning can be seen in the claim that favorable shifts in the "correlation of forces" will make additional international gains *easier* rather than harder, and in the corresponding belief that the growth of Soviet power "forced" the United States to accept detente in the 1970s. See William Zimmerman, *Soviet Perspectives on International Relations* (Princeton, N.Y.: Princeton University Press, 1969), 159–64; Raymond J. Garthoff, *Detente and Confrontation: American-Soviet Relations from Nixon to Reagan* (Washington: Brookings Institution, 1985), 36–53; and Coit D. Blacker, "The Kremlin and Detente," in *Managing U.S.-Soviet Rivalry: Problems of Crisis Prevention,* ed. Alexander L. George (Boulder: Westview, 1983). For evidence that some Soviet analysts recognized a tendency for states to balance, see Ted Hopf in chap. 6 of this volume.

13. See Waltz, *Theory of International Politics,* 126–27.

14. See Robert L. Rothstein, *Alliances and Small Powers* (New York: Columbia University Press, 1968), 11.

15. On the balance-of-power in the two world wars, see Paul M. Kennedy, "The First World War and the International Power System," *International Security* 9:1 (Summer 1984); and Kennedy, *The Rise and Fall of British Naval Mastery* (London: Allen and Unwin, 1983), 309–15.

16. The explanation, of course, is that the Allies were united by the common awareness that although Germany was ultimately less powerful, its aggressive actions made it more dangerous.

17. In 1950, the United States produced approximately 40 percent of gross world product; the Soviet Union managed only 13.5 percent. U.S. naval and air power were far superior, and the United States had a clear advantage in deliverable atomic weaponry.

18. The United States and its allies lead the U.S.S.R. and its allies by more than 3 to 1 in gross national product and nearly 2 to 1 in population. The two coalitions are roughly equal in number of men under arms, and the western alliance spends roughly 15 percent more each year on defense. For the evidence upon which this assessment is based, see Walt, *Origins of Alliances,* app. II.

19. As A. F. K. Organski puts it, "If we look at the whole sweep of international history for the past 150 years, we find that balances of power are the exception, not the rule." See his *World Politics* (New York: Alfred A. Knopf, 1968), 293.

20. An obvious example is the collapse of the U.S.-Soviet detente in the mid-1970s, amid mutual accusations that the other had exploited the relationship.

21. See Mohamed Heikal, *The Road to Ramadan* (New York: Quadrangle, 1975), 82–90.

22. Basic accounts of the Iranian crisis may be found in Bruce R. Kuniholm, *The Origins of the Cold War in the Near East* (Princeton, N.J.: Princeton University Press,

1980); R. K. Ramazani, "The Republic of Azerbaijan and the Kurdish People's Republic," in *The Anatomy of Communist Takeovers,* ed. Thomas T. Hammond (New Haven, Conn.: Yale University Press, 1975), 454–62; R. K. Ramazani, *Iran's Foreign Policy: A Study of Foreign Policy in Modernizing Nations* (Charlottesville: University of Virginia Press, 1975); George Lenczowski, *Russia and the West in Iran, 1918–1948* (Ithaca, N.Y.: Cornell University Press, 1949), chap. 11; Thomas A. Paterson, *Soviet-American Confrontation: Postwar Reconstruction and the Origins of the Cold War* (Baltimore: Johns Hopkins University Press, 1973); Richard Pfau, "Containment in Iran: The Shift to an Active Policy," *Diplomatic History* 1:4 (Fall 1977); and Robert Rossow, "The Battle for Azerbaijan," *Middle East Journal* 10:1 (Winter 1956).

23. Qavam visited Moscow in March 1946 and rejected Stalin's one-sided offer to withdraw from *some* of the occupied areas "pending examination of the situation." See U.S. Department of State, *Foreign Relations of the United States* [hereafter *FRUS*] *1946,* vol. VII (Washington, D.C.: U.S. Government Printing Office [hereafter U.S. GPO], 1969), 337 n. 36; Kuniholm, *Origins of the Cold War,* 313–15; and Ramazani, *Iran's Foreign Policy,* 135–36.

24. Qavam tried unsuccessfully to negotiate with the Azerbaijan and Kurdish republics in June and invited three members of the Tudeh party to join the cabinet in August. These measures may have been tactical concessions at best, as Qavam also formed his own "Democratic Party of Iran" at this time in order to oppose the Tudeh in the upcoming election.

25. According to U.S. Ambassador George V. Allen, Qavam began contemplating a "sharp change in policy" in September, because "he realized that [the] policy of conciliation towards Azerbaijan had not yielded favorable results." See *FRUS 1946* VII, 518.

26. Among other things, no oil had been discovered in Northern Iran at that time, and no significant amounts have been found to this day.

27. In 1943, the shah told U.S. officials that he would "like to see American interest in Iran continue and grow," and he also stated that a U.S. guarantee "would be most helpful in counteracting the ever-growing Soviet threat." See Ramazani, *Iran's Foreign Policy,* 57–58, 254. In November and December of 1945, Iranian officials in the United States warned that "the confidence of small countries" would be eroded if the United States did not help Iran. See Kuniholm, *Origins of the Cold War,* 279, 284–85.

28. Murray also noted that "we cannot provide Iran with an insurance policy against all dangers." See *FRUS 1946* VII, 374–75; and Kuniholm, *Origins of the Cold War,* 327.

29. According to Kuniholm, "Qavam and the Shah asked [Ambassador] Allen repeatedly what either U.S. or U.N. assistance meant in concrete terms. On 13 August, on 24 August, in early September, and on 29 September, Allen received pointed inquiries. But his cautious advice, together with Henry Wallace's speech of 12 September, were taken by the Iranians as evidence *that Iran could expect little in the way of concrete assistance from the United States.*" See *Origins of the Cold War,* 384 (emphasis added). At the beginning of October, Undersecretary of State Dean Acheson told the U.S. ambassador that "responsibility for maintaining Iran's independence and integrity rests primarily with the government of Iran." See *FRUS 1946* VII, 527. See also Pfau, "Containment in Iran," 362–63.

30. See *FRUS 1946* VII, 519–20.

31. A number of accounts conclude that Allen's behind-the-scenes activities were crucial in persuading Qavam and the shah to resist Soviet and Tudeh pressure in October. Allen pressed Qavam to take action against the Tudeh on October 11 and repeated his warnings to the shah three days later. According to the shah's version of this episode, Qavam was fearful of the Soviet reaction but the shah ordered him to oust the Tudeh from

his cabinet and restore the government's authority. See Pfau, "Containment in Iran," 365–68; Paterson, *Soviet-American Confrontation,* 177–83; and Kuniholm, *Origins of Cold War,* esp. 388–91.

32. Having ordered Qavam to oust the Tudeh on October 17, the shah made yet another request for U.S. support the following day. Ten days later, the United States finally announced that it would sell Iran several million dollars of military equipment, and Ambassador Allen told an Iranian newapaper that he thought the shah's decision to send troops into Azerbaijan was "perfectly normal and proper." See Kuniholm, *Origins of the Cold War,* 393–94.

33. The limited nature of U.S. support is revealed by Allen's September 30 request for "instructions which would justify [a] more favorable response to Qavam and also to [the] Shah." *FRUS 1946* VII, 519–20.

34. As Allen told Secretary of State James F. Byrnes: "we must keep in mind [that Qavam's] appeals to the U.S. for help have been answered by advice to depend on United Nations for security. Our advice has been best we could give, but Qavam's problems are immediate . . . ." *FRUS 1946* VII, 542.

35. Quoted in Kuniholm, *Origins of the Cold War,* 389 n. 18 (emphasis added).

36. Discussing his plans to oust the rebels, Qavam told Allen on November 23 that "he realized troops could probably not be sent to aid Iran but he felt Iran must bring to [the UN Security] Council's attention [a] situation which threatened world peace." *FRUS 1946* VII, 548.

37. In April 1947, Loy Henderson, Director of Near East and African Affairs in the U.S. Department of State, told a group of Iranian representatives: "It is desirable that Iran should keep the best possible relations with the Soviet Union . . . [economic or military] grants can be given only to those countries under direct threat and danger." *FRUS 1947* V (1971), 905. Similarly, Allen told the shah that "occasions arise when small states are called upon to defend their essential rights regardless of assurances . . . defending their essential interests even in the absence of airtight guarantees of help." *FRUS 1947* V, 922.

38. This theme is elaborated in R. K. Ramazani, *The Foreign Policy of Iran, 1500–1941: A Developing Nation in World Affairs* (Charlottesville: University of Virginia Press, 1966), 277–300.

39. R. K. Ramazani argues that the shah sought economic ties with the United States in order to deepen the U.S. political commitment to Iran. See his *Iran's Foreign Policy,* 163–64.

40. According to George McGhee, Assistant Secretary of State for Near Eastern Affairs, the shah told President Truman in 1949 that Iran had "always fought Russia with her bare hands," and that he would do so with or without American help. This statement suggests that U.S. credibility had little to do with Iran's interest in balancing against the U.S.S.R. See his *Envoy to the Middle World* (New York: Harper and Row, 1983), 69 and passim. See also Barry Rubin, *Paved with Good Intentions: The American Experience and Iran* (New York: Oxford University Press, 1980), 36–41, 49–51.

41. Although he had little sympathy for the U.S.S.R., Mossadegh balanced Anglo-American pressure by seeking support from the Tudeh party prior to his ouster. For accounts of this episode, see Richard J. Barnet, *Intervention and Revolution* (New York: New American Library, 1968), 226–29; Kermit Roosevelt, *Countercoup: The Struggle for Control of Iran* (New York: McGraw-Hill, 1979); Rubin, *Paved with Good Intentions,* chap. 3; and Ramazani, *Iran's Foreign Policy,* 247–50.

42. The Baghdad Pact was a treaty network linking Turkey, Pakistan, Iraq, Iran, and Great Britain, with the United States participating as an observer. Secretary of State John Foster Dulles opposed Iran's membership because he believed it would jeopardize the

shah's internal position, but the shah overcame this objection simply by announcing his desire to join. See Shahram Chubin and Sepehr Zabih, *The Foreign Relations of Iran: A Developing State in a Zone of Great-Power Conflict* (Berkeley: University of California Press, 1974), 90–92; and Rubin, *Paved with Good Intentions*, 97.

43. The Soviets offered Iran a fifty-year nonaggression treaty and substantial foreign aid if Iran would formally adopt a neutral position. Although the shah was concerned by the U.S. refusal to sign a formal treaty (the 1959 accord was an executive agreement), he declined the Soviet offer. See R. K. Ramazani, *The United States and Iran: The Patterns of Influence* (New York: Praeger, 1982), 38–39; Ramazani, *Iran's Foreign Policy*, 280–85, 295–99; Rubin, *Paved with Good Intentions*, 101–2; and Alvin Z. Rubinstein, *Soviet Policy Toward Turkey, Afghanistan, and Iran: The Dynamics of Influence* (New York: Praeger, 1982), 68–69.

44. See Chubin and Zabih, *Foreign Relations of Iran*, 77; and Sepehr Zabih, "Iran's International Posture: De Facto Non-Alignment Within a Pro-Western Alliance," *Middle East Journal* 24:3 (Autumn 1970): 313.

45. See R. K. Ramazani, "Emerging Patterns of Regional Relations in Iranian Foreign Policy," *Orbis* 18:4 (Winter 1975): 1047–48; Ramazani, *Iran's Foreign Policy*, 312–28; Rubinstein, *Soviet Policy Toward Turkey, Iran, and Afghanistan*, 69–70; and Rubin, *Paved with Good Intentions*, 108, 118–19.

46. The shah reportedly commented, "Now we know that the United States will not come to aid us if we are attacked." His interpretation of the war was faulty, however; Pakistan was the main aggressor in the 1965 war.

47. These tactics worked well: the United States offered a significant increase in arms shipments in 1967 and 1968. See Chubin and Zabih, *Foreign Relations of Iran*, 77–78.

48. See Chubin and Zabih, *Foreign Relations of Iran*, chap. 3, esp. 143–52, 156–62; Alvin J. Cottrell, "Iran, the Arabs, and the Persian Gulf," *Orbis* 17:3 (Fall 1973): 980–81. On Iran's relations with Israel, see Uri Bialer, "The Iranian Connection in Israel's Foreign Policy, 1948–1951," *Middle East Journal* 39:2 (Summer 1985); Nadav Safran, *Israel: The Embattled Ally* (Cambridge: Harvard University Press, 1981), 378–80; and Fred J. Halliday, *Iran: Dictatorship and Development* (New York: Penguin, 1979), 278–80.

49. See Ramazani, *Iran's Foreign Policy*, 339–44; and Rubin, *Paved with Good Intentions*, 118–21.

50. See Robert F. Litwak, *Detente and the Nixon Doctrine* (Cambridge: Cambridge University Press, 1984), 139–43 and passim.

51. Iranian arms imports averaged $146.5 million per year for the period 1965 to 1970. By contrast, arms imports for the period 1971 to 1977 were almost eight times greater, averaging $1.15 billion per year. See U.S. Arms Control and Disarmament Agency [ACDA], *World Military Expenditures and Arms Transfers* (Washington, D.C.: U.S. GPO, various years); and Leslie Pryor, "Arms and the Shah," *Foreign Policy*, 31 (Summer 1978).

52. See R. K. Ramazani, "Iran's Search for Regional Cooperation," *Middle East Journal* 30:2 (Spring 1976); Ramazani, "Emerging Regional Relations," 1051–54, 1060–62; Halliday, *Iran*, 270–77; and Tad Szulc, *The Illusion of Peace: Foreign Policy in the Nixon Years* (New York: Viking, 1978), 582–87.

53. See R. K. Ramazani, *Revolutionary Iran: Challenge and Response in the Middle East* (Baltimore: Johns Hopkins University Press, 1986), 21–22.

54. See Gary Sick, "Iran's Quest for Superpower Status," *Foreign Affairs* 65:4 (Spring 1987). As balance-of-threat theory would predict, Iran responded to U.S. naval

activity in the Persian Gulf (which led to a series of clashes between U.S. and Iranian forces) by expanding its diplomatic contacts and economic ties with the U.S.S.R.

55. The Islamic Republic has obtained military equipment from China, North Korea, Israel, *and* the United States.

56. Although this might appear to be an example of bandwagoning, it was in fact an effort to balance against the U.S.S.R. by obtaining British or American support. As the threat from Germany receded, the traditional threat from the Soviets dominated Turkish calculations. See Ferenc Vali, *Bridge Across the Bosporus: The Foreign Policy of Turkey* (Baltimore: Johns Hopkins University Press, 1971), 31–33; and Kuniholm, *Origins of the Cold War,* 21, 51–55, 68–72 and passim.

57. See Kuniholm, *Origins of the Cold War,* 287.

58. At the Potsdam Conference in July, the United States and Great Britain agreed that a revision of the Montreux Convention was in order, because it "failed to meet present-day conditions." See Rubinstein, *Soviet Policy Toward Turkey, Iran, Afghanistan,* 10; and Kuniholm, *Origins of the Cold War,* 260–70.

59. Although Turkish resolve was questioned by some U.S. officials, the Turks insisted they would "resist by force Soviet efforts to secure bases in Turkish territory even if Turkey had to fight alone." See *FRUS 1946* VII, 841.

60. See George S. Harris, *Troubled Alliance: Turkish-American Problems in Historical Perspective, 1945–1971* (Washington, D.C.: American Enterprise Institute, 1972), 17–29.

61. According to Ferenc Vali, "it was the Soviet threat, more menacing in its modern Stalinist form than the Tsarist pressures experienced in the past, that compelled Ankara to seek close political and military ties with the West." See Vali, *Bridge Across the Bosporus,* 35.

62. Turkey's strong anti-Soviet position and its active participation in the Korean War overcame resistance from France and Great Britain, who argued that Turkey was not a European country. See Bruce R. Kuniholm, "Turkey and NATO: Past, Present, and Future," *Orbis* 27:2 (Summer 1983); Rubinstein, *Soviet Policy Toward Turkey, Iran, Afghanistan,* 12; Harris, *Troubled Alliance,* 35–44; and Vali, *Bridge Across the Bosporus,* 36–37, 116–18.

63. See Alexander L. George and Richard Smoke, *Deterrence in American Foreign Policy: Theory and Practice* (New York: Columbia University Press, 1974), 332–33; Patrick Seale, *The Struggle for Syria: A Study of Arab Politics, 1945–1958* (London: Oxford University Press, 1965), 291–96; and Wilbur Clare Eveland, *Ropes of Sand: America's Failure in the Middle East* (New York: Norton, 1980), chaps. 19 and 23.

64. The military government that seized power in 1960 assured Turkey's allies that Turkey's existing commitments would be met. See Vali, *Bridge Across the Bosporus,* 126–28; and Harris, *Troubled Alliance,* 63–65.

65. See Vali, *Bridge Across the Bosporus,* 129; and Rubinstein, *Soviet Policy Toward Turkey, Iran, Afghanistan,* 132.

66. For the text of Johnson's letter, see *Middle East Journal* 20:3 (Summer 1966): 386–93. See also Harris, *Troubled Alliance,* chap. 5, esp. 112–15; Vali, *Bridge Across the Bosporus,* 130–31; and Richard C. Campany, *Turkey and the United States: The Arms Embargo Period* (New York: Praeger, 1986), 32–33.

67. See Rubinstein, *Soviet Policy Toward Turkey, Iran, Afghanistan,* 26–27, 29–31; and Vali, *Bridge Across the Bosporus,* 176–81.

68. See Andrew Mango, *Turkey: A Delicately Poised Ally* (Beverly Hills: Sage, 1975), 36; Kuniholm, "Turkey and NATO," 425.

69. See Campany, *Turkey and the U.S.*, chap. 4; and Michael Boll, "Turkey's New National Security Concept: What It Means for NATO," *Orbis* 23:3 (Fall 1979).

70. See Rubinstein, *Soviet Policy Toward Turkey, Iran, Afghanistan,* 27–29; and U.S. Central Intelligence Agency, *Communist Aid to Non-Communist Less Developed Countries, 1979 and 1954–1979* (Washington, D.C.: U.S. GPO, n.d.).

71. See Bulent Ecevit, "Turkey's Security Policies," *Survival* 20:5 (September–October 1978): 203–8; Boll, "Turkey's New National Security Concept," 619; and Rubinstein, *Soviet Policy Toward Turkey, Iran, Afghanistan,* 38–42.

72. See Boll, "Turkey's New National Security Concept," 615–16.

73. See U.S. House of Representatives, Subcommittee on Europe and the Middle East, 96th Cong., 2nd sess., *United States–Turkey Defense and Economic Cooperation Agreement, 1980* (Washington, D.C.: U.S. GPO, 1980), 35–69.

74. Among other things, nearly five hundred U.S. nuclear weapons are deployed on Turkish soil. See William M. Arkin and Richard W. Fieldhouse, *Nuclear Battlefields: Global Links in the Arms Race* (Cambridge: Ballinger, 1984), 232–33. See also Kuniholm, "Turkey and NATO," 436–45; and House Commitee on Foreign Affairs, *Turkey's Problems and Prospects: Implications for U.S. Interests* (Washington, D.C.: U.S. GPO, 1980), 14–28, 49.

75. Nonalignment was the brainchild of Prime Minister Jawarharlal Nehru, the dominant figure in Indian foreign policymaking and a leading spokesman for the "nonaligned movement." Useful guides to his thinking include J. Nehru, *India's Foreign Policy: Selected Speeches, September 1946–April 1961* (New Delhi: Ministry of Information and Broadcasting, 1961); Michael Brecher, *Nehru: A Political Biography* (London: Oxford University Press, 1959), chap. 19; and Taya Zinkin, "Indian Foreign Policy: An Interpretation of Attitudes," *World Politics* 7:1 (October 1955).

76. The most significant problem was the fate of Kashmir, a predominantly Moslem province that India occupied after independence, triggering a brief war between the two newly independent states. For accounts of the dispute, see Michael Brecher, *The Struggle for Kashmir* (London: Oxford University Press, 1952); Russell Brines, *The Indo-Pakistani Conflict* (London: Pall Mall, 1968), chaps. 4 and 5; and Lord Birdwood, *Two Nations and Kashmir* (London: Hale, 1956).

77. See William J. Barnds, *India, Pakistan, and the Great Powers* (New York: Praeger, 1972), 32–33.

78. The principles of *panch sheel* were (1) mutual respect for each other's territorial integrity and sovereignty; (2) mutual nonaggression; (3) mutual noninterference in each other's internal affairs; (4) equality and mutual benefit; and (5) peaceful coexistence. See Nehru, *India's Foreign Policy,* 99.

79. On Indian attitudes toward China, see Vidya Prakah Dutt, "India and China: Betrayal, Humiliation, Reappraisal," in *Policies Towards China: Views From Six Continents,* ed. A. M. Halpern (New York: McGraw-Hill, 1965), 202–9; Nehru, *India's Foreign Policy,* 303–12; Brecher, *Nehru,* 588–92; and Zinkin, "Indian Foreign Policy," 201–205.

80. See Brecher, *Nehru,* 419–20; and McGhee, *Envoy to the Middle World,* 46–52.

81. India supported the UN Resolution condemning North Korea's aggression in 1950, but viewed the Chinese intervention later in the year as justified. See Barnds, *India, Pakistan, and the Great Powers,* 61; G. W. Choudhury, *India, Pakistan, Bangladesh and the Great Powers* (New York: Free Press, 1975), 15, 74–77; S. M. Burke, *Mainsprings of Indian and Pakistani Foreign Policy* (Minneapolis: University of Minnesota Press, 1974), 127–29.

82. See Robert H. Donaldson, *Soviet Policy Towards India: Ideology and Strategy*

(Cambridge: Harvard University Press, 1974), chap. 3, esp. 70–76; and Choudhury, *India, Pakistan, Bangladesh,* 7–11, 15–16.

83. See Onkar Marwah, "National Security and Military Policy in India," in *The Subcontinent in World Politics: India, Its Neighbors, and the Great Powers,* ed. Lawrence Ziring (New York: Praeger, 1982); and Lorne J. Kavic, *India's Quest for Security, 1947–65* (Berkeley: University of California Press, 1967), 40–41.

84. See Barnds, *India, Pakistan, and the Great Powers,* 118.

85. For accounts of the Sino-Indian border dispute, see Kavic, *India's Quest for Security,* chap. 10; Richard Ned Lebow, *Between Peace and War: The Nature of International Crisis* (Baltimore: Johns Hopkins University Press, 1981), 184–92, 216–22; Klaus H. Pringsheim, "China, India, and Their Himalayan Border (1961–63)," *Asian Survey* 3:10 (October 1963); and Barnds, *India, Pakistan, and the Great Powers,* 141–55.

86. See Barnds, *India, Pakistan, and the Great Powers,* 152.

87. See Ian Graham, "The Indo-Soviet MIG Deal and Its International Repercussions," *Asian Survey* 4:5 (May 1964): 823.

88. On the Kennedy administration's efforts to improve U.S. relations in the Third World, see Gaddis, *Strategies of Containment,* 223–25; and Brown, *Faces of Power,* 198–204.

89. Border clashes between India and China had grown increasingly serious as relations deteriorated. Despite repeated Chinese warnings, Nehru ordered the Indian Army to outflank Chinese positions in the Aksai Chin (the main disputed area), which led the Chinese to take direct action to halt these deployments. See Neville Maxwell, *India's China War* (Garden City, N.Y.: Doubleday, 1972); and Allen S. Whiting, *The Chinese Calculus of Deterrence: India and Indochina* (Ann Arbor: University of Michigan Press, 1975).

90. India received $92 million worth of arms from the United States between 1962 and 1965, and $130 million from the Soviet Union between 1962 and May 1964. See S. Nihal Singh, "Why India Goes to Moscow for Arms," *Asian Survey* 24:7 (July 1984); and P. R. Chari, "Indo-Soviet Military Cooperation: A Review," *Asian Survey* 19:3 (March 1979): 236–37.

91. See Chari, "Indo-Soviet Military Cooperation," 232–35; and Kavic, *India's Quest for Security,* chap. 11.

92. The phrase was coined by President Ayub of Pakistan.

93. For an account of the Indo-Pakistani war of 1965, see Brines, *Indo-Pakistani Conflict,* chaps. 12–14.

94. See John E. Hill, "Military Aid and Political Influence: A Case Study of an Arms Embargo," *Pacific Community* 6:3 (1975).

95. For an account of the Soviet mediation effort, see Brines, *Indo-Pakistani Conflict,* chap. 16.

96. The text of the treaty is reprinted in Robert Jackson, *South Asian Crisis: India, Pakistan, and Bangladesh* (New York: Praeger, 1975), 188–91. For a discussion of its significance, see Ashok Kapur, "The Indo-Soviet Treaty and the Emerging Asian Balance," *Asian Survey* 12:6 (June 1972).

97. The desire to demonstrate U.S. credibility (especially to China) is apparent in Kissinger's extremely defensive account of the crisis. See Henry A. Kissinger, *White House Years* (Boston: Little Brown, 1979), chap. 21, esp. 853, 886, 895, 913–15, 918. For persuasive critiques of U.S. policy, see Christopher Van Hollen, "The Tilt Policy Revisited: Nixon-Kissinger Geopolitics and South Asia," *Asian Survey* 20:4 (April 1980); and Garthoff, *Detente and Confrontation,* chap. 8.

98. The Simla Accord was signed by Gandhi and Pakistani Prime Minister Bhutto in

July 1972. It committed both sides to settle differences through negotiation, not to interfere in each other's internal affairs, to refrain from the use of force, and to respect the December 17, 1971, cease-fire line. See *Keesing's Contemporary Archives,* August 19–26, 1972, 25432–33.

99. These trends should not be exaggerated. The Soviet share of Indian foreign trade remained fairly constant (at approximately 12 percent) through the 1970s, although it had dropped to 8.4 percent by 1982. See International Monetary Fund, *Direction of Trade Yearbook* (Washington, D.C.: International Monetary Fund, various years). The Soviet share of Indian military imports fluctuated, growing from 79 percent in the period 1965–1974 to 82 percent in the period 1976–1980, and then declining to 72 percent in the period 1979–1983. See ACDA, *World Military Expenditures;* Chari, "Indo-Soviet Military Cooperation"; and Glynn L. Wood and Daniel Vaagenes, "Indian Defense Policy: A New Phase?" *Asian Survey* 24:7 (July 1984).

100. India rejected Soviet proposals for a collective security system in Asia and consistently sought to reduce the superpower naval presence in the Indian Ocean.

101. On the Sino-Indian detente, see *Keesing's Contemporary Archives,* July 23, 1976, 27846; and Robert C. Horn, *Soviet-Indian Relations: Issues and Influence* (New York: Praeger, 1982), 123–24, 158–59.

102. Evidence of a fragile but distinct improvement in Indo-Pakistani relations is discussed in Jyotirmoy Banerjee, "Hot and Cold Diplomacy in Indo-Pakistani Relations," *Asian Survey* 23:3 (March 1983); *Keesing's Contemporary Archives,* March 1986, 34240; and the symposium entitled "South Asian Regional Cooperation: Four Views and a Comparative Perspective," *Asian Survey* 25:4 (April 1985).

103. Even before independence, Nehru recognized that great power rivalries could enhance India's security. In his words: "No country will tolerate the idea of another acquiring the commanding position [in India] which England enjoyed for so long. If any power was covetous enough to make the attempt, all the others would combine to trounce the intruder. This mutual rivalry would itself be the surest guarantee against an attack on India." Quoted in Marwah, "National Security and Military Policy in India," 73.

104. Convinced that the West was taking Pakistan for granted, Prime Minister Liaquat Ali Khan agreed to visit Moscow in 1950. This gesture convinced the United States to pay more attention to Pakistan, and Liaquat canceled the trip to Moscow and accepted an invitation to Washington. The Pakistani ambassador to the United States called this "a masterpiece of strategy . . . overnight Pakistan began to receive the serious notice and consideration of the U.S. government." Quoted in Choudhury, *India, Pakistan, Bangladesh,* 12.

105. On the origins of the U.S.-Pakistani alliance, see Choudhury, *India, Pakistan, Bangladesh,* 80–81; and S. M. Burke, *Pakistan's Foreign Policy: An Historical Analysis* (London: Oxford University Press, 1973), 126–35 and chap. 8. For a critical view, see Selig S. Harrison, "India, Pakistan, and the United States: Case History of a Mistake," *The New Republic* (Aug. 10, 1959).

106. According to Mohammed Ayub Khan, former Commander in Chief of the Army and President of Pakistan: "The crux of the problem from the very beginning was the Indian attitude of hostility between us; we had to look for allies to secure our position." See his *Friends Not Masters: A Political Autobiography* (London: Oxford University Press, 1967), 154. See also Choudhury, *India, Pakistan, Bangladesh,* 86 and passim; and George J. Lerski, "The Pakistan-American Alliance: A Reevalution of the Past Decade," *Asian Survey* 8:5 (May 1968): 405–6. The Pakistani government also faced internal threats from disaffected ethnic groups, especially a rebel movement among the

Pushtuns that received intermittent support from Afghanistan. See Khurshid Hasan, "Pakistan-Afghan Relations," *Asian Survey* 2:7 (July 1982): 14–16; and Barnds, *India, Pakistan, and the Great Powers,* 77–79.

107. See U.S. Agency for International Development, *U.S. Overseas Loans and Grants* (Washington, D.C.: U.S. GPO, various years).

108. China issued a $64 million interest-free loan in 1964, the first in a series of economic and technical agreements. See Ya'acov Vertzberger, "The Political Economy of Sino-Pakistani Relations: Trade and Aid 1963–1982," *Asian Survey* 23:5 (May 1983): 645 and passim.

109. On the origins of the Sino-Pakistani relationship, see Anwar H. Syed, *China and Pakistan: Diplomacy of an Entente Cordiale* (Amherst: University of Massachusetts Press, 1974), chap. 4; Ya'acov Vertzberger, *The Enduring Entente: Sino-Pakistani Relations 1960–1980* (New York: Praeger, 1983), 15–24; Khalid B. Sayeed, "Pakistan and China: The Scope and Limits of Convergent Policies," in Halpern, *Policies Towards China,* 236–48; and J. D. Armstrong, *Revolutionary Diplomacy: Chinese Foreign Policy and the United Front Doctrine* (Berkeley: University of California Press, 1977), 157–66.

110. As Ayub put it: "If we could not establish normal relations with all our three big neighbors, the best thing was to have an understanding with two of them . . . it was on this basis that I set out to normalize our relations with the PRC and the Soviet Union." See *Friends Not Masters,* 118 and passim. See also Burke, *Pakistan's Foreign Policy,* 359–60.

111. See Barnds, *India, Pakistan, and the Great Powers,* 212–16; G. W. Choudhury, "Pakistan and the Communist World," *Pacific Community* 6:1 (1974): 114 and passim; and Burke, *Pakistan's Foreign Policy,* chap. 15.

112. Quoted in Choudhury, *India, Pakistan, Bangladesh,* 142.

113. See Choudhury, *India, Pakistan, and Bangladesh,* 210–14; Jackson, *South Asian Crisis,* 94–96; and Vertzberger, *Enduring Entente,* chap. 4.

114. See Shirin Tahir-Kheli, "The Foreign Policy of 'New' Pakistan," *Orbis,* 20:3 (Fall 1976): 736–43.

115. See Vertzberger, *Enduring Entente,* 59–62; and "Political Economy of Sino-Pakistani Relations," 647–49; Tahir-Kheli, "Foreign Policy of 'New' Pakistan," 734–36; and William J. Barnds, "China's Relations with Pakistan," *China Quarterly* 63 (September 1975).

116. See M. G. Weinbaum and Gautam Sen, "Pakistan Enters the Middle East," *Orbis* 22:3 (Fall 1978): 601–3.

117. See Shirin Tahir-Kheli, *The United States and Pakistan: The Evolution of an Influence Relationship* (New York: Praeger, 1982), 54–62, 72–76; and Thomas B. Thornton, "Between the Stools?: U.S. Policy Towards Pakistan During the Carter Administration," *Asian Survey* 22:10 (October 1982).

118. Quoted in Alvin Z. Rubinstein, "Soviet Policy Towards South and Southwest Asia: Strategic and Political Aspects," in *The Great Game: Rivalry in the Persian Gulf and South Asia,* ed. Rubinstein (New York: Praeger, 1983), 88. See also W. Howard Wriggins, "Pakistan's Search for a Foreign Policy After the Invasion of Afghanistan," *Pacific Affairs* 57:2 (1984).

119. See Robert G. Wirsing and James M. Roherty, "The United States and Pakistan," *International Affairs* 58:4, (1982); Tahir-Kheli, *U.S. and Pakistan,* 97–104.

120. See Mehrunnisa Ali, "Soviet-Pakistani Ties Since the Afghanistan Crisis," *Asian Survey* 23:9 (September 1983): 1027–28.

121. See Wirsing and Roherty, "U.S. and Pakistan"; and Zubeida Mustafa, "Paki-

stan-U.S. Relations: The Latest Phase," *The World Today* (December 1980).

122. See W. Howard Wriggins, "The Balancing Process in Pakistan's Foreign Policy," in *Pakistan: The Long View,* ed. Lawrence Ziring et al. (Durham: Duke University Press, 1977).

123. The exception is the Iranian Revolution, which ended Iran's close relationship with the United States. This development was due primarily to domestic political events and ideological differences, however, and does not constitute an example of bandwagoning.

124. It is worth noting that the invasion of Afghanistan reversed these trends (at least temporarily) by reviving concerns about possible Soviet aggression.

125. During World War II, the shah of Iran told a group of U.S. officials that he viewed the United States as an especially valuable ally because the United States "was completely disinterested, having no contiguous frontiers and no selfish ends to serve in Iran." Quoted in Ramazani, *Iran's Foreign Policy,* 254

126. India was opposed to the Baghdad Pact, and Pakistan objected to U.S. military aid to India in the 1960s. India protested against the resumption of large-scale U.S. aid to Pakistan in 1982, despite the Soviet invasion of Afghanistan. In the same way, Soviet efforts to promote an "Asian Collective Security System" after the 1965 Indo-Pakistani war failed to overcome the rivalry or to weaken Pakistan's alignment with China.

127. See Steven David, "The Superpowers and Regime Realignment in the Third World," paper presented at the annual meeting of the American Political Science Association, The Palmer House, Chicago, Illinois, September 3–6, 1987.

128. On the European great power system, see Ludwig Dehio, *The Precarious Balance* (New York: Vintage, 1965); and F. H. Hinsley, *Power and the Pursuit of Peace: Theory and Practice in the History of Relations between States* (Cambridge: Cambridge University Press, 1963). On balancing behavior in the Middle East, see Walt, *Origins of Alliances,* chap. 5. One might add the formation of the Gulf Cooperation Council after the Iranian Revolution, or the emergence of ASEAN as an important regional organization after the U.S. withdrawal from Vietnam.

129. See Layne, "Atlanticism without NATO"; and Ravenal, "Europe without America."

130. For a more detailed analysis of this debate, see Stephen M. Walt, "The Case for Finite Containment: Analyzing U.S. Grand Strategy," *International Security* 14:1 (Summer 1989).

131. As Turkish Prime Minister Bulent Ecevit remarked in 1978: "Certainly a country always needs armaments and armies to insure her security. But I believe . . . that establishing an atmosphere of mutual confidence in our relations with the neighboring countries is at least as protective as and sometimes more protective than armaments." See Ecevit, "Turkey's Security Policies," 205.

4

Bandwagon Images in American Foreign Policy: Myth or Reality?

DEBORAH WELCH LARSON

In 1947, George Kennan warned that loss of Greece would "render a tremendous impetus to 'bandwagon' adherents to the communist movement:"

> It might well be sufficient to push both Italy and France across that fateful line which divides the integrity and independence of national life from the catastrophe of communist dictatorship. It might mean that final loss of our positions in North Africa; and the Iberian peninsula could then not long hold out. It might well make hopeless the position of other non-communist countries in northwestern Europe . . . . It would necessarily paralyze the political will of [England] and would probably make it impossible for it to do anything else than to cling to a precarious and unhappy neutrality.[1]

Since World War II American officials have acquired commitments to defend small states because they feared that communist victories might cause allies and friendly states to jump on the Sino-Soviet bandwagon. Were American policymakers right? Were U.S. allies vulnerable to Soviet intimidation or susceptible to Soviet political victories?

One way of approaching this problem is to consider the broader issue of when states bandwagon. Bandwagoning is alignment with the source of danger in contrast to balancing, which means allying with others against the major threat.[2] The question of when do states bandwagon has broader theoretical relevance as well. If, as Structural Realists argue, the uncoordinated acts of states produce an equilibrium of power, do minor shifts in the balance have any significance? Is the balance of power produced by the "invisible hand" of state competition for power?

Despite the importance of this issue, relatively little systematic research has been carried out on why states bandwagon.[3] Realist theory suggests two possible reasons. First, states may try to appease a threatening power to buy time and avoid invasion. Second, states may align with an aggressive, expanding power to acquire a share of the spoils.[4] I shall present an alternative explanation that challenges conventional balance of power theory by uncovering important intervening variables.

The interwar period in Europe is the exemplar for bandwagoning, as successive states in Eastern and Central Europe rushed to align with Hitler, allowing him to dominate the continent. In additon, American foreign policymakers were influenced by analogies to the 1930s. Consequently, I have compared states that bandwagoned in the interwar period with similar states that did not. What did

Hungary, Bulgaria, Rumania, Austria, Czechoslovakia, Yugoslavia, and France have in common that could account for their attempts to align with Nazi Germany? What distinguished Poland and why did it balance?[5] Deviant case analysis can refine and sharpen theory by revealing additional variables necessary to account for the dominant trend or suggesting revision of operational definitions.[6] By analyzing bandwagoning, I supplement balance of power theory by specifying some conditions under which it holds.[7]

Based on comparison of cases, I argue that states with weak domestic institutions are likely to align with a threatening power. Institutions are organizations that have been "infused with value" beyond the instrumental requirements of their assigned tasks.[8] An institutional framework explains additional cases and anomalies—for example, balancing by a small state with no allies—not well accounted for by balance of power theory.

I then apply this theoretical framework to crises in Greece; Korea; Dienbienphu, 1954–1955; and the Taiwan Straits, 1954–1955. Were American fears of bandwagoning justifiable? Because archival evidence is available and the outcomes are known, these cases allow us to assess the effects of American fears of bandwagoning on policy and to estimate the probability that allies and friendly states might have defected. If my argument is correct, there should be independent evidence that states with weak institutions were likely to bandwagon. Before presenting an alternative explanation, however, I would like to review the state of knowledge on why states bandwagon.

Realist Explanation

Realist theory suggests that states bandwagon to appease a threatening power or to acquire additional territory.[9] A state may hope to defer attack by allying with an external threat. If no alternative allies are available, the state may be forced to align with a menacing state.[10] Because they are vulnerable, small weak states are especially likely to align with a threatening power.[11] Since small states cannot affect the global balance of power through their own efforts, they have an incentive to "free ride" in hopes that major powers will provide for their security.[12]

The problem with the weak state hypothesis, however, is that it fails to account for various empirical anomalies. Major states, for example, sometimes bandwagon. Throughout the 1920s and 1930s, successive French leaders sought to accommodate and align with Germany, the state that most threatened France's hegemonic position in Europe.[13] Similarly, small states sometimes follow a balancing strategy despite the lack of credible allies. Poland refused Hitler's repeated offers of an anti-Soviet alliance, despite the lack of a credible French guarantee to come to their defense. Marshal Josef Pilsudski predicted that "France will abandon us, France will betray us."[14] Political instability and illegitimate authority are a source of state weakness that is missing from traditional balance of power theory, which treats the state as a unitary actor.

States may also ally with a revisionist power so that they can share the spoils of victory.[15] Thus, states are tempted to bandwagon with the winning side near the end of the war, when the outcome is visible. But after the war and division of available territories, victorious coalitions disintegrate.[16] This pattern seems to fit the evidence fairly well. Rumania and Bulgaria voluntarily fought alongside Hitler as his loyal allies, then changed sides in 1944 and marched with the Soviet Union against their former German partner. Hungary would have followed a similar strategy had not Admiral Horthy botched his 1944 attempt at a coup d'état by failing to arm his supporters against the Hungarian fascists.[17] On the other hand, as this example illustrates, it is not clear why a state's desire to acquire new territory should logically cause it to bandwagon rather than balance. What is important is that it ally with the *winning* side—not necessarily the same thing.

Both the weak state and "share the spoils" hypotheses do not explain why states align with a power that threatens their sovereignty during *peacetime,* when there is no immediate danger that a state will be invaded or imminent opportunity to scavenge for spoils. This consideration in itself limits the usefulness of these hypotheses, for states are not always engaged in war. Realist theory, for example, does not provide a convincing explanation for why Third World states bandwagoned with the Soviet Union or the United States in the postwar period. The superpowers' clients have not been threatened by invasion or attack. Cuba balanced by aligning with the Soviet Union against the United States *despite* attempted invasion and subversion.

Ad hoc explanations, of course, can always be adduced to explain cases in which states bandwagoned rather than balanced. But a more fruitful research strategy would be to obtain a better knowledge of cause–effect relationships than permitted by correlational methods or search for universal generalizations. One way to control for spurious correlation is to compare states who pursued different alignment strategies. Small size and weakness, for example, do not tell us much if these factors are present both when states balanced and bandwagoned.

An Institutional Explanation

Balance of power theory posits that states try to preserve their sovereignty and territorial integrity. International anarchy and differences in capabilities cause similarly situated states to behave the same way, regardless of different domestic structures. Balance of power theory holds that states should form a coalition against potential threats to their autonomy.[18]

But an institutionalist approach assumes that elites must try to stay in power. Consequently, political leaders' diplomatic strategies are constrained by their need to remain in office. Domestic structures vary, however, in their propensity to select and reward elites who will place the state's interests above those of class, ethnic group, or religion. It follows, then, that states that have similar capabilities may react differently to outside threats or opportunities for expansion. Elites bandwagon not to protect their state's territorial integrity or to enhance its power, but to preserve their rule.

Identity

When organizations have become institutionalized, they acquire a distinctive character or identity. One reason why institutions are valued for themselves is that they symbolize the community's identity and aspirations. Institutions also provide individuals with a distinctive identity apart from their family or place of residence. Individuals derive personal fulfillment from their role within the organization. They have personal ties and define themselves in terms of their place within the institutional network.[19]

Because institutions give people a sense of themselves, they become infused with noninstrumental value. Unlike organizations, institutions are not readily expendable for a more efficient organization. Destruction of an institution would cause the community to feel that it had lost something, that part of themselves was no longer there.[20] For example, no one objected when the Southern California department store Bullock's was taken over by Macy's. Even the doughty *Wall Street Journal,* however, complained that the corporate takeover of Bloomingdale's had caused the store to lose its distinctive glitz and trendiness, becoming just another bargain basement.

Similarly, the state embodies the collective identity of society. It is the state's representation of society that allows it to claim that its actions are in pursuit of the "national" interest rather than regional, ethnic, or class interests.[21] Also contributing to the state's role as the mirror of society is the function it fulfils as intermediary between domestic interests and other states. The state as a sovereign power is the only actor legally allowed to conduct relations and fight wars with other states.[22] In that role, the state acts for society in its dealings with other national groups and entities.

States have a distinctive national character that embodies cultural values. The German state is hierarchical, legal, formal, autonomous from society. The American state is segmentary, political, discretionary, competitive, and pluralistic.

Associated with the state's identity is an ideology that distinguishes the state from other national entities and locates individuals within a larger world scheme, providing them with a means of self-identification.[23] People derive their citizenship from the state.[24]

Widespread feelings of popular identification with the state buttress its authority.[25] Individuals must identify with something wider than their primary group to persuade them to give up their money and sacrifice their lives for an entity made up of people whom they will never meet.[26]

Not all states, however, adequately represent the identity of society. Institutions are an organic product of the path of development by which they have adapted to internal needs and external changes.[27] When institutions have been imposed on a society by an external power or minority group wielding the levers of coercion, it is unlikely that the fit between society and institutions will be very good. An institutional identity does not evolve by itself; intellectuals, politicians, historians, and propagandists create and diffuse common historial experience, which legitimizes national institutions. When domestic institutions are incongruent with the national identity, individuals do not identify with the state, but with their ethnic group, class, or political party. With no higher loyalty to restrain self-interest and the desire for aggrandizement, officials pursue particularistic goals at the expense of the state autonomy. If the gap between central organizations and popular culture is too extreme, revolution may be the result, as in Iran, where conservative Islamic mullahs overthrew the Westernized, modern, autocratic regime of the shah.

Lack of cultural self-identification with the state can affect diplomatic strategy in several ways. First, competing groups within society may use ties with external powers as a weapon in their domestic struggles. Second, lacking any noninstrumental attachment to the state, elites feel no scruples about making a deal with a more powerful state who will help them to retain their privileges and prerogatives. An obvious danger to the elites' rule is external subversion by an aggressive power. To bolster their domestic position, the state's elites try to align with the hostile power to induce it to refrain from subverting their authority. Thus, officials bandwagon in order to appease a hostile power, but the source of threat is *internal* not external as in more traditional balance of power theory.

Between the wars, for example, political institutions of Central Europe did not adequately represent their society's identity. In the interwar period, the successor states to the Austro-Hungarian and Russian empires were artificial creations, without a tradition of statehood. Ethnic groups and nations spilled across national borders and intermingled. These states lacked the unity and cohesion required to balance against Germany and to resist the Nazi onslaught.

Legally Czechoslovakia and Yugoslavia were composed of more than one "state nation"—in the former, Czechs and Slovaks, and in the latter, Serbs, Croats, and Slovenes—but one national group captured the state apparatus and imposed centralized institutions against the will of other "state nations." The task of establishing a national identity would have been difficult even if Czechs had accommodated the preferences of other national groups because the nations that made up Czechoslovakia had never been part of a unified state or had common borders. Czechoslovakia was made up of Czechs, Slovaks, Hungarians, Macedonians, Jews, and Poles. Over three and a half million Germans were included in Czechoslovakia.[28] But the Slovaks and Germans felt that the Czechs had run roughshod over their wishes. In 1918, Slovak leader Tomas Masaryk had signed an agreement with emigre Slovaks in Pittsburgh promising a Slovak diet, autonomous adminstration and law courts, and use of the Slovak lauguage in government and public schools. After the new state was formed, he denied that the document was legally binding or valid. Slovak nationalists objected to spelling "Czechoslovakia" as one word rather than hyphenated, because it symbolized Czech centralism. The Slovaks regarded the concept of "Czechoslovakia" as an ideological myth intended to perpetuate their political subordination.[29] The Czech constitution also denied Germans and Magyars the status of *Staatsvolker*, partners in the state, which they had passionately claimed, but instead designated them as merely "minorities."[30]

Even the dominant Czechs did not regard themselves as Czechoslovaks. In 1935 Czech Foreigh Minister Edvard Benes explained to Anthony Eden that it was Britain and France's responsibility to defend Czechoslovakia. The Czech people of Bohemia had lived before and survived within a German empire. But

Britain, Italy, and France could not remain great powers if the Germans controlled Czechoslovakia and Austria.[31]

Because of the lack of a Czechoslovak national identity, Hitler easily penetrated the state. Beginning in 1935, Nazis supported and advised Sudetan Germans and Slovaks.[32] To deal with this threat, the Czech leadership tried to reach a rapproachement with Germany. Foreign Minister Benes sought a rapprochement with Hitler in 1936 to 1937 and 1938 whereby the German leader would promise to refrain from stirring up separatism in return for a nonaggression pact. But Hitler was unwilling to bind himself even legally. At Hitler's instructions, Konrad Henlein provoked the Munich crisis by making demands for autonomy. In 1939, Hitler exploited a financial squabble between an autonomous Slovakia and the rump regime in Prague and granted the Slovak radical leaders' request for autonomy within a German empire.[33]

In Yugoslavia, the Serbs imposed centralized political institutions on a segmented, fissiparous society that also included Croats, Slovenes, Bosniaks, Montenegrans, and Macedonians. The Serbs conceived of the kingdom of Yugoslavia as a strong central government in which the monarchy and army would represent the continuity of Serbian statehood despite foreign occupation. The Croats, on the other hand, wanted a federal, republican system and were suspicious of the Serbian army. The Yugoslav constitution passed the constituent assembly only because the Croats had walked out. Believing that they had no future within Yugoslavia except as an autonomous state, the Croats retained their own political leaders, parties, religion, culture, and tradition of political obstructionism and passive resistance.[34]

Mussolini exploited the Serb–Croat conflict to penetrate the Yugoslav state. The Italian dictator gave the Croat separatists financial assistance and asylum from which to carry out terrorism, including the assassination of King Alexander.[35]

In confronting this threat, the Serbs placed retaining control of the Yugoslav state above maintaining its sovereignty. Instead of trying to accommodate the Croatian desire for autonomy, the Yugoslav foreign minister and Prince Paul aligned with Italy and Germany. To persuade Mussolini to stop trying to dismember Yugoslavia through subversion, the Yugoslav government signed a nonaggression pact with Italy. In 1934, the Yugoslav foreign minister also reoriented his country's alignment away from France toward Germany.[36]

In Bulgaria, the Macedonian minority defined themselves as a separate national identity. The Macedonians, after all, had a separate state in the fourth century B.C., when they were led by Philip and Alexander. Since that time, the Macedonians had been occupied by various empires, among them the Roman, Byzantine, and Ottoman. After World War I, Macedonia was divided among Greece, Bulgaria, and Yugoslavia, with the bulk of historic Macedonia going to the latter.[37]

The cohesive, committed Macedonians dominated political, adminstrative, military, commercial, and professional roles, exercising influence disproportionate to their numbers. No Bulgarian official dared repudiate or show a lack of enthusiasm for Macedonian irredentism. The one Bulgarian politician who tried to repudiate Macedonian territorial claims, radical peasant leader Stamboliski, was not only overthrown by a coalition of Macedonian terrorists and military officers, but dismembered. Militant Macedonian irredentist groups carried out raids and assassinations against Yugoslavia and Greece, alienating Bulgaria from its neighbors. Influence of the Macedonians led Bulgaria to ally with Hitler although most Bulgarians were pro-Russian for reasons of culture, religion, and history.[38]

Like the Bulgarian case, in Hungary a cohesive, committed minority also played a decisive role in their country's decision to bandwagon with Hitler. Because there were not enough educated, propertied Magyars, the Hungarian ruling class appointed the German Schwabs to positions in the government and military, rather than encourage social mobility among the peasants. The loyalty of the Schwabs to Hungary was always questionable. When he visited Hitler in 1933, Hungarian premier Gyula Gombos persuaded Hitler to promise not to stir up nationalism among the Schwabs. After Gombos died, however, Hitler felt himself released from the agreement. By 1938, the Schwabs were enthusiastically proclaiming their devotion to the Reich.[39]

The Schwabs ensured that Hungary would fight alongside Hitler against the West. The last chance for Hungary to avoid involvement in World War II on the side of the Nazis was in March 1941, when Hitler demanded that Hungarian troops assist in occupying Yugoslavia. Disobeying his orders from Count Pal Telecki, the German head of the general staff Henri-Werth commanded his troops to help Hitler. The Hungarian military, dominated by officers of German origin, complied with military rather than civilian leadership. Unable to fulfill his friendship treaty with Yugoslavia or to avoid war with Britain, Telecki committed suicide.[40]

Ethnic divisions alone will not lead a state to accommodate a stronger hostile power if the state's institutions create and embody the national identity. Between the wars, Poland included the most heterogeneous mix of ethnic groups, yet the Poles united against Germany. From 1795 until 1918, when the Polish state was partitioned among three empires, the Polish gentry kept its political and social identity, retaining distinctive culture and norms, making the political integration of the restored Polish state much easier.[41] A strong national identity enabled the Poles to unite against an external threat, despite ethnic diversity.

Thus, Foreign Minister Colonel Joseph Beck refused Hitler's repeated offers of an alliance, even when sweetened by the offer of spoils in the Ukraine, because Poland would lose her independence if allied with a much stronger power. Marshal Josef Pilsudski pursued a policy of equilibrium between Poland's two powerful neighbors, Germany and Russia.[42]

Austria differed from other Eastern European states in that it was ethnically homogeneous and had a previous history of sovereignty. On the other hand, the very nature of the Austro-Hungarian empire as a multiethnic conglomerate encouraged the development of national consciousness among the national components but not the center, where it would have undermined the very raison d'etre of the empire itself. Because of their weak national identity, Austria would have aligned with Germany if not prohibited by international treaty from seeking an *Anschluss,* or merger of the two states. The Austrians did not want a separate state and accepted their sovereignty only at the Entente's insistence. The allies also forced the Austrians to remove the first word from the name of their state, "German Austria." Statehood, moreover, did not engender national consciousness. The new Austrian state had not proved that it was economically and politically viable before the depression. As a result, most Austrians identified with the German nation with whom they had a common culture, history, and language rather than the puny and artificial "Austrian" nation-state.[43] Chancellor Kurt von Schuschnigg explained to Mussolini that "Austrians were not only a German-speaking people but actually a German people and as such, they could never accept an anti-German combine."[44] Austrians cheered Hitler and jubilantly greeted strangers on the street immediately after the *Anschluss*.[45]

In contrast, France was too ideologically polarized to form a coalition against German expansion into Central and Eastern Europe. A balancing strategy would have been to strengthen France's eastern alliances with Czechoslovakia and Poland while establishing a military connection with the Soviet Union. Historically, the national identity of France, a large country with many dialects and diverse climates, centered on Paris.[46] In the 1930s, ideas and culture from Paris could not unite the country because of the ideological mistrust of its politicians and officials. Initially the French right favored the eastern alliances and maintaining a strong defense to deter German aggression, while the left was pacifistic, antimilitaristic, and nationalistic.[47] In 1936, the growing electoral strength of Leon Blum's Popular Front, a coalition made up of Socialists and Radicals with some Communist support, aroused rightist fears that war against Germany would lead to the victory of communism in France. Indeed, the right feared victory over Germany even more than defeat because it would lead to the crumbling of authoritarian barriers to the spread of communism. Fear of bolshevism caused French rightists to oppose alliance with the Soviet Union against Germany. As William Evans Scott points out, the conservatives "seemed to place a higher value on defeating their domestic enemy than on defeating their national enemy. A consequence of this shift was renunciation of the free use of the balance of power."[48] The left, on the other hand, opposed the Eastern European alliances on the grounds that they strengthened French militarism and nationalism. The left was also internally divided. French Socialists opposed alliance with the Soviet Union because it might lead to a Communist take over in France.[49] As one historian commented, "Domestic and foreign policy thus had become intertwined, each sacrificing its integrity and coherence to the other."[50]

Legitimacy

The state's claim to legitimacy rests on the assumption that it alone represents the whole society and can carry out the public interest. The state is not only separate from society; at the same time it *is* the general will. By transcending separate factions and interest, it is the only institution that embodies the national interest.

Legitimate institutions can more easily enforce rules and property rights, because most individuals comply voluntarily without external coercion or supervision. Beliefs and ideology are more effective in inducing people to pay higher taxes and sacrifice their lives than brute force.[51]

States that do not represent the collective identity of society have more difficulty establishing their legitimacy. Thus, elites are drawn to alternative means of securing public consent—providing "bread and circuses," or stirring up jingoistic sentiments. Alignment with a more powerful, expansionist state can serve these purposes in various ways.[52] An expansionist power, for example may offer economic capital and trade on favorable terms in return for political subordination. Weak regimes may also try to bolster their domestic position by wrapping themselves in the cloak of an expanding ideological movement.[53] The elite may mobilize nationalist sentiment for the return of lost territories. To satisfy popular irredentist demands, the small state may then be forced to ally with a stronger revisionist power who will assist in reconquest of former territories.[54]

States that bandwagoned in the 1930s had governments perceived to be illegitimate by wide segments of the population. Regimes in Rumania and Hungary, for example, denied peasants and industrial workers participation in the political system or access to power. Right radicalist movements—the Iron Guard in Rumania and the Arrow Cross in Hungary—won the allegiance of the landless agricultural laborers, students, and nonskilled workers.[55]

Shortly after Hitler came to power, Hungary, Rumania, and Yugoslavia sought economic agreements in which Nazi Germany would purchase their agricultural surpluses on favorable terms. These agreements also had political significance; the Eastern European states wished to establish good relations with Germany while moving away from France. Germany's dominance over Eastern Europe was paved by these trade agreements because the satellite states' economies were then intermingled so that factories could not produce without German raw materials, machine parts, or spare parts nor market their agricultural produce anywhere else.[56] Although also an agricultural surplus state, Poland refused to accumulate a reichsmark balance, insisting on monthly meetings with German officials to insure that trade was exactly balanced. Thus, Poland avoided becoming dependent on trade with the Nazis.[57]

In the 1930s, the weak Balkan states admired Nazi Germany's domestic and diplomatic successes. Conservative elites inferred that fascism was the wave of the future and adopted the trappings and anti-Semitism of Nazism but not its mass mobilization or effective administration. Alignment with the stronger aggressive power further enhances the elites' legitimacy by allowing them to bask in its reflected glory and claim its official sanction for their rule. At the same time, the political instability, ideological polarization, and general strike movement of France had a "negative" demonstration effect, alarming conservative political elites of Poland and the Little Entente and causing them to shy further away from France.[58] Thus, Yugoslav Prime Minister Milan Stojadinovic confided to Italian Foreign Minister Edda Ciano that he admired Mussolini's ability to combine "force and consent" and promised that he would copy the fascist model. Stojadinovic borrowed the Roman salute, and his followers marched wearing green shirts while hailing him as leader. Ironically his political rival

Croat leader Vladko Macek inspected his Peasant Guards astride a white horse as they drilled wearing black shirts and acclaimed him as leader.[59] The Hungarian government was responsive to right–radical arguments that the best way to ingratiate the country to Nazi Germany was to imitate its institutions; thus, in 1938 the conservative regime passed anti-Semitic laws.[60]

In contrast to France, the Polish state at least was competent. Moreover, Poland was authoritarian, but by no means totalitarian. In prewar Poland, the press was independent, trade unions and political parties actively organized, and opposition leaders criticized the regime in the universities and published works. Further, the Polish peasants had a strong democratic tradition. Thus, the fascist movement did not enjoy support outside the urban middle class.[61]

In Hungary, the aristocracy tried to prevent the peasants and other disadvantaged groups from demanding economic and political reforms by reminding them of the territories lost in the Peace of Trianon.[62] The only way Hungary could regain Transylvania and Ruthenia was through alliance with Nazi Germany. Hungary nearly doubled its territory by 1940 thanks to Hitler's largesse. Hungary's ruling class accepted Hitler's Vienna Ward of Transylvania as their rightful due and did not intend to allow their country to become a German satellite. But accepting territorial spoils from Hitler without deferring to his leadership was like squaring the circle.[63]

Adaptability

Institutions do not change easily. The shared values that lead to homogeneity also lead to rigid ways of thinking and nonreceptivity to evidence indicating changes in the environment. Because their identity is bound up with the organization, officials develop a vested interest in existing rules and patterns of authority.[64]

But when organizations have become institutionalized, officials place its survival and health ahead of their own personal or group interests. Because officials derive part of their identity and self-worth from their role in the organization, destruction of the institution would cause them to feel that they had lost part of themselves. Thus, officials feel a need to accommodate internal interests and adapt to external pressures in order to preserve the instituion.[65]

In contrast, when a state's institutions lack identity and legitimacy, elites are not motivated to preserve the long-term interests of their state by restructuring its institutions. Instead, they despoil the state to maximize selfish group interests. National officials' concern for maintaining their positions blocks essential changes in the way institutions are structured and relate to society. Weak states are unable either to conciliate domestic foes or to overcome social resistance because they cannot reform themselves.

To illustrate, the weak states of Central and Eastern Europe were so preoccupied and self-absorbed with their domestic divisions that they could not carry out the reforms necessary to conciliate the oppostition and unite before the Nazi threat. For example, once in office, Czech President Benes was unable to fulfil his promise to give greater rights to the loyal Sudetan Germans and Slovaks because of the distrustful Czechs and the sluggish bureaucracy.[66]

After the right-radical leader Gombos died in 1936, the Hungarian aristocracy tried to reorient its policy toward Britain and France by placing a more conservative leader in power. But the groups that had benefited from aligning themselves with Germany—the marginal agriculture workers whom Germany had employed; the military, which secretly rearmed with German assistance; and the masses whose jingoist sentiments had been inflamed by promises of territorial spoils—would not permit it.[67]

The Serbs and Croats of Yugoslavia could not resolve their differences even under the risk of invasion by Germany, Italy, and Hungary. One day after Yugoslavia signed the tripartite pact, Serb officers carried out a coup in protest against an agreement providing the Croats with domestic autonomy, although the settlement was desperately needed to secure Croat assistance against Germany. Further, absorbed in their internal struggle with the Croats, Serb officers failed to realize that Hitler would interpret their action as a repudiation of the Axis and retaliate by invading.[68]

Cases

Truman Doctrine

The containment strategy tried to bolster other states' fragile institutions against the allure of Soviet power. The United States inaugurated the Truman Doctrine and sent military and economic assistance to Greece and Turkey to prevent Western Europe from accommodating to Soviet influence out of the belief that communism was the wave of the future.[69] Dean Acheson warned the cabinet that "if Greece fell within the Russian orbit, not only Turkey would be affected but also Italy, France, and the whole of western Europe."[70] A report by a special ad hoc State-War-Navy Coordinating Committee (SWNCC) also noted that "there is a 'bandwagon' quality attaching to the Communist movement . . . which is vulnerable to positive measures of aid and encouragement undertaken by U.S."[71]

American fears of bandwagoning were reasonable, because Western democratic institutions were fragile after the war. The French and Italians did not have confidence in their postwar political and economic institutions. Many French citizens favored an authoritarian regime since democracy appeared ineffective. The French gave only lukewarm endorsement to the constitution in a May 1946 national referendum, and Charles De Gaulle had presented a strong, convincing critique.[72] The Italian government had not succeeded in restoring production and employment. Italian officials' gross incompetence further decreased public confidence in the economic system, which retarded improvements in standard of living.[73] In short, European capitalists had not yet legitimized inequality and hierarchical management by proving that the capitalist system could substitute abundance for equality, the "politics of productivity."[74]

As a result of the popular distrust of the new postwar institutions, about one third of the electorate in France and Italy supported the Communist party. Communists held four Cabinet positions in France, including the posts of vice-premier and minister of defense. In the French elections of November 1946, the Communist party had received the largest number of votes. Columnist Anne O'Hare McCormick wrote in the *New York Times* that "the fight for survival is so primitive, the submergence of the middle class so general, the individual so hopeless, the sense of human dignity so blunted by inhuman transfers of people, the desire for change, and the feeling that any change must be for the better so overwhelming, that it is harder to stand fast than to follow the easier path—toward a Communist dictatorship or reaction."[75]

Conservatives in France and Italy could not govern effectively with Communist party membership, yet were afraid to toss them out because of the danger of strikes. Italian moderates were uncertain of American support and unwilling to offend the Soviet Union by opposing the communists. In both countries, the Communist party was in the unusual and unworkable position of being in the government yet free to mobilize the masses against it.[76]

France and Italy needed reassurance that the United States would provide them with economic assistance and military security while they rebuilt their economic and political institutions. The Truman Doctrine speech signaled to Western Europe that the United States was not returning to isolationism. From Paris, Harold Callender reported that diplomatic officials read Truman's speech with "amazement," viewing it as the most important diplomatic move since U.S. entry into World War II. One high government official who had been convinced that the United States was withdrawing from Europe commented that "this will convince Europeans that you are in to stay."[77]

Bolstered by the hope of American political and financial assistance, in May 1947 French Premier Paul Ramadier and Italian Prime Minister Alcide De Gasperi ousted communist members from their cabinets.[78]

Korean War

In June 1950, American officials feared that Europe would go neutralist if the United States allowed North Korea to absorb South Korea.[79] On June 25, 1950, a State Department intelligence report warned that the small Soviet satellite's successful military aggression would cause Europeans to question the might and will of the United States; West German neutralism would be strengthened. Secretary Acheson told congressional leaders that the United States had intervened with naval and air forces because "the governments of many Western European nations appeared to be in a state of near panic, as they watched to see whether the United States would act or not."[80]

How accurate were American fears? Would Western Europe have adopted a neutralist policy in reaction to U. S. refusal to intervene in Korea? For the United States to remain passive while South Korea was swallowed up would have weakened the infant North Atlantic alliance. The analogies to the 1930s were too powerful and recent, the parallels between divided Germany and Korea too obvious, for the United States to abandon South Korea without some loss of credibility.

Before the United States intervened with ground troops, several Western

European officials and influential European newspapers called for drastic action. Dutch Foreign Minister Stikker warned the U.S. ambassador that should the United States permit South Korea to fall, the consequences would be disastrous for all Asia, which the western world could "write off forever." Similarly, a ranking French Foreign Office official said that the loss of Korea would "irretrievably impair" Western prestige, and he compared the situation to Hitler's tactics in 1938. In France, the Gaullist paper *Ce Matin* voiced the fear that the failure of the United States to send ground troops to Korea might jeopardize the confidence aroused by initial U. S. action. Editorials in the British press stressed the importance of using ground forces to stop the northern invasion. Before Truman's announcement of naval and air support, a typical Belgian reaction was Minister of Public Works Coppe's statement that the United States had lost a great deal of face because of the Korean incident and Europeans would ask themselves which countries the United States intended to defend and then abandon.[81]

In addition to invoking analogies to the 1930s, many Europeans saw a parallel between divided Germany and Korea and used the U.S. reaction to the South Korean invasion as a test of American willingness to defend West Germany. For example, two influential Dutch newspapers, liberal *Nieuwe Rotterdam Secourant* and Catholic *De Tijd* stressed the parallel between the Korean outbreak and the German situation and suggested that the East German "people's police" might be used for the same task as the North Korean army. Germans worried about their own "38th parallel," the Elbe. Director of the Bundestag Administration Tressman explained that his government's concrern over Korea was based on the failure of U.S. intelligence in Korea, the inadequacy of Allied troops in Germany, and unrest near the Soviet zone border. Tressman complained that 25,000 federal police would be wholly inadequate to face 80,000 East German police. In July, East German leader Walter Ulbricht warned that the Federal Republic was about to share the same fate as South Korea. The Korean conflict helped to overcome European opposition to German rearmament.[82]

Western Europe was relieved and reassured by the U.S. decision to oppose North Korean forces. Norwegian Ambassador Wilhelm Morgenstierne informed Secretary of State Acheson that the smaller nations of Europe were much heartened, feeling that if the United States were capable of meeting the Korean situation so firmly, it certainly would not falter in meeting its commitments to the [NATO] area. According to the daily summaries of Western European official and press reactions prepared for President Truman and Secretary Acheson, Western Europe overwhelmingly approved U.S. actions. On June 27, the British press carried the theme that U.S. aid would be too little too late. The next day, the British press expressed satisfaction that the United States had decided to meet the communist challenge now, because it would have had to be met some day. The French press also approved the president's decision to send ground troops to Korea. A high French Foreign Office official described the U.S. action as "brilliant statesmanship." Foreign Minister Schuman told Ambassador Bruce that the U.S. move was the "only proper course of action." Similarly, the foreign minister of Denmark declared that his government was "extremely relieved" over the U.S. action in Korea and that other small states were "bound to feel assured." In

Sweden, liberal isolationist *Stockholm Tidningen* observed that resolute action by the United States was an "absolute necessity" if the United States did not wish "to lose the confidence its policy [had] achieved in Europe." The Brussels embassy reported that Belgians reacted with "relief and wholehearted support." In the *New York Times,* columnist Anne O'Hare McCormick reported that "neutralism and defeatism would have solidified from a vague tendency into a general movement toward making terms with the ascendant power of Moscow if Washington failed to react to a blatant stroke of aggression."[83]

Yet, although NATO might have been almost irretrievably weakened, it is improbable that Western European countries would have aligned with the Soviet Union even if the United States had failed to intervene in Korea. The reason is that Western Europeans identified strongly with democratic institutions, calling themselves "free peoples," and had acquired increasing self-confidence since the Truman Doctrine and the Marshall Plan. The evidence for this is that the U.S. intervention in Korea stimulated Western Europeans to spend more themselves for NATO. If Realist assumptions were correct, the smaller states should have tried to "free ride" on the alliance leader.[84]

Instead, the American demonstration of its willingness to expend its substantial resources to maintain noncommunist governments stimulated *greater* European support for defense spending. On July 19, Truman announced a $10 billion increase in U.S. defense expenditures. The increased U.S. defense effort not only reassured Western Europe, but stimulated greater defense efforts. For example, in Italy, the Defense Ministry announced that the army would be increased to full treaty limits of 250,000. The Catholic *Quotidiano* criticized "some European governments" for their attitude that "its up to America to defend Europe," while continuing to ask for and receive dollar aid. The paper said that the United States should tell its European allies that "America helps those who help themselves." In France, *Figaro* declared that July 19 marked a "major turning point in post-war history" and called on Western European nations to redouble their own military effort, coordinate their economies, and align their military policy with that of the United States. In Sweden, the liberal *Goteborgs Handelstidning* said that U.S. intent to strengthen its defense forces must not cause "the European democracies to shut their eyes to their own obligations." The conservative *Aftenposten* in Norway declared that "Norway must take a share of sentry duty to which the free world was summoned last night." In Britain, Attlee told the Commons that knowledge that America's immense resources were to be geared to the task of fulfilling the UN Charter would hearten free peoples throughout the world. He pledged that the British would do what they could to match U.S. resolve. Subsequently, the British committed themselves to spend 3,600 million pounds over three years, an increase of 1,100 million, *without* a firm commitment of U.S. military assistance.[85]

Dienbienphu

The Eisenhower administration exaggerated the danger that France and Asian countries would bandwagon if the French were defeated at Dienbienphu. American policymakers viewed East Asia through the lens of World War II. They had vivid, accessible memories of the 1930s in which successive states jumped on the Nazi bandwagon. If a foreign policy crisis superficially resembles previous cases in which small states accommodated to an aggressive power, policymakers will swiftly and automatically assume that the problem is similar and the appropriate response can be deduced accordingly.[86] The small, new, postcolonial states in the shadow of Sino-Soviet power evoked images of Central Europe between the wars. In the Dienbienphu crisis, U.S. officials explicitly referred to the World War II experience, pointing out the traditional propensity of the Thais to accommodate to superior power and French accomodation to the Nazis in 1940.

During the 1954 crisis, Eisenhower adminstration officials feared that the "psychological blow" of a French defeat by the Vietminh at Dienbienphu would lead them to withdraw from Indochina.[87] United States officials also thought that it might cause a shift in the balance of power in French politics. French Premier Joseph Laniel supported the European Defense Community (EDC) treaty, which would have rearmed West Germany within a multinational force and was awaiting ratification in the French assembly. Disaster at Dienbienphu might cause Laniel's government to fall to the anti-EDC, neutralist socialists and communists. Secretary of State John Foster Dulles worried that a leftist coalition might "collaborate with the Soviets just as the French government of the summer of 1940 collaborated with the Germans."[88]

Loss of Indochina might cause Asian countries to accommodate to the Sino-Soviet bloc, believing that communism was inevitable. The Policy Planning staff warned that communist conquest of Southeast Asia would "spread doubt and fear among other threatened non-Communiust countries and create the feeling that Communism was the 'wave of the future' and that the United states and the Free World were unable to halt its advance." Given the "traditional propensity of the Siamese ruling group to accommodate to superior power (as was the case in their turnover to Japan during the last war)," it was also certain that Thailand would "shortly accommodate itself to international communism." Countries in the Far East, South Asia, and elsewhere would be encouraged to accommodate to communist pressures. According to the official policy statement in Indochina, NSC 5405, the loss of one country could lead to alignment with communism by the remaining countries of Southeast Asia and Indochina.[89]

It could be argued that Eisenhower administration officials invoked analogies to the 1930s to legitimize policies pursued for other reasons. The military, in particular, could be expected to favor intervention when they could effectively carry out their missions without civilian interference.[90] But Admiral Radford was the only member of the Joint Chiefs who advocated American airstrikes at Dienbienphu.[91] Nor is it clear what bureaucratic interests were served by the NSC staff's support for U.S. intervention.

Perhaps anticommunist domestic sentiment motivated the Eisenhower administration to defend Dienbienphu to avoid a conservative backlash or charges of being "soft." But Eisenhower was doomed to be criticized by the American public no matter what he did in the Dienbienphu crisis. Loss of Indochina would arouse Democrats and McCarthyites into charging him with appeasement and selling out to communism. On the other hand, the American public strongly opposed sending ground troops to Indochina. Vice President Nixon's unauthorized reference to sending American combat troops to fight in Indochina aroused a storm of controversy. Dulles met with congressional leaders to get their approval of a broad "blank check" congressional resolution, which would give the president authority to deploy U.S. naval and air forces in Indochina. But the congressmen refused to give him the necessary authority until the secretary had obtained commitments of political and military support from U.S. allies, insisting that "we want no more Koreas with the United States furnishing 90% of the manpower."[92]

The British were immune to American bandwagon arguments. Foreign Minister Eden told Secretary of State Dulles that the British were confident that Malaya could be held if Indochina collapsed. He saw no parallel between the situations in Indochina and Malaya. Since the British believed that U.S. intervention could not save Dienbienphu or keep the French fighting in Indochina, they favored a negotiated settlement and partition.[93] Britain's refusal to participate in "united action" sealed the fate of Dienbienphu, which fell on May 7, 1954.

Largely because of British opposition, the United States did not intervene to help the French at Dienbienphu. Instead, the Eisenhower administration tried to reassure U.S. allies and friendly states by establishing a mutual security pact, the Southeast Asian Treaty Organization (SEATO). More important, the United States took measures to prevent South Vietnam from falling under communist domination.

But American predictions that France would bandwagon were alarmist; French support for democratic institutions and the Atlantic alliance was robust. Although EDC was defeated, the French government mobilized support for a different NATO institutional structure in which French sovereignty and nationalism would not be submerged within a supranational army. The French agreed to the participation of West German forces in NATO, an outcome wildly beyond the hopes of U.S. officials just three years previously.[94]

American policymakers also exaggerated the likelihood that Thailand and Malaya would jump on the Sino-Soviet bandwagon. Thailand's foreign policy has traditionally been compared to a bamboo "bending into the wind." On the other hand, the traditional institutions of the monarchy and Buddhism held powerful sway over the minds of Thais. Since Thailand had never been colonized by the West, nationalism was not tied to anti-Western feeling and communism had no basis for development. Had the United States refrained from establishing SEATO, Thailand would not have risked its sovereignty by allying with China.[95] Similarly, the Malayans also had a strong sense of national identity. Although Malaya was ethnically hetereogeneous, the feudal Malay elite, conservative Chinese businessmen, and traditional Islamic groups could unite behind their antipathy to communism.[96]

In sum, American policymakers interpreted national communist revolutions in Asia in light of the experience in Central Europe between the wars. Even the cliché referring to communism as the "wave of the future" was taken from Nazi propaganda. Once such schemas were evoked, American policymakers could not view Asia from a different perspective. They overlooked and failed to investigate differences in domestic or international context that distinguished East Asia in the 1950s from the interwar period and the rise of Hitler. In fact, despite the political instability of the French fourth republic, the French united behind democratic Western values. Moreover, many Asian countries—Japan, Thailand—had a strong sense of national identity, which motivated them to resist sacrificing their sovereignty by allying with more powerful communist countries.

Taiwan Straits

As in the Dienbienphu crisis, U.S. policymakers applied analogies from the 1930s to the 1954 to 1955 Taiwan Straits crisis. In the Taiwan Straits crisis, American policymakers feared both that the Taiwanese would lose the will to resist and that Chiang Kai-shek's regime would lose its legitimacy if he were forced to abandon his irredentism. The raison d'être and legitimating symbol of the Nationalist Chinese regime was return to the mainland. Chiang claimed that evacuation of the offshore islands would signal that the Nationalist Chinese must resign themselves to living on Taiwan, which would undermine the legitimacy of his rule. Unlike Taiwan and the Pescadores, the offshore islands had never belonged to Japan but had always been part of mainland China. The offshore islands were the only piece of Chinese territory that Chiang still owned, and he regarded them as a stepping stone to the mainland.[97]

The majority of the Joint Chiefs of Staff stressed that any further loss of territory to the communists would have a *psychological* impact on Chinese Nationalist Troops and other pro-U.S. Asian countries. Dulles claimed that the psychological repercussions of Chinese communist conquest of Quemoy and Matsu would result in the loss of Asia. He cabled the Department of State that "further retreat or loss of Formosa could convince Japan communism wave of future. Consequent effect on Okinawa and other parts of Asia obvious."[98] President Eisenhower invoked analogies to the 1930s in letters to Churchill.[99]

American policymakers worried that Taiwan was vulnerable to penetration by the People's Republic of China. Eisenhower administration officials believed that the PRC might be able to bribe or subvert the native Taiwanese, who outnumbered mainland Chinese by four to one.

American policymakers exaggerated Taiwan's susceptibility to subversion. In contrast to the previous Nationalist government on the mainland, Chiang Kai-shek's administration was effective, uncorrupt, and exercised extensive police powers and political control over the population. Further, Chiang Kai-shek's regime had carried out reforms giving the Taiwanese more rights.[100]

Despite Chiang's protests and complaints, loss of Quemoy and Matsu would not have forced him to accommodate to the Chinese communists because his institutional base was strong. Moreover, Chiang's confidence in his mission to return to the mainland was unshakable. Although sympathetic to Chiang's concerns, U.S. ambassador to Taiwan Karl Rankin believed that the Nationalist Chinese exaggerated the disastrous effects of loss of Quemoy and Matsu on Taiwanese morale. An intelligence report on Taiwanese morale predicted that while the loss of the offshore islands would be a major blow to the prestige and legitimacy of the Nationalist Chinese regime, Chiang would certainly retain his authority.[101]

As for the other Asian countries, a national intelligence estimate predicted that Taiwanese evacuation of the islands would be greeted with relief in Japan and would not affect the policies of the Philippines, South Korea, Thailand, South Vietnam, Cambodia, and Laos.[102] The danger that Asian countries would bandwagon in response to communist conquest of the offshore islands existed solely in the minds of U.S. officials.

Eisenhower decided not to intervene to defend Quemoy and Matsu, because letters he received from the American public argued against sending American boys to fight for Asians.[103] Nevertheless, to persuade Chiang to accept a UN cease-fire resolution, Dulles and Eisenhower agreed to the Taiwanese leader's longstanding request for a mutual defense treaty, limited to Formosa and the Pescadores.[104] The Eisenhower administration did not make a public commitment to Quemoy and Matsu. Instead, Dulles deliberately "fuzzed up" the language of the mutual defense treaty with Taiwan to imply that the United States might defend additional territories if necessary for the defense of Taiwan and the Pescadores.[105] Dulles reported to the National Security Council that he had decided that "it would be best not to nail the flag to the mast" by a detailed statement of our plans and intentions concerning the islands.[106] Instead, the resolution that President Eisenhower submitted to Congress on January 24 gave him authority to "employ the armed forces of the United States as he deems necessary for the specific purpose of securing and protecting Formosa and the Pescadores against armed attack," including "the securing and protecting of such related positions and territories" as he judged to be required to assure the defense of Formosa and the Pescadores.[107] Only Formosa and the Pescadores were specifically included in the resolution, Dulles explained to a bipartisan congressional meeting, "so that the flag and the prestige of the United States would not *necessarily* be involved in any operations pertaining to these islands."[108]

What Eisenhower actually would have done had the PRC invaded Quemoy and Matsu is not clear even in hindsight. The president was unwilling to decide until the Chinese actually invaded Quemoy and Matsu, when he would try to determine whether it was a preliminary movement to an invasion of Taiwan and the Pescadores. Further, Eisenhower said he would wish to see whether the Chinese Nationalists could win by themselves before intervening.[109]

Conclusions

Since World War II, many debates about American foreign policy have revolved around the issue of whether U.S. losses in peripheral areas would cause allies and friendly countries to climb on the Sino-Soviet bandwagon. Analysis of bandwagoning in the 1930s suggests that states that have weak institutions are likely to align with a threatening power because elites are more concerned about staying in power than with maintaining the sovereignty of the state. Alignment with a potential hegemon helps a weak regime retain authority in a variety of ways—by putting an end to external subversion, undermining the political position of domestic rivals, providing them with a source of economic assistance and an aura of invincibility by association with the great power's victories. Thus, when states do not follow the predictions of balance of power theory, an explanation may be found at the domestic level.

Further research is necessary, however, to determine if this argument also applies to Third World states or to the Soviet empire in Eastern Europe. Third World states are the remnants of former colonial empires. Their institutions have no tradition or history; inhabitants have no habits of loyalty. Riven by ethnic cleavages, these weak states are vulnerable to penetration from a hostile power. The elites, moreover, are self-serving, motivated only by the chance to acquire the spoils of office for themselves and their particular group. Similarly, conservative elites in Eastern Europe preferred that Mikhail Gorbachev's reforms not spread to their country, even if greater liberalization enhanced their state's autonomy vis-à-vis the Soviet Union.

A more fundamental and difficult question, of course, relates to the problem of establishing institutions. What types of institutions are best suited to particular societies? For example, should traditional, Islamic societies have political and economic institutions that mirror religious tradition, despite their incongruity with the modern world? What is the relationship between institutions and national identity? Can a national identity be created via appropriate cultural, political, and social institutions?

What are the implications for American foreign policy? Because their institutions are strong and legitimate, the advanced capitalist countries of Western Europe are unlikely to align with the Soviet Union unless abandoned by the United States. New states that emerge in the aftermath of a major war such as the former colonies in the Third World are more likely to bandwagon with a threatening state because their institutions are still unformed. As the process of state-building and nationalism comes to fruition, Third World countries should be more likely to balance.

Notes

1. George Kennan, "Comments on the National Security Problem," 27 March 1947, Lecture before the National War College, 868.00/3-2747, Record Group (RG) 59, National Archives (NA).

2. Stephen M. Walt, *The Origins of Alliances* (Ithaca, N.Y.: Cornell University Press, 1987), 17. The bandwagon metaphor could easily be confused with the domino theory. In the domino theory, the impetus for a country's fall comes from the *outside*. The domino theory implies that a loss to communist aggression in one country will embolden Soviet or Chinese leaders to attack or subvert adjacent areas. In contrast, bandwagoning occurs when successive countries align with a threatening state.

3. For an exception, see Stephen M. Walt, "Alliance Formation and the Balance of World Power," *International Security* 9:4 (Spring 1985): 3-43; Walt, *Origins of Alliances;* Stephen M. Walt, "Testing Theories of Alliance Formation: The Case of South-

east Asia," *International Organization* 42:2 (Spring 1988): 275-316. For surveys of the alliance literature, see Philip M. Burgess and David W. Moore, "Inter-nation Alliance: An Inventory and Appraisal of Propositions," *Political Science Annual* 3 (1973): 339-83; Ole R. Holsti, P. Terrence Hopmann, and John D. Sullivan, *Unity and Disintegration in International Alliances: Comparative Studies* (New York: John Wiley, 1973), chap. 1 and app. C, 7–9.

4. Walt, "Alliance Formation," 7–8.

5. The logic of inference is derived from John Stuart Mill's methods of difference and agreement. The method of agreement compares cases with a similar outcome on the dependent variable and eliminates noncommon factors. The method of difference contrasts cases with different outcomes and eliminates common factors, because they cannot explain the variance. For discussion, see Morris Zelditch, Jr., "Intelligible Comparisons," in *Comparative Methods in Sociology,* ed. Ivan Vallier (Berkeley: University of California Press, 1971), 267–307; Alexander L. George, "Case Studies and Theory Development," presented at Carnegie-Mellon University, October 15–16, 1982; Theda Skocpol, "Emerging Agenda and Recurrent Strategies in Historical Sociology," in *Vision and Method in Historical Sociolgy,* ed. Skocpol (Cambridge: Cambridge University Press, 1984), 378–79; Arend Lipjhart, "Comparative Politics and the Comparative Method," *American Political Science Review* 65 (September 1971): 682–93; Arendt Lipjhart, "The Comparable-Cases Strategy in Comparative Research," *Comparative Political Studies* 8:2 (July 1975): 158–77.

6. Lipjhart, "Comparative Politics and the Comparative Method," 692.

7. Kenneth Waltz, *Theory of International Politics* (Reading, Mass.: Addison-Wesley, 1979), 125–26; Walt, "Alliance Formation and the Balance of World Power," 3–43; Walt, *Origins of Alliances.*

8. Philip Selznick, *Leadership in Administration: A Sociological Interpretation* (Evanston, Ill.: Row, Peterson and Company, 1957), 17. See also Arthur L. Stinchcombe, *Constructing Social Theories* (Chicago: University of Chicago Press, 1968), 107; James G. March and Johan P. Olsen, "The New Institutionalism: Organizational Factors in Political Life," *American Political Science Review* 78:3 (September 1984): 739, 744; Stephen D. Krasner, "Approaches to the State: Alternative Conceptions and Historical Dynamics," *Comparative Politics* (January 1984): 223–46.

9. Robert L. Rothstein, *Alliances and Small Powers* (New York: Columbia University Press, 1968), 11; Walt, "Alliance Formation," 7–8.

10. Walt, "Alliance Formation," 17; Walt, *Origins of Alliances,* 30.

11. Annette Baker Fox, *The Power of Small States: Diplomacy in World War II* (Chicago: University of Chicago Press, 1959), 181; Michael Handel, *Weak States in the International System* (London: Frank Cass, 1981), 186; Walt, *Origins of Alliances,* 173; Rothstein, *Alliances and Small Power,* 26–27.

12. Walt, "Alliance Formation," 17; Walt, *Origins of Alliances,* 29, 173; Robert Jervis, "Systems Theory and Diplomatic History," in *Diplomacy: New Approaches in History, Theory, and Policy,* ed. Paul Gordon Lauren (New York: Free Press, 1979), 222.

13. Piotr S. Wandycz, *The Twilight of French Eastern Alliances: 1926–1936* (Princeton, N.J.: Princeton University Press, 1988), 456–57.

14. Wandycz, *The Twilight of French Eastern Alliances,* 26–27, 146–47, 152–53, 254.

15. Walt, "Alliance Formation," 8; George Liska, *Nations in Alliance: The Limits of Interdependence* (Baltimore: Johns Hopkins Press, 1962), 27; Jervis, "Systems Theory and Diplomatic History," 220.

16. Walt, *Origins of Alliances,* 31.

17. Hugh Seton-Watson, *The East European Revolution,* 3d ed. (New York: Frederick A. Praeger, 1956), 83, 89–90, 104.

18. Holsti, Hopmann, and Sullivan, *Unity and Disintegration in International Alliances,* 4–5.

19. Selznick, *Leadership in Administration,* 14, 17–19.

20. Selznick, *Leadership in Administration,* 18–19.

21. Krasner, "Approaches to the State," 233.

22. J. P. Nettl, "The State as a Conceptual Variable," *World Politics* 20 (July 1968): 563–64.

23. David E. Apter, "Introduction: Ideology and Discontent," in *Ideology and Discontent,* ed. Apter (New York: Free Press, 1964), 18–21.

24. Stephen D. Krasner, "Sovereignty: An Institutional Perspective," *Comparative Political Studies* (Spring 1988).

25. Nettl, "The State as a Conceptual Variable," 565–66.

26. Herbert C. Kelman, "Nationalism, National Sentiments, and International Conflict," paper presented at the Workshop on Nationalism and International Conflict, National Academy of Sciences, December 6–7, 1988.

27. Selznick, *Leadership in Administration,* 5–6.

28. Joseph Rothschild, *East Central Europe Between the Wars* (Seattle: University of Washington Press, 1974), 86–87; Anthony Tihamer Komjathy, *The Crises of France's East Central European Diplomacy: 1933–1938* (New York: Columbia University Press, 1976), 7; Komjathy and Rebecca Stockwell, *German Minorities and the Third Reich* (New York: Holmes & Meier, 1980), 22.

29. Rothschild, *East Central Europe Between the Wars,* 12, 118, 119n; C. A. Macartney and A. W. Palmer, *Independent Eastern Europe* (New York: St. Martin's Press, 1966), 193–94; Hugh Seton-Watson, *Eastern Europe Between the Wars, 1918–1941* (Cambridge: Cambridge University Press, 1945), 175–76.

30. Macartney and Palmer, *Independent Eastern Europe,* 193–94.

31. Rothschild, *East Central Europe Between the Wars,* 13; Gerhard L. Weinberg, *The Foreign Policy of Hitler's Germany: Diplomatic Revolution in Europe, 1933–1936* (Chicago: University of Chicago Press, 1970), 315.

32. Weinberg, *Foreign Policy of Hitler's Germany,* 225; Vera Olivova, *The Doomed Democracy: Czechoslovakia in a Disrupted Europe 1914–38,* trans. George Theiner (Montreal: McGill-Queen's Press, 1972), 190–94; Komjathy and Stockwell, *German Minorities and the Third Reich,* 27–28; J. W. Bruegel, *Czechoslovakia Before Munich* (Cambridge: Cambridge University Press, 1973), 120.

33. Komjathy, *Crises of France's East Central European Diplomacy,* 201–202; Weinberg, *The Foreign Policy of Hitler's Germany,* 225, 316–21; Bruegel, *Czechoslovakia Before Munich,* 177–81; Macartney and Palmer, *Independent Eastern Europe,* 398–99.

34. Rothschild, *East Central Europe Between the Wars,* 207; J. B. Hoptner, *Yugoslavia in Crisis: 1939–1941* (New York: Columbia University Press, 1962), 2–3, 7; Komjathy, *Crises of France's East Central European Diplomacy,* 21; Seton-Watson, *Eastern Europe Between the Wars,* 221–22; Ivo Banac, *The National Question in Yugoslavia* (Ithaca, N.Y.: Cornell University Press, 1984), 141–42, 144–145, 152–53. According to Hoptner, "It was the Serb–Croat divergence, although primarily an internal problem, that proved crucial in the formulation and operation of the new kingdom's foreign policy" (p.2).

35. Komjathy, *Crises of France's East Central European Diplomacy,* 10, 85–86;

Rothschild, *East Central Europe Between the Wars,* 246; Hoptner, *Yugoslavia in Crisis,* 27–28.

36. Hoptner, *Yugoslavia in Crisis,* 46–47,55–56, 58–60, 91–92; Konjathy, *Crises of France's East Central European Diplomacy,* 90–91, 95; Macartney and Palmer, *Independent Eastern Europe,* 316–17, 336, 356.

37. Seton-Watson, *Eastern Europe Between the Wars,* 311–12.

38. Macartney and Palmer, *Independent Eastern Europe,* 228; Rothschild, *East Central Europe Between the Wars,* 160, 323, 326; Seton-Watson, *East European Revolution,* 21; Seton-Watson, *Eastern Europe Between the Wars,* 244–47.

39. Rothschild, *East Central Europe Between the Two World Wars,* 176–77, 194; C. A. Macartney, *October Fifteenth,* Part I (Edinburgh: At the University Press, 1956), 14–17.

40. Macartney, *October Fifteenth,* 274–75, 474–90; Macartney and Palmer, *Independent Eastern Europe,* 443; Seton-Watson, *Eastern Europe Between the Wars,* 196, 409–410.

41. Rothschild, *East Central Europe Between the Wars,* 28–29; Henry L. Roberts, *Eastern Europe: Politics, Revolution & Diplomacy* (New York: Alfred A. Knopf, 1970), 173–74.

42. Roberts, *Eastern Europe,* 143–44, 160–61, 173–74; Weinberg, *Foreign Policy of Hitler's Germany,* 72–73; Anna M. Cienciala, *Poland and the Western Powers* (London: Routledge & Kegan Paul, 1968), 4–6; Macartney and Palmer, *Independent Eastern Europe,* 347.

43. Macartney and Palmer, *Independent Eastern Europe,* 270; Radomir Luza, *Austro-German Relations in the Anschluss Era* (Princeton, N.J.: Princeton University Press, 1975), 5–7, 10; Komjathy, *Crises of France's East Central European Diplomacy,* 12.

44. Komjathy, *Crises of France's East Central European Diplomacy,* 76, 215–16; Macartney and Palmer, *Independent Eastern Europe,* 270, 328–30.

45. Luza, *Austro-German Relations,* 44, 48, 52.

46. Fernand Braudel, *The Identity of France,* vol. 1, *History and Environment,* trans. Sian Reynolds (New York: Harper & Row, 1988).

47. Arnold Wolfers, *Britain and France Between Two Wars* (New York: Norton, 1966; Harcourt, Brace & World, 1940), 55, 61–62, 160; Wandycz, *The Twilight of French Eastern Alliances,* 455–57, 477; Charles A. Micaud, *The French Right and Nazi Germany* (Durham, N.C.: Duke University Press, 1943), 14.

48. Wandycz, *The Twilight of French Eastern Alliances,* 397–98, 426–47; Micaud, *The French Right and Nazi Germany,* 80–84, 222, 225–27, 230; William Evans Scott, *Alliance Against Hitler* (Durham, N.C.: Duke University Press, 1962), 261–62, 264–67 (quotation on 265).

49. Scott, *Alliance Against Hitler,* 253–54, 261–65.

50. Luther Allen, "The French Left and Soviet Russia," *World Affairs Quarterly* 29 (July 1959): 121.

51. Douglass C. North, *Structure and Change in Economic History* (New York: W. W. Norton, 1981), 53.

52. Liska, *Nations in Alliance,* 37. For examples of illegitimate Middle East regimes that bandwagoned with Nasser to induce him to refrain from trying to subvert their rule, see Walt, *Origins of Alliances,* 173–76, 208–9, 215–16.

53. Walt, "Alliance Formation," 20; Walt, *Origins of Alliances,* 39, 208–9.

54. Myron Weiner calls this pattern "The Macedonian Syndrome: An Historical Model of International Relations and Political Development," *World Politics* 23:4 (July 1971): 665–83.

55. Rothschild, *Central Europe Between the Two World Wars,* 178; Seton-Watson, *East European Revolution,* 44–46.

56. Weinberg, *The Foreign Policy of Hitler's Germany,* 115–18; Macartney and Palmer, *Independent Eastern Europe,* 313–15; Rothschild, *East Central Europe Between the Two World Wars,* 23–24; Hoptner, *Yugoslavia in Crisis,* 101–103; Macartney, *October Fifteenth,* 141–42.

57. David E. Kaiser, *Economic Diplomacy and the Origins of the Second World War* (Princeton, N.J.: Princeton University Press, 1980), 270–71.

58. Macartney and Palmer, *Independent Eastern Europe,* 346–47, 368.

59. Hoptner, *Yugoslavia in Crisis,* 87, 89, 121–22, 152–53.

60. Rothschild, *East Central Europe Between the Two World Wars,* 177.

61. Rothschild, *East Central Europe Between the Wars,* 72; Seton-Watson, *The East European Revolution,* 44–45.

62. Rothschild, *East Central Europe Between the Wars,* 160.

63. Rothschild, *East Central Europe Between the Wars,* 175–76.

64. Stephen Skowronek, *Building a New American State: The Expansion of National Administrative Capacities, 1877–1920* (Cambridge: Cambridge University Press, 1982), 12–13; Krasner, "Approaches to the State," 234–40.

65. Selznick, *Leadership in Administration,* 20–21.

66. Rothschild, *East Central Europe Between the Wars,* 128, 131n.

67. Seton-Watson, *The East European Revolution,* 98; Macartney and Palmer, *Independent Eastern Europe,* 443, 446; Rothschild, *East Central Europe Between the Wars,* 177.

68. Much to the new regime's embarrassment, Churchill interpreted the coup as a Serbian rejection of Prince Paul's signing of the tripartite pact, claiming that Yugoslavia had found its "soul." In fact, the foreign minister desperately tried to obtain an appointment with the German ambassador to assure him that Yugoslavia still adhered to its international obligations. The leader of the coup naively did not anticipate German retaliation. Hoptner, *Yugoslavia in Crisis,* 253, 265–66, 284; Roberts, *Eastern Europe,* 191; Rothschild, *East Central Europe Between the Wars,* 265.

69. Department of State, *Foreign Relations of the United States, 1947,* vol. V (Washington, D.C.: U.S. Government Printing Office) (hereafter cited as FRUS, followed by appropriate year and volume), 97–100; William D. Leahy diary, March 7, 1947, Library of Congress (LC); Notes on Cabinet Meeting, March 7, 1947, Matthew J. Connelly Papers, Harry S. Truman Library (HSTL), Independence, Mo.; James V. Forrestal diary, March 7, 1947, in *The Forrestal Diaries,* ed. Walter Millis (New York: Viking Press, 1951), 250–51; Robert A. Pollard, *Economic Security and the Origins of the Cold War, 1945–1950* (New York: Columbia University Press, 1985), 126–28. "The decision is to ask Congress for 250 million and say this is only the beginning," Truman explained to cabinet members on March 7. "It means [the] U.S. going into European politics." According to Admiral Leahy, the cabinet agreed that "financial assistance be given immediately to the Greek Government and that the people of America be fully and frankly informed that its purpose is to prevent Soviet domination of Europe."

70. Notes on cabinet meeting, March 7, 1947, Connelly Papers, HSTL. See also Senate Committee on Foreign Relations, *Legislative Origins of the Truman Doctrine,* executive sess., 80th Cong., 1st sess., 1973, 160; *FRUS 1947* II, 209–10; *New York Times* editorial, Mar. 11, 1947.

71. Report of the Special "Ad Hoc" Committee of the State-War-Navy Coordinating Committee, "Policies, Procedures and Costs of Assistance by the United States to Foreign Countries," April 21, 1947, *FRUS 1947* III, 217.

72. Caffery to Deputy Director of the Office of European Affairs Hickerson, March 6, 1947, *FRUS 1947* III, 693; Alfred J. Rieber, *Stalin and the French Communist Party 1941–1947* (New York: Columbia University Press, 1962), 300.

73. Dunn to Secretary of State, May 7, 1947, *FRUS 1947,* III, 899–901; James Edward Miller, *The United States and Italy: 1940–1950* (Chapel Hill: University of North Carolina Press, 1986), 192.

74. Charles S. Maier, "The Politics of Productivity: Foundations of American International Economic Policy After World War II, *International Organization* 31:4 (Autumn 1977): 607–33.

75. Joseph Marion Jones, *The Fifteen Weeks (February 21–June 5, 1947)* (New York: Harcourt, Brace & World, 1955), 79, 83–84, 88, 96; Scott Jackson, "Prologue to the Marshall Plan: The Origins of the American Commitment for a European Recovery Program," *Journal of American History* 65 (1978–1979): 1047; Rieber, *Stalin and the French Communist Party,* 302.

76. Miller, *The United States and Italy,* 190–91, 226; *New York Times* editorial, May 8, 1947.

77. Harold Callender, "Europe Is Amazed by Blunt Warning," *New York Times,* Mar. 13, 1947.

78. *New York Times* editorial, May 8, 1947; Harold Callender, "French Radicals Back Ramadier Despite Fears of Regimentation," *New York Times,* May 8, 1947; Rieber, *Stalin and the French Communist Party,* 350; Miller, *The United States and Italy,* 226, 228–29.

79. Harry S. Truman, *Memoirs,* vol. 1, *Years of Trial and Hope* (Garden City, N.Y. Doubleday, 1956), 333; George F. Kennan, *Memoirs 1925–1950* (Boston: Little, Brown, 1967), 486; Dean Acheson, *Present at the Creation: My Years in the State Department* (New York: W. W. Norton, 1969), 405; William Whitney Stueck, *The Road to Confrontation* (Chapel Hill: University of North Carolina Press, 1981), 173; Russell D. Buhite, "'Major Interests,' American Policy Toward China, Taiwan, and Korea, 1945–1950," *Pacific Historical Review* 47 (August 1978): 450–51; John Lewis Gaddis, "Korea in American Politics, Strategy, and Diplomacy 1945–50," in *The Origins of the Cold War in Asia,* eds. Yonosuke Nagai and Akira Iriye (New York: Columbia University Press, 1977), 288; Alexander L. George and Richard Smoke, *Deterrence in American Foreign Policy: Theory and Practice* (New York: Columbia University Press, 1974), 146, 148; James Irving Matray, *The Reluctant Crusade: American Foreign Policy in Korea, 1941–1950* (Honolulu: University of Hawaii Press, 1985), 251–52; Barton J. Bernstein, "The Week We Went to War: American Intervention in the Korean War, Part II," *Foreign Service Journal* 54 (February 1977): 9; Rosemary Foot, *The Wrong War: American Policy and the Dimensions of the Korean Conflict, 1950–53* (Ithaca, N.Y.: Cornell University Press, 1985), 59–60.

80. Intelligence Estimate Prepared by the Estimates Group, Office of Intelligence Research (INR), State Department, June 25, 1950, *FRUS 1950* VII, 149, 151, 153–54; John Lewis Gaddis, *Strategies of Containment* (New York: Oxford University Press), 109–110.

81. Summary of Telegrams, June 27, 1950, "Korea—Summary of Telegrams," Harry S. Truman Papers, President's Secretary File (PSF), HSTL; World Reaction to Korean Developments, July 1, 1950, prepared by the INR, Department of State, Korean War Documents file, ibid.; Brussels to Washington, June 29, 1950, Truman Papers, PSF, "Korea—Foreign Telegrams," HSTL.

82. World Reaction to Korean Developments, June 29, July 1, 2, 7, 1950, Department of State, Korean War Documents File, HSTL; Ann O'Hare McCormick, "The

European Backwash of the American Move in Asia," *New York Times,* July 1, 1950, 14; idem, "The Spotlight Shifts from France to Washington," *New York Times,* June 28, 1950, 26; Lawrence S. Kaplan, *The United States and NATO: The Formative Years* (Lexington: University Press of Kentucky), 150, 156–59; Robert McGeehan, *The German Rearmament Question: American Diplomacy and European Defense After World War II* (Urbana: University of Illinois Press, 1971), 23–24.

83. Memorandum of conversation, June 30, 1950, Dean Acheson Papers, "Memo of Conversation May–June 1950," HSTL; Summary of Telegrams, June 28, 1950, Truman Papers, PSF, "Korea—Summary of Telegrams," HSTL; World Reaction to Korean Developments, INR, June 29, June 30, and July 1, July 2, 1950, Department of State, Korean War Documents File, HSTL; Anne O'Hare McCormick, "The Spotlight Shifts from France to Washington," *New York Times,* June 28, 1950, 26.

84. Walt, *Origins of Alliances,* 33.

85. World Reactions to Korean Developments, July 21, 24, 27, 1950, Department of State, Korean War Documents File, HSTL; R. N. Rosecrance, *Defense of the Realm: British Strategy in the Nuclear Epoch* (New York: Columbia University Press, 1968), 134–39. From 1949 to 1953, European NATO countries' defense expenditures increased threefold. From 1950 to 1951, for example, Belgian military expenditures increased from 8,256 million to 13,387 million francs. French defense expenditures rose from 5,591 million to 8,811 million francs. See NATO Information Service, *NATO: Facts about the North Atlantic Treaty Organization* (Netherlands: Bosch-Utrecht, 1965), 112, 116–17.

86. Ernest R. May, *'Lessons' of the Past: The Use and Misuse of History in American Foreign Policy* (New York: Oxford University Press, 1973), 19–51; Robert Jervis, *Perception and Misperception in International Politics* (Princeton, N.J.: Princeton University Press, 1976), 261–71; Deborah Welch Larson, *Origins of Containment: A Psychological Explanation* (Princeton, N.J.: Princeton University Press, 1985), 50–57.

87. Minutes, NSC meeting, March 25, April 6, April 29, 1954, *FRUS 1952–1954* XIII, 1163, 1253, 1260.

88. Dulles to Washington, DULTE 9, April 23, 1954, Dwight D. Eisenhower Papers, Ann C. Whitman File, Dulles-Herter Series, "Dulles, John F. April 1954 (2)," Dwight David Eisenhower Library (DDEL), Abilene, Kans.; Dulles to Department of State, April 23, 1954, *FRUS 1952–1954* XIII, 1374; memorandum of discussion at NSC meeting, May 13, 1954, ibid., 1549; Dulles to Washington, DULTE 34, April 30, 1954, Whitman File, Dulles-Herter Series, "Dulles, John F. April 1954 (2)," DDEL; Richard H. Immerman, "United States Perceptions of its Interests in Indochina," in *Dien Bien Phu and the Crisis of Franco-American Relations: 1954–1955,* ed. Lawrence S. Kaplan and Denise Artaud. (Wilmington, DE: Scholarly Resources, 1990).

89. Charles C. Stelle, Policy Planning Staff, March 27, 1952, Draft—Indochina Section of NSC Paper, *FRUS 1952–1954* XIII, 83; Memorandum by Charles C. Stelle, Policy Planning Staff, March 23, 1954, *FRUS 1952–1954* XIII, 1146–48; NSC 5405, United States Objectives and Courses of Action with Respect to Southeast Asia, January 16, 1954, *FRUS 1952–1954* XII, 367; *FRUS 1952–1954* XIII, 971–72. See also "Further United States Support for France and the Associated States of Indochina," August 5, 1953, *FRUS 1952–1954* XIII, 717; SE 52, Probable Consequences in Non-Communist Asia of Certain Possible Developments in Indochina Before Mid-1954, November 16, 1953, ibid., 866–68, 871.

90. Richard K. Betts, *Soldiers, Statesmen, and Cold War Crises* (Cambridge, Mass.: Harvard University Press, 1977), 8–9, 120–23; Barry R. Posen, *The Sources of Military Doctrine: France, Britain, and Germany Between the World Wars* (Ithaca, N.Y.: Cornell University Press, 1984), 45–46.

91. Memorandum by the JCS to Secretary of Defense Wilson, March 31, 1954, *FRUS 1952–1954* XIII, 1198; minutes, NSC meeting, April 2, 1954, Whitman File, NSC Series, DDEL.

92. Memorandum of conversation by the Secretary of State, April 2, 1954, *FRUS 1952–1954* XIII, 1210–11; Draft Prepared in the Department of State, April 2, 1954 ibid., 1211–12; memorandum for the file of the Secretary of State, April 5, 1954, ibid., 1224; minutes, NSC meeting, April 6, 1954, ibid., 1254; George C. Herring and Richard H. Immerman, "Eisenhower, Dulles, and Dienbienphu: 'The Day We Didn't Go to War' Revisited," *Journal of American History* 71:2 (September 1984): 351–53, 355, 356, 360; memorandum of conversation, April 25, 1954, Whitman File, Dulles-Herter Series, "Dulles, John F. April 1954 (1)," DDEL.

93. Memorandum of conversation by Assistant Secretary of State for Far Eastern Affairs Robertson and the Counselor MacArthur, April 12, 1954, *FRUS 1952–1954* XIII, 1311; Minutes, NSC meeting, April 29, 1954, ibid., 1436–37; Geoffrey Warner, "Britain and the Crisis Over Dien Bien Phu April 1954: The Failure of 'United Action,'" in Kaplan and Artaud, *From Dien Bien Phu to Saigon*.

94. John T. Marcus, *Neutralism and Nationalism in France* (Glen Echo, MD.: Books Associates, 1958), 58–59, 83, 196; McGeehan, *The German Rearmament Question*, 234–38.

95. Donald E. Nuechterlein, *Thailand and the Struggle for Southeast Asia* (Ithaca, N.Y.: Cornell University Press, 1965), 103, 125, 129–31; Charles E. Morrison and Astri Suhrke, *Strategies of Survival: The Foreign Policy Dilemmas of Smaller Asian States* (New York: St. Martin's Press, 1978), 110, 115.

96. Morrison and Suhrke, *Strategies of Survival*, 148.

97. Don E. Kash, "United States Policy for Quemoy and Matsu," *Western Political Quarterly* 16 (December 1963): 915–16; J. H. Kalicki, *The Pattern of Sino-American Crises: Political-Military Interactions in the 1950s* (London: Cambridge University Press, 1975), 130, 133; George and Smoke, *Deterrence in American Foreign Policy*, 268–69, 277–78; *FRUS 1952–1954* XIV, 228–29; 585, 592.

98. *FRUS 1952–1954* XIV, 556, 557–58, 586, 599, 603–604, 605, 608; minutes, NSC meeting, September 12, 1954, ibid., 615–23; memorandum of conversation between Dulles and Eisenhower, March 6, 1955, *FRUS 1955–1957* II, 336; telegram from Dulles to Department of State, Bangkok, February 25, 1955, ibid., 308–309; memorandum of conversation with Dulles and Senator George, March 7, 1955, ibid., 337.

99. See, for example, Eisenhower to Churchill, February 18 and March 29, 1955, *FRUS 1955–1957* II, 294, 419–21.

100. Memorandum from Director of Central Intelligence Allen Dulles to Secretary of State John Foster Dulles, March 16, 1955, *FRUS 1955–1957* II, 383; NIE 100-4/1-55, "Morale on Taiwan," April 16, 1955, ibid., 481; A. Doak Barnett, *Communist China and Asia* (New York: Harper & Brothers, 1960), 394–95.

101. Letter from Rankin to Assistant Secretary of State for Far Eastern Affairs Robertson, March 13, 1955, *FRUS 1955–1957* II, 480.

102. NIE 100-4/1-55, April 16, 1955, *FRUS 1955–1957* II, 480.

103. Minutes, NSC meeting, September 12, 1954 *FRUS 1952–1954* XIV, 621. See also ibid., 501, 510, 516.

104. *FRUS 1952–1954* XIV, 731–32, 734, 753n., 929; Kalicki *The Pattern of Sino-American Crises*, 140–41.

105. *FRUS 1952–1954* XIV, 662, 828–29.

106. *FRUS 1955–1957* II, 86–91.

107. Dwight D. Eisenhower, *Mandate for Change: 1955–1956* (Garden City, N.Y.: Doubleday, 1963), 469.

108. *FRUS 1955–1957* II, 426–27.

109. Eisenhower to General Alfred M. Gruenther, February 1, 1955, *FRUS 1955–1957* II, 191; memorandum of conversation, Bipartisan Congressional Luncheon Meeting, March 30, 1955, ibid., 427–48. In "To the Nuclear Brink: Eisenhower, Dulles, and the Quemoy-Matsu Crisis," *International Security* 12:4 (Spring 1988): 112–13, Gordon Chang claims that Eisenhower was "disingenuous" in telling a group of senators that he could not know in advance whether he would intervene militarily in the offshore islands if the communists attacked. But Dulles told the Joint Chiefs that the "President did not wish to make this decision until a situation occurred which would clearly indicate that the defense of Quemoy and Matsu were related to the defense of Formosa." See memorandum of conversation, March 26, 1955, *FRUS 1955–1957* II, 402. Moreover, the commitment given to Chiang clearly states that "under present circumstances it is the purpose of the President to assist in the defense of Quemoy and Matsu against armed attack if he judges such attack is of a character which shows that it is in fact in aid of and in preparation for an armed attack on Formosa and the Pescadores and dangerous to their defense." By the time of the Radford–Robertson mission, Eisenhower had in fact changed his mind about defending the islands, and Chiang was so notified. See *FRUS 1955–1957* II, 512, 516, 522.

5

The Truman Administration and Global Responsibilities: The Birth of the Falling Domino Principle

DOUGLAS J. MACDONALD

On April 7, 1954, President Dwight Eisenhower spoke on Indochina at a press conference:

> you have broader considerations that might follow what you would call the "falling domino" principle. You have a row of dominoes set up, you knock over the first one, and what will happen to the last one is the certainty that it will go over very quickly . . . .
>
> But when we come to the possible sequence of events, the loss of Indochina, of Burma, of Thailand, of the Peninsula, and Indonesia following, now you begin to talk about areas that not only multiply the disadvantages that you would suffer through the loss of materials, sources of materials, but now you are talking really about millions and millions and millions of people.[1]

Thus the "falling domino principle" came into public view as a strategic concept.[2] The "domino principle" became one of the most controversial issues in U.S. politics because it was used by successive administrations as a justification for the Vietnam War. Despite this controversy, it apparently remains operative in the post-Vietnam era, as Ronald Reagan and others used similar logic to defend policies in Central America and elsewhere. In fact, virtually every U.S. president since 1954 has used the domino principle, or a variation of it, to defend policies associated with the containment of communism.

Despite the importance of this justification for U.S. foreign policy, surprisingly little research has been done to identify and analyze its origins. The metaphor used by Eisenhower has identified it in the popular imagination, journalistic circles, and among many scholars as a creation of his administration in reaction to the events surrounding the French defeat at Dienbienphu. But the principle had its origins in the Truman administration, and Eisenhower was simply articulating an important strategic premise in U.S. foreign policy that had been generally accepted by governmental decision makers, Congress and much of the public prior to his election in 1952.

The domino principle represented a perception of the nature of a growing global threat, intimately linked with the policy of containment, by a society and government that were quite unprepared to accept the global responsibilities thrust upon them in the wake of World War II. Governmental and public consensus-building evolves over time. For Americans, the political and geostrategic dust of World War II took five years to settle, with numerous intervening events. It settled first in Europe, then the Middle East, and finally in Asia. Governmental decision makers during the Truman administration began the postwar period with no clear policy consensus for dealing with the U.S.S.R. The years 1946–50 were a period of initial policy confusion that gradually became clarified by the adoption of a hard-line global containment policy, of which the domino principle is an integral part. Though the adoption of the hard-line consensus brought greater clarity of purpose to containment, it did not immediately end dissension within the government over the allocation of resources and basic geostrategic concepts, specifically, which areas of the world were most important to the containment effort.

A second stage thus was the gradual application of the lessons of early containment policy in Europe to the Middle East, and then to the most peripheral region to containment, Asia. The domino principle appeared first in Europe and was gradually applied to less important regions. The fall of China, the Soviet detonation of a nuclear device, and the outbreak of the Korean War in 1949 to 1950 settled a difference between hard-liners over an asymmetrical strongpoint strategy of containment that was relatively selective in determining which nations and regions were important to the security of the United States and a symmetrical perimeter strategy that suggested all areas were equally important because they were strategically interdependent. The former strategy suggested that resource allocation could remain relatively low; the latter that a much greater effort was necessary.[3] The adoption of the perimeter strategy and its requirement for greater resources symbolized the ascension of the domino principle as a strategic calculus in the periphery. Thus the acceptance of the domino principle was a logical antecedent to the adoption of the perimeter strategy.

From 1946 to 1950 decision makers were severely constrained in the adoption of the perimeter strategy by the relatively low levels of human and material resources that would be required to carry out a more ambitious policy.[4] The Truman administration was fiscally conservative and under consistent congressional pressure for more austerity still. Perceptions of an increased threat to U.S. interests, represented by the domino principle, gradually led to attempts to gain more resources for containment. Thus major events that caused the administration to request, and the public and Congress increasingly to approve, greater resources for containment will be analyzed as indicators of such changes in threat perception.

The divisions between strongpoint and perimeter strategists were based on differing views of this relationship between resource allocation and perception of threat to U.S. interests. Strongpoint strategists argued that limited resources should shape threat perceptions; perimeter strategists argued that threat perceptions should determine resource allocation. The Truman administration adopted the strongpoint strategy through 1948. By 1949, however, a series of intervening events had raised the specter of falling dominoes along the entire line of containment and strengthened the arguments of the perimeter strategists.

The Truman Doctrine (1947), the Czech coup and Berlin blockade (1948), the "fall" of China and the Soviet nuclear detonation (1949), and the outbreak of the Korean War (1950) represent watershed events in the evolution of a greater willingness of the United States to allocate more resources to containment as that policy was applied on a global scale. In all four periods, the growing scope of the strategic threat increasingly determined the level of resources to be made available. By 1950, these events were combined psychologically and politically into lessons that projected a pattern of communist expansion that threatened any vulnerable nation that stood in its path, that is, dominoes.

It was the integration of the strategic, psychological, political, and economic elements of these lessons that led to the adoption of the domino principle as a strategic calculus and justification for policy in the periphery as the line of containment spread to Asia. These lessons produced an important concept that has had great influence on U.S. policy in the periphery since then. An analysis of its origins will allow us to understand better its persistence in the face of skepticism from critics and why decision makers have found it useful as both rationale and justification for policy.

The Strongpoint Strategy (1945–1948)

The Contradictions of the Roosevelt Legacy

As the United States emerged from World War II, there were proponents of a hard line and of a soft line within its government, over the best way to approach the U.S.S.R. in the postwar period. The hard-liners wanted a firm but friendly diplomacy based on their prediction of a competitive balance of power relationship with the Soviets. The soft-liners wanted a less confrontational relationship, fearing that a hard-line policy would exacerbate Russian insecurities and render impossible the cooperative balance of power relations experienced during the war. Both groups wanted cooperation with the U.S.S.R.; the variance in policy prescriptions centered on means, not ends. Both saw themselves as correctly representing U.S. postwar goals.[5]

Franklin Roosevelt had kept his own counsel on issues dealing with postwar strategy, partly to avoid disrupting the wartime alliance with possible areas of disagreement, but also because he was well aware of the Wilsonian, universalistic propensities of his own people. He therefore struck a contradictory balance between Wilsonian idealism and a cooperative balance of power approach (represented by his plans for the United Nations) and a competitive balance of power approach toward keeping the postwar peace (represented by his "Four Policemen" concept).[6]

Roosevelt believed that the United States could not sustain large military commitments to keep the peace when the war ended. He was also aware that it alone could not prevent the Soviets from holding onto the areas they had already occupied in Eastern Europe and were about to occupy in the Far East.[7] He therefore aimed at balancing the power of the Soviet Union with the British Empire in Europe and the Middle East and China in the Far East. He planned to sell this idea to the American people through the United Nations, a concept he was quite skeptical about unless it reflected the power realities of the postwar world.[8] The decline of the British Empire, the failure of Chiang Kai-shek to unify China, and the ultimate absence of power realities in the United Nations system led the United States to a greater emphasis on the competitive balance of power approach in the postwar years.

Harry Truman inherited this internally contradictory policy of idealism and realism when he became president.[9] Though he was later criticized by some hard-liners for excessive reliance on the United Nations–soft-line approach to the Soviets at war's end, no president could have escaped an effort to establish a *modus vivendi* with the U.S.S.R. within that framework, given the state of U.S. public and world opinion.[10] In adopting both aspects of Roosevelt's contradictory policy, he believed he was fulfilling the aims of wartime diplomacy.[11]

The Origins of the Domino Principle in Europe

The hard line received its most consistent support from Europeanists within the State Department. As early as March 1943, former Ambassador to the U.S.S.R. William C. Bullitt warned that Europe would be communized unless Great Britain and the United States blocked "the flow of the Red Amoeba." After becoming ambassador to the U.S.S.R. in 1943, Averell Harriman also warned presidents Roosevelt and Truman of the potential for Soviet expansion.[12]

This advocacy of a hard line in Europe contained an early articulation of the underlying logic of the domino principle, that is, that areas contiguous to the U.S.S.R. (or its satellites) were inherently vulnerable to penetration and subversion. This would be accomplished through covert aid given to communist parties in the target nations, which would then subvert existing authority structures. Once in power, these Stalinist fifth columns would owe their allegiance to Moscow. With the Soviet army advancing throughout Eastern Europe in the final days of the war, this appeared to threaten the West also. As Harriman warned the president in April 1945: "Russian plans for establishing satellite states are a threat to the world and to us. The Soviet Union, once it had control of bordering areas, would attempt to penetrate the next adjacent countries."[13] According to Harriman and other hard-liners, the United States had to take a firm stand against such actions or it would only encourage further Soviet expansion.

This view, it should be noted, was seemingly vindicated by the increasing demands of the Soviets. Though they might have plausibly argued that their security would be threatened if they did not have compatible regimes in Eastern Europe (a concept for which most Americans had little sympathy), this argument would not support their territorial or concessionary demands in Turkey, Iran, Manchuria, and North Africa. The postwar actions of the Soviet Union confirmed the worst fears of American decision makers and gradually settled the contention within the government in favor of those arguing for a hard line.

Resources and the Response

The new emphasis on a hard line brought the dilemma of resource allocation to the forefront in policy circles. The hard-line response presupposed that the government could devote relatively large amounts of human and material resources to foreign policy goals until the postwar peace was settled. The problem for decision makers was that Congress and the public were undermining the means for implementing such a policy through demobilization and cuts in military spending. Secretary of the Navy James Forrestal complained that the American people were "going back to bed." At an October 1945 cabinet meeting, Truman himself complained that "demobilization" had turned into "disintegration." The U.S.S.R. also partly demobilized, but less extensively and less dramatically than the United States. In any event, U.S. leaders remained convinced that the Soviets were not demobilizing. The administration launched an unsuccessful campaign for Universal Military Training, which it would later resurrect occasionally, but the mood among congressional leaders forbade such an option.[14]

The shrinking resource share narrowed the options for responses to Soviet provocations and led to two major developments in immediate postwar policy: (1) a reliance on means other than conventional military strength to influence Soviet behavior; and (2) the reliance on a geostrategic rank-order calculus for determining interests, that is, some areas became more important than others. These were the basic underpinnings of the strongpoint strategy.

The new means of leverage were economic aid for reconstruction, the atomic bomb, and the force of world opinion.[15] The administration was not content with the reduced resource share, but acquiesced in the lead of congress. General George C. Marshall warned, "We are playing with fire while we have nothing with which to put it out."[16] Although internal and external pressures continued for a symmetrical perimeter strategy, the administration stayed with the asymmetrical strongpoint strategy until 1950 due to political and fiscal necessity.

This led to a Eurocentric policy that mirrored the wartime policy of meeting challenges on the European continent first, before becoming concerned with threats elsewhere. The policy was quickly reflected in Truman's China policy. Since the United States did not have the political will or resources to bolster Chiang Kai-shek, it sent General Marshall in 1946 to mediate between the Kuomintang (K.M.T.) and the Chinese Communist Party (C.C.P.).[17]

The Cold War

When the administration took a tough stand toward the Soviets in Europe and the Middle East in early 1946, the hard line again received a psychological boost among the public and within the government, but not enough to change policy direction. United States intelligence agencies had determined by December 1945 that the U.S.S.R. would consolidate its power in occupied territories "in preparation for further expansion" and then attempt to extend its influence on a global basis "by all means short of war."[18] In February, Stalin made a speech in which he compared the United States and Britain to Nazi Germany. It was within this context of rising tension between the superpowers that George F. Kennan wrote his famous "long telegram" of February 1946, which provided the intellectual underpinnings for the policy of containment. In the Middle East, the crisis over northern Iran, in which a tough Western approach eventually resulted in a Soviet withdrawal, was used by the hard-liners as an example of the efficacy of firmness. A few weeks later, Churchill made his "Iron Curtain" speech at Fulton,

Missouri. The U.S.S.R. was now more generally viewed as an inherently expansionist power that could only be stopped by a strong U.S. stand. Though this was already being argued by many in and out of government, Kennan's essay had an unusually strong effect on official thinking.

The growing tension was also reflected in the popular press. In April 1946, *Time* printed a map showing Iran, Turkey, and Manchuria as "infected" with the "Communist contagion," with other nations exposed. The Republicans launched an attack on the Democrats for "appeasement" of the Soviets and promised to make it an issue in the 1946 campaign. In a poll taken in March 1946, 70 percent of the public disapproved of the U.S.S.R. and 60 percent thought the U.S. response was "too soft." The cold war was under way.[19]

The Cold War and the Middle East

Though the Truman administration continued to follow a selective, asymmetrical and Eurocentric strongpoint strategy in dealing with the U.S.S.R., some within the government began calling for a universalistic, symmetrical and perimeter strategy of containment, that is, an acceptance that all regions, and increasingly by extension all nations within a region, were equally important to U.S. interests. Their basic argument was that to protect Europe from Soviet expansion in the long run, other areas must be considered strategically interdependent with that region. They therefore called for spreading the containment line further into the Middle East and Asia. In light of the onset of the cold war in early 1946, they went on the political offensive.

On April 29, 1946, Navy Secretary James Forrestal made a speech at the Foreign Policy Association of Pittsburgh in which he stated that the Soviets were inherently expansionist and were attempting to expand into four power "vacuums" in order to undermine the United States: (1) Central Europe, (2) the Middle East, (3) China and Japan, and (4) India and Indonesia. (In contrast, George Kennan's more selective strongpoint conceptualization excluded the Middle East, China, India, and Indonesia.) Forrestal followed the speech with a world inspection tour, after which he began vigorously promoting a perimeter strategy of containment.[20]

Shortly after Forrestal's return, Truman ordered a sweeping, top secret study of military requirements in those nations that ringed the Soviet Union. The Joint Chiefs replied on July 27, 1946, with a hawkish appraisal of Soviet intentions that gave more impetus to those advocating the perimeter strategy. The United States, these advocates argued, must contain Soviet influence on a global scale, strengthen ties with "naturally friendly peoples," seek bases around the world to protect its interests, and shore up the morale of nations under Soviet pressure. This policy review led to more U.S. support for Turkey in August and Iran in October. Although Truman told Forrestal on August 15, in the midst of the crisis over Turkey, that it would also be adopted in China, it was not. As it became obvious in late 1946 that the Marshall Mission to prevent civil war in China would fail, however, the military and hard-line diplomats again began pushing for a policy of containment in that region.[21]

As the containment effort began to be applied more vigorously to the Middle East, that is, "drawing a line" against Soviet expansion by "shoring up" vulnerable nations such as Iran and Turkey, and later Greece, some hard-liners called for its application to Asia in a mechanistic manner later associated with strong advocates of the domino principle. For example, the army's Operations and Planning Division estimated in September 1946 that if China fell to the communists, they would continue to expand "onwards from Manchuria, China and Korea, toward Indo-China, Malaya and India."[22] Many in the administration, however, were not yet willing to accept these dire predictions. Due to the objections of Marshall, Kennan, and the Far Eastern Division of State and stark fiscal constraints on policymakers, the universalistic perimeter policy of containment was not yet adopted. Asia was to remain peripheral for the time being.

The Truman Doctrine—Rhetoric and Reality

The major obstacle to the adoption of a symmetrical perimeter strategy remained: low levels of resources available to accept growing areas of responsibilities. A major increase in responsibility came in the spring of 1947 in a development that appeared to threaten Europe and the Middle East. The British informed the United States that they would no longer be able to afford the costs of aiding Turkey, under external Soviet pressure, and Greece, under internal pressure from a communist insurgency.

The U.S. response was debated within the goverment. Kennan and Marshall (now Secretary of State) were in favor of a limited, specific response to the crisis and warned of the demands that would emerge from any universal declaration of U.S. intentions to fight communism.[23] The public was being told that the United States would block the advance of communism on every front. The Truman declaration would come back to haunt the administration following the fall of China in 1949. All sorts of theories of treason and perfidy were accepted at face value. The administration's attempted explanations of the differences between Greece and China would be buried in the expectations raised by the Truman Doctrine.

The perceived necessity for excessive rhetoric was based on the need to mobilize public and congressional opinion to allocate more resources for a greater containment effort.[24] The Republicans had handily won both houses of Congress in 1946 and immediately began putting pressure on Truman to adopt the perimeter strategy, as promised in their campaign, while they denied him the means to do so.[25] In fact many of these critics were against providing the resources for a strongpoint strategy as well. This is one of the ironies of the whole Truman era. Many of the most extreme elements of the Republican party who later vilified Truman and Acheson for "appeasing" the Soviets were against the Truman Doctrine, the Marshall Plan, the North Atlantic Treaty Organization, the Mutual Defense Assistance Act, or any other programs for military and economic aid to contain the U.S.S.R.[26]

Given their campaign promises for reducing taxes, the Republicans wanted Truman to take responsibility for any new major tax programs. They were therefore skeptical of any major initiatives in foreign policy. At the meeting with congressional leaders to convince them to support the Truman Doctrine, then Under Secretary of State Dean Acheson made the first clear enunciation at such high levels of government of the logic of the domino principle, using only a different metaphor:

> Like apples in a barrel infected by one rotten one, the corruption of Greece would infect Iran and all to the East. It would also carry infection to Africa through Asia Minor and Egypt, and to Europe through Italy and France, already threatened by the strongest domestic Communist parties in Western Europe.[27]

The president, said Senator Vandenberg, would have to use this logic to "scare hell" out of the country.[28] He did. From its earliest appearance at the highest levels of government, the domino principle was used to convince Congress and the public of the importance of individual nations to the overall security of the United States by directly linking them to other nations and regions, as well as acting as a guideline for decision makers themselves for predicting future actions of adversaries. Thus from its earliest manifestations in American strategic thinking, the domino principle has often been simultaneously used as a strategic calculus, a policy justification, and cognitive tool for understanding reality.

The Strategic Debate Sharpens

The effects of the Truman Doctrine were immediate and profound. The Administration's plans until March 1947 were predicated on Roosevelt's idea of the combined efforts of the United States and Great Britain countering Soviet expansion, with a unified China balancing Japan and the U.S.S.R. in the Far East. The British Empire was now disintegrating and China was in the midst of a civil war. In April, the Joint Chiefs declared that the United States could no longer rely on the United Nations as the instrument for implementing the postwar peace.[29] Though no consensus was yet reached, the new policy debate over the strongpoint and perimeter strategies, begun in early 1946, became more heated.[30]

Both strongpoint and perimeter advocates believed in a competitive balance of power. The debate centered around the relationship between means (resources) and ends (threat perception.) The strongpoint strategists, arguing that means largely determine ends, suggested continuing the rank-order calculus for determining interests. The United States had to decide which areas of the world were important to it and apply its power at those points where its influence could be brought to bear. The perimeter strategists, arguing that ends largely should determine the means available, proposed that all nations ringing the U.S.S.R. were equally important and that U.S. power must be applied everywhere in order to ensure the national security.

The Truman administration, because of relatively fixed levels of governmental resources available, and its leader's fiscal conservatism, adopted the strongpoint strategy, but to mobilize public and congressional support adopted the rhetoric of the perimeter strategy in the Truman Doctrine. This created the huge gap between rhetoric and reality that would cause the administration so many problems with the fall of China in 1949.

The resources for the strongpoint strategy were to be primarily economic and were meant to lift the sagging morale of nations that ringed the U.S.S.R. The Joint Chiefs, though they now advocated a perimeter strategy, were asked to draw up a list of areas of strategic importance to the United States in June 1947. Asia was at the bottom of their list of regions and China was thirteenth of sixteen nations considered to be important to containment. Europe, including Greece, was at the top.[31]

One reason for this relatively sanguine attitude toward China and Asia was that the hard-line containment policy in Europe and the Middle East seemed to be working. By the end of 1947, it appeared to U.S. leaders that the policies adopted during the year were having an effect. Things had not gone well for the U.S.S.R. during 1946–47. The United States had made a public policy decision to aid Western Europe with billions of dollars that the Soviets could not match. Communism was declining in popularity throughout Europe. The U.S.S.R. had been forced to back down in Iran. The allies seemed to be getting their way in Germany and the Soviets continued to be excluded from Japan. Although there were continuing problems in Greece and China, Secretary Marshall announced at a cabinet meeting in November that the advance of communism had been stemmed in Europe and the Middle East and the U.S.S.R. was being compelled to reevaluate its policies.[32]

The Soviets Shift Strategy

Though Stalin's viewpoint remains an enigma, his policy decisions of 1948 suggest a growing insecurity over the Soviet position in the world. There was a precipitous increase in a Soviet hard-line policy throughout the world. In Eastern Europe, the Soviets and their satellites moved to destroy even the slightest ideological deviation from Stalinism, which in part led to the break with Tito in Yugoslavia. The pretense of cooperation with noncommunists in the region was quickly forgotten. To counter the allure of U.S. aid and the growing disillusionment with Soviet policies in Europe, there was an extremely harsh crackdown on dissent and moves toward "consolidation and orthodoxy" in the U.S.S.R., among communist governments in Eastern Europe, and among communist parties throughout the world.[33]

For the adoption of the domino principle, however, an even more important development was the creation of the Cominform in September 1947. This organization aimed at the coordination of policies among the Communist parties of the world, under Soviet control, to challenge the West on a global scale. Its "two camps" vision, of a world divided between "progressive" and "imperialist" forces, mirrored the growing bipolar view and use of the Nazi analogy in the West. As G. M. Malenkov told the founding session, the "Hitlerite" West "has taken the path of outright expansion . . . [in] Europe and the colonial and dependent countries." A. A. Zhdanov added: "The Communist Parties of France,

Italy, Great Britain and other countries . . . must take up the standard in defense of the national independence and sovereignty of their countries."[34]

The formal declaration of the meeting set forth a Soviet version of containment, which was similar to later U.S. rhetoric in the famous 1950 document, NSC 68: "The Truman-Marshall Plan is only a constituent part, the European subsection of the general plan for the policy of global expansion pursued by the United States in all parts of the world."[35] This policy, said the declaration, aimed at the "economic and political enslavement" of Europe, Asia and South America. In light of this, it was necessary for the Communist parties of the world to "close ranks, draw up an agreed program of actions and work out . . . tactics against the main forces of the imperialist camp, against American imperialism and its British and French allies . . . ."[36]

This was not hollow rhetoric; the effects of this policy shift were not long in manifesting themselves in Western Europe. Within weeks, the Communist parties in Italy and France used their positions in government and other organizations to precipitate widespread strikes, violence, and disorder in those nations.[37] The strong identification of these developments in the West with Stalin's policy shift added to the perception that all Communist parties were subservient to Moscow and therefore Stalinist fifth columns.

At the regularly scheduled December 1947 Meeting of the Foreign Ministers in London, the communist hard line became obvious as the Soviets attempted to veto virtually all U.S. and allied actions in Western Europe. Since this threatened the proposed implementation of the Marshall Plan, Britain and other allies began requesting a political union in the West to get on with postwar reconstruction.[38] Although the administration was interested, the continued blockage of funds in the U.S. Congress forced it to remain circumspect.

In Asia, however, the Soviet hard line became apparent only gradually throughout 1948.[39] The seeming end of any possible Western cooperation with communists in France and Italy, contrasted with the military success of the Chinese and Indochinese communists, suggested that the area of opportunity with the lowest costs for the Soviets lay not in Europe or the Middle East, but in Asia. But this was not immediately apparent to the Americans or their allies, as the Czech coup in February and the Berlin Crisis beginning in June heightened tensions in Europe precipitously. With Europe and the Middle East the primary areas of containment, Asia continued to be of tertiary concern. A subtle shift of policy, however, had begun to take hold in the Soviet Union.[40]

Marshall Sticks with the Strongpoint Strategy

George C. Marshall, the "Organizer of Victory" in World War II, was a man experienced in dealing within material limitations. Throughout his tenure as secretary of state, the Truman administration continued to cling to the risky, but cost-effective, strongpoint strategy. The underlying premises of this posture were four: (1) to avoid a depression, and because of congressional fiscal austerity, U.S. military spending would be kept low; (2) the U.S. preponderance of naval power would offset Soviet land power; (3) the U.S. public would not allow military conscription; and (4) the U.S. monopoly on the atomic bomb, which was believed to be safe for years, would deter the Soviets from starting a general war.[41] The United States would use its economic power to shore up the nations surrounding the U.S.S.R. and avoid using U.S. military forces to implement containment. This policy was to be implemented only in those areas that were deemed important and where it was believed economic aid would make a difference. In areas where governments were too corrupt to garner public support or use aid effectively, as in China, the United States must let the chips fall where they might.

However, this policy was coming under increasing attack at home, especially in the case of China. When the administration went to Congress for appropriation of funds for the European Recovery Plan in late 1947, a group of pro-Chiang congressmen threatened to block funds for Europe if China did not also receive aid. The China Aid Act of 1948 was promulgated when Marshall learned that to avoid aiding Chiang would mean a delay in aiding Europe. With the Italian elections due in 1948, stalling could have meant disaster.[42] Although he believed that aiding Chiang would only "prolong the agony" in China, against his better judgment he advised giving Chiang $550 million.[43] Thus congressional pressures for a perimeter strategy added to the growing consensus that many nations and regions were strategically interdependent.

Yet Marshall continued to support the more selective strongpoint strategy. In testimony before the House Committee on International Relations in February 1948, he answered a challenge that the United States should adopt a perimeter strategy:

> There is a tendency to feel that wherever the Communist influence is brought to bear—I am talking about a fundamental policy—we should immediately meet it head on, as it were. I think this would be a most unwise procedure for the reason that we would be, in effect, handing over the initiative to the Communists. They could, therefore, spread our influence out so thin that it could be of no particular effectiveness at any one point.[44]

He then compared the dilemma to that facing the United States during the war. Limits on resources required a hierarchy of interests; in the postwar period, as during the war, Europe and the Middle East would come first.[45] But four days later, Stalin made a move in Europe that would lend credence to those advocating the perimeter strategy and, increasingly, the domino principle.

The Czech Coup and More Lessons from Europe

On February 24, 1948, the elected Czechoslovakian government was overthrown in a coup by the Czech Communist Party. This event seriously affected U.S. strategic thinking because it was accomplished not by military invasion but by internal subversion by the Czech Communist party, probably under direction from Moscow.[46] This confirmed the suggestion that any nation contiguous to the U.S.S.R. or its satellites was highly vulnerable to penetration by the Soviets through fifth column communist parties. To Truman and his advisors it was reminiscent of Hitler's actions in Eastern Europe during the 1930s.[47]

The coup and seemingly related developments in the communist world also seriously alarmed the U.S. government and public. Within a few weeks, General Lucius Clay sent a telegram from Germany to Chief of Staff Omar Bradley saying that a distinct change had come over the Russians since the coup and that war could come with "dramatic suddenness." Bradley later said this telegram "lifted me right out of my chair." In addition, throughout 1948 and 1949 congressional leaders and many opinion leaders increasingly called for the extension of the Truman Doctrine to Asia. Although this recommendation was resisted until 1949, the administration was worried. At a cabinet meeting on March 12, 1948, Marshall expressed concern at the "passion" the coup had aroused in the United States. One side benefit of this "passion," however, was the passage of the European Recovery Plan in the spring of 1948 by the Republican-controlled appropriation committees, which thereby allocated unprecedented resources to Western Europe. In another request for increased resources, Truman asked Congress in March 1948 to reinstitute military conscription.[48]

June brought two more important developments that deeply altered U.S. perceptions. The first was the Soviet pressure leading to the eventual blockade of Berlin. Boldly Truman ordered around-the-clock airlifts of supplies to relieve the people of Berlin from starvation. The Berlin Blockade, following so closely the shock of the Czech coup, increasingly led the Truman administration to believe that Stalin's goals—like Hitler's—were unlimited. This was not a hysterical U.S. reaction, as often portrayed by "revisionist" historians with the luxury of hindsight. Even the left wing of the British Labour Party, traditionally loath to criticize the U.S.S.R., was increasingly convinced of the danger of Soviet expansion.[49] In the aftermath of the Czech coup and Berlin, even such a peace advocate as Bertrand Russell wondered whether a preventive war against Stalin might not be desirable.[50]

The second event that altered perceptions was the break between Tito and Stalin and the U.S. decision to aid the man who had been previously judged "more Stalinist than Stalin." Marshall saw the events as connected. At a July cabinet meeting, he stated that the "present tension" in Berlin was caused by three Soviet "losses of face" in recent months: (1) U.S. success in backing anticommunists in Italy, France, and Finland; (2) the Tito defection; and (3) Soviet "desperation" in the face of the successful passage of the Marshall Plan.[51] Thus Stalin was believed in need of foreign policy successes to regain international and domestic legitimacy.

In light of the Czech coup, Soviet pressure on Finland and the Berlin Blockade increasing tensions in Western Europe, the administration decided to "draw a line" by adding a specific military component to its containment effort which eventually led to the creation of NATO. Because increased interregional planning would be crucial to a global strategy, U.S. decision makers also became more concerned with the potential consequences in the periphery. The State Department told the British that the West should draw the line in Europe, but to do so publicly might make peripheral areas, including Asia, more vulnerable because the Soviets might conclude that everything outside the line was not of interest to the United States. State therefore suggested that the U.S. commitment to the defense of Western Europe be kept secret so as not to encourage Soviet opportunism in peripheral areas. The Europeans, and some Americans, argued that if the commitment were kept secret it would not deter Soviet expansion at the core of the containment effort. They therefore pressed for an overt Western alliance in Europe to improve the morale of that region and prevent the fall of another Czechoslovakia, in spite of the possible danger in Asia. By mid-1948, plans for the creation of NATO were going forward. In addition, Greece, Turkey, and Iran—the nations along the "line" drawn to block Soviet expansion in the Middle East—were given assurances of continued U.S. support.[52]

Despite the growing commitments in Europe, the resources were still not sufficient to extend the line of containment to Asia. That summer, Under Secretary of State Robert Lovett stated that the United States simply did not have the resources to finance European recovery, take care of its own defense needs, and aid all the nations that asked for help.[53] Thus the strongpoint strategy stood for the present, but the perception of a growing strategic threat and a growing potential for Soviet expansion was eroding its underlying premises.

The contradictions between the perimeter rhetoric and strongpoint strategy of Truman's first term were about to become a bitterly partisan political issue. Despite its problems, the administration was returned to office in Truman's surprise victory of November 1948. This made the Republicans even more critical of his containment policy and created even greater congressional pressures for a universal perimeter strategy of containment, while continuing to deny the resources to implement it.[54]

The Ascendance of the Perimeter Strategy

The Growing Specter of Dominoes in Asia

In the fall of 1948, the administration began to notice the militancy of Cominform policy in Southeast Asia and its correlation with communist uprisings in the region. As early as the Southeast Asian Youth Conference in Calcutta in February 1948, in the aftermath of the creation of the Cominform, various delegates gave special praise to the military successes of communist parties in China and Indochina. In ensuing months, many communist movements in Southeast Asia had taken to the jungle and begun armed insurgencies against existing governments, colonial or nationalist, as in Indochina, Malaya, Burma, and the Philippines. In India, a provincial revolt was instigated in large part by the Indian Communist Party shortly after the conference. Thus this meeting was later given special significance by U.S. decision makers and appeared at the time to be a sign of a coordination of communist global strategy.

In November 1948, Liu Shao-ch'i, Deputy Chairman of the Politburo of the C.C.P., wrote an article closely aligning the Chinese communists with the Soviet Union. By the fall of 1948, the C.C.P. was decisively defeating the K.M.T. on the battlefield, sooner than most in the United States, and perhaps even the C.C.P. itself, expected. The U.S.S.R. had already been taking a much more militant line in the Far East and elswhere. It appeared to increasing numbers in the administration that the Soviets were strategically probing Asia to offset setbacks in Europe and the Middle East, and were using the tactic that had proved successful in Czechoslovakia and Eastern Europe—internal subversion through Stalinist "fifth columns."[55] If Czechoslovakia, with relatively developed political institutions and a strong sense of nationalism, could be overthrown through internal subversion and Soviet pressure, what could be expected of the colonies, semi-colonies, and newly formed nations of Asia?[56]

Marshall, ailing and about to leave office, agonized over China policy, but in the end believed there was nothing the United States could do to "save" Chiang Kai-shek.[57] A number of unstable nations and colonial governments ringing the Chinese border appeared as vulnerable targets of opportunity for communist expansion. The task, as growing numbers in Washington saw it, was to limit the damage and prevent the fall of another.

Acheson's Asian Policy—"Titoism" Versus "Stalinism"

On January 21, 1949, the same day that Chiang Kai-shek "retired" to the island of Taiwan, Dean Acheson was sworn in as Secretary of State. The aroused Republican Right had no love for the dapper, caustic Acheson, and he did not command the respect or veneration that Marshall enjoyed. Yet Truman had enormous respect for him.[58] Although Acheson agreed with Marshall on China, their differences reflected the hardening U.S. view and were crucial to the application of the domino principle to Asia and the adoption of the perimeter strategy of containment that gradually became apparent under Acheson.

The first change was the increasing emphasis placed on the ideological component of containment throughout 1949. In the wake of the developments in Europe, the Middle East, and Cominform policy, Soviet expansion and worldwide communist subversion became synonymous to many in Congress and in the administration. Thus ideology became important as a predictor of communist behavior throughout the world for many Americans.[59]

Secondly, an increasingly global perspective precipitated by the collapse of the K.M.T. led to greater focus on the denial of communist influence in what had previously been considered a relatively unimportant region. Since Southeast Asia now appeared vulnerable to communist subversion, the entire region of Asia, including Japan and India, also seemed to be threatened through the potential denial of natural resources for postwar reconstruction. Strategic planning for Europe, the Middle East, and Asia became even more directly interrelated throughout 1949.[60]

Lastly, the increased interregional strategic planning led to greater difficulty in differentiating local conditions in the various Asian nations. This was in part because the Asian experts of the State Department were under political attack from the restless Republicans for having "lost" China. As many were removed from positions of influence, they were replaced by European-oriented diplomats who tended to think that every action of Asian communists was directed from Moscow. The linking of communist actions in Europe with communists in the periphery was a key element in the adoption of the domino principle as a universal calculus for U.S. policy, and therefore the perimeter strategy of containment.[61] Thus not only particular nations, but entire regions were perceived as threatened by communist subversion.

These shifts in perception and policy, however, were gradual. Acheson, like Kennan, was sincerely interested in the spread of "Titoism" in communist nations in early 1949, especially in China. He was not, however, particularly interested in Titoism in Southeast Asia where it appeared that Stalinism was spreading aggression and putting the West, if not democracy, on the defensive. In May 1949, for example, he approved a cable explaining his opposition to the argument that Ho Chi Minh was as much a nationalist as communist:

> [The] Question [of] whether Ho [is] as much nationalist or Commie is irrelevant. All Stalinists in colonial areas are nationalists. With [the] achievement [of] national aims (i.e., independence) their objective necessarily becomes subordination [of the] state to Commie purposes and [the] ruthless extermination [of] not only opposition groups but all elements suspected [of] even [the] slightest deviation.[62]

Although in the early months of 1949 there was some hope that China could be separated from Soviet influence, this idea gradually waned when the C.C.P. sided with the U.S.S.R. in the dispute with Tito, which had been made a litmus test for loyalty by Stalin. It was largely extinguished following Mao Tse-tung's "leaning to one side" speech in July, the public alignment of the C.C.P. with the Soviets, and the arrest of U.S. diplomats by the communist Chinese regime.[63] By summer, "Stalinism" appeared dominant in the communist parties of Asia.

The Principle Arrives in Asia

In February, State's Policy Planning Staff declared Southeast Asia "the target of a coordinated offensive plainly directed by the Kremlin." Loss of the area would critically affect the security of Japan, India, and Australia and eventually the United States. For the first time, this region was defined as "a vital segment on the line of containment." In June, Secretary of Defense Louis Johnson asked the National Security Counsil (NSC) to conduct a study on the effects of the fall of China on U.S. security in Asia. This document spelled out the domino principle in direct form. It argued that the fall of China would be felt throughout Asia and that it threatened the security of all nations in Southeast Asia. If one fell, it argued, all would eventually fall. The report was well received in the Defense Department, in which many members had been making a similar argument for months. It also received favorable attention at State. Within a month, Acheson wrote Ambassador-at-Large Philip Jessup that the United States could not allow another nation in Asia to fall to the communists.[64]

Thus the origins of application of the domino principle in Asia can be found in the difficult summer of 1949. Though Acheson and Truman continued to be relatively flexible toward the new regime in Beijing, they began to reinforce the beleaguered nations of Southeast Asia. The worry in Southeast Asia, and elsewhere, was the "bandwagon effect," that the failure of "democracy" in China would lead other nations to see communism as the wave of the future. Thus the *perception* of the global balance of power became as important as its reality[65] and was seen increasingly in ideological terms. In the language of the day, the "contagion" of the communist "amoeba" seemed to be spreading to peripheral areas after having been contained in central areas of concern. This was believed to be demoralizing all of the nations along the perimeter.

The perception of the strategic threat was changing not only within the government, but throughout U.S. society. Though the administration had not yet decided its policy in Asia, it was receiving increasing political heat at home. The publication of the "White Paper" on China in August 1949 brought down a storm of criticism on Truman and Acheson. Although much of the public remained apathetic toward the "fall" of China (a poll in September 1949 showed that 44 percent had no opinion or had never heard of Chiang Kai-shek), the rising clamor of hard-line Republicans in Congress was giving the administration real problems. Truman could largely ignore the extra-governmental "China lobby," but he could not, as he and Marshall had discovered in late 1947, afford to ignore the "China Bloc" in Congress. These groups' criticism of the administration's containment policy was increasingly accepted among conservatives, moderates, and some liberals.[66]

The Core and Periphery Are Joined: The Fall of China and the Soviet Nuclear Detonation

In the midst of growing international tension and criticism at home, the administration received yet more bad news. On September 22, 1949, Truman announced that the Soviets had exploded a nuclear device sometime in August. The strongpoint strategy had depended on the monopoly lasting for years. The attainment of a nuclear capability by the U.S.S.R. this soon was a shocking experience for Americans. Shortly thereafter, on October 1, Mao Tse-tung officially created the People's Republic of China (P.R.C.).

These two events, occurring so close together, led to the adoption of the perimeter strategy within the administration. Army General Omar Bradley later said that the twin disasters of the establishment of the P.R.C. and Soviet detonation had "set in train a government-wide reappraisal of our foreign and military policy," which later led to the promulgation of NSC 68, the premier document setting forth the perimeter strategy, in the spring of 1950.[67]

Prior to these events, the measure of the available resources had largely shaped the response to the perception of threat. In their aftermath, the perception of the threat increasingly shaped the measure of resources available.[68] On September 28, for example, Congress passed the Mutual Defense Assistance Act, which gave Truman some of the resources he had been attempting to get since 1947. Within two months, Acheson and Johnson had invited the French to seek military aid for Indochina.[69]

The domino principle was now firmly lodged in the minds of the administration's decision makers as a strategic calculus along the entire perimeter of the containment line, although the exact parameters of that line had yet to be drawn. Acheson accepted the European and Middle Eastern experiences as evidence of communist plans of take over Asian nations, as had been posited by the NSC that summer. When Prime Minister Nehru of India warned the secretary in October against the misapplication of the lessons of Europe in Asia, Acheson thought his arguments "specious." He argued that experiences with communists everywhere showed that "the attempt to take over would be inevitable."[70]

The Rise of Radicalism in Southeast Asia Raises the Fear of "Bandwagoning"

The adoption of the domino principle in Asia was not entirely due to domestic pressure or tensions in Europe, nor was it created in a vacuum. There *was* a communist threat of regional proportions in Asia in the wake of the fall of China. Intermittent communist insurgencies, of varying intensity, were already underway by 1949 in Malaya, Burma, Indochina, and the Philippines. At a communist conference in Beijing in November 1949, Cominform members, and those from the P.R.C., called for a militant line against Western colonialism and also against noncommunist nationalists like Nehru and Sukarno.[71] It is difficult to prove causal connections between the militant Cominform line and the uprisings, but they appeared to U.S. leaders to be directly linked[72] in the aftermath of the organization's call for greater consolidation of worldwide communist policy.

Secretary Acheson drew the perimeter line of containment along the island chain stretching from the Aleutians to the Japanese islands to the Philippines, and off the Asian mainland, in his January 12, 1950, National Press Club speech, including his famous exclusion of South Korea from direct strategic concerns. The traditional interpretation is that this demonstrated a lack of alarm over those nations that faced communist subversion on the Asian mainland. But this view is questionable.[73] In fact the administration was deeply concerned over the spread of communism in mainland Southeast Asia. The growing U.S. alarm over the entire region, and elsewhere, meant that the United States took actions in Korea and Southeast Asia as much for their effects outside as inside those particular nations. The domino principle provided the connection.

First, the Press Club speech clearly delineated U.S. *military* commitments, but not political or economic ones. In the immediate aftermath of the speech, for example, the House cut off economic aid to the Republic of Korea. The administration's successful struggle to restore it demonstrated its concern with the future of Korea. While military commitments were given only to the offshore island chain, the administration believed that the greatest threat came not from direct invasion but from internal subversion in nations contiguous to the Soviet sphere of influence. Therefore, because the *political* ramifications of backing "reactionary" regimes in the region would undermine Western influence throughout Southeast Asia, it refused to give military assurances to Taiwan.

Second, if the West were driven out of Southeast Asia, it was believed, demoralization would probably increase in Western Europe also. The military role of the West in Southeast Asia was still largely under the direction of the French and British, to whom the United States began granting military aid in the aftermath of the "fall" of China. This would continue throughout the first half of 1950 and increase precipitously following the outbreak of the Korean War. Aid to the newly formed governments in the region was also increased.

Last, though China had not been in and of itself considered strategically important, Japan certainly was. Even strongpoint strategists such as Kennan saw the latter nation as the key to stability, or the lack of it, in the region. Faced with a hostile, expansionist China, the futures of Southeast Asia and Japan became inextricably linked to U.S. planners. If Southeast Asia fell to the communists, it was believed, Japan and India would eventually "bandwagon" toward Moscow and Beijing in the long run to ensure access to natural resources. The demonstration of alarm in NSC 68 can be explained by recalling the *potential* disaster along the entire perimeter that faced the administration in early 1950.[74]

Developments in Asia appeared to justify such alarm. In January 1950 *Pravda* published Liu Shao-ch'i's November 1949 speech calling for the creation of "armies of liberation" in Southeast Asia. Mao was in Moscow in the early 1950s negotiating a friendship treaty with the U.S.S.R. In January, Ho Chi Minh, who had previously presented himself as a leader of a nationalist coalition, openly embraced a communist solution for Indochina and made public common cause with the P.R.C. Acheson observed that this proved his point of the previous May about Ho's subservient Stalinism. The collapse of the K.M.T. also "severely discredited" pro-Chiang and other nationalist political parties in Indochina and throughout Southeast Asia.[75] This movement away from noncommunist nationalists was seen as potentially shifting support toward indigenous communist parties, creating more Stalinist "fifth columns."

The pressure for a stronger U.S. stand in the region also came from allies, which increased fears of bandwagoning. Carlos Romulo, the Filipino diplomat, told the United States that the peoples of Southeast Asia were very worried over the seemingly tepid U.S. response to the fall of China, but he added a cautionary note against aiding the French in Indochina.[76] Allies in other regions were pressuring the United States to assert its leadership on a global scale. In December 1949, for example, Truman was informed that Latin American nations were "incensed . . . to the point of bitterness and disappointment" over what they perceived as a passive policy in the face of Soviet aggression in China.[77]

Thus the actions and staements of the P.R.C. and U.S.S.R., and widespread perceptions of growing Soviet global power relative to the United States, lent credence to those who were articulating the domino principle. Just as the communist parties in Greece, Czechoslovakia, France, and Italy seemed to take direction from Moscow, so did the communist parties of Southeast Asia seem to take direction from Beijing, which in turn appeared to be taking direction from Moscow. Though the idea of "monolithic communism" was much ridiculed in the retrospective view following the Sino-Soviet split of the 1960s, there appeared to be much truth to the charge in the late 1940s.

The U.S. Response—More Resources for Asia

The growth of radicalism in Southeast Asia in the wake of the establishment of the P.R.C. was viewed with alarm by the United States and added that region to the containment line. At a joint State-Defense meeting in late December 1949, the two departments reached consensus on U.S. policy toward Asia: (1) develop stable, self-sustaining states; (2) contain Soviet influence; and (3) maintain the current balance of power in the region. In February, the NSC reiterated its finding of the previous year that the communists were attempting to seize all of Southeast Asia. In March 1950, the CIA reached similar conclusions. Expecting to send economic aid, Truman approved the Griffin Mission to Southeast Asia to study what immediate economic actions would shore up the governments of the region.[78]

The administration also began requesting military aid for Southeast Asia. In early February 1950, Acheson and Johnson asked military planners to draw up a plan for extending military aid as soon as possible. From January to June, the United States granted $5 million to Indonesia to improve its constabulary, $3 million to Thailand, $3.5 million to Burma, $21 million to the French in Indochina, $6.5 million for the improvement of airfields in Japan, and $9.5 million for "psychological warfare" and unspecified "covert" actions in Southeast Asia. The administration's June 1 request for an additional $75 million for military aid for the region was pending when the Korean War broke out.[79] Though these amounts are small when compared with the Marshall Plan or NATO, and it should be understood that much less was expected, they do indicate an increase in the perception of threat in the region.

The administration was also moved to respond by domestic pressures. The contradictions between the strongpoint strategy and the perimeter rhetoric of the Truman Doctrine became increasingly apparent to Congress and the public with the fall of China. In early 1950, domestic criticism of Truman's containment policy increased precipitously. Spy scandals, the Alger Hiss trial, and a rising clamor of right-wing criticism moved the administration toward a harder line in the spring of 1950. The rhetoric of the Truman Doctrine had come back to haunt the administration. On January 8, James Reston of the *New York Times* pointed to the inconsistency of "blocking communism in Europe and letting it run wild in Asia."[80]

The Domino Principle Becomes Dogma—NSC 68 and Korea

In light of the increased threat in Southeast Asia, and criticism at home and abroad, the administration began contingency planning for a greatly enlarged effort to implement a perimeter strategy of containment. In January 1950 Acheson handed the problem to the Policy Planning Staff of the State Department. In an important personnel shift in the same month, Acheson replaced George Kennan, a leading advocate of the strongpoint strategy, with Paul Nitze. Nitze was a strong adovcate of the strategic interdependence of all areas of the world and his predilection was demonstrated in the document that resulted from Acheson's request: NSC 68.

The study was delivered to the president in April 1950. It completely rejected the strongpoint strategy in favor of the perimeter strategy and posited the strategic equivalence of all nations ringing the Soviet sphere of influence. Unless the United States took a firmer stand in what NSC 68 described as a direct, bipolar competition with the U.S.S.R., it would face a series of "gradual withdrawals under pressure until [it] discover[ed] one day that [it had] sacrificed positions of vital interest." "In the context of the present polarization of power a defeat of free institutions anywhere is a defeat everywhere."[81] Thus each and every nation along the entire perimeter was portrayed in the document as interdependent with U.S. security.

Although he retained reservations about the universalistic rhetoric of NSC 68, Acheson believed that the president at that point needed "communicable wisdom" that would "bludgeon the mass mind" of "top government" and warn American society of the potential danger that would overcome the United States within the next few years.[82] Though NSC 68 remained highly classified, Acheson initiated a series of speeches to gain support for the increases. The North Korean attack of June 25, 1950, solved the problem of convincing the public and Congress, though it was to cause him many more.[83]

The outbreak of the Korean War had a galvanizing effect on the U.S. foreign policy consensus and heightened the perception throughout society that much more had to be done to deny nations to the Soviet bloc. Unlike the uncertainty of the communist "penetration" arguments of the past, in which the evidence was ambiguous and the local noncommunist political groups often left much to be desired, the Korean invasion demonstrated outright communist aggression in an area of United Nations responsibility. It could also be met with an action easily understood by the Congress, the public and allies, that is, military action. Those who had been arguing for a universalistic perimeter strategy now appeared to have been prophetic in their warnings.

At a NSC meeting on June 29, Truman ordered the council to conduct "a resurvey of all policy papers affecting the entire perimeter of the U.S.S.R." Secretary of Defense Johnson replied that his deparmtent was already doing so in reaction to the president's earlier orders. At the same meeting, Acheson and Harriman also made clear connections they perceived between deterrence in the core and deterrence in the periphery. Before U.S. troops were sent to Korea, they argued, the Western Europeans had been increasingly demoralized by Soviet gains.[84] With greater U.S. commitment in the periphery, the Western Europeans, and the Soviets, would find commitments at the core more credible. George Kennan also emphasized the perceptual link between commitments at the core and in the periphery.[85]

The reaction to the Korean invasion set in motion a number of actions that led to the acceptance of the domino principle as dogma. In July, State's John Melby was sent to Southeast Asia to assess the military needs of the region. In his final report in December, he argued that if one nation in the region fell to the communists, all would eventually do so.[86] NSC 68 was adopted as policy in September. As the Korean War dragged on, the domino principle was increasingly accepted in the halls of government and in the minds of the public. The reservations over aiding the French in Indochina that had been expressed earlier within the State Department and by regional allies were forgotten. By June 1952, NSC 124/2 set forth the Principle in, according to the analysts in the Pentagon Papers, its "purest form":

> In the absence of effective and timely counteraction, the loss of any single country [in Southeast Asia] would probably lead to relatively swift submission to or an alignment with communism by the remaining countries of this group. Furthermore, an alignment with communism of the rest of Southeast Asia and India, and in the longer term, of the Middle East (with the probable exceptions of at least Pakistan and Turkey) would in all probability progressively follow. Such widespread alignment would endanger the stability and security of Europe.[87]

In addition, the loss of Southeast Asia would "make it extremely difficult to prevent Japan's eventual accommodation to communism."[88] Thus if any nation in Southeast Asia fell to communism, all might fall; if Southeast Asia fell, Japan and India might also; if Japan and India fell, most of the Middle East might be next; if the Middle East fell, Europe might surely follow; if Europe fell to communism, the United States would be surrounded.[89]

Thus direct strategic and psychological connections were drawn between every nation ringing the perimeter of the U.S.S.R and the security of the United States itself, in the gradual consensus the Truman administration created around the acceptance of global responsibilities. Eisenhower's remarks in April 1954 would be but a metaphorical description of what had been U.S. policy for at least four years.

Conclusions

The Evolution of the Principle

The United States emerged from World War II without a clear conception of the role it would play in the postwar world, but it gradually adopted a hard-line approach in the face of Soviet expansionist probes and an incresingly unilateral strategic position in Asia with the demise of the British Empire and the growing chaos in China.

In the process of dealing with a string of successive crises, U.S. decision makers developed and adopted a series of "worst case" predictions, all predicated on a central assumption, that were in essence the domino principle. The central assumption was that the U.S.S.R. was an opportunistic, expansionist nation with political control of numerous fifth column communist parties on a worldwide scale. Therefore, a nation vulnerable to subversion and contiguous to the Soviet sphere of influence, of which there were many in the aftermath of World War II, was inherently subject to communist penetration and was in danger of falling. This perception was reinforced in decision makers' minds by Soviet behavior, and that of its fifth columns, in Eastern Europe (especially Czechoslovakia), Western Europe (especially France and Italy), the Middle East (especially Greece and Iran), and Asia (after mid-1949, China and Southeast Asia). The apparent sequence of communist probes along the geostrategically expanding line of containment led to a perception of a symmetrical threat for which the strongpoint strategy was no longer considered adequate. The abrupt shift in the Truman administration's view of the amount of resources necessary for containment in the fall of 1949, which culminated in the planning goals of NSC 68, indicates that many accepted the perimeter strategy at that time.

The use of this logic as a domestic policy justification greatly increased the importance of the periphery, by tying it directly to the core in psychological and strategic terms. Once the perimeter strategy of containment was adopted, America's commitments became interdependent. If successfully challenged in one area, they would be increasingly, and possibly successfully, challenged in others. The loss of one might lead to the loss of all.

The Policy Functions of the Domino Principle

Within this context, the domino principle as a strategic concept became intimately linked with global containment policy, because it served several crucial functions for decision makers. First, it allowed the leading members of the Truman administration to perceive patterns in communist behavior through the use of analogic thinking. The lessons of the 1930s and the Munich analogy weighed heavily on the minds of U.S. decision makers;[90] ample instances of communist behavior in the postwar world suggested parallels. Attitudinal change is most likely to occur when discrepant information arrives in swift and clear fashion.[91] The strongpoint strategy appeared to be risky, but acceptable, as long as the U.S.S.R. did not have nuclear weapons and China was in chaos. The sudden shift in these variables in the fall of 1949, however, promoted acceptance of the perimeter strategy for which the adoption of the domino principle in Europe and the Middle East were psychological antecedents. The earlier experiences with the communists were then viewed within the context of a global pattern of aggression through the use of internal subversion. The attack on South Korea seemed to confirm those beliefs further and added the fear that a direct invasion might further Soviet aims in Asia. It also convinced the public and Congress that much greater resources had to be allocated in the face of a greater strategic threat.[92]

Second, the domino principle offers a crude but serviceable strategic calculus for policymakers in situations characterized by a high degree of uncertainty. It is extremely difficult to determine a priori the strategic worth, to the United States and other allies, or the relative vulnerability to communist subversion, of individual nations, especially in developing areas. In 1961, for example, President Kennedy at times privately believed, though never publicly stated, that the United States was overextended in Asia and was deeply involved in societies to which it should never have been committed. The problem for him, as it is for other presidents, was exactly how to separate those nations that were important from those that were not. In an August 1961 off-the-record press briefing he admitted his puzzlement: "I don't know where the non-essential areas are."[93] The domino principle solves that psychological and political problem by making all regions and, by extension, each nation within a region, strategically important.

If an allied nation is evaluated discretely, it might appear to be unimportant to the security of the United States.[94] The decision maker must decide not only in terms of the allied nation's importance to the United States, but also its importance to the security of its region, which may make it crucial to the security of the United States. In the Truman administration, the strategic value of Southeast Asia was greatest not to the United States, but to Japan. Even strongpoint strategists argued that Japan was crucial to American national interests. Thus intraregional and interregional analyses are necessary to determine strategic worth to the United States. The domino principle provides decision makers with the means for making those connections.

A common criticism of the domino principle is that it is impossible to predict with any authority whether a potentially vulnerable nation is likely to fall.[95] The problem for the decision maker is that it is impossible to predict with any authority that it *won't* collapse or bandwagon. Given the high degree of uncertainty, and the stakes involved, it might appear better to the decision maker to follow what appears to be a prudent course and assume it will.

Accepting short-term costs to prevent greater long-term costs can be a reasonable choice. This "rational hedging"[96] allows the decision maker to deal with the uncertainty and make a decision. Machiavelli recognizes this in his praise of the Roman diplomatic practice of intervening sooner rather than later:

> For the Romans did in these cases what all wise princes should do: they not only have to have regard for present troubles but also for future ones, and they have to avoid these with all their industry because, when one foresees from afar, one can easily find a remedy for them but when you wait until they come close to you, the medicine is not in time because the disease has become incurable. And it happens with this as the physicians say of consumption, that in the beginning of the illness it is easy to cure and difficult to recognize, but in the progress of time, when it has not been recognized and treated in the beginning, it becomes easy to recognize and difficult to cure. So it happens in affairs of state, because when one recognizes from afar the evils that arise in a state (which is not given but to one who is prudent), they are soon healed; but when they are left to grow because they were not recognized, to the point that everyone recognizes them, there is no longer any remedy for them.[97]

While it may not be very satisfying intellectually, to a decision maker it might be better to have a crude strategic calculus than to have none at all.

Third, the domino principle gives a decision maker arguments for domestic support for the resource allocation necessary for a global containment policy. Acheson used it for this purpose with Congress in the spring of 1947; Eisenhower used it with the public in April 1954. A largely uninformed and lethargic public was a real problem during the late 1940s and Republicans won both houses of Congress due to the popularity of tax reduction. The irony rubbed on President Truman. At an early NSC meeting on Korea, Secretary of the Air Force Stuart Symington complained that the lack of military preparation had undermined the ability to meet the crisis. Apparently irked, Truman "questioned whether Mr. Symington may have forgotten that this is a democracy." He and General Marshall, said the president, had been attempting to garner the resources for a greater effort since 1945, but had always been faced with "a hostile Congress."[98] It is difficult to explain the complexities of international politics and to ask for resources in "giveaway" programs for nations that seemingly have no direct connection with the security of the United States. The domino principle provides an easily understandable informational instrument for making those connections and preventing the public, and Congress, from ignoring peripherally important security problems that potentially might lead to centrally important security problems.

As Truman and Acheson discovered, however, there is a real danger in raising expectations to such levels. The problem is that the domino principle is *too easily* understood, and simplistically applied, by the general public and partisan political opponents. Though he later complained of the lack of "delicacy" in the public mind in understanding the Truman Doctrine, in a very real sense Acheson had only himself to blame.

Last, it should be noted that many nations contiguous to the U.S.S.R. or its satelittes *were* under pressure from internal communist subversion during the time of the domino principle's adoption. The existence of a "sanctuary" from which insurgents can be trained, protected, and supplied is a crucial element in fighting a guerrilla war or subverting a government. Though indigenous factors remain the most important variables, a contiguous border with a friendly power is, to say the least, a major plus for communists acting against existing governments. The Czech coup would not have been as likely had Czechoslovakia not had a common border with other communist nations. The Chinese communists might not have triumphed without a common border with the U.S.S.R. The Communists in Indochina might not have triumphed in the early 1950s without a common border with China. In contrast, when the borders of Yugoslavia were closed to the Greek communist insurgents in 1949, following the split of the former from the Soviets, the insurgency was rather easily defeated. In Malaya and the Philippines in the 1950s, where no common border with a communist nation existed, the guerrillas were also defeated. Thus assuming the vulnerability of nations in unstable regions to internal and external communist subversion is not a foolish concern.

The Effects of the Principle

It is arguable that the application of the domino principle, which originated in Europe, in a curious way generated a policy that worked in Southeast Asia. From the perspective of the 1980s, the programs adopted in 1949 to 1950 essentially succeeded in preventing the fall of the *region* to communism. The insurgencies that began in Thailand, Burma, Malaya, and the Philippines in 1948 to 1949 were all defeated. The communists won only in Indochina, where the anticolonialist struggle witnessed the ideological marriage of communism and nationalism in the most powerful nation of that regional grouping, Vietnam. It was in Indochina that the lack of historical perspective and mechanistic application of the domino principle failed spectacularly. Where decolonization went relatively smoothly, as in Burma, Malaya, Indonesia, Singapore, and the Philippines, and Western support was granted to the fledgling noncommunist governments of the region, however, relatively moderate nationalist groups prevailed. Those governments and groups *were* vulnerable and ready to fall in the late 1940s and early 1950s. Though indigenous political forces remained the most important factor, Western support was also crucial in preventing the advent of communism in Southeast Asia during decolonization. The use of the domino principle as a strategic calculus and policy justification may exaggerate the actual threat to a worst case potential threat, but it is arguable that it is necessary in a democracy to provide the resources and political will to meet a real, though lesser, crisis situation. Oversell may in fact be a rational policy choice. Clearly decision makers in the United States have seen and used it in this way.

Ironically, the very time Eisenhower was publicly articulating the domino principle was when it might have been questioned, at least in Southeast Asia. But 1954, much of the revolutionary ardor of the P.R.C. had cooled and it switched in 1955 to the "Bandung spirit" of relative peace with noncommunist nationalists in Asia, at least outside Indochina, due to the failure of a militant policy and the costs of its role in Korea. In fact, the P.R.C.'s militant policy had been shifting since 1952.[99] The insurgencies in Southeast Asia were by and large dissipated, again excepting Indochina, with the additional exception of Malaya which was decided in favor of noncommunists in 1960. By the mid-1950s, many Asian nations saw their traditional rivalries with other Asian societies as a greater threat than China.[100]

However, by that time the domino principle had gained a momentum of its own, because it provided a strategic calculus for decision makers in situations with a high degree of uncertainty, a means to garner the resources necessary for containment, the basis for a foreign policy consensus, and was seemingly based in an earlier reality. The domestic furor over the loss of China and the fear of failure in containment policy created a dynamic in U.S. political life whereby policy makers are held to the standards of the domino principle whether they believe in it or not. The irony is that it was partly formulated to increase the perception of the strategic threat in congressional and public circles, but came to dominate so much of American strategic thinking. The domino principle was "sold" too well and trapped decision makers into a containment strategy with little flexibility. That is not to say that decision makers did not agree with the domino principle; they did. By the time of Eisenhower's public declaration in 1954, however, the exigencies of the domestic cold war consensus made this more or less irrelevant.

The domino principle was discredited for many in the mid-1970s by the American involvement in Vietnam. Within a few years, however, the Soviet invasion of Afghanistan, the fall of the shah of Iran (even though not to communists), and the Sandinista revolution in Nicaragua raised fears of a strategic threat and engendered the belief among many that the United States was not being tough enough in its world posture. In the 1980s, Ronald Reagan was elected and vowed to overcome this weakness and prevent the fall of more allied nations to communism, using the domino principle as a justification.[101] This may or may not be wise, but it is likely to continue until an alternative strategic calculus, acceptable to decision makers, Congress, allies, and the public, is developed to determine our interests in the periphery. It would seem, then, that the domino principle—or some variation—will be with us for some time.

Notes

I would like to thank Richard Betts, Dorothy Borg, the late William T. R. Fox, John Garofano, Samuel P. Huntington, Robert Jervis, Theresa Johnson, Robert Kaufman, Timothy Lomperis, James W. Morley, Robert Ross, Peter Trubowitz, James Wirtz, and Howard Wriggins for their constructive discussions and comments. Any mistakes are mine. The article was written while the author was a John M. Olin Postdoctoral Fellow in National Security Studies at the Center for International Affairs, Harvard University.

1. Dwight D. Eisenhower, *Public Papers of the Presidents of the United States, 1954* (Washington, D.C.: U.S. Government Printing Office [hereafter referred to as U.S. GPO], 1960), 383.

2. The "domino principle" is also often referred to as the "domino theory," for example, in other chapters in this volume. I use the term domino principle because its advocates eventually raised it to the level of a general policy principle. It therefore has connotations of certitude not captured in the term domino theory. It also follows Eisenhower's own usage in the passage quoted above. Either usage, however, is acceptable.

3. The "strongpoint" and "perimeter" strategies are analyzed in John Lewis Gaddis, *Strategies of Containment: A Critical Analysis of Postwar American National Security Policy* (New York: Oxford University Press, 1982), 54–88.

4. Ibid., 3–126; Samuel P. Huntington, *The Common Defense: Strategic Programs in National Politics* (New York: Columbia University Press, 1961), 1–64.

5. For the distinction between the "competitive" and "cooperative" conceptions of the postwar balance of power, see Alexander L. George, "Domestic Constraints on Regime Change in U.S. Foreign Policy," in *Change in the International System,* ed. Ole R. Holsti, Randolph M. Siverson, and Alexander L. George (Boulder, Colo.: Westview Press, 1980), 238–51. See also Jervis's treatment of the concepts of "deterrence" (hard-line) and "spiral" (soft-line) models of decision making in theoretical terms in Robert Jervis, *Perception and Misperception in International Politics* (Princeton, N.J.: Princeton University Press, 1976), chap. 3. For an excellent analysis of the splits between competitive and cooperative balance of power approaches in the Truman administration, see Deborah Welch Larson, *Origins of Containment: A Psychological Explanation* (Princeton, N.J.: Princeton University Press, 1985), 66–125.

6. Daniel Yergin, *Shattered Peace: The Origins of the Cold War and the National Security State* (Boston: Houghton Mifflin, 1978), 45, 48, 58, 68; for the "Four Policemen" concept see also, Gaddis, *Strategies of Containment,* 10. The "Four Policemen" were to be Great Britain, the U.S.S.R., China, and the United States. For a similar confusion between realism and idealism in Roosevelt's colonial policy, see John J. Sbrega, "The Anticolonial Policy of Franklin D. Roosevelt: A Reappraisal," *Political Science Quarterly* 101:1 (1986): 65–84; and William Roger Louis, "The Special Relationship and British Decolonization: American Anti-colonialism and the Dissolution of the British Empire," *International Affairs* (London) 61:3 (Summer 1985): 397–98.

7. Yergin, *Shattered Peace,* 58; Charles Dobbs, *The Unwanted Symbol: American Foreign Policy, the Cold War, and Korea, 1945–1950* (Kent, Ohio: Kent State University Press, 1981), 18–19.

8. Yergin, *Shattered Peace,* 45.

9. For splits between the soft-line and hard-line approaches in the early postwar days, see Larson, *Origins of Containment,* 213–18. These divisions of opinion were also present within the government bureaucracy. Poole demonstrates it was the State Department, not the military leadership, that most forcefully advocated a hard line in the early period; Walter S. Poole, "From Conciliation to Containment: The Joint Chiefs of Staff

and the Coming of the Cold War, 1945–1946," *Military Affairs* 42:1 (February 1978): 14–15. However, the soft-line approach dominated in the Far Eastern Division of the State Department. In a guideline for field personnel in Asia produced late in 1945, the four main elements of U.S. policy were: (1) a demilitarized Japan; (2) "close and friendly relations with Russia"; (3) U.S. retention of all islands captured from Japan; and, (4) a grouping of "national elements" in Southeast Asia under the United Nations. Harry S. Truman Library, President's Secretary's Files, China, 1945: Box 173 (hereafter, HSTL, PSF, File Title, Box no.)

10. I am indebted to the late William T. R. Fox for this point.

11. Yergin, *Shattered Peace,* 17–41, 71–73; Gaddis, *Strategies of Containment,* 15.

12. Bullitt quoted in Yergin, *Shattered Peace,* 42. For the hard line view, see Larson, *Origins of Containment,* 76–125.

13. Quoted in Yergin, *Shattered Peace,* 85. Harriman issued a similar warning about Soviet penetration of China if U.S. attempts to unify it were to fail, see Russell Buhite, *Soviet-American Relations in Asia, 1945–1954* (Norman: University of Oklahoma Press, 1981), 32.

14. Walter Millis, ed., *The Forrestal Diaries* (New York: Viking, 1951), 100, 110, 316–17; Huntington, *The Common Defense,* 33–47; see the early discussion of Universal Military Training at the cabinet meetings of August 31, 1945, September 7, 1945, and September 26, 1945, in HSTL, Michael J. Connelly Files (hereafter referred to as MJC), White House Files, Set II: Box 2. For a contrary view of the conventional Soviet military threat in Europe, see Matthew A. Evangelista, "Stalin's Postwar Army Reappraised," *International Security* 7:3 (Winter 1982/83): 110–38.

15. Gaddis, *Strategies of Containment,* 15–17, 23.

16. Quoted in Millis, *The Forrestal Diaries,* 373.

17. Tang Tsou, *America's Failure in China* (Chicago: University of Chicago Press, 1963), 365–66.

18. "Intelligence Estimate of the World as of December 1, 1945," National Archives, Decimal Files, Record Group 59, Marshall Mission Records, 1944–1948: Box 2 (hereafter, NA, DF, RG 59, File Title: Box no.).

19. George F. Kennan, *Memoirs: 1925–1950* (Boston: Little, Brown and Co., 1967), 271–97; Yergin, *Shattered Peace,* 171; Ernest May, *"Lessons" of the Past: The Use and Misuse of History in American Foreign Policy* (New York: Oxford University Press, 1973), 47. Nikita Khrushchev later related that it was Churchill's speech in Fulton, Missouri, that led the Soviets to believe that the cold war had begun; Nikita Khrushchev, *Khrushchev Remembers: The Last Testament* (Boston: Little, Brown and Co., 1976), 401–402.

20. Millis, *The Forrestal Diaries,* 155–56, 177, 179–80, 187.

21. War Department Cable 97428 (August 14, 1946), Colonel Marshall Carter to General George Marshall, NA, DF, RG 59, Marshall Mission Records, 1944–1948: Box 2; see also, War Department Cable 99514 (September 5, 1946), ibid.; War Department Cable, "Gold 2055," Underwood (Nanking) to Carter (February 9, 1947), NA, DF, RG 59, Marshall Mission Records, 1944–1948: Box 7; Poole, "From Conciliation to Containment," 14–15; Millis, *The Forrestal Diaries,* 192.

22. Memo (unsigned) to Secretary of the Navy Forrestal and Secretary of War Patterson (c. September 13, 1946), NA, DF, RG 59, Marshall Mission Records, 1944–1948: Box 2.; Memo (unsigned) to General Marshall (September 14, 1946), ibid.

23. For example, Marshall thought Truman overstated his case in his appearance before Congress, as did John Carter Vincent, the head of the China Division of the State Department; see Gary May, *China Scapegoat* (New York: New Republic Books, 1979),

156–57; Kennan, *Memoirs,* 311–24; see also Walter LaFeber, "American Policy-Makers, Public Opinion, and the Outbreak of the Cold War, 1945–50," in *The Origins of the Cold War in Asia,* ed. Yonosuke Nagai and Akira Iriye (New York: Columbia University Press, 1977), 53–54.

24. On the perceived need to "oversell" a crisis and proposed remedy in order to gain domestic support generally, see Theodore J. Lowi, "Making Democracy Safe for the World: National Politics and Foreign Policy," in *Domestic Sources of Foreign Policy,* ed. James N. Rosenau (New York: Free Press, 1967), 295–331.

25. For example, Senator Arthur Vandenberg, the leading Republican spokesman on foreign policy in Congress, made a "shift of emphasis" speech in January 1947 (following Marshall's failure in China), in which he advocated a more pro-Chiang policy. At the same time he noted in his diary, "It seems to me that we might just as well begin to face the communist challenge on *every* front." Quoted in John R. Skretting, "Republican Attitudes toward the Administration's China Policy, 1945–1949" (Ph.D. diss., University of Iowa, 1952), 38–39. On the fiscal austerity of the 80th Congress, see David Caute, *The Great Fear: The Anti-Communist Purge Under Truman and Eisenhower* (New York: Simon and Schuster, 1978), 562; Millis, *The Forrestal Diaries,* 236, 238–40, 250.

26. Athan G. Theoharis, *The Yalta Myths: An Issue in U.S. Politics, 1945–1955* (Columbia: University of Missouri Press, 1970), 82–83.

27. Dean Acheson, *Present at the Creation* (New York: Norton, 1969), 219.

28. Walter LaFeber, *America, Russia and the Cold War, 1945–1980*, 4th ed. (New York: Wiley, 1980), 54.

29. Gaddis, *Strategies of Containment,* 57. See also Forrestal's summation of a Defense Department report in August in which he states that the United Nations concept "is no longer valid" and that the United States had to realize "that we are in political fact facing a division into two worlds." The State Department and General Eisenhower, among others, generally agreed with this view. Millis, *The Forrestal Diaries,* 307.

30. Gaddis, *Strategies of Containment,* 54–88.

31. U.S. State Department, *Foreign Relations of the United States* (hereafter *FRUS*, vol. I, 746), *1947*. See also Nancy B. Tucker, *Patterns in the Dust* (New York: Columbia University Press, 1983), 183.

32. Millis, *The Forrestal Diaries,* 340. For Marshall's policies during this period, see Forrest C. Pogue, *George C. Marshall: Statesman, 1945–1959* (New York: Viking Press, 1987), 144–257; for U.S. policy in the Middle East, see Bruce Kuniholm, *The Origins of the Cold War in the Near East* (Princeton, N.J.: Princeton University Press, 1980), 383–431.

33. Zbigniew K. Brzezinski, *The Soviet Bloc: Unity and Conflict* (Cambridge: Harvard University Press, 1974), 58–64; Louis J. Halle, *The Cold War as History* (New York: Harper, 1967), 149–51; Vojtech Mastny, "Stalin and the Militarization of the Cold War," *International Security* 9:3 (Winter 1984/85): 112–15.

34. Quotes from Halle, *The Cold War as History,* 150–51.

35. Quoted in ibid., 155.

36. Ibid., 155.

37. Ibid., 87–88, 156.

38. John Baylis, "Ernest Bevin and the Origins of NATO: Britain, the Brussels Pact and the Continental Commitment," *International Affairs* (London) 60:4 (Autumn 1984: 619–21.

39. J. H. Brimmell, *Communism in South East Asia* (London: Oxford University Press, 1959), 249–78.

40. On the relative caution in the new Soviet militancy in Europe and the Middle East and the opportunism in Asia, see, Adam B. Ulam, *Expansion and Coexistence: Soviet Foreign Policy, 1917–1973,* 2d ed. (New York: Praeger, 1974), 488–89. For the new emphasis on Asia, see also Joseph L. Nogee and Robert H. Donaldson, *Soviet Foreign Policy Since World War II* (New York: Pergamon Press, 1981), 71–77; William O. McCagg, Jr., *Stalin Embattled, 1943–1948* (Detroit: Wayne State University Press, 1978), 286–87.

41. See, for example, Forrestal's ideas on this strategy in December 1947 in Millis, *The Forrestal Diaries,* 350–51.

42. For the crisis atmosphere over the Italian election, see James E. Miller, *The United States and Italy, 1940–1950: The Politics and Diplomacy of Stabilization* (Chapel Hill: University of North Carolina Press, 1986), 243–49.

43. This figure was later cut by Congress. Memorandum for the President, "China Policy—NSC 6" (April 2, 1948), HSTL, PSF, NSC Meetings, 1948: Box 220; HSTL, Walton Butterworth Oral History, 41–42; Cabinet Meeting (November 14, 1947), HSTL, MJC, White House File, Set II: Box 2; U.S. House of Representatives, *U.S. Policy in the Far East, Part One, Historical Series* (Washington, D.C.: U.S. GPO, 1976), 166–67, 173, 333, 355–56. See also Omar Bradley with Clay Blair, *A General's Life* (New York: Simon and Schuster, 1983), 517–18; Harold L. Hitchens, "Influences on the Congressional Decision to Pass the Marshall Plan," *The Western Political Science Quarterly* 21:1 (March 1968): 51–68.

44. U.S. House of Representatives, *U.S. Policy in the Far East,* 165.

45. Ibid., 165–66.

46. For example, following a government crisis contrived by the Czech communists, the Soviet deputy foreign minister arrived in Prague. The coup quickly followed. The timing of these developments strongly suggested coordination of policy between the Soviets and the Czech communists. Halle, *The Cold War as History,* 75. On the Czech coup, see also Hugh Seton-Watson, *Neither War Nor Peace* (New York: Praeger, 1960), 203–207; Mastny, "Stalin and the Militarization of the Cold War," 115–19.

47. On the application of the Nazi analogy to the Soviets in Eastern Europe, see Ernest May, *"Lessons" of the Past,* 50. On the effects of the coup on the perceptions of U.S. decision makers, see Jervis, *Perception and Misperception,* 308.

48. Halle, *The Cold War as History,* 180; Bradley with Blair, *A General's Life,* 477; Lester Foultos, "The Bulwark of Freedom: American Security Policy for East Asia, 1947–1950" (Ph.D. Diss., University of Illinois at Urbana-Champaign, 1980), 270; HSTL, MJC, White House File, Cabinet Meetings, Janaury 9–December 31, 1948: Box 2. On the connection between the Czech coup and the Marshall Plan in Congress, see Acheson's remarks on July 2, 1953, in HSTL, Dean Acheson Papers (hereafter, DA): Princeton Seminars (July 2, 1953): Box 74.

49. Alan Bullock, *Ernest Bevin: Foreign Secretary* (New York: Norton, 1983), 530–31.

50. Mastny, "Stalin and the Militarization of the Cold War," 121.

51. HSTL, MJC, White House Files, Cabinet Meetings, Janaury 9–December 31, 1948: Box 2.

52. *FRUS 1948* III, 35–42, 48, 51, 65, 103–5, 108, 184, 197.

53. Gaddis, *Strategies of Containment,* 59; *FRUS 1948* III, 103, 105, 108.

54. Acheson, *Present at the Creation,* 354, 369. Assistant Secretary of State for Far Eastern Affairs Walton Butterworth later observed that the Truman administration had only limited problems with the Republicans until the president's reelection. It was then that the "China lobby" started gaining real influence among the press, Congress, and

public, but not within the administration. HSTL, Walton Butterworth Oral History: 39–40. See also David McLellan, *Dean Acheson: The State Department Years* (New York: Dodd, Mead and Co., 1976), 142; Millis, *The Forrestal Diaries,* 520.

55. For the concern and confusion during the period, see Marshall's remarks at the NSC Meeting of November 26, 1948, HSTL, PSF, NSC Meetings, 1948: Box 220; Charles B. McLane, *Soviet Strategies in Southeast Asia* (Princeton, N.J.: Princeton University Press, 1966), 357–60; Tucker, *Patterns in the Dust,* 28; HSTL, Philip Sprouse Oral History: 21; see Walton Butterworth's remarks on the C.C.P. view of the Kuomintang collapse, HSTL, Roundtable Discussion on American Policy toward China (October 6–8, 1949): vol. II; Buhite, *Soviet-American Relations in Asia,* 70–71.

56. I am indebted to Howard Wriggins for making this point.

57. See his remarks at a cabinet meeting on November 26, 1948, HSTL, MJC, Notes on Cabinet Meetings, 1948: Box 2.

58. HSTL, Matthew J. Connelly Oral History: 329–30.

59. Gaddis, *Strategies of Containment,* 70. The new emphasis on ideology had begun in earnest in Europe in mid-1948; see *FRUS 1948* III, 154.

60. On the connection between the "fall" of China and the adoption of the domino principle in Southeast Asia, see the "Pentagon Papers," U.S. Department of Defense, *United States–Vietnam Relations, 1945–1967* (Washington, D.C.: U.S. GPO, 1971) (hereafter, PP/GPO), vol. I, Part IIA, A-2. See also, Tucker, *Patterns in the Dust,* 19; Andrew J. Rotter, *The Path to Vietnam: Origins of the American Commitment to Southeast Asia* (Ithaca, N.Y.: Cornell University Press, 1987), 35–48.

61. For the lack of historical perspective in U.S. containment policy in Asia, see David P. Mozingo, "Containment in Asia Reconsidered," *World Politics* 19:2 (April 1967): 361–77. The process of eliminating expertise within the Far Eastern Division of State had begun in November 1945, when Ambassador to China Patrick Hurley resigned, charging that "pro-communist" elements were undermining U.S. policy. Throughout the 1940s, Asian specialists were removed to other areas of concern in a failed attempt to protect them from criticism and political attack; many nevertheless had their careers ruined. The effects of these attacks can be seen in the fact that the first two Assistant Secretaries of State for Asian Affairs, Walton Butterworth and Dean Rusk, were chosen because they did *not* have long experience in Asia. See, HSTL, Walton Butterworth Oral History: 53–54; remarks by Dean Rusk, HSTL, DA, Princeton Seminars (March 14, 1954): Box 74. See also, HSTL, John F. Cady Oral History: 34–40. On the "China hands" and their fates, see E. J. Kahn, Jr., *The China Hands* (New York: Viking Press, 1975).

62. *PP/GPO,* vol. I, pt. IC, C-5.

63. Tucker, *Patterns in the Dust,* 31–32; HSTL, Richard Weigle Oral History: 21. For an analysis that properly emphasizes the internal and external political constraints in both the U.S. and China that precluded an early rapprochement, see Steven M. Goldstein, "Chinese Communist Policy Toward the United States: Opportunities and Constraints, 1944–50," in *Uncertain Years: Chinese-American Relations, 1947–1950,* ed. Dorothy Borg and Waldo Heinrichs (New York: Columbia University Press, 1980), 235–78.

64. The document is excerpted and summarized in *PP/GPO,* vol. I, pt. II, A3, A45–A46. See also Robert Blum, *Drawing the Line* (New York: Norton, 1982), 112–18. On Acheson's cable, see Philip Jessup, *The Birth of Nations* (New York: Columbia University Press, 1974), 29. The cable was sent at the time of Mao's public alignment of the C.C.P. with the Soviet Union.

65. Gaddis, *Strategies of Containment,* 85; Tucker, *Patterns in the Dust,* 23. For the

"bandwagon effect" in terms of alliance formation and an argument that fear of it may be exaggerated by decision makers, see Stephen M. Walt, *The Origins of Alliances* (Ithaca, N.Y.: Cornell University Press, 1987); esp. 147–80.

66. Acheson, *Present at the Creation,* 302–7; Theoharis, *The Yalta Myths,* 79–81; Tucker, *Patterns in the Dust,* 157–64. See also Samuel F. Wells, Jr., "Sounding the Tocsin: NSC 68 and the Soviet Threat," *International Security* 4:2 (Fall 1979): 141–51.

67. Bradley with Blair, *A General's Life,* 518–19.

68. Huntington, *The Common Defense,* 48–49.

69. Acheson, *Present at the Creation,* 312–13, 345; Bradley with Blair, *A General's Life,* 518–19, 523; McLellan, *Dean Acheson,* 185; Theoharis, *The Yalta Myths,* 70–72; see Acheson's remarks, HSTL, DA, Princeton Seminars (October 10–11, 1953): Box 75; Blum, *Drawing the Line,* 125–42, 211; Tucker, *Patterns in the Dust,* 182 and n. 42; Russell H. Fifield, *Americans in Southeast Asia: The Roots of Commitment* (New York: Thomas Y. Crowell Co., 1973), 141.

70. Acheson, *Present at the Creation,* 335.

71. For the militant Cominform line taken after 1947 and the communist uprisings in 1948 and 1949, see Brimmell, *Communism in South East Asia,* 249–78; McLane, *Soviet Strategies in Southeast Asia,* 275, 351–474; Oliver E. Clubb, Jr., *The United States and the Sino-Soviet Block in Southeast Asia* (Washington, D.C.: Brookings Institution, 1962), 12–20; Evelyn Colbert, *Southeast Asia in International Politics, 1941–1956* (Ithaca, N.Y.: Cornell University Press, 1977), 125–51; John F. Cady, *The History of Post-war Southeast Asia* (Athens: Ohio University Press, 1974), 60–82; Jay Taylor, *China and Southeast Asia* (New York: Praeger, 1976), 1–10, 251–60; Fifield, *Americans in Southeast Asia,* 57–147.

72. For the argument that they were not directly linked, see Tanigawa Yoshihiko, "The Cominform and Southeast Asia," in *The Origins of the Cold War in Asia,* ed. Nagai and Iriye, 362–77.

73. See, for example, Blum, *Drawing the Line.*

74. Acheson, *Present at the Creation,* 354–58. Acheson's speech is contained in *Department of State Bulletin* 22:551 (January 23, 1950): 111–18; see also, Blum, *Drawing the Line,* 183–84. On the administration's concern over Japan and its interdependence with Southeast Asia, see Dean Rusk's remarks, HSTL, DA, Princeton Seminars (March 14, 1954): Box 74; *PP/GPO,* vol. I, pt. II, A3, A47–A48; Foultos, "The Bulwark of Freedom," 247–51, 276; Gaddis, *Strategies of Containment,* 77; Rotter, *The Path to Vietnam,* 127–40. On the potential effects in Southeast Asia of U.S. aid to the K.M.T., see Acheson's and Truman's views in NSC Meeting (December 30, 1949), HSTL, PSF, NSC Meetings, 1949: Box 220. On the Korean aid cuts, see Dobbs, *The Unwanted Symbol,* 182–88.

75. The quote is from the "Pentagon Papers," *PP/GPO,* vol. I, pt. IC, C-5, pt. IB, I, B-66.

76. Memo, Melby to Lacy (March 27, 1950), HSTL, John F. Melby Papers, Philippines (Cowen–Melby Correspondence, 1949–1950): Box 7.

77. Memo, Corrigan to Austin (December 7, 1949), HSTL, PSF, Subject File (China I): Box 173; Memo, Corrigan to White House (December 22, 1949), ibid.

78. Acheson, *Present at the Creation,* 347–48; Blum, *Drawing the Line,* 168–70; see also the remarks of Dean Rusk, HSTL, DA, Princeton Seminars (March 14, 1954): Box 74; Memo, John Melby to William Lacy (March 27, 1950), HSTL, John F. Melby Papers: Philippines (Melby–Cowen Correspondence, 1949–1950: Box 7. For the Griffin Mission, see Memo of Conversation, Acheson and Truman (February 20, 1950), HSTL, DA, Memoranda of Conversations, 1950: Box 65. This action was caused by a combina-

tion of concern for the security of the area and Republican pressure (R. Allen Griffin, the head of the mission, was a Republican) for bipartisanship from Senator William Knowland and Representative Walter Judd; Fifield, *Americans in Southeast Asia,* 143–45. On June 5, Truman signed the necessary legislation to authorize $40 million for China and Formosa, $40 million for the "general area of China," and $35 million for the "Point IV" program in Southeast Asia (later cut to $27 million). Some earlier aid meant for the Nationalists in China was also switched to Southeast Asia. Blum, *Drawing the Line,* 200–202.

79. Blum, *Drawing the Line,* 202–4, 213. The request, with more to follow, was passed by Congress in July 1950.

80. Reston quoted in Thomas G. Patterson, "If Europe, Why Not China?," *Prologue* 13:1 (Spring 1981): 35.

81. *FRUS 1950* I, 237–92; see also, Gaddis, *Strategies of Containment,* 91, 97, 108; Wells, "Sounding the Tocsin," 124–26, 137–38.

82. Acheson, *Present at the Creation,* 347–48, 374.

83. See, for example, his speech on "total diplomacy" in *Department of State Bulletin* 22:559 (March 20, 1950): 427–30. On the gaps between Acheson's rhetoric to unite the government and society around a stronger stand and his own reservations prior to Korea over the capability of the United States to adopt the perimeter strategy, see Gaddis, *Strategies of Containment,* 114–15. For Acheson's account of the speaking tours and his defense of the excessive rhetoric, see Acheson, *Present at the Creation,* 375–81. See also, Wells, "Sounding the Tocsin," 126.

84. NSC Meeting (June 29, 1950), HSTL, PSF, NSC Meetings, 1950: Box 220; see also, Robert Jervis, "The Impact of the Korean War on the Cold War," *Journal of Conflict Resolution* 24:4 (December 1980): 563–92; HSTL, Robert Lovett Oral History: 27. For a theoretical treatment of the psychological links between commitments in the core and at the periphery in dealing with adversaries, see Patrick M. Morgan, "Saving Face for the Sake of Deterrence," in *Psychology and Deterrence,* ed. Robert Jervis, Ned Lebow, and A. Stein (Baltimore: Johns Hopkins University Press, 1985), 125–52.

85. When John Carter Vincent, the former head of State's China Division (and who was later driven out of the foreign service), warned against a universalistic hard line in the region, Kennan told him: "John Carter, your views on Asian policy are quite sound . . . but the immediate problem is to maintain the morale of Europe and its will to resist the communist challenge." Quoted in Ross Terrill, "John Carter Vincent and the American ,'Loss' of China," in *China and Ourselves,* ed. Ross Terrill and Bruce Douglas (Boston: Beacon Press, 1969), 130.

86. Melby Mission Final Report (December 11, 1950), HSTL, John F. Melby Papers, Chronological File, 1950: Box 10.

87. *The Pentagon Papers,* vol. I (Gravel Edition) (Boston: Beacon Press, 1971), 83–84.

88. Ibid., 84.

89. See also, Melby Mission Final Report (December 11, 1950); *PP/GPO,* vol. I, pt. II, A3, A47–A48.

90. On the Truman administration, see May, *"Lessons" of the Past,* 19–86; more generally on the lessons of history, Jervis, *Perception and Misperception,* 217–315.

91. Ibid., 308–10.

92. These sequential lessons of dealing with the Soviets during the Truman administration long outlasted the late 1940s. Eisenhower, justifying the intervention in Lebanon in 1958, called attention to the "Communist takeover of Czechoslovakia, the Communist conquest of the China mainland in 1949 and their attempts to takeover Korea and Indo-

china." Quoted in Stanley Hoffmann, *Gulliver's Troubles: Or the Setting of American Foreign Policy* (New York: McGraw-Hill, 1968), 137 n. 52.

93. Quoted in Herbert Parmet, *JFK: The Presidency of John F. Kennedy* (New York: Dial Press, 1983), 328.

94. For treatments that employ this technique to advocate a less active U.S. role in the developing world, see Jerome Slater, "Dominos in Central America: Will they Fall? Does It Matter?," *International Security* 12:2 (Fall 1987): 105–34; Robert H. Johnson, "Exaggerating America's Stakes in Third World Conflicts," *International Security* 10:3 (Winter 1985/86): 32–68.

95. For example, Bernard Brodie, *War and Politics* (New York: Macmillan, 1973), 151; Robert H. Johnson, "Exaggerating America's Stakes in Third World Conflicts," 40.

96. The term is Jack Snyder's; see his introductory and concluding chapters in this volume.

97. Niccolo Machiavelli, *The Prince,* trans. Harvey C. Mansfield, Jr. (Chicago: University of Chicago Press, 1985), 120. I am indebted to Robert Kaufman for pointing out this passage to me.

98. NSC Meeting (November 24, 1950), HSTL, PSF, NSC Meetings, 1950: Box 220.

99. Brimmell, *Communism in South East Asia,* 249–78. It should be noted that Chinese policy again turned relatively militant in the late 1950s. Russell H. Fifield, *Southeast Asia in United States Policy* (New York: Praeger, 1963), 40–67.

100. Mozingo, "Containment in Asia Reconsidered," 363–65.

101. On President Reagan and the use of the domino principle, see S. Neil MacFarlane, *Superpower Rivalry and Third World Radicalism: The Idea of National Liberation* (Baltimore: Johns Hopkins University Press, 1985), 200.

6

Soviet Inferences from Their Victories in the Periphery: Visions of Resistance or Cumulating Gains?

TED HOPF

Since World War II, American decision makers' perceived need to counter Soviet activities in peripheral areas of the globe has led the United States into a continual string of conflicts, from the Korean War to the Grenada operation. American statesmen did not perceive any strategic interests at stake in these conflicts, but instead, continue to be haunted by the "lessons of Munich," which teach that any sign of weakness before a potential foe will lead to the latter's ultimate challenge for global hegemony.[1]

During the postwar years American policymakers have consistently feared that an American failure to respond in a peripheral conflict would generate an image of American weakness in the eyes and decision making calculus of their Soviet counterparts. For instance, President Johnson, in a July 1965 cabinet meeting, argued that "if we run out on Southeast Asia, there will be trouble ahead in every part of the globe—not just in Asia, but in the Middle East and in Europe, in Africa and Latin America. I am convinced that our retreat from this challenge will open the path to World War III."[2] Ten years later, Secretary of State Kissinger, in his efforts to convince Congress to finance covert operations in Angola, contended that the "inability to respond in Angola will show we have lost all capacity to respond to anything less than a direct and substantial challenge."[3] Most recently and with respect to a different adversary, Secretary of State Shultz justified the bombing of Tripoli and Benghazi: "We must remember, and of course Europeans particularly remember, that tolerance or appeasement of aggression has historically brought more aggression."[4]

In sum, American policymakers believe that the world is a place where, as a consequence of American defeats in the periphery, the credibility, for the Soviets, of American resolve and capabilities to resist future Soviet expansion will be weakened, where American allies will bandwagon with a strengthened opponent, and where dominoes will fall to the Soviets.[5] American decision makers rarely have been specific about how they expect these phenomena to derive from such defeats, but one can suggest a number of plausible possibilities about their beliefs.

First, the Soviet leadership itself might be emboldened to embark on new adventures, because American credibility to resist Soviet expansion had waned. Similarly, Soviet allies might become more aggressive as they sense that greater victories are possible.

Americans might fear, second, the bandwagoning of their own allies and third, that dominoes will fall to the Soviets. Faced with the threat of Soviet expansion, strategic allies who are continually being lured by Soviet political blandishments and coerced by its military power, will accommodate themselves to this menace, rather than resist it. American allies in the region of the most recent defeat who are fighting insurgencies of their own will fall victim to revolutionary events, rather than redoubling their efforts to resist such an outcome. For example, it was argued that an American loss in Vietnam would impel American allies around the world to question the reliability of American guarantees of protection against Soviet aggression, and hence they would try to work out arrangements with the Soviet Union that would undercut American interests. It was further assumed that geographically contiguous countries, such as Thailand and Malaysia, would fall into the Soviet camp soon after South Vietnam.

But in fact, as this study demonstrates, Soviet perceptions of the consequences of their victories in Vietnam, Angola, and Ethiopia reveal an enormous bias toward perceiving a world that counters their victories, rather than one that reinforces them. At most, the fall of Saigon in April 1975 did cause the Soviets to see an America unable to repeat an intervention on the scale of the Vietnam War, but even then the Soviets did not form the view, so feared by American policymakers, of an irresolute America bereft of military power and allies, besieged by the invincible forces of national liberation.

In fact the evidence is that American policymakers have grossly exaggerated the effects on Soviet thinking of American defeats in the periphery, and hence greatly overestimate the stakes involved in any given conflict. Moreover, their failure to think through just how Soviet gains might cumulate has led them to neglect a vast array of foreign policy instruments that the Soviets themselves recognize as effective in countering their further efforts at expansion.

In the next section, I describe the propositions of deterrence theory about cumulating gains and the few empirical tests of them that others have performed. I also outline a set of hypotheses derived from an alternate theory of balancing. In the following section, I explain the tests for assessing which theory best describes actual Soviet perceptions, evidence of which is gleaned from a review of the relevant Soviet literature. I explain how I use attribution theory to analyze Soviet perceptions during four specific periods. In the section "Soviet Inferences from Their Victories in the Periphery," I summarize the results for the four cases: Vietnam, 1969–1972; Vietnam, 1972–1975; Angola, 1975–1976; and the Horn of Africa, 1977–1978. (The Appendix presents the raw data for each of the four periods.) In the final section, "Soviet Perceptions," I present the conclusions of this study.

The Validity of Deterrence Theory's "Cumulating Gains"

In this section, I describe the propositions of deterrence theory about cumulating gains that have driven American foreign policy in the periphery. This theory predicts that, after an American loss in the Third World, Soviets will see an incapable and irresolute America, American allies ready to bandwagon with the Soviet Union, and falling dominoes in countries contiguous to the region of the latest American defeat. I recount the few empirical tests of these propositions that have been executed. I then present an alternative "balancing" theory, which predicts that Soviets will maintain images of a highly credible America, despite these defeats, and will also perceive American allies balancing against the Soviets and regional actors cooperating with one another to compensate for the latest Soviet victory in the region.

The predictions of these two alternative theories are compared in Table 6.2.

Deterrence Theory

The policies rooted in the widespread use of the Munich analogy have been reinforced by traditional deterrence theory. Thomas Schelling and Glenn Snyder distinguished material or strategic interests from deterrent or reputational interests, arguing that protection of the former requires the maintenance of the latter: American resolve must be demonstrated in peripheral areas in order to deter the Soviets from acting aggressively elsewhere.[6] Deterrence theory, however, says nothing about the choices of other countries: whether dominoes will fall and allies will bandwagon. It encompasses only Soviet perceptions of American credibility. But American foreign policymakers have gone beyond traditional deterrence theory to assume that American resistance in the Third World is necessary to teach the right lessons about American credibility, to American and Soviet allies as well as to the Soviets themselves. In this study, I test all three propositions—credibility, bandwagoning, and dominoes—as if they are derived from deterrence theory directly.

Surprisingly, there is little or no historical evidence that, in fact, statesmen infer an opponent's general irresoluteness and weakness from encounters in the periphery. Even Hitler is a questionable case, as his plans for conquest after the March 1936 remilitarization of the Rhineland appear not to have been contingent on whether he was resisted or not. Moreover, Czechoslovakia could hardly be considered to be in the periphery of Europe at the time.[7]

There have been only two attempts to investigate empirically whether a victor in a confrontation in fact draws general inferences about a defeated state's probable future behavior in a conflict. The first study, by Paul Huth and Bruce Russett, found that in twenty-three cases where deterrence failed, there was no correlation between a previous victory by the attacker and its decision to challenge the would-be deterrer in the present case.[8] They establish only the lack of a correlative relationship between victories and subsequent challenges, but are not able to demonstrate whether or not there is any causal significance.

In a later work, Huth used comparative case studies to test whether or not the past behavior of a defender of the status quo enters into the calculations of a would-be challenger. If either the defender or challenger has been forced to retreat in a previous confrontation with the other involving force of arms, deterrence in the future is less likely to be successful. In the four cases examined here, however, there were no direct clashes: armed conflicts were only between the allies and clients of the United States and Soviet Union. The American defeat in Vietnam might not meet Huth's criteria for selection as a case, for he further finds that the past behavior of the defender in conflicts with someone other than the attacker has no effect on the attacker's decision making calculus.[9]

A Theory of Balancing

A theory of balancing makes predictions about American credibility, the behavior of American allies, and regional dynamics precisely contrary to those of deterrence theory.

First, Soviet leaders would not see a defeat in a peripheral area as indicative of American irresoluteness or incapability. On the contrary, as a consequence of that very defeat, the Soviets should expect the United States to redouble its efforts at the next opportunity as a way to counter any shift in the balance of power. In other words, American credibility should not be expected to suffer from defeats in the periphery.

Second, American allies around the world should be expected to increase their resistance to Soviet and Soviet-allied expansion as a consequence of a Soviet victory, as the threat appears more imminent. Rather than bandwagoning with or accommodating themselves to an apparently enhanced Soviet power position, American allies will balance against the perceived menace.

Third, Soviet allies should be encouraged by the fact that their corevolutionaries succeeded in besting the United States and its allies. However, they should also recognize that the very victory that inspires them to action also has a bracing effect on their opponents, the United States and its allies. The perceptions of a Soviet ally are very dependent on local conditions. So, falling dominoes is a variable to be tested, not an axiom to be assumed.

Testing the Validity of Cumulating Gains

In this section, I explain how I selected the four historical cases and describe my use of attribution theory as a way to analyze the evidence drawn from the Soviet literature. I enumerate predictions about these perceptions based on the two competing theories. I also show how I employ Soviet speeches and articles in order to derive Soviet perceptions of the international arena.

A Crucial Case for Deterrence Theory

I have chosen four cases for this study. These four cases, taken together, constitute a crucial case for deterrence theory postulates.[10] The American military defeat in Vietnam was the first battlefield defeat suffered by the United States since World War II and came despite an expenditure of $150 billion and the loss of over 50,000 American lives. Thus I test Soviet perceptions from the Vietnam War from 1969 to 1972, and from the American withdrawal from Vietnam in 1973 and the fall of Saigon in 1975. Thereafter, the United States failed to stop a pro-Soviet guerilla force from wresting control of Angola from two other pro-Western armies and failed to prevent the Soviet Union from affecting the outcome of the war on the Horn of Africa. So my third case examines Soviet perceptions from the abortive American intervention in Angola in 1975 to 1976, and the fourth and last case, Soviet perceptions from their support for Cuban intervention on the Horn in 1977 to 1978 to help the Ethiopian government defend itself against a Somali invasion.

If the Soviets were ever to infer the kinds of lessons for credibility, bandwagoning, and dominoes predicted by deterrence theory in the postwar period, this string of American losses should have evoked them. Indeed, American decision makers themselves and the American foreign policy elite refer to the "post-Vietnam syndrome" and the subsequent Soviet gains in Africa as evidence that deterrence theory is valid. If, however, Soviet perceptions after these American losses are not consistent with deterrence theory predictions, then the theory has failed its test in a crucial case.

Attribution Theory

Attribution theory concerns the processes whereby people develop images of others, their capabilities, their degree of motivation and effort, and amount of ultimate responsibility for their actions and their consequences. It postulates that an observer of an event assumes it was caused by the conditions present and not by those that were absent. When that event or a similar one is repeated, the observer compares the conditions present with those that were assumed to cause the prior one, and through a process of elimination determines the necessary or sufficient cause(s) of that phenomenon or class of phenomena. Given a sufficient number of cases, the observer becomes quite confident of what causes a particular event.[11]

This model was used to assign causal weights to the various Soviet perceptions derived from Soviet speeches and articles.

One of the most robust experimental findings of attribution theory is that people's confidence in their predictions of someone's future behavior increases with how stable and enduring they perceive to be the conditions that produced that behavior.[12] This suggests two ways to order Soviet perceptions in terms of stability, one derived from the attribution literature, the other arrived at inductively from the Soviet literature itself.

Attribution theorists distinguish between behavior caused by characteristics of the individual, or "disposition," and that caused by external environmental condition(s), or "situation."[13] The experimental evidence shows that dispositional attributions are more stable, and hence of greater predictive power, than situational ones.

The other way to find out how stable the tendencies toward balancing or domino behavior are thought to be is to derive these data directly from the Soviet literature. If Soviet analysts speak of a particular condition as durable or as being uncountered by any opposing condition, then one may assume that Soviet analysts place high predictive value on that variable. If they describe a particular condition as ephemeral, or as being engaged in a struggle with countervailing forces, then there is reason to place less weight on that condition in Soviet expectations about the tendencies in the international system.

This model is reproduced in Table 6.1 as a matrix that contains all the logical possibilities for Soviet inferences. Soviet statements about the dispositional elements listed have the most causal weight because they are indicators of American dispositions to resist future Soviet foreign policy adventurism in the Third World. The categories of diplomatic and military actions and military expenditures are signs of American elite capacity to actualize its dispositions. The domestic situational factors listed are critical only to the degree that they constrain the elite's ability to advance its preferences above. Soviet views of external situational influences on American behavior, namely, the resolve and capabilities of Soviet allies and of American allies and of national liberation movements are important insofar as Soviets see these other actors as preventing the American elite from implementing its dispositional preferences. They are also an indicator of whether Soviets expect bandwagoning by American allies, or regional dynamics that resemble falling dominoes in response to American defeats.

The attitude of the American elite is derived from statements by Soviet observers about the reasons for American behavior made in terms of characteristics inherent to the nature of imperialism or to the dispositions of the American governing elite. These elite dispositions, along with the dispositions of Congress and the American public, define the resolve component of American credibility, that is, the inherent propensity of the United States to resist revolutionary changes in the Third World.[14]

American diplomacy, its military actions, including deployments abroad and military aid to American allies, and the size and content of its military budget, are indicators of governmental elite dispositions. They are the most direct expressions of American intentions with respect to future behavior because the governing elite itself has direct control over their employment. These elements, along with American economic capacity, constitute the variable of American capabilities, which with resolve, yield a Soviet measure of American credibility.

The categories at the right in Table 6.1 are elements that act as opportunities for the American elite to realize its preferences, situational constraints on these opportunities, and also as autonomous causal factors in their own right. For

Table 6.1. Categories of Soviet Perceptions

	Internal to the U.S.	External to the U.S.
Dispositional	Ruling Elite's Attitudes	
	Diplomatic Actions	
	Military Actions	
	Military Expenditures	Soviet Allies
		National Liberation Movement
Situational	Public Opinion	American Allies
	Congress	
	Economic Capacity	

example, America's allies can resist Soviet expansionism independent of the United States, or they can facilitate an American predisposition to resist. The dispositions and capabilities of America's allies constitute the bandwagoning variable in this study. Soviet observers' descriptions of American allies helping the United States to resist Soviet expansionism refute deterrence theory's assumption of allied accommodation after an American defeat.

Soviet perceptions of the relative strengths of regional Soviet and American allies are indications of whether or not Soviet observers expect more dominoes to fall in the region of the last American defeat. The weakness or strength of regional American clients or allies is an unstable situational variable that denotes the potential for falling dominoes, which is also affected by the dispositions and capabilities of regional national liberation movements.

Deterrence and Balancing Theory: Explicit Predictions

Deterrence theory and balancing theory make competing predictions as to how the categories in Table 6.1 would reflect Soviet perceptions after the cases of Vietnam, Angola, and Ethiopia. The alternative predictions are indicated below and then each one's predictions for the individual categories are given.

In the most extreme case, beliefs in cumulating gains would see imperialism as a system disposed to retreat and an American governmental elite disposed to accommodate to the expansion of Soviet power. The U.S. government's actions would reflect this disposition. American allies and clients would also accommodate themselves to their respective threats; Soviet radical allies and clients would be emboldened by a Soviet victory to challenge American and allied positions elsewhere in the world. Moreover, all the unstable situational variables would reinforce the elite dispositions. There also should be no instances of Soviets observing these events and failing to draw inferences from them as to future American behavior and developments in the Third World. Instances in which Soviet observers initially are uncertain as to the ultimate outcome of the struggle between indicators of resistance and signs of cumulating gains should be ultimately resolved in favor of the latter.

If the findings of this study conformed to that sketched out above, then American policymakers' beliefs in cumulating gains would be supported by irrefutable evidence. But this is too high a standard against which to measure either theory. Beliefs in cumulating gains would be strongly validated even if only the dispositional variables, that is, the attitudes of the American ruling elite and its capacity to advance its preferences, pointed in that direction, given the assumption that observers place greater reliance on dispositional evidence.

The weakest validation for deterrence theory would be if only the situational variables were seen as compelling the actors to operate against their predispositions to resist. This points out the enormous importance of evaluating the struggle the Soviets perceive between dispositional and situational factors when they make contrary predictions about future American behavior. If Soviet observers note that there are certain situational factors compelling American leaders to act against their desires to resist, and these factors either disappear or are in subsequent analyses noted as having been countered effectively, then it implies that the Soviets expect resistance to be the American response in the future.

To test the opposing theory of balancing, the standards of measurement outlined above are applied to look for statements that predict resistance. In addition, cases in which Soviet observers comment on any one of the three conflicts without making any predictions or inferences at all about future American resistance also disconfirm deterrence theory. This is an important category, because it implies that many Soviet analysts see little utility in trying to predict, based on past experiences, how the world will react to any further attempts at expansion. These instances disconfirm deterrence theory because it argues that it is precisely the certainty of such Soviet inferences that demands an American response.

Table 6.2 displays the contrary predictions offered by the two theories with respect to each of the categories in Table 6.1.

Table 6.2. Deterrence and Balancing Theory: Contrary Predictions

Categories	Predictions of Deterrence Theory	Predictions of Balancing Theory
Imperialist Disposition	Imperialism, by its very nature, is inclined to retreat in the face of future Soviet expansion.	Imperialism, by its very nature, is inclined to respond with force in the face of future Soviet expansion.
Elite Disposition	The American governing elite is inclined not to respond in the face of future Soviet expansion.	The American governing elite is inclined to resist any further Soviet efforts at expansion.
Diplomacy	U.S. diplomacy will be aimed at pursuing accommodation to Soviet expansion in the future.	U.S. diplomacy will try to prevent any future Soviet successes at expansion.
Regional Military Actions	American force deployments in the region of the last conflict will be diminished, as will military aid to that region.	American force deployments and military aid will be increased in the region of the last conflict to compensate for the losses suffered.
Global Military Actions	U.S. force deployments outside the region of the latest conflict and military aid in general will be cut.	U.S. force deployments and military aid will be increased to compensate for the losses suffered.
Military Expenditures	American defense allocations will be reduced in recognition of the futility of trying to resist future Soviet aggression.	American defense budget will be increased to better counter efforts at future Soviet expansion.
Public Opinion	U.S. public opinion will prevent it from resisting any future Soviet expansion.	U.S. public opinion will support American efforts at countering future Soviet expansion.
Congress	Congress will prevent the U.S. from resisting future Soviet expansion.	Congress will support U.S. efforts at countering future Soviet expansion.
Economic Capacity	The American economy cannot sustain efforts to resist future Soviet expansion.	The American economy can support such efforts.

Global Allies	West European and Japanese allies of the U.S. are likely to accommodate themselves to future Soviet expansion.	West European and Japanese allies of the U.S. are likely to resist further Soviet efforts at expansion.
Global Clients	American clients far afield from the region of latest conflict (after Vietnam, e.g., Zaire, in southern Africa) will bandwagon with, or accommodate themselves to, increased Soviet power in their region.	Extra-regional American clients will respond to Soviet gains elsewhere in the world by increasing their resistance to any signs of Soviet encroachments in their own regions.
Global National Liberation Movement (NLM)	NLMs outside the area of the latest Soviet victory (after Vietnam, e.g., the MPLA in Angola) will be inspired to increase their efforts.	Extra-regional NLMs will fear that any efforts by them to gain further victories will be countered.
Regional Allies	American allies in the region of the last conflict (in Southeast Asia, e.g., Australia) will bandwagon with, or accommodate themselves to, increased Soviet power in the region.	American regional allies will increase their resistance to any further accretions of Soviet power in the region.
Regional Clients	American clients in the region of the last conflict (in southern Africa, e.g., Zaire) will bandwagon with, or accommodate themselves to, increased Soviet power in the region.	American regional clients will resist any further Soviet encroachments in the region.
Regional NLM(s) National Liberation Movement(s)	NLMs in the region of the latest conflict (in Southeast Asia, e.g., the Pathet Lao) will be encouraged to increase their efforts at subverting American clients and allies in the region.	Regional NLMs will be increasingly cautious about attempting any further gains in that region.
Conflict Between Observed Tendencies	The struggle between the conditions that favor resistance and those that favor expansion will be resolved in favor of the latter.	The struggle between cumulating gains and resistance will be resolved in favor of the latter.
No Inference	There should be very few or no instances in which inferences are drawn from these cases.	There will be a significant number of instances of no inference.

The Use of Soviet Sources in This Study

Well over 500 articles and 300 leadership speeches were coded in terms of the matrix in Table 6.1.[15] I divide the group of Soviet inferences into two categories, the party leadership and the general academic and daily press. Each article or speech was assigned to one of these three—internal-situational, internal-dispositional, or external—and identified as supporting one of the two theories or coded as a "struggle" between two tendencies or as a "no inference" from the case considered. The article was further coded with whatever causal factors it contained. This process generates a picture of Soviet inferences for each of the four periods included in this study—Vietnam, post-Vietnam, post-Angola, and post-Ethiopia.

Cases coded as "no inference" only include those articles and speeches in the three newspapers that dealt with American foreign policy or the conflicts occurring in the region of the case. If the writer or speechmaker, given this opportunity, failed to note the consequences of the conflict for future American behavior, then it was coded as no inference.[16] The "no inference" category can be especially revealing. For example, General Secretary Brezhnev spoke at a dinner for Angolan President Agostinho Neto in Moscow and praised the enormous victory won by the MPLA, yet made no reference to the consequences of this event for future developments in southern Africa; this absence is a very strong disconfirmation of the domino component of American beliefs.

Soviet Inferences from Their Victories in the Periphery

Constructing a Baseline: Vietnam, 1969–1972

From 1969 to 1972, the Nixon administration was searching for an "honorable" way to withdraw from Vietnam. Steady American troop withdrawals and the enunciation of the Nixon Doctrine were combined with increased bombing by American and South Vietnamese aviation and the Vietnamization of the war, which entailed increased American supplies of military equipment to the Saigon government.

Deterrence theory's predictions for Soviet perceptions in this period are ambiguous. On the one hand, the Soviets should see cumulating gains, as the Americans were indeed withdrawing from the conflict. On the other hand, the South Vietnamese army had become far stronger and the use of air power against the North Vietnamese was increasing. These factors should cause the Soviets to see continued resistance in the region. Balancing theory would assume that the Soviets should be more concerned with the elements of resistance to their efforts.

The evidence is mixed. The Soviet political leadership's perceptions were dominated by images of resistance in the period, but these were in decline from 1969 to 1971. These images of continued balancing behavior, however, increase again in 1972 to pre-1970 levels. Soviet academics and journalists, however, see resistance peaking in 1970 and secular decline subsequently. The data in Table 6.3 in the Appendix give a detailed breakdown of Soviet inferences for the period. Figure 6.1 in the Appendix represents graphically the relative proportions between Soviet images of balancing and cumulating gains.

General Perceptions

At the most general level of analysis, Figure 6.1 shows that Soviet observers saw an external arena characterized by strong resistance. The American governmental elite was disposed to counter perceived Soviet expansion, and it advanced this desire through military activities in Southeast Asia and through healthy defense budgets. Moreover, American allies and clients in the area reinforced these American efforts. However, Soviet analysts identified three situational factors that potentially hindered these efforts. America's NATO allies objected to the continuation of the war in Vietnam, as did a significant segment of the American public. Moreover, it appeared to Soviet observers as if the economic costs of the war were becoming unbearable. These factors militating against further resistance to Soviet expansion were insufficient, however, to change American elite preferences or to blunt the activities of American allies abroad. It is important to note that American public pressures had not yet been converted into effective congressional opposition to the war, at least in Soviet eyes. This absence of congressional pressure allowed the American government to realize its preference to resist.

An examination of Soviet commentary reinforces these points:

O. Bykov, a frequent contributor to MEiMO, describes the dispositions of American elites in early 1971.

> Efforts, to any degree, to realize the need for curtailing the excessive level of foreign policy activities evokes, in certain circles of the United States, the fear that this can weaken their international positions and undermine faith in the ability of the country to assume its role of "superpower." Hence, any plans for the redeployment of American forces abroad are accompanied by invariable affirmations of the inviolability of their "obligations" abroad. "We don't intend to leave the world arena," declared President Nixon, in his foreign policy message to Congress.
>
> If one is to judge not only by official statements, but also by concrete deeds, then one cannot draw the conclusion that Washington is thinking at all of giving up its "global mission."[17]

Thus Bykov indicated that there is American behavior that is good evidence of its intentions on the international stage. It is interesting that what American analysts in retrospect saw as a signal of American retreat in the period—Nixon's promulgation of the Guam Doctrine in 1969—Soviet analysts saw as a device to perpetuate American aggression in the region, and thus, as a way to realize American dispositions: "It isn't surprising that the proclamation of the 'new' doctrine has not led to a curtailment of the American military presence in the region of the Pacific Ocean. On the contrary, together with the escalation of the war against the Vietnamese people, the total number of American armed forces in Southeast Asia and the Far East has increased and at the beginning of 1969, it surpassed one million."[18] "The American invasion of Cambodia is a matter of course for the 'Guam Doctrine' and the policy of 'Vietnamization.' "[19]

American military activities in an area of conflict are an important variable that Soviets use to gauge American credibility throughout this study. Another indicator of elite ability to realize its plans is the state of the military budget. Both, in this period, were perceived to be evidence of American intent and ability to continue the aggression in southeast Asia and also to prevent additional Vietnams in the Pacific region overall.

Soviet commentators also noted that American allies in the Pacific region were reinforcing American efforts aimed at preventing further Soviet gains in the area. Losev and Sergeev, for example, noted that Nixon, in his February 1970 foreign policy message to Congress, had stressed that Japan was "the key to the success of the Guam Doctrine in Asia." Moreover, Japan was willing and able to "make a concrete contribution for the implementation of this doctrine" by supplying aid to Laos, Cambodia, and Vietnam. This "military-political accord" between Washington and Tokyo is "directed against the Asian national liberation movement (NLM)."[20]

Kobrin argued that American political commentators have admitted that the American rapprochement with China was being used to "undermine the . . . revolutionary and liberation forces in Southeast Asia" and was directed against the "Soviet Union first of all."[21]

Along with America's Japanese, Chinese, and Indonesian allies, Soviet observers noted that American local clients were also continuing or increasing their resistance to "progressive" change in the region:

> It's a fact that the very newest doctrines of the "Vietnamization" type not only have not weakened the stake of American imperialism on bases . . . , but have as their real goal the activization of pacts and alliances forged long ago.
>
> At the June 1972 regular session of SEATO, Secretary of State Rogers and Minister of Foreign Affairs Alec Douglas-Home called for a new build-up of the "joint efforts" of its participants. Recent events, including the holding of huge maneuvers code-named "Sea Scorpion" in the South China Sea in October, showed that the slogan of "the revival of SEATO" weren't only "encouraging words."
>
> It is proposed to tie SEATO more closely to the policy of the United States in Indochina and to subordinate the organization to the needs of the "Guam Doctrine."
>
> This is reflected in the transfer of the American armed forces being withdrawn from South Vietnam to Thailand. This country, according to *United States News and World Report,* is rapidly being turned into a "new center of American power in Southeast Asia." The American military clique, reports *Newsweek,* hopes "to replace" South Vietnam with Thailand as its main military base in Southeast Asia.[22]

The elements that combined to constitute the Soviet image of a resistant world in this period were American elite dispositions, American military activities, and the actions of American allies and clients in the Pacific region. Soviet observers identified three potential counters to these dynamics—the opposition of America's NATO allies, domestic public opinion, and burdensome economic consequences. To put it in different terms, American credibility was seen as high, by virtue of elite preferences and its demonstrated military capabilities. Moreover, American allies and clients in the region were balancing against, not bandwagoning with, the threat posed by North Vietnam, hence preventing any possible tumbling of dominoes. But public opposition to the war and the strains to which the economy was subjected in prosecuting it posed future threats to American credibility.

Opposition to the war by American allies could suggest two quite different conclusions, neither one of which Soviet analysts identified. On the one hand, it could reflect allied balancing propensities if American allies were averse to the further dissipation of American resources in Southeast Asia when the Central Front merited greater attention and expenditures. On the other hand, the allies could have seen American adventurism as an obstacle to accommodation with the Soviets in Europe.

Trofimenko, for instance, argues that the United States can no longer rely on its allies in Europe to support its Third World adventurism, but he does not explain why this is the case.

> The practice of the postwar years shows that the interests of the United States and its possible local partners have not completely or even substantially coincided in many conflicts. More often than not one observes a rather strong divergence of interests, even if one is to examine the regional policies of such states as Britain, Germany, and Portugal, which have been the most active supporters of the general foreign policy course of the United States in the postwar epoch. All this makes the reliance of strategists [in Washington] on the effective military power of American partners aimed against "third parties" very tenuously grounded.[23]

Trofimenko analyzed the announcement by Defense Secretary Laird of a new policy of "realistic containment," which foresaw increased burden-sharing among American allies and clients to counter the Soviet threat. Trofimenko identified the domestic political and economic situation in the United States as the primary causes for this reassessment of tactics by the American government.

> "We," says Laird [in May 1971], "call it realistic because it was drawn up to take into account the most important factors of reality with which America clashes. . . . [These] four main factors are: the strategic reality, financial reality, the actual situation with manpower, and the political reality" . . . .
>
> In the category of "political reality" goes the domestic political situation in the United States, where the popular masses all the more decisively and loudly are demanding the renunciation of military adventures abroad and for the government to turn its face toward domestic socioeconomic problems. In recognizing that reality, President Nixon says: "We must not undertake abroad more than public opinion in our own country is able to evaluate positively . . . ."
>
> The "third reality"—the financial one—is the direct result of the dollar crisis, which was caused by the excessive military expenditures of the United States abroad during the entire postwar period. Washington is clashing with the real problem of the lack of resources for the realization, at its previous level, of its functions as the world gendarme.[24]

Public opinion and economic costs notwithstanding, the American government continued to pursue a course aimed at thwarting Soviet expansion. One important reason for this was that the public had not yet been able to influence Congress to represent its opposition to adventurism to the relevant powers in Washington. That this is apparent to Soviet observers is evident from the absence of any mention of congressional pressure from their commentaries in this period. Trofimenko offered other reasons for the ability of the elite to override this public opposition.

> This recognition of the president [of the need to stay within the bounds of domestic opinion] of course does not mean that the American government will always attentively obey the opinion of society in the formulation of its foreign policy. On the contrary, the optimal course for any bourgeois government is either to ignore public opinion or to create an artificial climate of support in the country for official policy by the propagandistic manipulation of public opinion. In an effort to take into account this financial reality, the American government, on the one hand, by means of persuasion and exhortation, and also by means of unilateral financial-economic measures, is striving to put part of its expenditures, including military, onto its partners, putting on their shoulders an additional financial burden.[25]

The argument that Soviet analysts were most attentive to the struggle between American public opinion and the actions and desires of the American government is further supported by the nine instances of indecision. Over three-quarters of these delineate lines of battle drawn between these two tendencies. For example, Lev Stepanov writes:

> The mass antiwar movement has achieved such a scale that official Washington is forced to reexamine the course affirmed earlier of unrestrained escalation of American participation in military activities in Indochina. The basic formula worked out under Nixon and expressed by the concept of "Vietnamization" is calculated to put out the fire of antiwar activities in the United States itself and at the same time preserve for the government the possibility of continuing aggression.[26]

Vitalii Zhurkin, writing in 1969, was not able to determine definitively whether the consequences of Vietnam for American behavior would facilitate or impede further "progressive change" in the world. He enumerated several factors that would hamstring American efforts to intervene in the periphery in the future, but then hastened to add that it was too soon to tell whether the United States had learned the appropriate lessons from its experience in Vietnam.

He noted that "the Vietnam adventure has significantly affected the economic position of the country, aggravating its monetary-financial complications." America's global allies have deserted it. "The United States, having entered into alliances with more than forty states, has ended up in Vietnam with practically no allies at all." Domestic political unrest in the United States "serves as a warning to the leading circles of what will threaten them if they decide on new foreign adventures of such a type."

But there is substantial evidence that the Soviets felt that these constraints were not recognized by the policymaking elite.

> In political circles in the United States there exists an aspiration to reduce the lessons of the Vietnam failure only to a single elementary conclusion about the need, so far as is possible, to avoid the repetition of concrete situations of the Vietnam type. Such evaluations, on the one hand, speak to the scope of the sobering influence of the Vietnam failure on the ruling circles of the United

> States, but on the other hand—to the aspirations of representatives of these circles to limit to the particular, as much as is possible, the conclusions from the political and military defeat which the United States suffered there.[27]

By the middle of 1972 Zhurkin had resolved that the United States was unable to repeat its Vietnam adventure, and more important, that the American ruling elite had largely resigned itself to this constraint. He argued that since such conflicts cannot be fought on the cheap, the United States could not afford to initiate them. "In Vietnam the hopelessness of the 'limited' aggressive actions of imperialism graphically manifested itself. A local intervention, which the Pentagon counted on realizing without expending great energies or resources, took away the lives of tens of thousands of American soldiers and consumed . . . almost $200 billion." It also caused "a painful domestic political crisis; it struck at the economy of the country." The lack of support rendered by America's closest allies should give the United States pause before it begins any new adventures. "Washington should be convinced of this when it measures its efforts to create such a coalition for intervention in Indochina with the yardstick of the times of the Korean War." In sum, he wrote, "Some of the representatives of realistically thinking groups very likely would go into conflicts if they would bring success and if there were the possibility of both little bloodshed and small expenditures. But in the present-day situation this is excluded."[28]

The findings for this period identify a number of crucial variables used by Soviet observers to predict the prospects for future unimpeded expansion. By 1972, they saw the elements that facilitated resistance—elite dispositions, regional military actions, and the activities of American regional allies and clients—as effectively countering those factors that undermined American capabilities to resist Soviet expansion—allied and domestic political opposition and economic costs. But there are those, such as Zhurkin by 1972, who saw these situational constraints as overriding American elite desires.

Party Leadership Perceptions

The Soviet party leadership also saw a world characterized by resistance. Figure 6.2 shows that such perceptions were always the most prevalent ones across the four years and that there were only three inferences of cumulating gains as a consequence of the ongoing war in Vietnam. But some interesting differences with the general view emerge under analysis. First, it is clear that Soviet leaders were far more undecided than were the journalists and academics surveyed here about the outcome of the war in Vietnam and the willingness of the United States both to continue it and to repeat such an adventure elsewhere.

In all twenty cases of indecision (see Table 6.3 in the Appendix), Soviet leaders perceived an elite fully resolved to continue the war in Vietnam or repeat such interventions in the future. What prevented Soviet leaders from making a clear inference were the continued military efforts of the North Vietnamese and Vietcong. Essentially, Soviet leaders were convinced of their allies' continued resistance, but they were equally convinced that the United States had no intention of leaving any time soon. Typical of this uncertainty was a speech made by Podgorny while in Hanoi:

> In the face of ever more serious defeats, and having ended up in a military and political deadend, American ruling circles are trying different maneuvers. But the facts say that they have not renounced their neocolonialist plans in Washington. The intensive military operations in South Vietnam by the American militarists, air attacks against the DRV, the invasion of Cambodia, and the mass attacks against Laos, all testify to this. All these actions shed light on the true essence of the "Guam Doctrine" and show the real value of "peacemaking" American-style.
>
> [But] this is a futile policy. In Vietnam, Laos, and Cambodia today the United States is farther from the achievement of its aims than ever before. And there is no doubt that the Vietnamese people will achieve the complete ruin of the notorious policy of "Vietnamizing" the war.[29]

Also telling was what the Soviet leadership neglected to consider in drawing conclusions about Vietnam. Unlike journalists and academics, who paid a great deal of attention to such elements of American credibility as public opinion and economic capability, Soviet leaders appeared far more focused on elite resolve and the military capabilities it demonstrated in resisting Soviet expansion. In addition, the leadership did not consider American allies and clients to be of great importance in reaching conclusions about the consequences of Vietnam for future American resistance—again, quite different from the arguments of Soviet academics and journalists about the contributions made to the American cause in Southeast Asia by the South Vietnamese themselves, Thailand, Australia, South Korea, and others. Moreover, NATO opposition to the war did not appear to have been weighed heavily by the leadership either.

Hence, when making a general assessment about the international arena based on the lessons of Vietnam, the party leadership focused on the elements that constitute American credibility, namely, its resolve and capabilities, while ignoring the behavior of European allies and American allies in Southeast Asia. In essence, Soviet leaders focused on American credibility, not on those factors that constitute the dynamics of possible bandwagoning or falling dominoes.

On only three occasions did Soviet political leaders conclude that events in Vietnam implied continued success for progressive change in the periphery. The most limited of these lessons was drawn by Podgorny during the same October 1971 visit to North Vietnam. While in Haiphong, he concluded from its successful defense against air attacks that socialism in North Vietnam was secure from American aggression—not exactly a very optimistic projection of future success.[30]

Ulyanovsky drew more far-reaching conclusions in two long articles about the national liberation process in general. In 1970 he wrote that "the experience of the struggle in Vietnam shows . . . the extraordinary significance of the alliance between the socialist system, the international working class, and the national liberation movement for dealing a rebuff to imperialist forces. Imperialism does not have the power equal to the might of this alliance."[31]

The following year he drew a conclusion more limited in goegraphical scope, arguing that the national liberation movement was assured of victory in Southeast Asia, given the same conditions he indicated above.[32] Ulyanovsky, however, was in the smallest minority in inferring any loss of American capability and the prospect of falling dominoes triggered by events in Vietnam.

The Height of Cumulating Gains—Vietnam, 1973–1975

In January 1973, the United States concluded a peace agreement with North Vietnam that entailed the withdrawal of all American forces. In a little over two years, the North Vietnamese army entered Saigon, having overrun the South Vietnamese army in the process. Deterrence theory would predict that Soviet observers should perceive an America bereft of the will and the capacity to prevent future Soviet adventurism in the Third World. Soviets should see American allies around the world questioning the utility of American security guarantees. Soviet observers should also see other countries in Southeast Asia, such as Thailand, as good candidates for victorious national liberation struggles.

Balancing theory, on the other hand, predicts that Soviet observers would perceive an America resolved and able to prevent any "future Vietnams." They would expect American strategic allies and allies in Southeast Asia to rally their forces to balance against the ascendant threat, rather than moving to accommodate themselves to it.

The evidence in Figures 6.1 and 6.2 and Tables 6.4 through 6.6 in the Appendix does not strongly support the predictions of deterrence theory. While images of cumulating gains outnumbered those of balancing in both 1973 and 1975, the situation was briefly reversed in 1974, that is, soon after the American withdrawal from South Vietnam. Moreover, while American capabilities to repeat another adventure on the scale of Vietnam were questioned by Soviet observers, the latter also saw the United States as militarily capable of arming regional powers to prevent any domino effects. Nor did Soviet observers doubt an American elite will to intervene to resist Soviet expansion in the future, though such predispositions were situationally constrained at that time by economic and domestic political circumstances. Finally, although Soviets saw national liberation movements around the world as encouraged by the Vietnamese victory, they also saw American allies around the world, backed by the United States, balancing against these progressive forces. In sum, Soviet observers in this period saw a struggle ahead, both within America, and in the international arena, between forces of progressive change and forces of reaction.

General Perceptions

At the most general level, one can see what strong effects the signing of the peace treaty in Paris in January 1973 and the evacuation of Saigon in April 1975 had on Soviet images of American capabilities. In the previous period of 1969 to 1972, over 60 percent of the indicators supported an image of resistance. By 1973, this situation was reversed, with over two-thirds of all factors pointing to cumulating gains. And again after the North Vietnamese victory in 1975, almost two-thirds of all the elements supported images of further expansion. The evidence for 1974, however, illustrates a very important point. The fact that in that year neither theory received clear-cut support in Soviet writings demonstrates the extreme fragility of Soviet images of cumulating gains. The evidence further outlines the limited nature of such inferences as Soviet analysts did make.

Efforts by the South Vietnamese army in 1974 generated images of balancing among Soviet academics and journalists. After the fall of Saigon, Soviet inferences were bounded by the fact that they did not see dominoes falling in the region past Laos and Kampuchea, and saw China and Japan as important autonomous sources of balancing power.

Many Soviet analysts saw the signing of the Paris accords as proof of imperialism's inability to resist future progressive change in the periphery. For example, V. Pavlovskii wrote that "the victory of the Vietnamese people clearly says that one cannot conquer a people which is struggling for its freedom and independence and relying on the mighty support of the U.S.S.R. and other socialist countries and all the progressive forces of the world."[33]

But even this seemingly stark image of the unlikelihood of further resistance to Soviet expansion was subject to certain conditions, namely that it required the "mighty support" of the Soviet Union and Eastern bloc, plus diplomatic and domestic political pressure on the imperialist governments to give up the fight. If these were the conditions seen as necessary for Soviet expansionism to succeed, then such a combination of circumstances would still be relatively rare.

Perhaps the most frequently derived conclusion from this assessment of imperialism was that the United States would be willing in the future to negotiate on other areas of conflict in the world, most notably in the Middle East. In its lead editorial concerning the signing of the Paris accords, *Pravda* wrote that "the liquidation of one of the dangerous hotbeds of war is yet another striking confirmation of the fact that in international relations the aspiration to resolve arguable questions by peaceful means, by negotiations, is getting stronger."[34] This expectation was short-lived, however. Once Kissinger started his shuttle diplomacy in the Middle East, Soviet commentary all but dropped any mention of an increased American readiness to negotiate as a consequence of the Vietnam War.

One of the more prevalent indicators of falling dominoes cited by Soviet observers in this period was the idea that the Paris treaty and then the fall of Saigon both acted to inspire NLMs in Southeast Asia and around the world. But once again it is important to emphasize the limits of these inferences. After the signing of the Paris accords, Soviet analysts spoke only of the National Front for the Liberation of South Vietnam as being assured of ultimate victory. No allusion was made to possible subsequent victories by NLMs, even in Laos or Cambodia, let alone Thailand or farther afield.[35]

Even after the fall of Saigon, domino inferences were still limited, first just to Cambodia and then extending only to Laos.[36] Again, Soviet expectations went no farther than those countries already on the brink of collapse and those regimes that had already been written off by the American Congress and public.

With respect to NLMs elsewhere in the world, Soviet commentators used the same formulaic language they had used to describe the disposition of imperialism in the period. "The victory [of the South Vietnamese patriots] is convincing evidence of the invincibility of the NLM, on the side of which is the Soviet Union, other socialist countries, and all the progressive and peaceloving forces of the planet."[37] These are the same restrictive conditions Soviet analysts cited as necessary for an imperialist disposition to allow future Soviet expansionism in the Third World.

In addition to being limited to a narrow geographic scope and laden with conditions very difficult to meet, the increasingly militant NLMs in the region had to confront American military activities in the area. Soviet observers continued to see American military activities in and around Southeast Asia as evidence of the American elite's ability to realize its inherent disposition to resist in the area. Soviet analysts frequently cited a renewed and increased American military presence in Japan,[38] the transfer of American troops from South Vietnam to Thailand, the continued presence of the Seventh Fleet in the coastal waters of Asia[39] and the redeployment of American forces to South Korea[40] as demonstrative of American plans in the region.

Soviet observers also identified the autonomous balancing behavior of American allies in the area as another counter to the falling of dominoes in the region. They perceived both China and Japan as active partners of the United States in stemming the tide of progressive change in the region, with China balancing against the Soviet Union directly, and Japan providing military and economic aid to American clients in the region, particularly South Korea.[41]

The two most important factors that gave rise to an image of an America unable to respond to future Soviet adventurism were public and congressional opposition to any further involvement of the United States in such operations in the periphery. Domestic political unrest and congressional efforts to tie the hands of the administration in Southeast Asia were seen as effective constraints on the elite's disposition to continue the war in Vietnam and to maintain military support for the threatened regimes in Indochina. R. Vasiliev and I. Seregin noted that the

> stern reality of the Vietnam War promoted the growth of sentiments among wide circles of American society against the involvement of the United States in new military adventures abroad and in favor of a curtailment of the American "military presence" in other regions of the world . . . .
>
> The legislation of Congress and the public speeches of senators and representatives attest to the fact that in Congress, as in the entire country, feelings are strengthening in favor of the noninvolvement of the United States in new military conflicts abroad, in favor of a curtailment of American military obligations abroad and for an expansion of domestic socioeconomic programs. Congress passed a law ending the financing of military operations in Indochina by the United States. A law was passed which provides for limiting the power of the president in the use of American armed forces abroad.[42]

Soviets argued that Congress itself reflected the American public's growing opposition to the war and to its renewal, and that it was thus able to force the governmental elite to adopt policies contrary to its own preferences. Soviet analysts clearly believed that the desires of the American public and its representatives were an important condition to watch in gauging probable American responsiveness in the future to peripheral challenges.

Some Soviets initially identified lack of American economic wherewithal as one of reasons for the American decision to withdraw from Vietnam. These Soviets, however, did not subsequently pursue this line of argument. Commenting in *Izvestiya* one month after the conclusion of the Paris accords, V. Matveev wrote that the United States had been compelled to sue for peace once the myth of conducting a war at "little cost" had been dispelled.[43] But after 1974, economic costs no longer appeared in Soviet explanations of why the United States was forced to end the war. Perhaps they already realized that the revised American strategy, to avoid such costly protracted affairs and instead to rely on less expensive instruments such as regional military activities and the power of its clients and allies in the area, made economic considerations no longer relevant.

The most important boundary on inferences was the Soviets' consistent recognition that the American elite was disposed to continue resistance even after the Vietnam debacle. There were some, like V. Kobysh, who believed that

> the defeat in Indochina graphically demonstrated to the powers that be in America that military force is not almighty, that in the present-day world, detachments of marines and even rockets are not a decisive argument. An understanding of this by the sensibly thinking part of the ruling class logically leads them to the acceptance of the "categorical imperative" of detente.[44]

But the vast majority of Soviet analysts rejected the notion that the American elite was learning the true lessons of its defeat in Vietnam. More representative of Soviet views were the thoughts of L. Semeiko, then a senior researcher at the Institute of the U.S.A. and Canada. He argued that instead of coming to grips with changed reality, "there is resistance from highly influential circles in the West. American military theoreticians are searching for new forms and means for furthering the build-up of its military might and its use. However, we are not talking about radical changes."[45]

In sum, Soviet academics and journalists felt that the United States was not as credible after Vietnam, due to the evaporation of congressional and public support for future interventions of the same scale and cost as Vietnam. This erosion of credibility was limited, however, by the simultaneous recognition that elite dispositons to resist remained unchanged and that American military activities in the Far East and around the globe demonstrated significant capability to resist. Moreover, Soviet analysts again remarked on the balancing, not bandwagoning, behavior of American allies and clients in the region, namely China, Japan, Thailand, and South Korea. In addition, any domino inferences were limited only to Laos and Cambodia, and were not being ascribed to Thailand, let alone globally, as American foreign policymakers assumed.

Party Leadership Perceptions

The inferences made by the Soviet political leadership follow the same general trend as those made by academics and journalists.[46] After both the signing of the Paris peace accords and the fall of Saigon, Soviet leaders saw a significantly less resistant international environment. In 1974, however, just as in the case of academics and journalists, though to an even more dramatic degree, they rebounded to pre-1973 levels of pessimism about easy expansion. As in the 1969 to 1972 period, the Soviet political elite had a view quite different from Soviet academics and journalists about the degree of change in American credibility and what the consequences of Vietnam were for potential bandwagoning of American allies and falling dominoes in Southeast Asia.

The two most important elements of resistance that Soviet leaders continued to see in the period were the balancing behavior of America's regional clients and American military activities in the area. In the speeches for this period, it is quite striking how long it took Soviet leaders to become convinced that the United States was really going to leave South Vietnam, that it was not going to reintroduce either ground or air forces, and that the Vietcong were going to drive the Thieu government out of the country.

For example, in a speech during his visit to India in November 1973, Brezhnev argued that there were still foreign forces "interfering in the internal affairs of the peoples of Indochina."[47] Much more prevalent than beliefs that the United States was not through in Vietnam were perceptions that the South Vietnamese government was acting, either autonomously or in collusion with the Americans, to thwart the aims of the Paris accord. Podgorny argued, for example, that "the Saigon regime, with the support of the imperialist powers, is sabotaging the Paris accords and preventing the establishment of a stable peace in this region."[48] In fact these concerns that the war was not ending in Vietnam continued almost until the fall of Saigon itself.[49]

As before, the Soviet leadership did not pay attention to the two elements of American resolve that were accorded the greatest importance by journalists and academics, namely, congressional and public opposition to the war. Moreover, mention of elite dispositions were also largely absent from leadership explanations for the outcome in Vietnam.

There were two kinds of gains Soviet leaders saw as deriving from the American defeat in Vietnam. The first, and most frequently cited, was the perception that the war's end would be a great spur to detente in Southeast Asia, Asia as a whole, and the world in general. The second, and far less prevalent belief, was that the Vietnamese victory would inspire other liberation movements around the world in their struggles.

The most frequent inference made by Soviet leaders in this period was that the end of American aggression in Vietnam signified a new era of negotiations on a global scale. In fact, the top three Soviet leaders, Brezhnev, Kosygin, and Podgorny, along with Gromyko, included the advancement of detente in every one of their inferences about cumulating gains ensuing from the end of the war. They only differed on how broad a swath detente was going to cut in the world.

In his June 1974 election speech, Kosygin asserted that "as a result of the end of aggression in Indochina . . . there is a turn from war to peace, toward a general improvement of the situation in Southeast Asia."[50] In an election speech the following year Podgorny stated that "the liquidation of the military hotbed in Vietnam has led to an enormous step in the direction of detente in Asia."[51] Brezhnev linked detente to "the creation of conditions for the further improvement of the international atmosphere."[52] Gromyko further linked the outcome in Vietnam to the situation in Europe, arguing that "the reestablishment of peace in Vietnam released additional energies for the further advancement of detente, including in Europe."[53] Both Gromyko and Brutents made direct inferences from Vietnam to the enhancement of prospects for a negotiated solution in the Middle East.

Brutents, in a long article on detente and the national liberation movement, wrote:

> It's well-known that the end of the Vietnam War removed a most serious obstacle to the broadening of detente . . . . It is not at all accidental that now, when the flames of the Vietnam War have been extinguished, . . . pressure in the world is increasing in favor of a just [Middle East] solution, and the isolation of the ruling circles of Israel is getting deeper and deeper.[54]

In the same speech in Paris in which Gromyko concluded that the global national liberation movement had been inspired by the Vietnamese victory, he also remarked that "as a result of the agreement, new opportunities are created for the deepening of detente." He then immediately turned to the Middle East, suggesting that "the settlement and reestablishment of peace in the Middle East can be achieved [on the same bases] as in Vietnam."[55]

Typical of the less prevalent set of encouraging lessons from Vietnam were statements like that of Brezhnev during the official celebrations commemorating the thirtieth anniversary of the end of World War II: "It is time to recognize a simple truth: in our time, attempts to suppress the liberation movement are doomed to failure. And the best evidence of that is the victory of the Vietnamese people."[56]

While the Soviet leadership drew conclusions from the victory in Vietnam concerning the potential future gains for liberation movements around the world and about how the road was now being cleared for deeper and broader detente, in fully one-third of their speeches that touched on the Vietnam War, they failed to draw any conclusions whatsoever about the effects of this victory on the international environment. This occurred in a variety of contexts. In some of these one would not expect them to have expressed any such conclusions, as, for example, in Brezhnev's television address to the American people in June 1973.[57] But this is a rare context indeed for Soviet leaders to make such kinds of public statements. Most telling are the cases in which their audiences were radical Third World allies or organizations, such as Brezhnev's speech in Cuba before Castro and his official message to an Afro-Asian People's Solidarity Organization (AAPSO) conference,[58] Kosygin's speech before Kaddafi in Libya,[59] Podgorny's addresses before the Afghani Prime Minister Daoud and President Barre in Somalia[60] and Ponomarev's keynote address on the occasion of Lenin's one hundred fourth birthday.[61] Most revealing, of course, would be a failure to mention any cumulating gains from Vietnam before a Vietnamese audience, which is exactly what occurred when Brezhnev greeted the Society of Vietnamese-Soviet Friendship in Hanoi on the occasion of its twenty-fifth anniversary.[62]

This serves to illustrate the crucial point that the Vietnam War, no matter what inferences the Soviets derived from its outcome, was of second-order importance when the Soviet leadership characterized the nature of the international system. Throughout the period after the American withdrawal from Vietnam, the Soviet political elite's foreign policy attention was focused on arms control with the United States, political and military detente in Europe, the emergent Chinese threat, and to a lesser degree, the Middle East. For example, from 1973 to 1975 Brezhnev made forty-one speeches in which he spoke at some length on foreign policy issues. Of these, in only eight did he make inferences from the Vietnam War, while in all of them the above list of issues was always present—even when addressing exclusively Third World audiences.

This helps to explain in part why the most dominant inference Soviet leaders made after Vietnam was not about falling regional dominoes or bandwagoning American allies, but about the prospects of detente with the United States and Western Europe, and negotiated settlements in "hotbeds of tension."

The Return Toward an Image of Pure Resistance: Angola, 1975–1976

Throughout 1975 a civil war raged in Angola. The Soviet Union provided military supplies to one faction in the conflict, the Popular Movement for the Liberation of Angola (MPLA), and to Cuban troops fighting alongside this group. The United States provided covert military assistance to the two other factions competing with the MPLA for power, the National Union for the Total Independence of Angola (UNITA) and the National Front for the Liberation of Angola (FNLA). By March 1976, after Congress had passed the Clark Amendment ending all American aid to the FNLA and UNITA, the MPLA established itself in Luanda as the legally recognized government of the People's Republic of Angola.

Deterrence theory would predict that Soviets should learn from this American failure that the United States is both unwilling and unable to resist Soviet efforts to promote revolutionary change in the periphery. Soviet observers should expect American strategic allies to question the vitality of American security guarantees and that other countries in the region, such as Zimbabwe, Namibia, and South Africa, had become ripe for liberation movement victories of their own.

Balancing theory, on the contrary, would predict Soviet images of an America resolved and capable of preventing any future revolutionary change in the Third World. Soviet observers would see both global allies and regional actors making efforts to balance against the ascendant threat created by this latest Soviet victory.

Soviet perceptions of the consequences of the MPLA victory in Angola completely contradict the predictions of deterrence theory.[63] Soviet observers saw an American government both willing and able to resist future revolutionary change in the Third World. Indeed, the United States had developed a new diplomatic instrument to prevent future liberation movement victories. The situational constraints identified by some Soviets as hindering the American ruling elite's ability to advance its preferences had been overcome or qualitatively changed. Soviet observers also saw regional actors, South Africa and Rhodesia, in particular, as powerful opponents of any future Soviet gains in the region.

General Perceptions

The abortive efforts of the United States to intervene covertly in the Angolan civil war caused a reversal in Soviet perceptions of American and allied capabilities. Virtually all the variables Soviet analysts had previously identified as partially constraining a resolute elite shifted toward predictions of future resistance. That this dramatic turnabout occurred in the face of what had been widely recognized by the American public and policy community as an American defeat only reinforces just how fragile the Soviet images of a world of cumulating gains are, and how strong the Soviet inclination toward images of a resistant world.

As a consequence of Vietnam, some Soviet analysts had perceived imperialism as disposed to allow Soviet gains to go unchallenged. As a consequence of events in Angola, these were replaced by perceptions that ascribed to imperialism both the will and cability to resist such expansion, that is, American credibility was high. As L. Tamarin describes it: "Events of recent years show that imperialism is in no way prepared to resign itself to the loss of its positions in countries which, not so long ago, were colonies or semi-colonies, and will do everything possible to prevent their development along the path of independence and progress."[64]

Soviet observers were unanimous in seeing the American governmental elite as disposed to resist. Gennady Trofimenko, in a lengthy piece devoted to an analysis of American foreign policy in the 1970s, concluded that

> much of the so-called re-examination of [military] obligations has not meant a disavowal of hegemonic schemes and plans, but rather the advancement of only more camouflaged, more sly schemes, called on to prolong the life in the international arena of the same American policy of "positions of strength."
>
> The practice of American foreign policy in the first half of the 1970s shows that there were very few cases when the United States in fact—and voluntarily, rather than under compulsion—manifested restraint, when their conduct in approaching regional crises in any important way differed from their approaches in the previous decade.[65]

After Vietnam, many Soviet observers predicted that this American loss meant that the United States would now be willing to reach diplomatic settlements in other regional conflicts, especially in the Middle East. After the American loss in Angola, however, these same Soviet observers identified diplomacy as one of the new instruments adopted by the United States to stave off future "Angolas" in the region. Indeed, it is most revealing that several Soviet analysts compared American efforts to gain unilateral advantage for the United States by managing the peace process between the Arabs and Israel, with similar efforts with respect to southern Africa aimed at thwarting the natural forces of violent revolution in Zimbabwe, Namibia, and South Africa.[66] M. Vishnevskii, for example, argued that the victory in Angola had "demonstrated the resolve of Africans to liquidate the racist regimes" in South Africa and Rhodesia as well. But, he wrote, the American government also realized this and had sent Secretary of State Kissinger to southern Africa to "seize the initiative from the socialist community by suggesting American mediation of the situation in southern Africa." While Kissinger supported majority rule in Zimbabwe, he advocated this be done "only by peaceful means." Most discouraging of all to Vishnevskii, however, "the leaders of the countries which Kissinger visited [undeniably] approved of his program for solving the 'Rhodesian problem.' "[67]

Clearly the Soviets were concerned that Kissinger's efforts would render Soviet military aid irrelevant to the liberation struggle that they expected in southern Africa as a consequence of the events in Angola. References to such "inspired regional NLMs" accounted for almost one half of all Soviet inferences of cumulating gains recorded for this period. Hence the great chagrin with which Soviet analysts watched the Americans effectively counter this opportunity. This struggle between American diplomacy and liberation forces in southern Africa was accorded great importance by Soviet analysts, attested to by the fact that more than a quarter of the selections coded "Indecision" in this period concerned just this conflict.

Also frequently noted as an indicator of American capability for this period were the regional military activities of the United States in Angola, namely the provision of covert support to the FNLA and UNITA. Only public opinion and congressional pressure prevented the American government from realizing its preference of continuing this aid. As Arkady Butlitskii put it,

> the government of the United States had to take into account the sentiments which predominated in the halls of the Capitol, especially with respect to the defeat of American imperialism in Vietnam. The Senate and House, despite the efforts of the White House and State Department, decisively rejected appropriations for the Angola adventure.[68]

While Soviet analysts were ascribing a primary role to American public opinion for thwarting the plans of the American government, they also recognized for the first time that there was domestic political support within the United States for efforts to counter Soviet expansion. This marks a very important turning point in Soviet perceptions as one of the most important constraints on the American government's policies of resistance began to erode, thus enhancing American credibility still more.

Georgii Arbatov, in commenting on the consequences of the 1976 presidential campaign for Soviet-American relations, reported that,

> American observers are indicating certain shifts in the sentiments of the American people which have occurred over the past year. In one of the surveys, conducted in September by the Public Agenda Foundation, it was noted in particular that, although the public is for the continuation of detente, distrust in the Soviet Union and also support for an American military build-up guaranteeing American military superiority has increased among some.[69]

He noted that detente as a policy was largely left undefended by both candidates in the election, so hard-liners such as Ronald Reagan were able to cultivate anti-Soviet feelings among the electorate without any counterattacks from defenders of detente. Soviet observers could no longer be so sanguine that the American public would impede an administration's efforts at countering Soviet adventures.

Two external balancing factors contributed to the Soviet images of a resistant world in this period. First, global allied opposition to American efforts at such resistance disappeared completely. Indeed, opposition was even replaced by some open support. Soviet commentators did not report any NATO opposition to the Angola operation, while they repeatedly mentioned the alliance of Beijing with Washington as evidence that China had chosen for itself a new global role to advance the interests of American imperialism.[70] Soviet observers exaggerated the Chinese role in Angola considerably, as well as Chinese coordination with Washington, but the fact remains that they saw Chinese aid to the FNLA as an additional factor balancing against the Soviet Union in the periphery.

Soviet observers ascribed an enormously important balancing role to South Africa. Pretoria's own efforts to counter the MPLA in the civil war and to deal with the deleterious effects of having lost the Portuguese colonial buffer helped dash Soviet hopes for the armed liberation of the rest of southern Africa.

Soviet analysts recognized that both Pretoria and Salisbury were intent on resisting their own NLMs. As the editors of *Pravda* wrote in December 1975, "The last racist bastions of Rhodesia and South Africa are undertaking desperate efforts to withstand the wave of the NLM and to preserve their domination."[71] South Africa and Rhodesia were a threat to the Southwest African Peoples' Organization (SWAPO) in Namibia, the African National Congress (ANC) in South Africa, and the Patriotic Front in Zimbabwe and also conducted aggression against the newly decolonized states of Mozambique and Angola.[72]

Perhaps the most compelling examples of the Soviet return to an image of resistance were the writings of Zhurkin and Arbatov. Both described in detail how the American elite was able to design around any remaining weak constraints against pursuing their own preferences to resist. Zhurkin, writing in the last months of 1976, noted that American foreign policy had still to cope with the legacy of Vietnam by "avoid[ing] directly involving itself in those international conflicts which threaten long, direct involvement of American armed forces. The Unites States . . . prefers to replace military operations . . . with political, diplomatic, and other measures of interference" to advance its interests. While the "logical conclusion from the 'post-Vietnam syndrome' should have been the complete disavowal of the policy of force in international conflicts," the American elite refused to learn these lessons. In the case of Angola, wrote Zhurkin, only Congress prevented American involvement in another "intervention of the Vietnam type." But there remain "extremely persistent efforts in the leading circles of the United States to . . . leave loopholes for the possible application of force in that or another concrete situation. Indeed, the interference of Washington in Angola attested, in the final analysis, to stubborn attempts to thwart the action of the 'post-Vietnam syndrome.' " The only type of intervention forsworn by the American government was "the nonrational massive interference of

American armed forces in an international conflict which can lead to 'new Vietnams.' "

Zhurkin saw American diplomacy as a "preventive policy" to be "called into play before the beginning of conflicts to secure their development in directions favorable to the United States." Such measures included American covert actions (such as in Angola and Chile), increased arms sales to the Middle East, and finally "so-called shuttle diplomacy," citing the September 1975 Sinai II disengagement accord and Kissinger's negotiations in southern Africa in the summer of 1976. These were aimed at preserving Western positions in the region and "weakening the mighty wave of the NLM in southern Africa."[73]

Arbatov had written in July 1973 that, as a consequence of Vietnam, American decision makers were convinced of the futility of intervening in such conflicts against NLMs.[74] But three years later he had entirely reversed course: "Failures in American foreign policy, in particular in Southeast Asia, are causing clear relapses of thinking into categories of the 'cold war' among some American officials. Certain circles . . . again are beginning to speak of the need for the United States to assume responsibility for the 'maintenance of order in the world' by 'containing' the Soviet Union." Moreover, "judging by the reaction of the United States to the events in Angola, American policy in no way can get out of the well-trodden anti-Communist rut."[75] Arbatov also identified as crucial the shift in American public opinion toward a hard line against Soviet adventurism.

Party Leadership Perceptions

The Soviet leadership also saw a credible America, expected no falling dominoes in southern Africa and foresaw balancing against, not bandwagoning with Soviet power, by American allies. As in previous years, Soviet leaders paid no attention to the congressional and public components of American resolve. In their comments on the international situation, even more so than in the case of the Vietnam War, they paid little attention to the Angolan events in general. In fact, of the sixty-nine speeches surveyed for this period, in only fourteen of them was Angola even mentioned, and five of those times no inference at all was made. Unlike the case of Vietnam, no Soviet leaders asserted that the victory of the MPLA was an inspiration for liberation movements on a global scale.

Soviet elite views conformed to the overall picture presented above, with the exception of attention to Congress and public opinion. At the Conference of Communist and Workers' Parties held in East Berlin in June 1976, Brezhnev commented on NATO's contribution to American efforts in Africa:

> Our common class enemy—the international bourgeoisie—shows more than a few examples of coordinated international activities in the fight against revolutionary forces. Where an exploitative system is threatened and where the forces of national and social liberation are gaining ascendancy, imperialism . . . coordinates its counterattacks, of which there are examples . . . both in Europe [Portugal] and in Africa.[76]

Gromyko spoke in the United Nations about how the further unfolding of the liberation process in southern Africa was being hindered.

> The rulers of the RSA and Rhodesia and those who support and arm them now act as though they will reckon with the inevitability of the process of national liberation and are trying to bring it about. But in reality, as before, they are doing everything to restrain the struggle of the peoples of Zimbabwe, Namibia, and RSA. They use any means, from direct pressure to political tricks and economic bribes, to derail the NLM from true independence and freedom.[77]

Brezhnev expressed the heart of the matter when he complained at a dinner with Agostinho Neto that:

> Now, when Africa has shown that it can deal by itself with the vestiges of colonialism and racism, some people, under the flag of aiding this process, have begun to try to replace the true liberation of southern Africa with a fiction—essentially to preserve the positions of imperialism and to maintain . . . the RSA.[78]

Soviet leaders also failed to draw any conclusions from the events in Angola in front of audiences before which one would expect them to have been most eager to express such beliefs. These included Gromyko's address at the UN General Assembly session in September 1975, Brezhnev's greetings to the meeting of the Non-Aligned Conference in Sri Lanka in August 1976 and his message to the AAPSO Conference a year earlier, and Podgorny's speech at a breakfast for the Congo's president, Marien Ngouabi.[79] Most revealing is the fact that Kosygin, at a dinner for the Angolan prime minister, Lopo do Nascimiento, did not make any mention of the influence of the MPLA's victory on events either in southern Africa or on the international scene.[80]

An Image of Pure Resistance: The African Horn, 1977–1978

In November 1977, the Soviet Union airlifted Cuban troops and Soviet matériel to Ethiopia to help drive Somali armed forces from Ethiopian territory. The Soviets took this action despite an American warning to the Soviet leadership that it would undermine detente between the two countries. By March 1978, Cuban and Ethiopian forces had driven the Somali invaders out of the Ogaden and back into Somali territory.

As in the cases of the American withdrawal from Vietnam, the fall of Saigon, and the MPLA victory in Angola, deterrence theory would predict that the Soviets would learn from their successful intervention in the Horn of Africa that the United States was irresolute and incapable of resisting Soviet adventurism abroad. They should also expect that American strategic allies would question American security guarantees and that other states in the region, such as Kenya and the Sudan, would be ripe for revolutionary eruptions. Deterrence theory assumptions should be especially clearly borne out here because this was the third consecutive defeat for American foreign policy in the periphery in the 1970s.

Balancing theory would predict Soviet images of a highly credible America, with its allies helping it balance against the enhanced Soviet threat. The Soviets should also see regional actors increasing their resistance to revolutionary movements in the area.

The evidence in this period clearly provides solid support for the balancing alternative and contradicts the predictions of deterrence theory. After Angola, Soviet observers had begun to return to their pre-1973 images of a resistant world. In 1977 to 1978, they saw a world of nothing but resistance.[81] All sixty-three coded inferences indicated such behavior. Such an undiluted image is striking in itself, but what is even more impressive is that these perceptions were being generated during a time that many American analysts consider to be one of American retreats and aggressive Soviet adventurism. In fact, it turns out that American, Western, and regional responses to the war on the Horn and the two Shaba[82] incursions very effectively demonstrated to Soviet observers both high American credibility and the balancing propensities by American allies and clients.

General Perceptions

Expectations that the Carter administration would resist Soviet efforts to gain influence in the periphery were reflected in the analysis of P. T. Podlesnyi:

> It is becoming increasingly obvious that Washington is taking the course, to use the words of official representatives of the administration, of making a "decisive challenge" to the Soviet Union in the regions of the world which have "decisive significance for the United States now or can have such significance in 15–20 years." American efforts to resist the Soviet Union in developing countries has been invigorated. This is most graphically manifested in American policy in the Middle East and Africa, which is aimed at weakening the positions and influence of the Soviet Union, to incline the countries and NLMs of these regions toward the West, and to not allow the development of a political situation in these regions in a direction that would be contrary to the interests of American imperialism.[83]

Moreover, the American elite was no longer impeded from realizing its ambitions by congressional and domestic pressure. The absence of these necessary conditions for American restraint would be evidence enough for Soviet inferences of high American credibility, but Soviet analysts went even farther and acknowledged that both the American public and Congress were urging the government to resist further Soviet expansion. Soviet analysts now believed the American elite to be on the defensive against anti-Sovietism arising from society, where previously, the masses were seen as restraining the elite's inherent hard-line tendencies. Iu. A. Ivanov describes how

> members of Congress are subject to a greater degree [than the president and government] to the tangible pressure of the dominant ideology of anti-Communism. For they depend on re-election in their congressional district or state, where the decisive role can be played by conservative businessmen or simply

rich and influential adherents of primitive anti-Communism from the extreme Right of the political spectrum.[84]

Whereas before, American leaders at least had to appear to reflect popular sentiments in favor of restraint, Soviets saw these very same representatives as compelled to take a hard line to gain votes in the upcoming midtern elections. Vasiliev wrote:

> Recent polls show that the president's personal popularity has fallen to its lowest level. In these conditions, experts [here in Washington] explain as political devices the administration's and Democrats' efforts to raise their stock by bowing to conservative elements and by manifesting "a hard line in foreign policy." It is no secret that anticommunist and chauvinistic sentiments sit deeply within the consciousnesses of many Americans and that "demonstrations of muscles" are an old and tested device for winning votes.[85]

Soviet observers continued to believe that the American diplomatic instrument employed after events in Angola posed obstacles to the falling dominoes of national liberation revolutions there. In this period, however, Soviet analysts did not even see any inspired NLMs as a consequence of Soviet actions on the Horn. For the first time, Soviets saw NLMs as being completely on the defensive against the imperialists and their regional clients and allies.

M. L. Vishnevskii (sounding like his colleagues in the post-Angola period) emphasized that the Western plan for Zimbabwe, while calling for majority rule, did so "only by peaceful means." Soviet analysts had evaluated Kissinger's policy in post-Angola Africa as an attempt to preserve the status quo in southern Africa, or to manage the change occurring there in such a way as to protect Western interests. But Carter's policy was seen by Vishnevskii as aimed at rolling back Soviet gains in the area by "developing contacts with African countries of socialist orientation [in this region, Angola and Mozambique], which would be the best solution to the problem of eliminating communist influence in Africa. According to [Cyrus] Vance [in a July 1977 speech before the NAACP], the development of all possible contacts with these countries must lead to the transformation of their foreign policy orientation."

Vishnevskii described how the United States and the Western Contact Group[86] were also trying to dissuade SWAPO from effecting violent soical revolution in Namibia. While the Soviets overestimated Carter's ability to develop contacts with Angola and Mozambique, it illustrates how they perceived a change in the terms of engagement in the region. Not only was the United States successfully averting violent revolutions, which would have played to the Soviet strong suit of arms transfers, but it also threatened the gains already made in Angola.[87]

One way the United States displayed its intent to resist after the Soviet intervention in the Horn was to begin to establish a military relationship with Somalia. Soviet observers noted the negotiations with President Siad Barre throughout the first half of 1978 and remarked upon the potential threat to Ethiopia of an American naval presence in Somalia.[88]

Beyond the actions undertaken by the United States itself which so strongly affected Soviet perceptions of American credibility, the United States also enjoyed the benefits of the autonomous balancing efforts of its regional clients, allies, and members of NATO. Soviet observers identified the Sudan, Egypt, and after November 1977, Somalia itself, as hostile regional actors operating in the interests of imperialism. They saw the Sudan as providing arms and sanctuary to the Eritrean separatists in northern Ethiopia and staging armed provocations across its border with Ethiopia. Egypt supplied American arms to Somalia. Once Somalia abrogated its Treaty of Friendship and Cooperation with the Soviet Union, the latter saw it as a client of the United States and of reactionary Arab regimes in the Gulf and Africa. Soviets described Somalia as performing its patrons' bidding in the effort to roll back the progressive gains made in Ethiopia.[89]

In 1978 Soviets saw a wider array of instruments reinforcing America's capabilities. Besides paying heed to the actions of regional actors on the Horn, they paid enormous attention to the actions of the United States and its allies in response to the Shaba insurgency in Zaire. Soviet analysts were impressed that the Carter administration did not experience any public or congressional resistance to its participation in the airlift of troops and matériel to Zaire, and in fact received support from both these quarters. In addition, Soviets noted how quickly and effectively France and Belgium responded to Mobutu's requests for military assistance and how closely Washington and its European allies cooperated in this endeavor to quash a threat to a mutual client.

Soviet observers identified the participation of the imperialists' regional clients in this mission as an additional element of resistance to progressive change in Africa. In particular, the use of Moroccan ground troops and Egyptian pilots were evaluated as the beginnings of an intra-African interventionist force, which could be used by the United States and its allies to protect clients and even to launch counteroffensives against the positions of African progressive states.[90]

Party Leadership Perceptions

The Soviet political elite in this period did not remark on a single instance of gains cumulating from Ethiopia's victory on the Horn. Here, again, they saw an America highly resolved and capable of resisting future Soviet expansion, and American allies and clients intent on balancing against, rather than bandwagoning with, progressive change.

Two speeches in this period demonstrate the power of these images of resistance. Both were delivered at dinners honoring Ethiopia's Mengistu in Moscow, that is, before an audience where one would expect the most optimistic assessments of the contributions of Ethiopia's progressive development to the world revolutionary movement. Instead, both Podgorny and Brezhnev dwelt on imperialism's threat to such gains, rejecting the more delicate route of simply not drawing any conclusions. Podgorny, in May 1977, declared:

> In its efforts to restrain the progressive development of Ethiopia, the domestic counterrevolution appeals for the support of certain imperialist and other reactionary forces which do not like the strengthening of the NLM and their socio-

> economic progress. Here, as everywhere, these forces employ the old arsenal: inciting national hostility, provocations and blackmail, and setting countries and peoples against each other.
>
> Recent events attest that the imperialists, using certain Arab countries, first of all Saudi Arabia, are trying to establish their control in the Red Sea region . . . . They are trying to create some kind of closed military-political bloc in the region and holding naval excercises off Ethiopian shores. It is not hard to see that the real aim of the organizers is to fight against countries which have chosen the progressive path of development, to fractionate and weaken them and make short work of each of them in turn.[91]

Podgorny then turned to the collective efforts of imperialism in Zaire, showing that he did not concur with Mengistu's assertions that the events on the Horn had proven the inherent weakness of imperialism.

Sixteen months later, Brezhnev also remarked how the imperialists used these territorial conflicts "for their own ends, pitting African countries against each other." And the imperialists, he said, continue to use the tension maintained on the Horn in their own interests. He denounced the Western initiative on Zimbabwe independence as a sham, saying that these Western efforts were "reduced to preserving the previous essence of the racist regimes, but only behind new signs."[92]

Soviet leaders saw two other consequences of events on the Horn, neither of which had been mentioned before. In an interview while in New York for a special UN session on disarmament, Gromyko attacked the United States for using events on the Horn as a pretext for increasing its military budget and "whipping up the arms race." While of course Gromyko saw the American response as illegitimate, he still recognized it as a real consequence of the intervention on the Horn.[93] Brezhnev, meanwhile, saw the United States using the Horn as a pretext for undermining detente in general. Whereas Soviet leaders had seen the end of the Vietnam War as a spur to the deepening and broadening of detente, these Soviet leaders now recognized that the successful defense of the Ethiopian government by Cuban forces was deleterious to the cause of detente, especially to arms control. Of course Brezhnev argued this was a spurious connection created by the Americans to conceal their true motives.[94]

Soviet Perceptions: An Inclination to See a Balancing World

This study demonstrates that Soviet observers—academics, journalists, and party leaders alike—do not draw the kind of inferences predicted by deterrence theorists and assumed by American policymakers who believe in the "lessons of Munich," the bandwagoning of allies and the falling of dominoes. Such Soviet inferences were limited after American defeats by a number of factors. Even at the height of cumulating gains, after the Paris accords and the fall of Saigon, Soviets never doubted American elite resolve to resist. Instead, they attributed the American defeat to transitory public and congressional constraints on the government that compelled it to withdraw. By 1975 to 1976, these restraints were being eroded, and by 1977 to 1978, they were replaced by public and congressional support for the elite's preference to resist Soviet adventurism in the periphery.

The Soviets saw the United States as having powerful capabilities at its disposal, even when it was operating under congressional and public pressure. The Soviets viewed the American use of diplomacy to change the rules of the game in such a way as to render Soviet military involvement irrelevant, as an effective weapon against any NLM that had drawn strength from a nearby NLM victory. The other important capability used effectively by the United States was its military presence abroad, including its forces at sea, its air and ground bases around the globe, and arms transfers to allies and clients.

The Soviet image of a balancing world was further strengthened by its view of regional reactions to the victories of its allies. Again and again Soviet observers noted how such gains evoked balancing behavior by American allies and clients in the region—Thailand in Southeast Asia, the RSA in southern Africa, the Sudan on the Horn. These autonomous balancing dynamics only further reinforced the already strong Soviet images of a world that countered their gains.

Other contributors to the Soviet image or resistance were the balancing efforts of China, Japan, and several NATO allies. China's involvement with the FNLA in Angola, Japan's economic aid to South Korea, France and Belgium's intervention in Zaire, and Britain's engagement in Zimbabwe all helped convince the Soviets that America's strategic allies would respond with balancing efforts in the face of threats to their shared interests in the Third World.

There is one image of cumulating gains that did persist throughout the period. This was the belief that neither the American people, Congress, nor the American ruling elite would ever consciously choose to repeat an intervention on the same scale as Vietnam. Soviet observers clearly assumed that the United States had neither the resolve nor the capability to repeat such an adventure. This helps to explain why Soviet writers analyzed so closely the American efforts to design around this one enormous constraint.

It should not be surprising that the Soviets' only stable and unconditional attribution about American capabilities derived from the Vietnam War. As Fritz Heider demonstrated some thirty years ago, inferences about another's inability to perform a task are not likely to be made unless the observer sees great effort followed by failure.[95] It was the fact that the United States spent $150 billion and suffered 60,000 dead in a losing cause that allowed the Soviets to infer what images of weakness they did.

The Soviet images of low American credibility turned out be extremely ephemeral, soon to be replaced with very robust perceptions of both high resolve and strong capabilities. This phenomenon also has a basis in attribution theory. First, it has been found that there is an enormous bias to ascribe negative traits to another's neutral behavior.[96] Thus Soviet leaders, or American leaders for that matter, often perceive the most hostile intent behind even innocuous actions by the other.

Moreover, desirable traits (in this case, Soviet images of an international environment characterized by cumulating gains) are difficult to acquire and easy to lose. Likewise, unfavorable ones (like American power and a willingness to use it) are easy to acquire and difficult to lose. Far more behavioral instances are required to infer favorable attributes about another than unfavorable ones. Hence, one should expect that a lengthy string of American defeats or nonresponses would be necessary to produce an impression of American weakness on the Soviet leadership. Furthermore, it is much easier for people to imagine disconfirming behavior for favorable traits than for unfavorable ones. This implies that Soviet decision makers are very receptive to information that disproves notions of American restraint, while maintaining a skeptical attitude toward evidence in favor of such notions.[97]

Soviet perceptions over this ten-year period strongly confirm these findings of attribution theory. That images of cumulating gains are hard to generate is demonstrated by the limited nature of Soviet inferences from the American failure in Vietnam. That they are easy to lose is confirmed by the fact that another American failure, in Angola, resulted in a return toward perceptions of resistance. That an image of resistance is easy to establish is shown by both the case of Angola and the extremely powerful inferences drawn from the Shaba events—the latter being a contributor to indicators of a resistant world that was quite unexpected by American observers.

In terms of prescriptive theory, those who believe in dominoes, deterrence theory, and bandwagoning argue that the United States must respond to peripheral challenges in order to generate a reputation for resistance. This study finds, however, that such actions on the part of the United States are not necessary for Soviet observers to maintain images of a resistant world. Thus, the United States need not intervene in the periphery based on the fear of creating images of low American credibility, falling dominoes, and bandwagoning allies in the minds of Soviet decision makers.

Several additional conditions, however, if present, might require the United States to intervene in the periphery.[98] If the Soviet Union would infer from American defeats in the periphery that the United States will not defend the status quo in strategic areas, then the United States should intervene in the periphery. If American allies and clients would lose confidence in American security guarantees as a consequence of such defeats, then the United States should intervene.[99] If the Soviet Union demonstrates the ability to convert peripheral gains into strategic ones, then the United States should intervene. If Soviet allies and clients will become emboldened as a result of American failures in the periphery, then the United States should intervene if any one of the above conditions is true.

However, this study suggests that these additional conditions are also not likely to prevail after American defeats as perceived by the Soviets. First, there were absolutely no cases of Soviets making the inferential leap from peripheral to strategic areas. Second, the Soviets consistently saw America's regional and global allies and its clients increase their commitments and energies to resist further Soviet expansion after a Soviet victory. The Soviets did not predict accommodative stances on the part of American friends. While the Soviets did believe their foreign allies and clients had become inspired by Soviet victories, they also recognized that a wide range of obstacles simultaneously were being erected in their path.

Finally, are Soviet images of cumulating gains necessary or sufficient conditions for a Soviet decision to intervene in the periphery? In the case of Angola, it is reasonable to argue that the Soviet image of the United States was a necessary condition for the Soviet Union to decide to commit itself to the MPLA. But it can hardly be called a sufficient condition, given the numerous other factors that permitted and encouraged the Soviets to act as they did, including the lack of any definable status quo in Angola itself, the Soviets' long historical relationship with the MPLA, the perceived Chinese competition; parallel Cuban interests, cooperation of the Portuguese governor-general in Angola, the "absolution" of South African intervention on the other side, support by the Organization for African Unity, and Soviet air and sealift capabilities.

More troubling is the fact that the Soviet Union chose to intervene on the Horn even when it expected a resistant world. An image of resistance is thus neither necessary nor sufficient to deter the Soviet Union from peripheral adventurism, but may in fact be simply irrelevant. This finding parallels the conclusions of Richard Ned Lebow, that states often challenge deterrent positions even if all the indicators point to a guaranteed response by the defender.[100] In the case of the Horn, the Soviets' loss of their position in Egypt, the threat to their position in Somalia due to Saudi efforts directed at the subornation of Barre, and the rapid closing of windows of opportunity previously thought available in southern Africa might have impelled the Soviets to opt for adventure even in the face of acknowledged resistance.

Notes

The author would like to express his gratitude for the helpful comments of Jack Snyder, Rick Herrmann, Doug Blum, Robert Jervis, and Chaim Kaufman. Teresa Johnson deserves special thanks for her acute editorial eye.

1. I use "strategic" to refer to the material value to either power of that land, its population, natural resources, and industry. The United States has a strategic interest in a territory insofar as its loss to the Soviet Union would increase Soviet military power potential to such a degree as to greatly threaten American physical or economic welfare. Hence, for the United States, only Western Europe, the oil-producing regions of the Middle East, Japan, and perhaps, China fit this description. For the Soviet Union, only Eastern Europe and perhaps China are appropriately termed strategic interests. Areas contiguous to one or the other power have no inherent military power potential, but can be converted into such a potential if the other power so chooses and gets away with it. For example, Castro's overthrow of Batista in 1959 was not a strategic loss to the United States, but if Khrushchev had been successful in deploying IRBMs there in 1962 and if the Soviet Union had not agreed to renounce the use of Cuba as a strategic base, Cuba would have been a strategic loss. Hence, it was inappropriate for the Soviet Union in the

case of Afghanistan or the United States in the case of Nicaragua, to assert they were facing strategic losses—unless the United States and the Soviet Union choose to make those respective areas into one of strategic value. Neither has had a realistic notion of achieving such a goal.

2. Lyndon Baines Johnson, *The Vantage Point* (New York: Holt, Rinehart and Winston, 1971), 147–48.

3. "Angola," *Hearings Before the Subcommittee on African Affairs of the Senate Foreign Relations Committee,* 94th Congress, second session, January 29, 1976, 15.

4. *New York Times,* Apr. 15, 1986.

5. I define credibility in the conventional sense as a combination of relevant military capabilities and the demonstrated resolve to use them.

6. See Schelling, *Arms and Influence,* (New Haven, Conn.: Yale University Press, 1966); and Snyder, *Deterrence and Defense* (Princeton, N.J.: Princeton University Press, 1961). Snyder also identifies what he calls "political interests," that is, the American interest, in this case, in maintaining its allies' and clients' confidence in American resolve to defend them. Here I am concerned with Soviet perceptions of American allies' propensities to bandwagon, not the factual issue of whether or not allies are so inclined. Stephen Walt, "Alliance Formation and the Balance of World Power," *International Security* 94:4 (Spring 1985): 3–43, demonstrates that there is an overwhelming propensity to balance among such allies. See also his chapter (chap. 3) in this volume.

7. Thanks to Robert Jervis for bringing the doubtfulness of even this case to my attention.

8. Huth and Russett, "What Makes Deterrence Work," *World Politics* 36:4 (July 1984): 517.

9. Paul K. Huth, "The Dilemma of Deterrence: Credibility versus Stability, Escalation and Conflict Resolution in Crises from 1885–1984" (Ph.D. diss., Yale University, 1986), 109–29, 228–77.

10. Harry Eckstein, "Case Study and Theory in Political Science," in *Handbook of Political Science,* vol. 7, ed. Fred Greenstein and Nelson Polsby (Reading, Mass.: Addison-Wesley, 1975), 113–20.

11. Harold H. Kelley, "Processes of Causal Attributions," *American Psychologist* (February 1973).

12. See Bernard Weiner, "Achievement Motivation as Conceptualized by an Attribution Theorist," in *Achievement Motivation and Attribution Theory,* ed. Weiner (Morristown, N.J.: General Learning, 1974), 21; Irene Frieze and Weiner, "Cue Utilization and Attributional Judgements for Success and Failure," Ibid., 73–80; Valerie A. Valle and Frieze, "The Stability of Causal Attributions as a Mediator in Changing Expectations for Success," *Journal of Personality and Social Psychology* (May 1976): 579–87; John P. Meyer, "Causal Attributions for Interpersonal Events of Varying Magnitudes," *Journal of Personality and Social Psychology* (May 1980): 704–17.

13. Edward E. Jones and Daniel McGillis, "Correspondent Inferences and the Attribution Cube: A Comparative Reassessment," in *New Directions in Attribution Research,* ed. John H. Harvey, William J. Ickes, and Robert F. Kidd, vol. I (Hillsdale, N.J.: Erlbaum, 1976).

14. The governing elite here is defined as the president, Pentagon, State Department, and White House, including the national security adviser.

15. The tables of contents of *Mirovaya Ekonomiya I Mezhdunarodnye Otnosheniya (MEiMO), Narody Azii I Afriki (Naia),* and *Kommunist* were scanned from 1969 to 1978 for all articles dealing with Soviet or American foreign policy, American domestic politics and the regions of Southeast Asia, southern Africa, and the Horn of Africa. The same was done for *SShA* from 1970 to 1978 and *Kommunist Vooruzhenykh Sil (KVS)* from 1971

to 1978. *Letopis Gazetnykh Statei* was used to find articles on the same topics and speeches by the party leadership from 1969 to 1978 in *Pravda, Izvestiya,* and *Krasnaya Zvezda (KZ)*. The party leadership includes: General Secretary Brezhnev, Prime Minister Kosygin, Foreign Minister Gromyko, and two other senior Politburo members, Podgorny and Suslov, plus Ponomarev, Chairman of the Central Committee's International Department; his deputy, Ulyanovsky; and a section head, Brutents.

16. Articles that dealt only with the domestic developments of, say, Angola, were not coded as no inference, as it was judged not to have been a real opportunity for such inferences to be made by the writer.

17. O. Bykov, "O Nekotorikh Chertakh Vneshnepoliticheskoi Strategii SShA," (On Certain Aspects of the Foreign Policy Strategy of the U.S.), *MEiMO* (April 1971): 55. All translations from Russian are the author's, unless otherwise noted.

18. N. Fedulova, "Evoliutsiya ili Zamknutii Krug?: Poslevoennaya Politika SShA v Iugo-Vostochnoi Azii," (Evolution or Vicious Circle?: Postwar American Policy in Southeast Asia), *MEiMO* (July 1971): 32.

19. V. Gantman, "Tekushchie Problemi Mirovoi Politiki," (Current Problems of World Politics), *MEiMO* (October 1970): 82.

20. Sergei Losev and L. Sergeev, "Tekushchie Problemi Mirovoi Politiki," (Current Problems of World Politics), *MEiMO* (January 1971): 88.

21. M. Kobrin, "Tekushchie Problemi Mirovoi Politiki," (Current Problems in World Politics) *MEiMO* (October 1971): 82. M. Andreev argues that Indonesia is also helping the U.S. balance against progressive forces in the region in: "ASEAN—Ekonomicheski Blok c Politicheskimi Tselyami," (ASEAN—An Economic Bloc with Political Aims) *MEiMO* (February 1969): 91.

22. E. Pavlovskii, "Opasny Anakhronizm v Iugo-Vostochnoi Azii," (A Dangerous Anachronism in Southeast Asia) *MEiMO* (December 1972): 99–102.

23. Henry Trofimenko, "Politicheskii Realizm i Strategia 'Realisticheskovo Sderzhivaniya,' " (Political Realism and the Strategy of "Realistic Containment") *SShA* (December 1971): 12.

24. Ibid., 5–7.

25. Ibid., 6 and 7.

26. L. Stepanov, "Tekushchie Problemy Mirovoi Politiki," *MEiMO* (April 1972): 80–85.

27. V. Zhurkin, "Budut Li Izvlechoni Uroki?," (Will the Lessons be Learned?), *MEiMO* (April 1969): 15–25.

28. V. Zhurkin, "Imperializm i Mezhdunarodno-Politicheskie Krizisy," (Imperialism and International Political Crises), *MEiMO* (August 1972): 14–18.

29. *Pravda,* Oct. 5, 1971, 4.

30. *Pravda,* Sept. 7, 1971, 1.

31. "Natsionalno-Osvobiditelnoe Dvizhenie—Primety XX Stoletiya," (The National Liberation Movement—Signs of the Twentieth Century), *Izvestiya,* Feb. 12, 1970, 3.

32. "XXIV Syezd i Mirovoi Revoliutsionnyi Protsess-Kogda Sbrosheny Tsepi," (The 24th Party Congress and the World Revolutionary Process—When the Chains Are Thrown Off), *Izvestiya,* Apr. 28, 1971, 3.

33. V. Pavlovskii, "Azii—Kollektivnuiu Bezopasnost," (Collective Security for Asia), *Kommunist,* no. 16 (1973): 58. This phraseology became something of a ritual incantation for the period, accounting for almost all the instances of this category of inference.

34. "Bolshaya Pobeda Pravovo Dela Vietnama," (The Great Victory of the Just Cause of Vietnam) *Pravda,* Jan. 28, 1973, 1.

35. For a representative example, see E. Vasilkov, "Iuzhnoi Vietnam: Realnost i

Perspektivi," (South Vietnam: Reality and Prospects), *Kommunist,* no. 11 (1973): 98–108.

36. For a representative example, see R. Vasiliev, "Laos: Po Puti Nezavisimosti," (Laos: On the Path of Independence) *KZ,* Oct. 11, 1975, 3.

37. Lead Editorial, "Zakrepit Mir vo Vietname," (To Consolidate Peace in Vietnam) *Izvestiya,* Mar. 6, 1973, 1.

38. For examples, see V. Ovchinnikov, "Narashchivanie pod Vidom Sokrashcheniya," (A Build-up under the Guise of a Cutback) *Pravda,* Feb. 28, 1973, 4; and A. Malyshkin, "Opasnoe Prisutstvie," (Dangerous Presence) *KZ,* Feb. 8, 1975, 3.

39. Colonel Leontiev, "Soglashenie Nado Vypolnat," (The Accord Must Be Fulfilled) *KZ,* Apr. 4, 1973, 3. Colonel Leontiev, "Tragediya ne Dolzhna Povtoritsya," (The Tragedy Must Not Be Repeated) *KZ,* April 15, 1973, 3.

40. See Vyacheslav Razubaev, "Obosnovannoe Bespokoistvo," (Justified Uneasiness) *Pravda,* June 5, 1974, 5.

41. See V. Kassis, "Za Kulisami Sobytii—Opasnyi Treugolnik," (Behind the Scenes of Events—A Dangerous Triangle) *Izvestiya,* Oct. 30, 1975, 4.

42. R. Vasiliev and I. Seregin, "SShA: Protivoborstvo Tendentsii," (The U.S.A.: A Battle of Tendencies) *Pravda,* Nov. 15, 1973, 4.

43. V. Matveev, "Moguchaya Sila Solidarnosti s Vietnamom," (The Mighty Force of Solidarity with Vietnam) *Izvestiya,* Feb. 23, 1973, 2.

44. V. Kobysh, "SShA: Razryadka Stanovitsya Deistvitelnostiu," (The U.S.A.: Detente Is Becoming a Reality), *Kommunist,* no. 8 (1975): 112.

45. L. Semeiko, "Formy Novye, Sut Prezhnyaya—O Nekotorykh Amerikanskikh Voenno-Strategicheskikh Kontseptsiyakh," (New Forms, [But] the Essence Is as Before—On Certain American Military-Strategic Concepts) *KZ,* Apr. 8, 1975, 3. The very title reveals how Soviet analysts believed that American leaders only modified their tactics, while pursuing the same strategy of balancing.

46. See Figures 6.1 and 6.2 and Tables 6.4 through 6.6 in the Appendix.

47. *Pravda,* Nov. 28, 1973, 2. See also Podgorny speaking in Bulgaria, *Pravda,* Sept. 9, 1974, 3.

48. Ibid. For other such expressions of concern about this "continuing hotbed of tension," see Ponomarev's Supreme Soviet election speech *Pravda,* June 11, 1974, 3; Podgorny's election speech *Pravda,* June 14, 1974, 2; Kosygin's speech before the visiting Guinean head of state *Pravda,* Feb. 20, 1975, 4; and Podgorny's joint message with Kosygin to the fourth AAPSO Conference *Pravda,* Sept. 5, 1973, 1.

49. See Podgorny's speech before the Congo's President Marien Ngouabi *Pravda,* Mar. 26, 1975, 4.

50. *Pravda,* June 13, 1974, 2. For another inference with respect to detente in Asia, see Brezhnev's speech before the DRV's delegation led by Le Zuan. This speech is particularly strong evidence of the predominance of detente as a lesson from the Vietnam outcome, as Brezhnev makes no references to the global liberation movement or to regional dominoes and bandwagoning, before an audience to which one would expect him to describe the most far-reaching images of cumulating gains. *Pravda,* Oct. 29, 1975, 1–2.

51. *Pravda,* June 13, 1975, 2. For other references to the Vietnamese victory's affects on detente in Asia, see Podgorny's speech before Afghani Prime Minister Daoud, *Pravda,* December 10, 1975, 4; Gromyko's speech at the UN General Assembly in the fall of 1975, *Pravda,* September 24, 1975, 4; Brezhnev's speeches on receiving the Order of Lenin and in the Indian Parliament *Pravda,* July 12, 1973, and Nov. 30, 1973, 3 and 2.

52. *Pravda,* May 9, 1975, 2.

53. In his speech at the CSCE, *Pravda,* July 4, 1973, 5.

54. "Razryadka Mezhdunarodnoi Napryazhennost i Razvivaiushchiesya Strany," (Detente and Developing Countries), *Pravda,* Aug. 30, 1973, 4–5.

55. *Pravda,* Feb. 28, 1973, 4.

56. *Pravda,* May 9, 1975, 2. For virtually identical statements that also stress as preconditions for such victories the unity of the socialist community, international workers' movement, and "all progressive mankind," see Podgorny's speech at a dinner for Afghanistan's Prime Minister Daoud *Pravda,* Dec. 10, 1975, 4; Gromyko at the UN General Assembly in the autumn of 1975 and a month after the signing of the Paris accords at an international conference on Vietnam in Paris—*Pravda,* Sept. 24, 1975, and Feb. 28, 1973, 4 and 4.

57. The text is reproduced in *Pravda,* June 25, 1973, 1.

58. *Pravda,* Jan. 31, 1974, and Sept. 18, 1975, 2 and 1.

59. *Pravda,* May 14, 1975, 4.

60. *Pravda,* June 6 and July 13, 1974, 4 and 4.

61. *Pravda,* April 23, 1974, 1–3.

62. *Pravda,* May 22, 1975, 1.

63. See Figures 6.1 and 6.2 and Tables 6.7 through 6.9 in the Appendix.

64. L. Tamarin, "Raschyoti i Proschyoti Imperialistiov v Afrike," (The Calculations and Miscalculations of the Imperialists in Africa), no. 18, *Kommunist* (1976): 96.

65. G.Trofimenko, "Vneshnyaya Politika SShA v '70-e Gody: Deklaratsii i Praktika," (American Foreign Policy in the '70s: Declarations and Practice) *SShA* (December 1976): 22.

66. See, for example, Tomas Kolesnichenko, "Mezhdunarodnaya Nedelya—'Chelnochnye' Operatsii H. Kissinger," (International Week—The "Shuttle" Operations of H. Kissinger) *Pravda,* Sept. 26, 1976, 4.

67. M. L. Vishnevskii, "O Novykh Tendentsiyakh v Afrikanskoi Politike SShA," (On New Tendencies in the African Policy of the U.S.) *SShA* (August 1976): 69–71.

68. A. Butlitskii, "Angola—Sryv Proiskov Imperialisticheskoi Reaktssi," (Angola—Thwarting the Intrigues of Imperialist Reaction) *MEiMO* (May 1976): 87.

69. G. Arbatov, "Sovetsko-Amerikanskie Otnosheniya Sevodnya," (Soviet-American Relations Today) *Pravda,* Dec. 11, 1976, 4–5.

70. See, for example, M. Kobrin and Iu. Oleshchuk, "Tekushchie Problemy Mirovoi Politiki," (Current Problems of International Politics) *MEiMO* (January 1976): 105.

71. Obozrevatel (Observer), "Golos Svobodnoi Afriki," (Voice of Free Africa) *Pravda,* Dec. 19, 1975, 4.

72. See, for example, Captain Gavrilov and V. Berezin, "Rodeziiskii Ochag Napryazhennosti," (Rhodesian Hotbed of Tension) *KZ,* Mar. 14, 1976, 3.

73. V. Zhurkin, "Razryadka i Politika SShA v Mezhdunarodnykh Konfliktakh," (Detente and American Policy in International Conflicts) SShA (February 1977): 4–13. This article was signed to press on January 10, so was most probably written in the latter half of 1976.

74. "Sovetsko-Amerikanskie Otnosheniya na Novom Etape," *Pravda,* July 22, 1973, 4.

75. G. Arbatov, "O Sovetsko-Amerikanskikh Otnosheniyakh," (On Soviet-American Relations) *Pravda,* Apr. 2, 1976, 4–5.

76. *Pravda,* June 30, 1976, 2.

77. *Pravda,* Sept. 29, 1976, 4.

78. *Pravda,* Oct. 8, 1976, 2.

79. All *Pravda,* Sept. 24, 1975, 4.; Aug. 16, 1976, 1.; Sept. 18, 1975, 1; and Mar. 26, 1975, 4.

80. *Pravda,* May 25, 1976, 4.

81. See Figures 6.1 and 6.2 and Tables 6.10 through 6.12 in the Appendix for details.

82. In March 1977 and again in May 1978, Cuban- and Angolan-trained insurgents from the Katangan people of Zaire's Shaba province infiltrated from Angola and tried to seize control of the province from Mobutu's government in Kinshasa. During the first incursion, the Carter Administration limited itself to sending small quantities of military supplies to Mobutu. In May 1978, however, it provided air transport for French and Belgian paratroopers to Zaire, who succeeded in quashing the rebellion.

83. P. T. Podlesnyi, "Borba v SShA Vokrug Perspektiv Razryadki," (The Struggle in the U.S. Around the Prospects for Detente) *SShA* (September 1978): 53–60.

84. Iu. A. Ivanov, "Congress: Labirinty Vlasti i Vneshnyaya Politika," (Congress: Labyrinths of Power and Foreign Policy) *SShA* (June 1978): 91.

85. G. Vasiliev, "Zigzagi na Potomace," (Zigzags on the Potomac) *Pravda,* June 7, 1978, 5.

86. The other members are Britain, Canada, France, and West Germany.

87. M. L. Visnevskii, "SShA i Natsionalno-Osvoboditelnoe Dvizhenie v Afrike," (The U.S. and the NLM in Africa) *SShA* (August 1978): 36–44.

88. See, for example, G. Leonidov, "Proiski Pentagona na Afrikanskom Roge," (Intrigues of the Pentagon on the Horn of Africa) *KZ,* July 25, 1978, 3.

89. Pavel Mezentsev, "Opasnye Plany," (Dangerous Plans) *Pravda,* July 16, 1977, 5; M. L. Vishnevskii, "SShA i Natsionalno-Osvoboditelnoe Dvizhenie," 38.

90. L. M. Kuznetsov, "Afrikanskaya Maska Washingtona ('Negritud' na Vooruzhenii Amerikanskikh Ideologov)," (The African Mask of Washington [American Ideologists Armed with "Negritude"]) *SShA* (March 1978): 19; O. Anichkin, "Kto Ugrozhaet Afrike," (Who Threatens Africa) *Izvestiya,* June 7, 1978, 3; N. Vladimirov, "Na Otkup Monopoliyam," (Under the Complete Control of Monopolies) *Izvestiya,* June 21, 1978, 3; candidate Politburo member V. V. Kuznetsov's speech in Addis Ababa reproduced *Izvestiya,* Sept. 12, 1978, 4; Major Iu. Gavrilov, "Interventy v Zaire," (Intervenors in Zaire) *KZ,* May 26, 1978, 3.

91. *Pravda,* May 5, 1977, 4.

92. *Pravda,* Nov. 18, 1978, 2.

93. *Pravda,* June 3, 1978, 4.

94. While visiting the Soviet Pacific Fleet, *Pravda,* Apr. 8, 1978, 1.

95. See Heider, *The Psychology of Interpersonal Relations* (New York: John Wiley, 1958), 111–16.

96. Jonathan L. Freedman, David O. Sears and J. Merrill Carlsmith, *Social Psychology* (Englewood Cliffs, N.J.: Prentice-Hall, 1981), 92.

97. Myron Rothbart and Bernadette Park, "On the Confirming and Disconfirming of Trait Concepts," *Journal of Personality and Social Psychology* (January 1986): 137.

98. See note 1 for a discussion of the distinction between peripheral and strategic areas.

99. Stephen Walt shows in his work that American allies do not bandwagon with the Soviet Union after American defeats, but rather assiduously work to tighten their alliances with the U.S. See Walt, "Alliance Formation," 1985, and chap. 3 in this volume.

100. Richard Ned Lebow, *Between Peace and War* (Baltimore: Johns Hopkins University Press, 1981).

APPENDIX

Table 6.3.

	Factors Internal to U.S.	Deterrence Theory	Balancing Theory	Factors External to U.S.	Deterrence Theory	Balancing Theory
Party Leadership Perceptions: Vietnam, 1969–72[a]						
Dispositional	Elite Attitudes	0	9	Regional Allies	0	1
	Regional Military	1	26	Southeast Asia	1	0
	Military Expenditures	0	4	Global National Liberation Movement (NLM)	1	0
Situational						
General Perceptions: Vietnam, 1969–1972[b]						
Dispositional	Elite Attitudes	2	11	Regional Allies	3	20
	Regional Military	0	8	Global Allies	3	1
	Military Expenditures	0	3			
Situational	Public Opinion	3	0			
	Economic Capacity	3	0			

Notes: "Factors Internal to the U.S." are divided into dispositional and situational attributions. "Factors External to the U.S." are not differentiated in this way, as they are at once situational with respect to American behavior, and dispositional with regard to the actors themselves. "Regional" refers to the geographic area around Southeast Asia. Cases of indecision are those in which Soviets did not unequivocally infer lessons that support either theory; instead, they saw a struggle between cumulating gains and balancing behavior.

[a] Cases of indecision, 20; cases of no inference, 4 of 51.

[b] Cases of indecision, 9.

Table 6.4.

	Factors Internal to U.S.	Deterrence Theory	Balancing Theory	Factors External to U.S.	Deterrence Theory	Balancing Theory
Party Leadership Perceptions: Vietnam, 1973[a]						
Dispositional	Elite Attitudes	1	0	Regional Allies	0	1
	Detente	5	0	Dem. Rep. Vietnam	1	0
				Global NLM	1	0
Situational						
General Perceptions: Vietnam, 1973[b]						
Dispositional	Elite Attitudes	16	4	Regional Allies	0	2
	Regional Military	0	4	Global Allies	1	0
				Regional NLM	3	0
				Global NLM	1	0
Situational	Public Opinion	9	0			
	Congress	2	0			
	Economic Capacity	3	0			

Notes: "Detente" refers to inferences that the American elite now accepts detente as the defining characteristic of international relations. "Dem. Rep. Vietnam" refers to inferences that socialism is safe in North Vietnam.

[a] Cases of indecision, 2; cases of no inference, 8 of 22.

[b] Cases of indecision, 5; cases of no inference, 71 of 122.

Table 6.5.

	Factors Internal to U.S.	Deterrence Theory	Balancing Theory	Factors External to U.S.	Deterrence Theory	Balancing Theory
Party Leadership Perceptions: Vietnam, 1974[a]						
Dispositional	Detente	2	0	Regional Allies	0	7
	Regional Military	0	4			
Situational						
General Perceptions: Vietnam, 1974[b]						
Dispositional	Elite Attitudes	2	3	Regional Allies	0	4
	Regional Military	0	4	Global NLM	1	0
	Military Expenditures	0	1			
Situational	Public Opinion	3	0			
	Congress	2	0			
	Economic Capacity	1	0			

[a] Cases of indecision, 4; cases of no inference, 8 of 25.

[b] Cases of indecision, 5; cases of no inference, 52 of 77.

Table 6.6.

	Factors Internal to U.S.	Deterrence Theory	Balancing Theory	Factors External to U.S.	Deterrence Theory	Balancing Theory
Party Leadership Perceptions: Vietnam, 1975[a]						
Dispositional	Detente	3	0	Regional Allies	0	4
	Regional Military	0	1	Detente in SEA/ Asia	2	0
				Southeast Asia	1	0
				South Vietnam	1	0
				Global NLM	3	0
Situational						
General Perceptions: Vietnam, 1975[b]						
Dispositional	Elite Attitudes	9	6	Regional Allies	4	6
	Regional Military	0	2	Regional NLM	3	0
	Global Military	0	1	Global NLM	3	0
Situational	Public Opinion	6	0			
	Congress	2	0			

Notes: "Detente in SEA/Asia" refers to Soviet expectations of an outbreak of detente in Southeast Asia and in Asia m generally. "SEA" refers to Soviet expectations of liberation movement victories in Laos and Cambodia. "South Vietn refers to Soviet expectations of a Vietcong victory in South Vietnam.

[a] Cases of indecision, 1; cases of no inference, 8 of 24.

[b] Cases of indecision, 2; cases of no inference, 18 of 40.

Table 6.7.

	Factors Internal to U.S.	Deterrence Theory	Balancing Theory	Factors External to U.S.	Deterrence Theory	Balancing Theory
Party Leadership Perceptions: Angola 1975–76[a]						
Dispositional	Elite Attitudes	0	2	Regional Allies	0	1
	Regional Military	0	1	Regional NLM	1	0
	Diplomacy	0	1	Global Allies	0	1
Situational						
General Perceptions: Angola, 1975[b]						
Dispositional	Elite Attitudes	0	5	Regional Allies	0	7
	Regional Military	0	1	Regional NLM	2	0
	Diplomacy	0	2	Global Allies	0	1
Situational	Public Opinion	1	0			
	Congress	1	0			
General Perceptions: Angola, 1976[c]						
Dispositional	Elite Attitudes	2	13	Regional Allies	0	8
	Regional Military	0	5	Regional NLM	5	0
	Military Expenditures	0	1	Global Allies	0	3
	Diplomacy	0	8			
Situational	Public Opinion	2	2			
	Congress	2	0			

Notes: "Regional" refers to southern Africa. "Diplomacy" refers to U.S. and allied efforts to bring majority rule to Zimbabwe, Namibia, and South Africa.

[a] Cases of indecision, 2; cases of no inference, 5 of 14.

[b] Cases of indecision, 7; cases of no inference, 24 of 33.

[c] Cases of indecision, 21; cases of no inference, 26 of 54.

Table 6.8.

	Factors Internal to U.S.	Deterrence Theory	Balancing Theory	Factors External to U.S.	Deterrence Theory	Balancing Theory
Party Leadership Perceptions: Horn of Africa, 1977–1978[a]						
Dispositional	Elite Attitudes	0	3	Regional Allies	0	4
	Regional Military	0	2			
	Military Expenditures	0	1			
	Detente	0	1			
Situational						
General Perceptions: Horn of Africa, 1977[b]						
Dispositional	Elite Attitudes	0	3	Regional Allies	0	13
Situational						
General Perceptions: Horn of Africa, 1978[c]						
Dispositional	Elite Attitudes	0	8	Regional Allies	0	14
	Regional Military	0	3	Global Allies	0	11
	Military Expenditures	0	1			
	Diplomacy	0	2			
	Global Military	0	3			
Situational	Public Opinion	0	3			
	Congress	0	1			

Notes: "Regional" refers to the area around the Horn and Arabian Peninsula.

[a] Cases of indecision, 0; cases of no inference, 9 of 25.

[b] Cases of indecision, 2; cases of no inference, 25 of 40.

[c] Cases of indecision, 11; cases of no inference, 46 of 66.

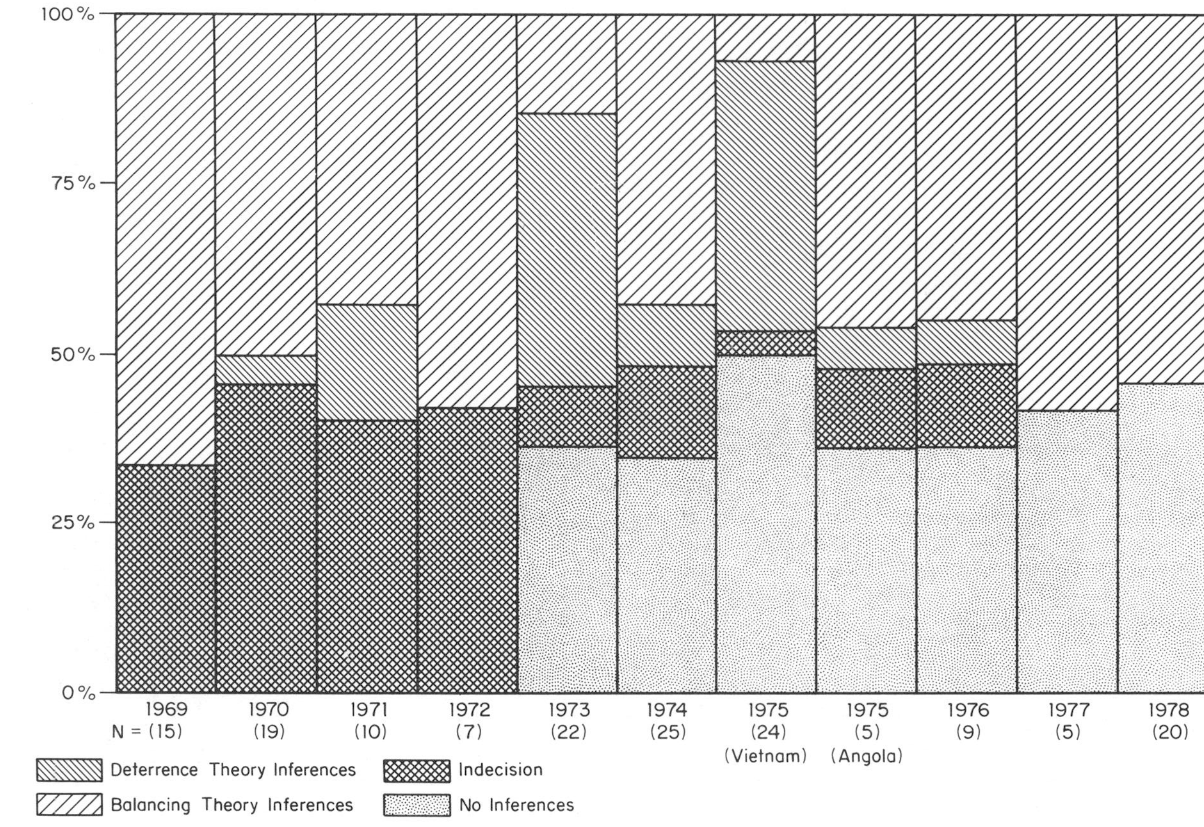

Fig. 6.1. Perceptions of the Soviet Party Leadership, 1969–1978.

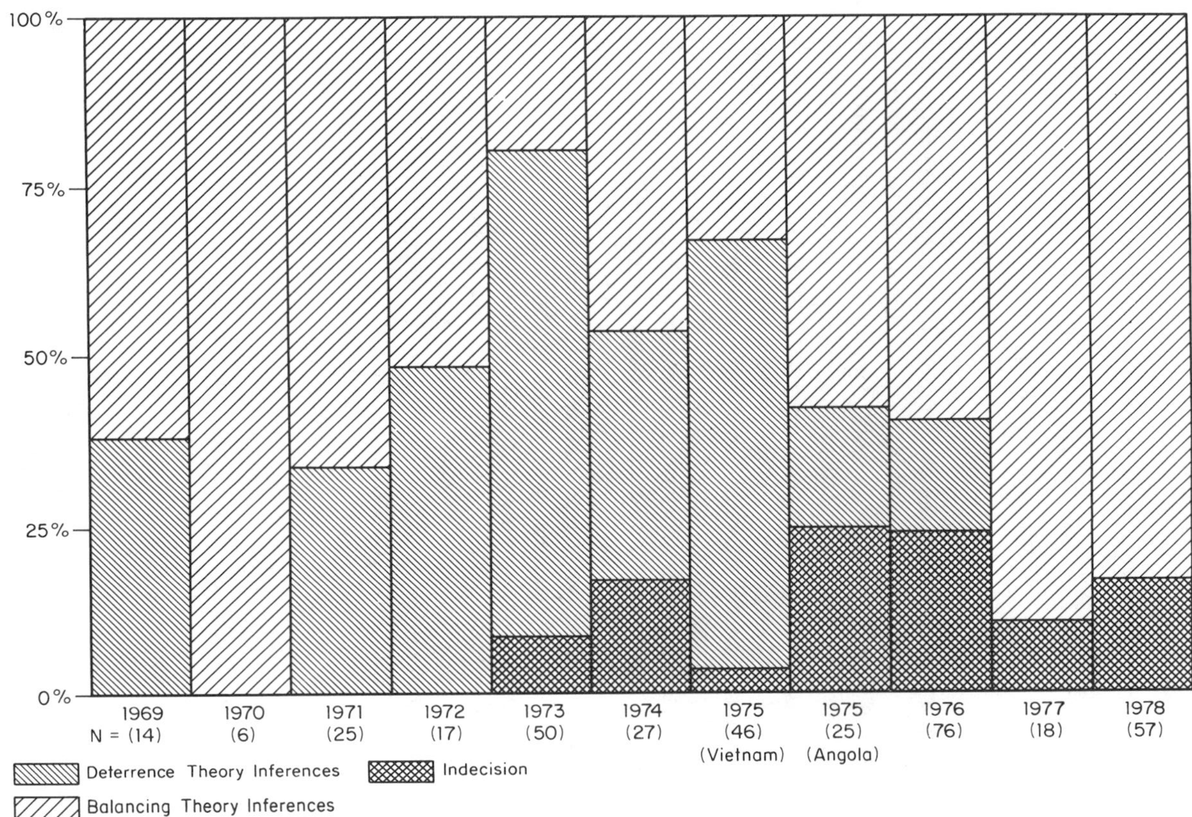

Fig. 6.2. General Soviet perceptions, 1969–1978.

7

Soviet Perceptions of American Foreign Policy After Afghanistan

DOUGLAS BLUM

At first, the hue and cry over the Soviet invasion of Afghanistan can have occasioned little surprise in Moscow. Not necessarily because it was legitimate, but simply that it was so utterly predictable, coming from the querulous administration in Washington. Indigenous radical movements, Soviet weapons modernization, Cuban brigades, hostage crises: all events, great or small, were greeted by the same chorus of shrill voices. Had that been the end of it, one can imagine that nothing more than the standard Soviet response would have been issued, with its characteristic blend of vitriol and wounded innocence. But the package of sanctions that President Jimmy Carter announced, and perhaps the sheer intensity of the outcry itself, made the American reaction to Afghanistan noteworthy. Coming as it did at the precise turning of the decade, the entire episode lent itself to the musings over change and continuity in U.S.-Soviet relations that were obligatory anyway. For these reasons it continued for some time to stand out as a landmark against the background of the later 1970s.

As the 1980s wore on and the invasion receded into the past, it was gradually subsumed by the deterioration in bilateral relations into a broader context of affronts and unpleasantries, until it lost much of its earlier specificity. The continued Soviet presence in Afghanistan kept the issue alive, but it was no longer topical in the same way. Already by 1983 the subject was seldom encountered in the Soviet press and policy journals, and even then mostly in passing.

The initial U.S. response produced no major impact on Soviet behavior, nor was it ever expected to. Yet it did compel a serious consideration of the effect of Soviet behavior on U.S.-Soviet relations. Because the intervention necessarily occurred all at once instead of unfolding over time, and because the sanctions were concrete and imposed almost instantly as retribution, Soviet analysts had to grapple with the issue as posed by the American side. Therefore, beyond the bristling rhetoric that appeared in the policy-relevant journals, some important matters were discussed. What lessons did Soviet analysts draw concerning the intervention and its aftermath? What impact was it seen to have had on Soviet-American ties? What was the nature and meaning of the U.S. response to the intervention? From the perspective of Soviet analysts, what did the answers to these questions imply for policy? These are the main issues this paper seeks to address.

This discussion makes use of certain insights from attribution theory, which provide guidelines for assessing the substance of Soviet debates in the open policy-relevant literature. At best, they allow one to go beyond the standard "between the lines" reading, by providing a systematic basis for identifying distinct viewpoints and gauging their associated policy prescriptions. At least, they render transparent the rules of thumb upon which this analysis rests.

In brief, the argument contained in these pages can be summarized as follows:

Soviet analysts held a range of views concerning the reasons for the shift in American policy after Afghanistan. According to the largest group, American policy was shaped by basic structural, ideological, and motivational factors that remained essentially constant despite changes in the world outside. For authors who made this kind of dispositional attribution, the "sharp turn" in U.S. behavior was mainly a matter of form rather than substance, and in any case was not caused by Soviet behavior. This point of view reflected the official line and was shared by individuals at all levels of the policy making community. A second, much smaller group, composed of institute specialists and journalists, attributed the change in policy primarily to situational factors. In this view Soviet behavior—including the invasion of Afghanistan—had exerted a substantial impact on American conduct. There was also a third, fairly diverse group of writers who described a combination of situational and dispositional factors.

Many of the writings surveyed contained implicit or explicit prescriptions for future Soviet policy. These prescriptions were closely correlated with authors' attributions regarding the reasons for the shift in U.S. policy. Those who stressed dispositional factors tended to propose a "unilateral" Soviet response, including heightened force posture, active pursuit of gains in the Third World, and willingness to accept moderate risks of confrontation with the United States in the process. Those who emphasized situational factors tended to prescribe a "bilateral" approach involving restrained competition along with extensive cooperation, so as to reduce the risk of conflict. These writers also advocated modification of Soviet behavior in the Third World. Authors who saw a mixture of situational and dispositional factors proposed a "management" policy, typically supporting the cautious pursuit of unilaterally defined objectives, a modicum of cooperation, and avoidance of potentially provocative military actions.

Attribution theory, and its distinctions between dispositional and situational explanations for behavior, made it possible to predict the correlations between the types of attributions and the types of prescriptions that were evident in the press. Such use of attribution theory may help to support or confirm inferences regarding Soviet policy debates. In addition, it may partially explain why individual authors advance the positions they do.

This study is based on material drawn from the Soviet press between 1980 and 1984, in particular the policy-relevant journals and monographs intended for the elite. Although the military literature is not included, this nevertheless represents a considerable cross section of contemporary views and attitudes. The authors surveyed include a broad range of civilians and officials at various levels of the Soviet hierarchy, and their writings should provide some important insights into the prevailing climate of opinion during this period.

Soviet Explanations of American Foreign Policy

Attribution theory has developed over the past twenty-five or thirty years as a way of understanding how people explain events and behavior.[1] Attribution theory distinguishes two alternative types of explanations for others' behavior. A "dispositional" explanation is one that attributes an actor's behavior to his or her inherent characteristics or personality. A "situational" explanation attributes behavior to external factors, which are said to have caused or influenced the actor to behave in a certain way.

This distinction is useful for predicting and explaining conflict behavior. Actors who make dispositional attributions for an opponent's behavior tend to respond in confrontational ways, while those who make situational attributions are likely to behave in a more accommodative manner. When actors in the latter category accept some responsibility for conflict (that is, see their own behavior as part of the situation that caused the other's acts), they tend to be conciliatory.[2] But the overwhelming tendency for people involved in conflict is to attribute hostile intentions to the adversary, that is, to explain behavior of the adversary in dispositional terms. Several psychological biases combine to account for this.

First, in what is known as the "fundamental attribution error," observers generally exaggerate the extent to which the actions of others are caused by dispositional factors. Actions are assumed to be voluntary, and outcomes are assumed to be intentional.[3] A partial exception occurs in conflict situations: although the adversary's unfavorable acts are attributed to his disposition, his favorable acts are ascribed to situational causes.[4] Second, attributions are "self-serving": People are more likely to accept responsibility for positive than for negative outcomes.[5] People also typically overestimate their own importance in others' eyes, and assume that behavior that affects them is specifically directed at them. Thus most people—including policymakers—take more than their fair share of credit for cooperative outcomes and see their own influence as the primary cause of an adversary's restraint. However, when the adversary behaves unfavorably, they tend to perceive intentional, irreducible, and unjustifiable hostility.[6]

All of the above tendencies are supported by substantial evidence, but there remain important qualifications. Not all unfavorable acts committed by adversaries are attributed to dispositional causes, and not all people are equally inclined to deny responsibility for negative outcomes.[7] Thus not only general tendencies for perception and behavior, but also significant exceptions to such tendencies, need to be borne in mind when assessing psychological factors involved in conflict. Different individuals do perceive events differently.

In the particular examples examined in this chapter, it would seem that Soviet authors who attribute U.S. involvement in Third World crises to situational factors have essentially different policy outlooks than those who make dispositional attributions for the same behavior. Therefore, this chapter identifies the kinds of attributions that appear in the Soviet press regarding superpower conflicts, and general tendencies for Soviet policy will be inferred on this basis.

One would expect most Soviet analysts to attribute U.S. behavior to a militaristic disposition. Those who do would likely find little point in attempting to resolve conflicts cooperatively. Some form of unilateral approach would appear to them to be more advisable. From the viewpoint of such analysts, there would be no point in forswearing the pursuit of Soviet objectives in hopes of pacifying the aggressor; in fact if it were possible to weaken the United States by promoting progressive change in the developing countries, there should be all the more reason to embrace indigenous radical movements. Substantial cooperation, accommodation, and compromise must be out of the question. Instead, an essentially hostile United States ought to be opposed by a resolute show of strength. In addition to deterring military encroachment and rebuffing it when it occurs, it might also appear possible to ensnare the aggressor in a web of diplomatic maneuvers. A skillfully orchestrated anti-war campaign or peace program might create enough political pressure to effectively hamper American freedom of action.

One would expect situational attributions in the Soviet literature for this period to be less numerous, but those that do appear may reflect a less antagonistic image of the opponent. A situational explanation leads to an entirely different set of options. By definition, if the situation can be adjusted, so can the opponent's behavior. Insofar as Soviet policy is recognized as an important element in the overall situation, part of the preferred approach should involve a modification of Soviet behavior. In this way it ought to be possible to regulate the general interaction in such a way as to decrease the likelihood of triggering a conflict in the future. Should a conflict arise, it ought to be possible to resolve it bilaterally by addressing the root cause. Despite the persistence of competition, there should be no fundamental obstacles to achieving extensive cooperation.

In the traditional work on attribution theory, situational and dispositional explanations are generally distinct. However, in the "real" world of politics, some analysts grappling with the complexities of events and patterns of relations may explain U.S. behavior by a combination of situational and dispositional factors.[8]

Analysts in this group can be expected to take a stand somewhere between the two extremes. To the extent that an interactive component of the competition is recognized, a given author might favor some adjustment in Soviet behavior or, at least, argue that international tensions should not be needlessly exacerbated. At the same time, the dispositional aspect of U.S. policy would suggest that Soviet defense must continue to be a high priority. And while the means of pursuing Soviet objectives might be altered, the basic agenda need not be.

In defining the relevent variables, the basic distinction is between behavior that is viewed to be characteristic of an actor and behavior that is viewed to be essentially conditioned or determined by external factors—in this case by the political environment. Virtually all of the articles in the Soviet journals during this period that focused on the subject of American policy included some dispositional reference to the "nature of imperialism," or the like. And almost all made some mention of the "changing correlation of forces," or the triumphs of national liberation movements, situations that were seen as provoking American hostility. The issue in identifying dispositional attributions therefore is not simply whether a given analyst mentioned external factors that influenced U.S. behavior, but rather whether U.S. behavior was considered to be explicable even without the particular situation involved. If the external factor—in this case the Afghanistan intervention, either alone or in conjunction with the other revolutionary advances of the 1970s—is seen as having merely afforded the United States an opportunity to vent its imperialist wrath, then we can say that the analyst has made a dispositional attribution. In contrast, a situational attribution would stress a U.S. policymakers' perception of threat, instead of their hostility. While a situational attribution does not necessarily *ignore* dispositional factors, it places a strong emphasis on environment and interaction. In the case of a mixed attribution, both situational and dispositional factors should be present, with neither one predominant.

An obvious example of a dispositional attribution is the official explanation that the Soviet intervention was simply a pretext for the reactionary American policy that followed. A situational explanation would discuss a direct American response (however unjustified) to Soviet actions, or would treat the United States as reacting to events in the Third World or to Soviet policy. However, the arguments one finds in Soviet journals are almost never that clear-cut. After all, the official line on such matters must be toed to some extent. No analyst would flatly deny that Afghanistan merely furnished a convenient pretext for United States aggression, and even a direct statement that echoes the official explanation cannot be accepted as conclusive evidence of an author's position. Furthermore, in many if not most cases a writer may not clearly articulate his underlying attribution; indeed, he may not be fully conscious of it. In any case he may choose to make the point implicitly instead of stating it outright. For all of the above reasons it is necessary to pay close attention to context, wording, and emphasis. In this way it is often possible to arrive at a judgment regarding an author's basic explanation for American policy.

Dispositional Attribution

The largest and most influential group was composed of authors who made dispositional attributions for the shift in American conduct. It included the senior leadership and represented the official Soviet line. There were of course nuances within this group, such as the precise nature an author ascribed to the United States, or the underlying reasons given for American malice. A number of authors practically revelled in the U.S. reaction, which suggests it was a vindication for those who had always harbored doubts about the viability of detente. A few even professed concern about a possible military threat. But the common theme among these writers was that America's "true character" was revealed in its response to the Afghan affair.

Several months after the intervention in Afghanistan, S. Modenov wrote an article in the (then) propagandistic journal *International Affairs* on the "slander campaign" unleashed by the United States. It "raises the question," the author mused, "what is behind such a stormy reaction to an incident so far from American borders."[9] The unsurprising conclusion that Modenov reached was that Afghanistan supplied a convenient pretext for the subsequent U.S. assault against detente and progressivism everywhere.[10] There was nothing more to the analysis; the foreign policy context was not presented as a significant factor in shaping American policy. One was left with the impression that the U.S. reaction to the successful defense of the Afghan revolution was simply in keeping with its violent hatred for radical change. Here then was a clear example of a dispositional explanation of American policy, which started and ended with the contention that Afghanistan was merely a pretext.

Other authors went on to specify the precise disposition underlying the shift in policy. Most characterized it as a combination of expansionism and antiprogressivism. Boris Ponomarev, for many years head of the International Department of the Central Committee, tended to emphasize the "class roots" of American behavior. In his view, this accounted for a kind of reflexive response, whereby "the progressive changes in the world . . . evoke the fear and hatred of the chief monopolies, the thieving capitalist businesses," and so on.[11] Authors who shared this perspective argued that America was indeed reacting to national liberation movements but was doing so for essentially dispositional reasons. Progressive change did not represent an external factor that "determined" American behavior. Instead, what these authors were saying was that imperialism *always* behaves aggressively toward national liberation movements: such was the nature of the beast. When academicians like Georgii Kim and journalists like Viktor Sidenko alternatively discussed expansionism and reaction to revolutionary movements, they were simply referring to two sides of the same coin.[12]

Analysts who saw U.S. policy as intrinsically aggressive tended to minimize the shift after Afghanistan and instead dated the turnabout from the start of the Carter administration or even earlier. Viktor Shamberg of the Institute of the World Economy and International Relations (IMEMO) was one of those who asserted in retrospect that detente had been merely a tactical ploy all along. A limited moderation of East–West tensions had been pursued in the hopes that it would free the United States to engage in imperialism—and others were said to have opposed any agreement whatsoever. In any case, when this tactical expedient backfired it was simply discarded.[13] Former *Pravda* editor Lev Tolkunov suggested that a change in the world correlation of forces had "forced" the United States to accept detente under Nixon and Ford, but that since then an increasing "re-ideologization" had steered policy on a more militaristic course.[14] The "anticommunist crusade" of the 1980s merely "demonstrates the essence of American foreign policy." For Tolkunov, neither Afghanistan nor the advent of the Reagan administration marked any real watershed: "The leaders of the U.S.A., as before, see the world through the prism of confrontation . . . [as a means of] finding a way out of the historical dead end in which they find themselves."[15] And even authors who did recognize a change after Afghanistan depicted it as one of form rather than substance. Boris Koval, deputy director of the Institute of the International Workers' Movement, noted the onset of a "frontal counterattack," which he felt represented merely a "shift of the strategic phase of the struggle."[16]

Writers who stressed dispositional factors generally seemed to regard the military-industrial complex (MIC) as a dominant force behind the American state. It was often alleged that militarism had become an increasingly pervasive element in American political thought since the mid-1970s, largely in reaction to detente and arms control. But whether construed as the product of a monolithic MIC or of a broader social-political process, these writings tended to present military means and ends as absolutely central to U.S. policy. For example, one institute scholar contended that the Afghan intervention provided an eagerly awaited excuse for repudiating the SALT II treaty. It was implied that the latter motive stemmed from a perverse refusal to accept parity as a fact of life.[17] Nikolai Lebedev, then rector of the Moscow State Institute for International Relations, subscribed to the notion that "if there had been no Afghanistan, the militaristic circles in the United States and NATO would surely have found another excuse" for heightening the arms race.[18] Another writer argued that the "myths" concerning Soviet expansionism had been fabricated in order to conceal the "appetite" of the military industrial complex for "military adventurism."[19] According to this image, aggression was virulent and yet somewhat diffuse; global in scope but not a direct and immediate threat to the Soviet Union itself.

Others, however, went farther in ascribing a deep-seated anti-Soviet sentiment to U.S. policymakers. Seen in this light, American "military intrigues" in and around Afghanistan took on a still more ominous meaning. This in fact was the heart of the official Soviet justification for intervention, as enunciated by Brezhnev. In the short run, according to Brezhnev, the United States (in collusion with the Chinese) meant to topple the revolutionary regime and to insert a reactionary one in its stead. But this was merely a step toward establishing a base on the sourthern border of the U.S.S.R., which would represent a "serious threat to the security of the Soviet state."[20] At the highest level, in what probably reflected the original consensus on intervention, Andrei Gromyko and Ponomarev wrote articles pointing to the threat of the "transformation of Afghanistan into a pro-imperialist base," and the U.S. desire to establish an "active military center," in the region.[21] Others such as Pavel Demchenko, a *Pravda* editor who writes on Asian and African affairs, depicted an American attempt to compensate for the loss of facilities in Iran by garnering new ones nearby.[22] Nor did the prevalence of such views diminish over time. Rostislav Ulianovskii, then the venerable first deputy head of the International Department under the CPSU Central Committee (CCID), charged in a 1983 article that American counterrevolutionary activity in Afghanistan was inspired by a desire to bring the country within an "orbit of anti-Soviet blocs and alliances."[23]

None of the writers in this category, who attributed American behavior to dispositional factors, saw American policies as in any way responsive to Soviet behavior—at least not in terms of any causal connection between, say, the invasion of Afghanistan and the U.S. reaction. Often there was no reference whatsoever to any Soviet actions during the 1970s as having any bearing on the course of American conduct. When there was, it took the form of an explicit refutation of the idea that superpower relations were essentially interactive. Thus Vadim Zagladin, first deputy head of the CCID, flatly rejected the views of "some comrades" who argued that "the Soviet Union did not use all possibilities it possessed to strengthen detente, undertook 'rash' actions which 'provoked' imperialism and 'forced' it to take a course toward confrontation."[24] Apparently, it depended on what one meant by "provoked." "It is entirely natural," Zagladin declared, "that the support of socialism for the revolutionary struggles of such countries as Angola, Ethiopia, and Afghanistan 'provoked' imperialism. This is not surprising—truly it undermined [imperialism's] plans" to foster counterrevolution and neocolonialism.[25]

Mixed Attribution

A second, smaller group of authors explained the U.S. reaction in somewhat more sophisticated terms. This group included a variety of figures at different levels of prominence, and appeared to represent a substantial current of disagreement within the policymaking elite. Although none of the individuals in this group saw Soviet misdeeds as a real factor in the U.S. response, they all went beyond simple, monocausal explanations. Indeed, for these authors the deterioration in superpower relations revealed a complex array of American needs, fears, and vulnerabilities as well as sinister aims.

Genrikh Trofimenko, department head at the Institute of the U.S.A. and Canada, started off the decade with a dim view of American objectives and gradually progressed to still dimmer views. At times, he wrote about the United States's new "policy without prospects" as if it were an entirely trumped-up crusade against socialism and progressivism everywhere, dating back to the beginning of the Carter administration.[26] At other times, though, he attributed the shift in U.S. policy to a number of factors, both internal and external. On the one hand there were dogmatic ideological tenets, combined with a historical legacy of imperial tendencies.[27] On the other hand changing circumstances created social and political pressures. "To a sizeable degree," he conceded at one point, the turn away from detente "was connected with the crisis of U.S. foreign policy, with the series of its failures and defeats in the international arena"; these had been widely interpreted as being the "results of detente."[28] In particular, Trofimenko singled out the Iran hostage crisis as an important event in fueling the public demand in the United States for a more militarist posture. Situational and dispositional elements blended together in this analysis.

Unlike authors who explained U.S. behavior in exclusively dispositional terms, those who made mixed attributions displayed some awareness of American perspectives and sensitivities. Viktor Kremeniuk, a colleague of Trofimenko's, described America as having grown increasingly dependent upon natural resources in the developing countries. For this reason, he explained, the national liberation movements acquired particular significance in the calculations of American policymakers.[29] This in turn affected U.S. perceptions of Soviet behavior. Kremeniuk recognized that there were differing interpretations of Soviet policy, and although he argued that the rejection of detente was not a "'legitimate response' to injury to [the United States's] position . . . in the liberated countries," he acknowledged that these events and the interpretations of them "played a not insignificant role" in turning American away from detente.[30] While it was undeniable that the national liberation victories were "disadvantageous for imperialist interests," it was nevertheless "totally untrue" and "arbitrary" for the United States to blame the U.S.S.R. and to desert detente on this basis.[31] Kremeniuk also pointed to "other factors" contributing to the American response: the MIC, imperialistic ambitions, and so forth.[32] This was a veritable hodge-podge of causality.

Authors who saw a combination of internal and external factors did not describe a monolithic state dominated by big monopolies or the military sector. Instead they tended to perceive a variety of influences on policy, including shared understandings of American policymakers that transcended narrow institutional interests. These qualities were evident in the writing of Vadim Kortunov, who had been a close advisor to Podgorny in the 1970s. In answer to the question of why "precisely in recent years" anti-detente forces had surfaced, Kortunov paid lip service to the explanation that focused on the military-industrial complex, but added that this explanation "did not exhaust the whole problem."[33] A further part of the explanation lay in the U.S. refusal to accept the irreversibility of progressive changes in the world, but even this was secondary. The crux of the matter was the widespread "false understanding [in the United States] . . . of the historical significance of the changes that occurred in the international arena during the years of detente."[34] Kortunov implied that those changes were regarded as detrimental to those who hoped to split the socialist community via political and economic means. Again, it was partly the negative flow of events that undermined Western support for detente and prompted the "counterattack against socialism."[35]

Yet another distinction concerns the characterization of U.S. objectives. Those who attributed U.S. policy to mixed factors tended not to discuss American behavior as being solely aggressive or expansionist in intent. Aleksei Kiva, a deputy editor of the journal *Aziia i Afrika segodnia,* wrote two articles in August and September 1980 on the imperialist threat in the developing countries. The first article described an all-out militarist assault and explained U.S. objectives along official lines: promoting conflict, staging counterrevolution, scrambling for bases, and so forth.[36] But the second article was far more nuanced in its appraisal of American policy, seeing its fundamental goal as the prevention of further revolutionary developments and the preservation of the status quo; the chief instrument in this campaign was propaganda, not guns.[37] Even this varied to some extent, depending on situational factors: "The more serious the imperialist defeat in this or that region, the fiercer the anti-Soviet and anticommunist propaganda."[38]

One final distinction concerns the nature and function of ideology. Whereas dispositional attributions treat ideology as immutable, derived from socioeconomic factors, and aggressively expansionist, mixed attributions depict a complex set of tendencies, the interrelations among which were susceptible to change. Thus Iuri Zamoshkin began a 1982 article by stating that ideology in the United States developed with "relative independence," even though it also reflected "structural characteristics" and "objective processes." The "zig-zags" in U.S. policy, he suggested, could best be understood from this perspective.[39]

Behind this arcane phraseology, Zamoshkin was in effect arguing that American ideology was dynamic, that it was partially shaped by events, and that it in turn exerted an influence on policymakers. Therefore despite its messianic-imperialist foundation, ideology shifted under the impact of the Vietnam war and the social contradictions of the period, and this eventually meant that "pushing through the arms race and militaristic activity" became "too difficult" for the ruling elite.[40] The late 1970s brought a new shift, Zamoshkin argued. National liberation triumphs restricted the scope of American activity abroad; the Warsaw Pact gained in strength relative to NATO; there were mounting social and economic problems at home. The result was a "crisis of national self-consciousness," and subsequently a "neurotic" reaction to events that exposed American weaknesses.[41] Zamoshkin did not disregard dispositional factors, but saw a complicated interplay among various ideological currents and social groups in response to the political environment.

It should be noted that the attributions appearing in the literature are not always easily categorized. Perhaps because the attribution itself is not always consciously selected by the analyst as a specific point of discussion, it is sometimes left ambiguous or implicit. In some cases, such as when dispositional attributions blend into mixed attributions, the interested reader's judgment must be based on a few key passages or phrases—if indeed it is possible to make any judgment at all. An example of a borderline case is the writing of Richard Ovinnikov, at present the rector of the Moscow State Institute of International Affairs (MGIMO). Ovinnikov dated the "sharp turn" in policy at the end of the 1970s, and portrayed it (rather mildly) as an attempt to "turn back the clock" to the halcyon days before national liberation.[42] He often suggested that the "key to major policy" was "in the hands of big business,"[43] but he also recognized the existence of conflicting views among "right-wingers" and "realists,"[44] and stressed the significance of disagreements between Vance and Brzezinski.[45] Furthermore, he elaborated on the difficult situation confronting the ruling circles: social ferment at home, the Vietnam debacle, the rise of the Third World, the strengthened position of world socialism. In these circumstances, Ovinnikov declared, the leadership's "inability, and more precisely . . . unwillingness" to find a "reasonable" solution to its problems led it to resort to "hegemonistic adventurism."[46] This was presented as something of a desperate last resort rather than a premeditated, dispositionally explicable outcome. In fact, Ovinnikov stated that it was the need to justify the shift in policy that led to the rise in anti-detente and anti-Soviet sentiment, rather than vice versa.[47] Again, the categorization was ambiguous, but on the whole it leaned to the mixed rather than the dispositional side.

Situational Attribution

As already discussed, no analysis of American policy in the Soviet media between the years 1980 and 1984 would have been allowed to attribute the "sharp turn" explicitly and exclusively to situational factors. Perhaps no author would have chosen to do so even if the opportunity had existed. But a small group of authors during this period, including some prominent academics and journalists, did seem to place special emphasis on situational factors. Once more the categorization is unavoidably problematic. While a dispositional attribution can be immediately ruled out, the distinction between a situational and mixed attribution is not clear-cut. However, a differentiation can be made by paying attention to wording and weighting.

Along with the emphasis on situational factors, authors in this group stressed the importance of stark divisions within the U.S. policymaking community. They clearly pointed to interaction between Soviet behavior and the American turn away from detente after Afghanistan in a way that suggested that the United States was, to an important extent, truly responsive to Soviet policy initiatives. The writings of the well-known journalist Aleksander Bovin furnish a good illustration of this. In an article published in the central party journal in July 1980, Bovin reviewed a recent edition of Lenin's essays on foreign policy and took advantage of the occasion to discuss their profound relevance in light of present-day events. It was essential, Bovin warned his readers, to bear in mind Lenin's admonition concerning the effect of Soviet policy on internal politics in the West. Not all capitalists were alike: there were "different strata, groups, factions of the bourgeoisie"; each was marked by a different political orientation, degree of militancy, and attitude toward relations with the U.S.S.R. It was here that Bovin's own attribution became apparent:

> The correlation of forces between "reasonable capitalists" and "the warlike party" is a changeable quantity which is determined by many factors. A part of them are outside the limits of influence of socialist foreign policy. But the other part is accessible for its influence. This is why Lenin warns against ill-thought-out, hasty steps [which] can frighten [and] antagonize the "reasonable capitalists" [and] give a trump card into the hands of the "warlike party."[48]

When Bovin remarked obliquely that this insight remained extremely "topical" in conditions of the "struggle for detente," it seemed clear that he was referring to the Afghan intervention.[49]

A general recognition of interaction in superpower relations was evident in the writings of several other commentators on foreign affairs, particularly analysts at the Institute of the U.S.A. and Canada. Andrei Melvil, writing shortly after the invasion of Afghanistan, noted that the current state of world politics reflected the "tight mutual influence and intertwining" between the "internal and external policy courses of capitalist and socialist countries."[50] Andrei Kokoshin made a similar point when he discussed America's growing vulnerabilities resulting from victories of national liberation movements and increased U.S. dependence on natural resources in the developing countries.[51] Against this background, the fall of the shah was perceived as a major blow to America's international economic and political standing.[52] This in turn led to heightened U.S. sensitivity, which contributed to a widespread "anti-Soviet mood" and "distortion of the policy of the Soviet Union."[53] However unjust such accusations might be, Kokoshin did not consider them disingenuous. Even relative moderates, he acknowledged, "consider the 'Soviet threat' to be real, but suggest that the United States 'overreacts' to it."[54] Elsewhere, Kokoshin noted that anxiety created by the oil crisis exacerbated this reaction: Soviet "aid" to Afghanistan "was interpreted by the majority of [U.S.] organs of mass information as a step allegedly directed toward an exit to the Persian Gulf for the purposes of establishing control over the main supplies of oil for the 'free world.'"[55]

The mechanism whereby the United States translated these perceptions into a hostile shift in policy was easily identified. Like Bovin, Melvil and Kokoshin sharply distinguished between realists and reactionaries within the American elite and detailed the process whereby external events could have a decisive influence in shaping foreign policy outcomes. For Melvil, it was a "dialectical" process in which domestic politics influenced foreign policy and vice versa.[56] In the aftermath of Afghanistan, the aggressive-reactionary camp had been able to prevail over the pacifistic camp after a "fierce struggle."[57] Kokoshin too rejected the view that "foreign policy is strictly determined only by economic factors," given the "complex political system" in the United States.[58] In a later monograph he argued that it was only after all of the setbacks of the 1970s that the transnational corporations, "many of whom saw the Soviet Union as the main source of their misfortunes," aligned with the military-industrial complex against the supporters of detente.[59] Elsewhere he described a division between far-sighted realists and right-wingers, and pointed to the sudden increase in the interventionist mood in the Senate following the Iran crisis.[60]

In addition to the above-mentioned external factors, two institute directors—Georgii Arbatov and Evgenii Primakov—recognized the importance of American notions of "resolve." Essentially, Arbatov and Primakov saw the events of the 1970s interacting with strategic beliefs to bring about a shift in U.S. policy. Primakov, then of the Institute of Oriental Studies and currently head of the Institute of the World Economy and International Relations (IMEMO), asserted that the United States had not intervened on behalf of the shah despite its concern over access to oil supplies, largely due to Soviet warnings against doing so. However, this stiffened U.S. resolve not to allow any repetition of Iran; Primakov implied that Afghanistan had been perceived in this light.[61] He elsewhere indicated an awareness of America's intent to "counterattack the revolutionary forces" so as to "defend" its "vital interests," however arbitrarily and unilaterally it defined them.[62] Primakov also criticized U.S. adherence to the "domino theory," which he argued only backfired and actually led to greater instability.[63] Still, he plainly saw it as a set of beliefs that underlay militaristic reactions to particular events.

Arbatov, director of the Institute of the U.S.A. and Canada, wrote in a similar vein, rejecting the notion that "weakness" and a "lack of resolve" were the real causes of American failures in the Third World. Rather, the explanation lay in America's penchant for high-handedness and its support of dictatorships.[64] Nevertheless, he recognized that the "panicky affirmations" and visions of "Soviet tanks and soldiers on the shores of the Persian Gulf" reflected real fears and were not merely propaganda.[65] Arbatov also appreciated the interaction between Soviet behavior and the American response. "Nobody," he admitted, "expects the Americans . . . to approve of the April Revolution in Afghanistan and the help provided to it by the Soviet Union."[66] Yet this was no reason to scuttle detente.

Prescriptions for Soviet Policy After Afghanistan

The shift in American policy required a response on the Soviet side, even if only a decision to stay the course. Considering the dramatic worsening of relations and the confrontational tone in Washington that extended well into the Reagan presidency, the response must have been carefully worked out in stages over the next several years. As Raymond Garthoff has suggested, the June 1980 plenum was most likely convened in order to address this issue, and certainly Brezhnev dwelt at length on the future of U.S.-Soviet relations at the Twenty-Sixth Party Congress in February 1981.[67] The conclusion initially reached and steadily affirmed thereafter was that "detente" was not dead—that negotiation still offered a potentially profitable avenue for the resolution of outstanding differences. After Brezhnev's death the Soviet leadership continued to hold out hope that the Reagan administration would come around. Not until the fall of 1983, after the KAL 007 incident and the heated American recriminations that followed, did Andropov finally sound the death knell of detente.[68]

During this almost four-year period there was substantial fluidity in Soviet policy, and commentators advanced a range of competing views in the media. Detente was a notoriously vague term, and the interpretation an author placed on it allowed a lot to be said with a little. Beyond this there remained some latitude for independent positions and veiled criticisms—provided they were sufficiently "principled" in nature—even after Andropov's signal that an impasse had been reached. By that time, however, relations had reached such a low point that little more was ventured in the press than the acerbic official line. Until 1984 then, there was a debate on Soviet policy vis-à-vis the United States.[69]

In assessing the stands taken by the participants in this debate, it is not necessary to assume that the perceptions or prescriptions that were advanced reflected an author's private views accurately. As Franklyn Griffiths has pointed out, statements may have a "transactional" quality, intended for intra-elite consumption and esoteric communication at the highest level.[70] This should not in principle render them inaccessible. It is true that not all articles contain policy prescriptions, and many of those that can be identified are couched in vague and implicit terms. Yet by paying attention to programmatic endorsements, the alleged remediability of conflict, and the status accorded to proponents of detente within American politics, it is often possible to piece together a plausible advocacy position. As has already been discussed, one should expect prescription to vary with attribution. Those who made dispositional attributions for American conduct should be expected to support stern, uncompromising Soviet measures in return, whereas those who made mixed attributions might be expected to endorse a more subtle, modulated response. And those who saw external factors at work, including possibly an element of Soviet responsibility, ought to favor mutual accommodation instead. The following sections will examine the relationship between attribution and policy prescription in greater detail.

Unilateralism

Associated with dispositional attributions is the prescription to unilaterally pursue an uncompromising, potentially confrontational course of action. Since the adversary is dispositionally and unswervingly aggressive, it would be folly to attempt a conciliatory policy. Instead the first priority must be defense. That much assured, the zero-sum nature of the competition underlined the need to extend Soviet power and influence at the adversary's expense. Opportunities should be created as well as exploited, with no exercise of restraint beyond the minimum required to avoid war. Detente could be instrumental in this regard, in so far as it tied the aggressor's hands and accelerated the inevitable process of progressive change. On the other hand, only marginal cooperation could be anticipated due to the overwhelmingly competitive nature of the relationship.[71]

A few analysts combined a dispositional view of American foreign policy with what amounted to a clarion call to arms. One author, for example, expounded upon the importance of ensuring an adequate defense of the homeland and praised the Warsaw Treaty Organization for enforcing the peace in Europe and providing support to the revolution in Afghanistan. He described the work of the CPSU as being dedicated to achieving solidarity among all anti-imperialist forces and declared that the ability to defend the gains of socialism with military might was a crucial deterrent to imperialist aggression.[72] Others were less inflammatory, but still emphasized the need to counter a possibly imminent threat. Initially, this often took the form of a hearty endorsement of—and perhaps elaboration upon—Brezhnev's statement of preparedness to put down aggression by force, enunciated at the Twenty-Sixth Congress. Radomir Bogdanov, a deputy director of the Institute of the U.S.A. and Canada, hailed Brezhnev's declaration and added his own call for "uncompromising exposure of and struggle to uproot all manifestations of the chronic ailment of hegemonism."[73] Lev Tolkunov, warning his readers of a "new anticommunist 'crusade,'" insisted that "the necessity of strengthening the defensive might of the homeland . . . becomes all the more apparent."[74] By the beginning of 1984 such statements were particularly prevalent on all levels and were often unmodulated by any accompanying plea for a return to detente.[75]

Throughout this period analysts who condemned America's dispositionally driven policy advocated vigorous support of Third World radical movements, even if this meant involvement in regional conflicts. According to this point of view, detente in no way prevented the U.S.S.R. from providing aid to national liberation movements; in fact American intrigues necessitated the extension of Soviet assistance.[76] An unsigned editorial in the weekly *New Times* averred that the United States should not have the "slightest doubt" that the Soviet Union "will be able to uphold its legitimate interests and the interests of its allies and friends."[77] The same notion was frequently presented in terms of a willingness to rally to the defense of a friendly regime under attack from imperialism without or counterrevolution within. Often the lessons of Chile and Kampuchea under Pol Pot were invoked.[78] The immediate reference was to Afghanistan, but its applicability to future cases was made explicit as well.

Others extended the argument to urge not only the defense of established gains, but also the support of those who were struggling to achieve such gains. Viktor Sidenko, for example, implied this when he warned of American plans to use the "Afghan question" in the UN as a "smoke screen" to hide military preparations in the Near and Middle East. For Sidenko the lesson of Afghanistan was the necessity of providing military aid to national liberation movements in the future.[79] As another author remarked, Afghanistan demonstrated the fact that historical progress occurred "not by evolutionary means, but through fierce class struggle."[80] An authoritative endorsement came from Ponomarev, who cited Lenin on the need to carry out the historical mission of socialism. In addition to strengthening the economic and military might of the U.S.S.R., he urged that it was essential to strengthen the solidarity of the international communist movement, and to "strive for the maximum utilization . . . of the enormous potential . . . of the contemporary working class and national liberation movement."[81]

No author, however, evinced a cavalier disregard for the dangers of military involvement. No one suggested that the United States could be bullied, or that a Soviet ability to prevail made it safe to disregard utterly the risks of escalation inherent in regional conflict. The point was rather that the U.S.S.R. must be prepared to respond to all challenges in order to guarantee the progress of national liberation and to prevent America from reversing the "correlation of forces." The trick was to promote radical change without unduly provoking the enemy. Although conflict might well be unavoidable in the end, this was not the same thing as marching in with guns blazing. Thus Boris Koval quoted Lenin on the inevitable resolution of historical questions "by force." However, Koval insisted that "such force must not, of course, be construed vulgarly—as a direct physical influence or coercion."[82] Such vulgar displays were inexpedient. Koval instead called for a united front of anti-imperialist forces, apparently for its deterrent as well as persuasive value. "The issue," he declared, "is one of the political potential of force."[83] But if the imperialists resorted to violence, there was no reason to quail. As another writer put it, "Today the confrontation between the two systems has acquired a universal character. This means that attempts at suppressing revolution . . . from outside can be attacked by international solidarity."[84]

Occasionally it was possible to catch a glimpse of the strategic beliefs that appeared to underlie the unilateralist prescription. Iuri Katasonov, who warned of a "constant threat" of American use of force, saw the extension of Soviet military aid as a crucial deterrent against the transformation of this threat into reality.[85] Katasonov asserted that the U.S.S.R. was the United States's "single major military opponent," and that radical movements and regimes were assessed by American strategists in terms of their relations with the U.S.S.R. and the likelihood of Soviet armed support.[86] The implicit message was that allies were automatically prime targets of imperialist attack, and that willingness to demonstrate resolve was essential not only in order to avoid losses but also to accumulate gains. In this view, Soviet aid might be key in enabling national liberation movements to successfully "balance" against American aggression.[87] Similarly, Georgii Kim wrote of the need to remove sources of "instability" in the liberated countries, which diverted resources, prevented independent development, and stymied progressive political change.[88] Soviet aid, in his view, had "allowed the stabilization of the situation in Afghanistan" and paved the way for further economic and political transformation.[89] For Kim, the lesson was a general one. In the face of mounting imperialist military pressure, he argued, "Socialist friendship with its willingness to grant necessary material—including military—help . . . serves as a stabilizing factor."[90] Like Katasonov, Kim seemed to be suggesting that regional military involvement should not be a last resort in cases of extreme defensive exigency, but could play a salutary role in advancing or ensuring the interests of the U.S.S.R. and its allies. It is interesting to note that in many respects, the image of the adversary contained in these policy prescriptions resembles that of the "paper tiger." The United States was perceived to be pressing ahead, rapaciously devouring everything in its path. And yet with a resolute show of strength the tiger could be contained, or perhaps even forced to retreat.

Another factor that helps to explain the unilateralist prescription is the associated view that a dispositionally hostile American leadership would be unreceptive to a moderate policy. Nor was any prospect of internal change foreseen. Many of these authors did not draw a distinction between "hawks" and "doves" in American politics. Others recognized that some differences existed, but minimized their practical significance. As Iuri Melnikov argued, "Even the most 'liberal' American presidents and governments, inclined or compelled toward realism . . . invariably continued at the same time to strive for an increase in the military potential of the U.S. [and] the attainment of military superiority over its opponents."[91] Therefore only Soviet force was able to deter American aggression.[92] Even Aleksandr Iakovlev, one of the few who perceived the presence of "realistic forces" among the ruling elite, concluded (in late 1983) that "there is not much hope for the strength of their influence for the time being."[93]

With these ideas in mind, the unilateralist endorsement of detente after Afghanistan takes on a clearer meaning. The prototypical example was Brezhnev's 1981 proposal for a joint "code of conduct" in the Third World. Its essential elements were noninterference in the domestic affairs of states, recognition of territorial integrity, respect for the policy of nonalignment, and general support for the developing countries.[94] While this had some propaganda value, it in no way constricted Soviet options in the Third World and did not address the problematic issues of superpower relations. The writings of other unilateralists provided additional insights into this approach.

Boris Ponomarev enthusiastically welcomed Brezhnev's call for a code of conduct and the elimination of sources of conflict. At the same time he righteously defended Soviet involvement in the "legitimate struggle of the peoples for their national and social liberation."[95] Elsewhere, he rejected the notion that the U.S.S.R. had to "pay a price" for detente by forsaking the liberation movement.[96] The real instrumental value of detente for Ponomarev was revealed when he soberly appraised the international political ramifications of the U.S. "'cold war' campaign." "The danger of the maneuvers and propagandistic vagaries of the imperialist centers . . . must not be underestimated," he warned.[97] However, all was not lost. Soviet proposals for detente served to undermine this "campaign." With satisfaction, Ponomarev reported that Brezhnev's peace overtures at the Party Congress had evoked "confusion" *(vmeshatelstvo)* among the imperialists.[98]

A similar point was made by Konstantin Zarodov, an old ideologue who died in 1982 after serving for years as the editor of *Problemy mira i sotsializma,* the organ of the international communist movement. Writing in a publication intended for a domestic audience, Zarodov took note of the perception of Soviet behavior abroad. He detailed the point of view according to which "the exacerbation of tensions was in equal measure the responsibility of 'both sides'—NATO and the Warsaw Pact."[99] Of course it was absurd, he argued, to judge such matters on the basis of "diplomatic protocol," without understanding the "class nature" of the opposing policies. Unfortunately though, "errors" of this kind were apparently widespread, and they were serious: Zarodov warned that there was a danger of such ideas "disorienting" the working class movement.[100]

The lesson was twofold. First, there was the Leninist duty not to allow "another Chile," by which Zarodov clearly meant that military force continued to be justifiable in certain circumstances.[101] Second, he asserted that despite increased imperialist aggression, "never in the past" had there been "such potential for removing the danger of war."[102] This seeming paradox was merely a reflection of the "dialectic of international life." Thus, by pursuing a "peace-loving policy," the Soviet Union could both actively foster radical change in the Third World and hinder any hostile American response; meanwhile, national liberation victories themselves helped erode American capabilities. Here was Zarodov's rationale for promoting a "reconstruction of international relations on the basis of peaceful coexistence."[103] In this way the unilateralist prescription evoked an image of "offensive detente."

Management

A second cluster of prescriptions, associated with mixed attribution, endorsed what might be called a "managerial" approach to U.S.-Soviet relations. Writers who took this approach departed from the unilateralist position on the issue of conflict in the Third World. Whereas the unilateralists accepted the risks inherent in regional intervention (implicitly, on the grounds that such risks were both necessary and manageable), these writers were less adventuristic. Many of them indicated an unwillingness to sacrifice the gains of the 1970s, even if this meant that conflict could ultimately not be avoided. However, while they were ready to accept risks in order to avoid losses, they were reluctant to do so in order to achieve gains.[104] All of them advocated a dynamic policy in the Third World, presumably including political and economic support for chosen national liberation movements. But they also shared the belief that with skill, prudence, and self-restraint, this activism could be insulated from confrontation. Authors who took a management approach wanted a strong defense, but were relatively optimistic about the prospects of cooperation with the United States. In this view it was worthwhile to make long-term adjustments to scale down the intensity of competition.[105]

The degree of caution an analyst deemed advisable, or the danger of military confrontation, is difficult to assess. No commentator on foreign policy would advocate simply letting a client twist in the wind. And there may well have been a near unanimity within the policymaking and academic communities that something had to be done to advance the revolutionary cause in the developing countries. But even then, the *way* it was done might matter almost as much as the fact *that* it was done, in terms both of triggering a hostile American response and inflaming world opinion.

Vadim Kortunov's writing provides an illustration of this viewpoint. Kortunov insisted that Western notions equating detente with solidification of the status quo were mistaken: "Social trends in the world are an objective phenomenon," he wrote; these "in no way contradict detente, but on the contrary are its most reliable guarantee."[106] That such objective phenomena might involve Soviet participation was implied by Kortunov's congratulatory catalogue of progressive change in the 1970s. However, he also observed that "Western politicians" wrongly tended to assume that detente was "limited," encompassing only economic and social matters, or only regional politics (for example, European politics).[107] In reality, he claimed, all global problems were interconnected and thus "any local conflict unavoidably affects the other centers of world politics."[108] Obviously this was an argument that cut both ways. The point seemed to be that cautious activism was indicated, provided that it did not lead to military intervention. Only in this way was it possible to reconcile his statement that as a result of progressive change, "international security . . . suffers not in the least, but on the contrary gains."[109]

It is noteworthy that authors who attributed the shift in U.S. policy to mixed factors generally presented a less extreme image of the U.S. threat than those who made dispositional attributions. Henry Trofimenko, as we have already seen, was increasingly inclined to paint a very bleak picture of American intentions. However, he also discerned several factors that combined to "place rather severe limits on American possibilities."[110] These factors included the "active foreign policy course" of the U.S.S.R., the "greater influence" of the liberated countries, and increased economic power of the West Europeans and Japanese.[111] The implication was that the Soviet Union ought to maintain an active foreign policy, in particular one aimed at further boosting the "influence" of certain developing countries. Also, Trofimenko avoided any favorable mention of Soviet military involvement or overt supply of military aid to Third World clients. The "limits on American possibilities" seemed to imply that armed intervention should not be necessary and that the United States would not respond drastically unless provoked.

Another implication of the argument that American military capabilities were effectively limited, whether by political factors or by Soviet parity, was that the U.S.S.R. could and should provide military assistance in certain cases. For example, Viktor Kremeniuk wrote that the United States was flexing its military muscles as a way of threatening the U.S.S.R. against intervening on behalf of embattled national liberation movements.[112] On the other hand, he pointed to increasing opposition to the use of force, from within both the United States and the Atlantic Alliance.[113] Apparently, American militarism was not likely to run amok, and the Soviet Union need not be intimidated into deserting its friends. Kremeniuk therefore defended Soviet aid to Afghanistan during the "critical period" in December 1979.[114] He also quoted Brezhnev to the effect that the U.S.S.R. did not seek superiority, but would not allow the United States to achieve it either.[115] The overall position seemed to be that a massive military buildup was unnecessary and that the use of force should be avoided wherever possible, but that Soviet interests should not be sacrificed due to a loss of either parity or nerve. Here it is important to bear in mind the distinction, which was never made explicit in Soviet writings, between rallying to the defense of an established client and engaging in reckless adventurism. Kremeniuk seemed to be clearly advocating only the former. Others who endorsed the Afghan intervention in qualified terms were probably taking the same position.

M. D. Lvov, a deputy editor at *Novyi mir,* was fairly forthcoming on this score. He wrote in *New Times* in January 1980 on the "growing imperialist threat"; in fact his article was quite restrained compared to others appearing in the journal at that time. In it, Lvov praised the "political, economic, and moral assistance" provided to the liberated countries by the socialist community.[116] However, he added that "in exceptional cases" where a revolution was directly threatened, "military aid too can be granted."[117] Lvov conveyed his sober appraisal of the "danger arising" from such crises and stressed the "urgency" which accompanied "the question of helping the newly free states . . . while at the same time not allowing imperialism to provoke major armed conflicts."[118] The wording left open to doubt the advisability of becoming involved in conflicts such as those in Ethiopia and Angola in the future. In fact the opposite may have been implied by Lvov's pronouncement that the solution to the above question "will always require a principled approach, restraint, and a high sense of responsibility."[119]

Writers in this group intimated that moderation on the Soviet side might be reciprocated by the United States. Vladimir Petrovskii, then a department head in the Ministry of Foreign Affairs and now Deputy Foreign Minister, wrote in a review essay that the rise of right-wing conservatism did not mean the eclipse of liberalism. On the contrary, he accepted the argument of the authors under review (one of whom was Iuri Zamoshkin) that the predominance of one group could actually promote consolidation and reemergence of the opposition.[120] Furthermore he agreed with the authors that politicians are generally pragmatists motivated by political pressures.[121] Petrovskii concluded that "Soviet peace initiatives" could "play an enormous role in further activating [peace-loving] forces" in the United States.[122]

Zamoshkin himself, in another article not referred to by Petrovskii, seemed to offer a similar strategy aimed at moderating American policy. Zamoshkin argued that reactionary circles had managed to foster mass anti-detente sentiment by skillfully associating the detente period with setbacks in U.S. foreign policy.[123] This, he felt, posed a serious obstacle to any future improvement in relations. However, he also pointed to the still important forces favoring detente and asserted that they "may be becoming activated."[124] The chances of confirming a pro-dente attitude, according to Zamoshkin, depended on success in "destroying the association" of detente with negative developments in domestic and foreign affairs.[125] Although Zamoshkin never said so, the implication was that Soviet behavior in the Third World and direct ties with the United States could be instrumental in this regard. Of course, Zamoshkin and Petrovskii may have intended nothing more than an empty propaganda campaign, along the lines advocated by the unilateralists in the preceding section. But the evidence of a mixed attribution along with a relatively nuanced image of the American policymaking process suggests that something more substantial was meant.

Finally, the management approach combined an emphasis on defense and cooperation. Nikolai Inozemtsev, the director of IMEMO until his death in 1982, was a prominent representative of this point of view. In a speech delivered before the Academy of Sciences in May 1980, Inozemtsev expressed the hopeful opinion that detente was not yet dead.[126] He praised the contribution of the Warsaw Pact in deterring American aggression, but he also pointed out that such hostile designs had proven futile in the past, even when the United States had been relatively more powerful.[127] In addition, he noted with satisfaction that the international standing of the socialist community had risen during the 1970s along with the increased stature of the liberated countries.[128] The upshot seemed to be that defense should be an important but not paramount concern, and that the Soviet Union could successfully compete for influence abroad without resorting to force. In this way it should be possible to maintain a substantial amount of cooperation. Inozemtsev again mentioned the desirability of economic and scientific-technical cooperation with interested parties in the West in an article written following the Twenty-Sixth Congress.[129] Pehaps it might be worth paying a price for this kind of detente.

Bilateralism

Some Soviet analysts in the period following the invasion of Afghanistan seem to have been interested in reaching a cooperative modus vivendi with the United States. This does not mean they assumed that competition might be abandoned. On the contrary, for certain authors it apparently represented a safer way of pursuing political gains than before, when too many of what were thought to be implicit understandings turned out to be frank misunderstandings. Perhaps, it was thought, some sort of institutionalized arrangement could prevent the eruption of a potentially disastrous confrontation. This might involve a considerable moderation of Soviet conduct in the Third World. While competition would not be eliminated thereby, it might have to be regulated to an extent, and each side would have to take into account the legitimate interests of the other. This would include mutual restraint in terms of ends as well as means. The crucial point was to remove sources of conflict and to allow progressive changes to evolve while avoiding the dangers of militarism and reaction. Extensive cooperation should be established as well, for both the benefits it offered and its ability to help stabilize the relationship. In this way it might be possible—to use the elliptical Soviet phrase—to make detente "irreversible."

Is it justified to grant a lofty title, such as "bilateralism," to a relative handful of ideas appearing in the Soviet journals during the early 1980s? Not many writers dealt extensively with the issue of maintaining detente, and even when they did, changes in the structure of U.S.-Soviet relations were not often implied. However, those who did raise the possibility of something new were not just obscure, insignificant analysts (most were from the institutes, but were relatively prominent). In short, there was just enough smoke to suggest the presence of a small fire within the policymaking community at large.

Georgii Arbatov was one of the few writers who indicated an appreciation of the complexity of security issues. He justified the Afghan intervention on grounds of defense, but he did so in a way that reflected a perception of the dangers of unilateral action as well as an awareness of the inescapably bilateral nature of the resolution of security problems. Arbatov pointed out that much of the "so-called 'arc of crises'" was contiguous to Soviet borders and at the same time overlapped with America's self-declared "vital interests."[130] The point was not simply the standard allegation that U.S. "vital interests" were arbitrarily defined. Arbatov seemed to be implying that there were legitimate concerns on both sides, and that this was a problem to be wrestled with. His insistence that stable relations must be maintained despite the existence of tensions implied that problems should be managed mutually.[131]

Several writers suggested that, even in the short run, interventionist or destabilizing policies did not pay. Those who took this position tended to quote Lenin frequently, perhaps in self-defense. Thus Evgenii Primakov quoted Lenin on the futility of trying to export revolution, since after all, "without ripe internal conditions . . . revolution cannot succeed."[132] Similarly, Aleksander Bovin argued that war by itself was ineffective as a means of speeding up revolutionary change. As he instructed the reader, "Lenin did not at all deny that the victorious proletariat should help its class brothers abroad. He only stressed that the form of this help should have nothing in common with 'export' of revolution."[133] Furthermore, involvement in local conflicts was dangerous. First of all, it tended to arouse American fears of spillover unrest and falling dominoes. Arbatov, as mentioned above, pointed to "panicky affirmations" in the United States concerning "Soviet tanks and soldiers on the shores of the Persian Gulf."[134] Second, regional conflicts could easily get out of hand, perhaps inadvertently resulting in superpower confrontation. Bovin argued that local wars "intensify international tensions" and raise the danger of general war. He acknowledged that imperialist intrigues were usually responsible, but he also stated that one could not discount the "general instability" of emerging regimes, arising from a variety of purely indigenous factors.[135]

Although proponents of management often alluded to "realistic" politicians as a potential source of change in American policy, bilateralists emphasized the point much more strongly. Andrei Melvil contended that, despite the enunciation of the Carter doctrine, "there is no unity within the U.S. on what policy to pursue vis-à-vis the U.S.S.R."[136] Elsewhere, he noted the existence of "objective" conditions for detente, as well as "subjective" conditions. The latter included "certain shifts in the political thinking of the ruling elite of the West, [and] the strengthening of realistic impulses, in no small degree conditioned by a recognition of the constricted possibilities of capitalism in the world arena."[137] Andrei Kokoshin stated that "the most farsighted representatives of the ruling elite . . . despite their disillusionment with many elements of detente as it developed in the seventies, do not see in principle another way of avoiding a direct confrontation with the Soviet Union."[138] Apparently, an accommodative Soviet strategy would find a large, immediately receptive audience.

What bilateralists were suggesting was that Soviet initiatives could be enormously influential in shaping the character of U.S.-Soviet relations. Bovin cited Lenin on the importance of avoiding "ultimatums" that could allow imperialists to say that negotiation was impossible.[139] Furthermore, he again quoted Lenin on the need to exercise "the utmost caution, circumspection, and restraint" so that an "unconsidered or hasty step" should not "aid the extreme elements."[140] Kokoshin even quoted Bovin quoting Lenin on the need to isolate militarist politicians and encourage "reasonable" ones who favored detente.[141]

The general thrust of the bilateralist policy appeared to combine normalization, efforts to eliminate sources of conflict, and extensive cooperation with peaceful competition. Kokoshin suggested that an important factor in the decline of detente had been the failure to establish greater collaboration in the areas of trade and scientific and technical exchange. If achieved, he felt that this might have a stabilizing influence on U.S.-Soviet relations.[142] Melvil also explicitly advocated expanded cooperation in a variety of areas: economic, scientific, technical, cultural, and "to some extent in the area of political regulation of conflict situations."[143] However, this would in no way diminish "ideological competition."[144]

The idea of institutionalized, mutual regulation of competition as a means of avoiding serious conflict was strongly endorsed by Primakov. He stated that the Reagan adminsitration had reached the conclusion that "'restraint' on a global level is insufficient to guarantee the national interests of the U.S.A."[145] This created a highly volatile situation in which the dangers of unilateral American action were incalculable. Therefore Primakov stressed "the necessity of political regulation of international conflict."[146] He proposed a set of measures for this purpose, including the establishment of procedures for joint resolution of conflict, limits on the scope of military testing and maneuvers, "zones of peace," and so forth.[147] Not all of them were new or particularly substantive, but in the context of the overall discussion they represented an appeal for bilateral management as opposed to going it alone. Bovin too indicted a preference for some sort of systematic arrangement. He accepted the existence of ongoing competition. However, he insisted that it be accompanied by adherence to "principles of international relations"—including equal rights, respect for sovereignty and territorial integrity, and so forth—"not as pleasant wishes, which are recalled from time to time but which are not fulfilled, but as the active, real basis of intercourse of states."[148] He further expressed the hope that it would be possible to avert confrontation in the future by "making more widespread and firm . . . the principles of peaceful coexistence and cooperation."[149] Clearly it was a far cry from this position to one that flatly rejected any notion of "rules of the game."[150]

Conclusion

What does all of this tell us about the nature of Soviet motivations and the range of elite views at the end of the Brezhnev era? The answer, in the most general terms, is that knowing how an author views the adversary reveals a lot about how he interprets specific aggressive behavior and knowing how an author interprets the adversary's aggressive behavior says a lot about how he views the adversary. In the latter case the pattern of attribution reveals an underlying image that constitutes a key element of the author's worldview. This is worth knowing about because such images of the adversary are quite stable; in fact they will not change except in the face of powerful, persistent challenges, and even then only in conjunction with extensive changes in other central beliefs. But most of all, such attributional tendencies are closely associated with policy preferences, as can be gathered from implicit or occasionally explicit prescriptions that were found in the Soviet press. In short, knowing what kinds of images prevail gives the outsider an important insight into the assumptions and cognitions that inform elite decision making.

Such images are contained in beliefs about the dynamic of international politics, including the concepts that underlie the "domino" and "bandwagon" metaphors. From the Soviet point of view, after the invasion of Afghanistan the United States was balancing against the U.S.S.R. and its policy of offensive detente. On this point there was virtual unanimity. Where the various schools of analysis parted company was in regard to the explanations they offered for American conduct, and this in turn appears to have been associated with a divergence of views about both the degree of interconnectedness in world politics and the stability of the status quo.

More precisely, to those who held the dispositionally hostile "enemy" image, the United States was trying to roll back the gains of national liberation and was attempting to trigger a negative domino effect that the U.S.S.R. had to balance against. In this view the pattern of outcomes in world politics is highly interconnected, and gains as well as losses tend to snowball. Partly this dynamic is seen to be the result of external pressures, such as U.S. imperialism versus Soviet-sponsored "proletarian internationalism," but partly it is due to internal forces and the encouragement they draw from victories elsewhere. Consequently, according to those who share such an outlook, the superpower's behavior plays the key role in initiating a process that, once set in motion, tends to gather momentum. In the Soviet Union's case this meant two things. First, it involved aiding the national liberation movement in the Third World through a variety of political, military, and economic means. Second, once underway, it meant offsetting the adversary's balancing actions in order to safeguard the favorable process of change and to prevent dominoes from falling in reverse.

From the standpoint of those who held more complex images of the adversary, the dynamic of dominoes and bandwagons appeared differently, as did the range of desirable options. For those who made situational attributions, the pattern of political change in general appeared much less interconnected. Thus, gains and losses were not perceived to be so tightly linked together or likely to gather momentum once initiated by outside intervention. On the other hand these analysts tended to see more interaction and contingency in the superpower relationship itself. In particular, they perceived American balancing to be caused by, and directed against, Soviet activism, rather than against either Soviet power per se or indigenous radicalism. At the same time, they regarded internal factors, rather than external superpower influences, as being crucial for determining the outcome of "progressive" impulses in the Third World. Consequently they tended to discount the significance of domino tendencies.

According to this view Soviet activism is neither necessary for progressive outcomes, nor even desirable given its deleterious effect on bilateral relations. In sum, because analysts in the situational group did not have an enemy image, they did not have a zero-sum outlook, and therefore did not exaggerate the significance of gains and losses. Instead the situational group emphasized the importance of internal factors and saw the external factor as unnecessary and counterproductive. American balancing was viewed as being the result of external (especially Soviet) involvement, whereas the key variables that actually determined progressive outcomes had to do with internal developments in Third World societies. In contrast, for the dispositional group the relationship was just the opposite: balancing was the result of internal progressive tendencies in Third World states, and the critical variable determining outcomes was the presence or absence of Soviet support.

The mixed attribution group regarded both internal and external factors as equally important in the process of national liberation gains. Likewise, they saw balancing as occurring in response to external factors (although not including Soviet involvement) as well as internal factors. Like those with undifferentiated enemy images, individuals in this group also saw domino tendencies, but perceived them as operating internally rather than externally. The difference was that because this group did not perceive essential Soviet responsibility for American balancing, they advocated a shift in tactics rather than strategy. That is, they suggested avoiding provocative moves, but their prescription to proceed with greater caution did not imply an abandonment of radical activism. On the contrary these analysts continued to call for Soviet involvement to facilitate change in the political status quo. However because they stressed the importance of internal processes, they were more willing than the dispositional group to reduce the level of Soviet involvement and to let the maturation of immanent political processes determine the final result. Particularly if American balancing was triggered they were willing to downplay the issue rather than risk confrontation.

The conclusions just summarized have been stated rather sharply, and the categories that frame them may be overly neat and tidy. Anyone familiar with the nature of Soviet policy discussions knows that the reality is often murky and ill-defined, and this was especially true in the pre-"glasnost" period. Yet despite the normative constraints in the Soviet press at the end of the Brezhnev era, real differences were aired and stands were taken, many of which foreshadowed the "new thinking" under Gorbachev. In retrospect and as a guide to the future, knowing how these positions emerged and were played out helps us to understand the sources of past Soviet conduct and the dramatic reorientation of policy now.

Notes

1. Deborah Welch Larson has written an admirably clear and concise overview of attribution theory which suggests its broad applicability to foreign policy research. See her *Origins of Containment: A Psychological Explanation* (Princeton, N.J.: Princeton University Press, 1985), 34–42.

2. M. Snyder, E. Tanke, and E. Berscheid, "Social Perception and Interpersonal Behavior: On the Self-Fulfilling Nature of Social Stereotypes," *Journal of Personality and Social Psychology* 35 (1977): 656–66; R. Dyck and B. Rule, "Effect on Retaliation of Causal Attributions Concerning Attack," *Journal of Personality and Social Psychology* 36 (1978): 521–29; A. Sillars, "Attribution and Interpersonal Conflict Resolution," in *New Directions in Attribution Research,* ed. J. H. Harvey, W. Ickes, and R. Kidd, vol. 3 (Hillsdale, N.J.: Erlbaum, 1981), 285–86.

3. E. E. Jones and R. Nisbett, "The Actor and the Observer: Divergent Perceptions of the Causes of Behavior," in *Attribution: Perceiving the Causes of Behavior,* ed. E. E. Jones et al. (Morristown, N.J.: General Learning Press, 1972), 79–94; L. Ross, "The Intuitive Psychologist and His Shortcomings: Distortions in the Attribution Process," in *Advances in Experimental Social Psychology,* ed. L. Berkowitz, vol. 10 (New York: Academic Press, 1977), 173–220.

4. For a review of relevant psychological studies and an application to international conflict, see S. Rosenberg and G. Wolfsfeld, "International Conflict and the Problem of Attribution," *Journal of Conflict Resolution* 21:1 (March 1977): 75–103.

5. D. Miller and M. Ross, "Self-Serving Biases in the Attribution of Causality: Fact or Fiction?" *Psychological Bulletin* 82:2 (March 1975): 213–25.

6. On this tendency, the self-serving bias, and their effects on statesmen, see Robert Jervis, *Perception and Misperception in International Politics* (Princeton, N.J.: Princeton University Press, 1976), 343–55.

7. S. Schwartz, "Words, Deeds, and the Perception of Consequences and Responsibility in Action Situations," *Journal of Personality and Social Psychology* 10:2 (October 1968): 232–42.

8. A. W. Kruglanski, "The Endogenous-Exogenous Partition in Attribution Theory," *Psychological Review* 82:6 (November 1975): 387–406; G. Weary and J. H. Harvey, "Evaluation in Attribution Processes," *Journal for the Theory of Social Behavior* 11:1 (March 1981): 93–98.

9. S. Modenov, "Imperialist and Reactionary Schemes Fall Through," *International Affairs,* No. 4 (April 1980): 82–87.

10. Ibid.

11. B. Ponomarev, "Kommunisticheskaia pechat—glashatai mira," *Kommunist,* no. 12 (August 1981): 18.

12. G. Kim, "Sovetskii Soiuz i natsionalno—osvoboditelnoe dvizhenie," *Mirovaia ekonomika i mezhdunarodnye otnosheniia,* no. 6 (June 1980): 29. See also V. Sidenko, "Leninskii vneshnepoliticheskii kurs i natsionalnoe osvoboditelnoe dvizhenie," *Mirovaia ekonomika i mezhdunarodnye otnosheniia,* no. 2 (February 1980): 10–11.

13. V. Shamberg, "SShA v sovremennon mire," *MEiMO,* no. 7 (July 1980): 52–54.

14. L. Tolkunov, "Zamysly i dela novoiavlennykh 'krestonostsev'," *Kommunist,* no. 6 (April 1983): 106–7.

15. Ibid., 112.

16. B. I. Koval, "Leninskaia kontsepsiia mirovogo revoliutsionnogo protsessa i sovremennost," *Rabochii klass i sovremennyi mir,* no. 3 (May–June 1980): 8–9.

17. Iu. V. Katasonov, "Voenno-politicheskaia strategiia SShA na rubezhe 70–80kh godov," *SShA*, no. 2 (February 1980): 10.

18. N. I. Lebedev and S. V. Kortunov, "Problema razoruzheniia i ideologicheskaia borba (Kritika apologetov gonki vooruzhenii)," *Novaia i noveishaia istoriia*, no. 4 (July–August 1980): 8.

19. E. Lavrov, "Mifi protiv razriadki," *MEiMO*, no. 12 (December 1980): 108–10.

20. "Otvety L. I. Brezhneva na voprosy korrespondenta 'Pravda,'" *Kommunist*, no. 2 (January 1980): 13–14.

21. A. Gromyko, "Razoruzhenie: nasushchaia problema sovremennosti," *Kommunist*, no. 11 (July 1980): 8; B. Ponomarev, "Sovmestnaia borba rabochego i natsionalno-osvoboditelnogo dvizhenii protiv imperializma, za sotsialnyi progress," *Kommunist*, no. 16 (November 1980): 34–35.

22. P. Demchenko, "Afghanistan: na strazhe zavoevanii naroda," *Kommunist*, no. 5 (March 1980): 77.

23. R.Ulianovskii, "Razvitie revoliutsionnogo protsessa v Afghanistane," *MEiMO*, no. 8 (August 1983): 26.

24. V. Zagladin, "Sovremennyi mezhdunarodnyi krizis v svete leninskogo ucheniia," *MEiMO*, no. 4 (April 1984): 4.

25. Ibid., 17.

26. G. Trofimenko, "Politika bez perspektivy," *MEiMO*, no. 3, (March 1980): 18–24.

27. G. Trofimenko, "Osnovnye postulaty vneshnei politiki SShA i sudby razriadki," *SShA*, no. 7 (July 1981): 3–6.

28. Ibid., 14.

29. V. A. Kremeniuk, "Sovetsko-amerikanskie otnosheniia i nekotorye problemy osvobodivshikhsia gosudarstv," *SShA*, no. 6 (June 1982): 9–10.

30. Ibid., 15.

31. Ibid.

32. Ibid.

33. V. V. Kortunov, "KPSS v borbe za razriadku: protivoborstvo dvukh tendentsii v mezhdunarodnoi zhizni," *Voprosy istorii KPSS*, no. 10 (October 1980): 34.

34. Ibid.

35. Ibid., 35.

36. A. Kiva, "Imperializm i strany sotsialisticheskoi orientatsii," pervaia statia, *Aziia i Afrika segodnia*, no. 8 (August 1980): 6–9.

37. A. Kiva, "Imperializm i strany sotsialisticheskoi orientatsii," vtoraia statia, *Aziia i Afrika segodnia*, no. 9 (September 1980): 9–10.

38. Ibid., 6.

39. Iu. A. Zamoshkin, "Ideologiia v SShA: za razriadku i protiv nee," *SShA*, no. 4 (April 1982): 3.

40. Ibid., 4–5.

41. Ibid., 11–13.

42. R. Ovinnikov, "Za kulisami aggressivnoi politiki Vashingtona," *Kommunist*, no. 14 (September 1981): 77–78.

43. R. Ovinnikov, "Vnimanie: 'iastreby'," *Kommunist*, no. 2 (January 1983): 94; see also idem, *Uoll-strit i vneshniaia politika*, Moscow, Mezhdunarodnye otnosheniia, 1980.

44. Ovinnikov, "Vnimanie," 102–4.

45. Ovinnikov, "Za kulisami," 78–79.

46. Ovinnikov, "Vnimanie," 94.
47. Ibid.
48. A. Bovin, "Neprekhodiashchee znachenie leninskikh idei," *Kommunist,* no. 10 (July 1980): 75.
49. Ibid.
50. A. Iu. Melvil, "Leninskaia kontsepsiia vneshnei politiki i sovremennost," *SShA,* no. 4 (April 1980): 8.
51. A. A. Kokoshin, *SShA: za fasadom globalnoi politiki* (Moscow: Politizdat, 1981), 56–66.
52. Ibid., 53–55.
53. Ibid., 154.
54. Ibid., 160.
55. A Kokoshin, "Gruppirovki amerikanskoi burzhuazii i vneshnepoliticheskii kurs SShA," *SShA,* no. 10 (October 1981): 14.
56. Melvil, "Leninskaia kontsepsiia," 7.
57. Ibid., 15.
58. Kokoshin, "Gruppirovki," 3.
59. A. A. Kokoshin, *SShA v sisteme mezhdunarodnykh otnoshenii 80-kh godov* (Moscow: Mezhdunarodnye otnosheniia, 1984), 27.
60. Kokoshin, *SShA za fasadom,* 71–72, 147–48.
61. E. Primakov, "Blizhnii vostok: dalneishaia militarizatsiia politiki SShA," *Kommunist,* no. 9 (June 1980): 108.
62. E. Primakov, "Zakon neravnomernosti razvitiia i istoricheskie sudby osvobodivshikhsia stran," *MEiMO,* no. 12 (December 1980): 47, 39.
63. Primakov, "Blizhnii vostok," 113–14.
64. G. Arbatov, "Vneshniaia politika SShA na poroge 80-kh godov," *SShA,* no. 4 (April 1980): 52.
65. Ibid., 54.
66. Ibid.
67. R. Garthoff, *Detente and Confrontation: American-Soviet Relations from Nixon to Reagan* (Washington, D.C.: Brookings Institution, 1985), 998–1001.
68. Ibid., 1014–17.
69. See J. Hough, *The Struggle for the Third World: Soviet Debates and American Options* (Washington, D.C.: Brookings Institution, 1986), 13–26; see also T. Bjorkman and T. Zamostny, "Soviet Politics and Strategy toward the West: Three Cases," *World Politics* 36:2 (January 1984), 189–214.
70. F. Griffiths, "The Sources of American Conduct: Soviet Perspectives and Their Policy Implications," *International Security* 9:2 (Fall 1984): 42–43.
71. I use the term "unilateralism" to distinguish the following analysis from Griffiths's discussion of "coercive isolationism." Ibid., 27–30. The major difference concerns the image of detente, which in the early 1980s was almost unassailable although, as I discuss, was clearly an offensive manipulative detente. In this sense "unilateralism" also incorporates elements of Griffiths's "expansionist internationalism"; see his pp. 30–34. A similar, very suggestive, but rather sketchy approach is T. Milburn, P. Stewart, and R. Herrmann, "Perceiving the Other's Intentions," in *Foreign Policy U.S.A./U.S.S.R.,* ed. C. Kegley and P. McGowen (Beverly Hills, Calif.: Sage Publications, 1982), 51–63. See also C. Jonsson, "Foreign Policy Ideas and Groupings in the Soviet Union," in *Soviet Foreign Policy and East-West Relations,* ed. R. E. Kanet (New York: Pergamon, 1982), 3–26.

72. V. K. Germanov, "Borba KPSS za obespechenie blagopriiatnykh vneshnepoliticheskikh uslovii stroitelstva kommunizma," *Voprosy istorii KPSS,* no. 8 (August 1980): 31–42.

73. R. Bogdanov, "Zastarelyi nedug gegemonizma," *Kommunist,* no. 11 (July 1981): 117.

74. L. Tolkunov, "Zamysly i dela," 113.

75. For example, see A. Iakovlev, "Rakovaia opukhol imperskikh ambitsii v iadernykh vek," *MEiMO,* no. 1 (January 1984): 14.

76. Again for example, see Lavrov, "Mifi," 109.

77. "The People's Will Cannot Be Shaken," *New Times,* no. 2 (January 1980): 1.

78. Modenov, "Imperialist and Reactionary Schemes," p. 83; R. Ulianovskii, "Sovetskaia sotsialisticheskaia federatsiia i osvobodivshiesia strany," *Narody Azii i Afriki,* no. 6 (November–December 1982): 16. Ulianovskii, referring to U.S. efforts to "divide and conquer," added the examples of UNITA in Angola and the Eritreans in Ethiopia.

79. Sidenko, "Leninskii vneshnepoliticheskii kurs," 14, 17.

80. B. S. Popov, "Aktualnye problemy proletarskogo sotsialisticheskogo internatsionalizma," *Voprosy istorii KPSS,* no. 4 (April 1981): 28.

81. B. Ponomarev, "Velikaia zhiznennaia sila leninizma," *Kommunist,* no. 7 (May 1980): 15. See also Ponamarev, "Kommunisticheskaia pechat," 20.

82. Koval, "Leninskaia kontsepsiia," 9.

83. Ibid.

84. N. Ivanov, "Schemes of the Enemies of the Afghan Revolution," *International Affairs* (Moscow), no. 10 (October 1981): 129–30.

85. Katasonov, "Voenno-politicheskaia strategiia," 10.

86. Ibid., 12–13.

87. On "balancing" and "bandwagoning" tendencies, see Stephen M. Walt, "Alliance Formation and the Balance of Power," *International Security* 9:4 (Spring 1985): 3–43.

88. G. Kim, "Sovetskii Soiuz," *MEiMO,* no. 6 (June 1980): 2–4.

89. Ibid., 29.

90. Ibid.

91. Iu. M. Melnikov, *Sila i bessilie: vneshniaia politika Vashingtona 1945–1982 gg.* (Moscow: Izdatelstvo politicheskoi literatury, 1983), 362.

92. Ibid., 362–63.

93. Iakovlev, "Rakovaia opukhol," 16.

94. *Pravda,* July 23, 1981, 4–5.

95. Ponomarev, "Kommunisticheskaia pechat," 20.

96. B. Ponomarev, "O mezhdunarodnom znachenii 26 sezda KPSS," *Kommunist,* no. 5 (March 1981): 13–14.

97. Ibid., 14.

98. Ibid., 11.

99. K. I. Zarodov, "O nekotorykh perspektivakh razvitiia mirovogo revoliutsionnogo protsessa v svete idei XXVI sezda KPSS," *Voprosy istorii KPSS,* no. 9 (September 1981): 31.

100. Ibid., 32.

101. Ibid., 33.

102. Ibid.

103. Ibid., 34.

104. On this general tendency, see A. Tversky and D. Kahneman, "The Framing of

Decisions and the Psychology of Choice," *Science,* no. 211 (1981), 453–58. The fact that unilateralist authors appeared more willing to accept risks for gains underlines the importance—and subjective nature—of individual expectations and perceptions of base rates. I would like to thank Robert Jervis for bringing this point to my attention.

105. Again with regard to Griffiths's analysis, this position is obviously similar to "reformative internationalism." I essentially subdivide Griffiths's category into two parts, "management" and "bilateralism," where the latter is distinguished by its emphasis on institutionalization in both the competitive and cooperative spheres. See Griffiths, "Sources of American Conduct," 34–39.

106. Kortunov, "KPSS v borbe," 34. Kortunov also subscribed to the view that detente is "in no way a neutral factor," but rather one that accelerates the ineluctable progress of national liberation, etc. Kortunov, "Pagubnye retsidivy politiki sily," *Kommunist,* no. 10 (July 1980): 102.

107. Kortunov, "KPSS v borbe," 30.

108. Ibid.

109. Ibid., 34.

110. Trofimenko, "Osnovnye postulaty," 27.

111. Ibid.

112. Kremeniuk, "Sovetsko-amerikanskie otnosheniia," 16.

113. Ibid., 17.

114. Ibid., 14.

115. Ibid., 16.

116. M. Lvov, "Entering the New Decade," *New Times,* no. 2 (January 1980): 7.

117. Ibid.

118. Ibid.

119. Ibid.

120. V. Petrovskii, "SShA: politika i politicheskoe soznanie," *Kommunist,* no. 16 (November 1981): 125.

121. Ibid.

122. Ibid., 128. See also Ovinnikov, "Vnimanie," 102–4.

123. Zamoshkin, "Ideologiia v SShA," 16.

124. Ibid.

125. Ibid.

126. N. N. Inozemtsev, "Doklad Akademika N. N. Inozemtseva," *MEiMO,* no. 6 (June 1980): 13.

127. Ibid.

128. Ibid., 12.

129. N. Inozemtsev, "26 sezd KPSS i nashi zadachi," *MEiMO,* no. 3 (March 1981): 12–13.

130. Arbatov, "Vneshniaia politika SShA," 45.

131. Ibid., 54.

132. E. Primakov, "Osvobodivshiesia strany v mezhdunarodnykh otnosheniiakh," *MEiMO,* no. 5 (May 1982): 22.

133. Bovin, "Neprekhodiashchee znachenie," 72.

134. Arbatov, "Vneshniaia politika SShA," 54.

135. Bovin, "Neprekhodiashchee znachenie," 77.

136. A. Melvil, "The Two Aspects of American Hegemonism," *New Times,* no. 31 (August 1980): 19.

137. Melvil, "Leninskaia kontsepsiia," 11.

138. Kokoshin, "Gruppirovki," 14.

139. Bovin, "Neprekhodiashchee znachenie," 74.
140. Ibid., 75.
141. Kokoshin, *SShA v sisteme,* 10.
142. Ibid., 27–28.
143. Melvil, "Leninskaia kontsepsiia," 11.
144. Ibid.
145. Primakov, "Osvobodivshiesia strany," 20.
146. Ibid., 22.
147. Ibid., 23.
148. Bovin, "Neprekhodiashchee znachenie," 73.
149. Ibid., 77.
150. Iu. P. Babich, "Mogulshchiki razriadki za rabotoi," *SShA,* no. 9 (September 1981): 70.

8

The Soviet Decision to Withdraw from Afghanistan: Changing Strategic and Regional Images

Richard Herrmann

In 1988 the Soviet Union decided to withdraw its troops from Afghanistan. One question addressed in this chapter is why. But more fundamentally this chapter is about how we interpret superpower behavior in countries along the Asian rimland and about how perceptions of global strategies are translated into the images of regional conflicts. I plan to begin with a discussion of the enemy image and its effects on the interpretation of an adversary's behavior. My key point here will be that our assumptions about the adversary's motives may effect our estimate of its relative capabilities. I will then turn to an empirical examination of Soviet perceptions of Afghanistan. By beginning with an examination of our own proclivities for misperception and a theoretical conception of the relationship between strategic beliefs and tactical regional images, I hope to have also set the stage for interpreting the Soviet decision to withdraw from Afghanistan.

The second part of this chapter will open with a study of the Soviet perceptions that led to the decision to intervene. The third part will then offer a parallel study of the decision to withdraw. I plan to analyze the changing Soviet strategic beliefs about the United States, the southwest Asian region, and domestic Afghan politics in each time period.

Competing Hypotheses About Soviet Strategic Beliefs: Naive or Romantic?

When Soviet troops rolled into Kabul in 1979 the American president expressed his outrage and shock. Jimmy Carter explained that this act of Soviet aggression had fundamentally changed his view of Soviet intentions.[1] Most Americans joined the president in concluding that Brezhnev had betrayed the spirit of detente and had revealed his expansionist ambitions. Gorbachev's decision to withdraw has not had a comparable effect on American assumptions about Soviet motives. The intervention reinforced well-learned cold war assumptions. The withdrawal does not really contradict American conclusions about Soviet foreign policy. I want to explore why this is the case and to examine critically the lessons we might draw from the Soviet withdrawal.

The Cold War Hypothesis: Deterrence Works

The prevailing American understanding of Soviet strategic beliefs is best captured in Nathan Leites operational code of the Politburo.[2] It assumes that Bolsheviks are always determined to expand but do so in an opportunistic fashion.[3] They test their adversary's resolve, and when they find weakness they exploit it. When they confront steel they retreat. They seek the spoils of conquest without the costs. The Gorbachev decision to abandon Kabul in this conception is not problematic. The explanation for the withdrawal is self-evident. The costs were too high. And these costs were directly increased by America's military aid for the mujahadeen.[4]

Washington and the mujahadeen taught the Soviets a lesson. It is a tempting conclusion for Americans and Afghans alike. Certainly real costs and constraints played a major role in Soviet decision making.[5] The urgent demands of the economy at home; domestic dissatisfaction with the casualties; the direct costs in terms of troops and resources; and the opportunity costs the Soviet had to pay in American-Soviet, Sino-Soviet, and Soviet-Islamic relations surely surpassed the threshold of costs that new Soviet leaders were willing to pay. But it is also true that this threshold is a variable that is determined by the priority Soviet leaders grant to this theater. No one should doubt that Moscow could have deployed vastly more force to Afghanistan. The most important question is why the Gorbachev regime decided that the continuing costs in Afghanistan were no longer worth the effort.[6]

When the Americans left Vietnam, Soviet analysts concluded that the will and courage of the national liberation forces and the resolute support of the U.S.S.R. had forced Washington to retreat.[7] They had taught Americans a lesson about the limits of American power and post-war hegemony.[8] Some Soviet observers felt that "realistic" Americans had learned their lesson and would change course. Others felt that Washington would only pursue new and more clever tactics. Both views agreed that Washington had been beaten and that the episode demonstrated the limits of American power.[9]

In Washington, the Soviet withdrawal from Afghanistan generated a similar debate. Much of the argument turned on judgments about what the adversary had learned and whether it would produce any lasting change in its foreign policy. The mainstream of the debate in both cases assumed that the adversary was defeated and wondered whether or not the lessons about the need to give up their aggressive and expansionist adventures would really sink in. The parameters of the debate were set by the basic assumptions of the enemy image.[10] The image describes the adversary as permanently aggressive and as ready to seize opportunities if available. It also implies that when the adversary retreats it is because it has been forced to. In the enemy image the notion that our strength produces their restraint and their withdrawal is symptomatic of their weakness is the central assumption about the dynamics of interaction.

We, of course, need to avoid accepting too quickly a romantic notion that we simply bloodied the enemy's nose and, being a paper tiger, it quickly folded.

This could lead to a dangerous underestimation of the adversary's power. It would be a grave mistake to allow our national egos and our motivational assumptions about Soviet motives to determine our assessment of their capabilities. But the enemy images of the cold war can lead us in this direction and they can also blind us to changes in the adversary's intentions.

The pullback from Afghanistan is not the first Soviet retreat in southwest Asia. Stalin withdrew his troops from Azerbaijan and Kurdistan after a short-lived confrontation in 1946. This event is traditionally remembered as an American victory and attributed to both the strength of President Truman's threats to use force and the diplomacy of Iranian Prime Minister Ahmad Qavam.[11] It is not necessary to digress into the details of this case to make my central point that Americans are inclined to perceive the Soviet pullback as caused by American compellence. For most of them, the alternative interpretation, that Stalin moved in Iran to protect Baku and the southern front from British encirclement, is seen as naive.[12] But the romance of our traditional interpretation would probably appear obvious to George Allen, the American ambassador to Iran, back in 1946.

Ambassador Allen understood that Washington had no options for compelling a Soviet pullback.[13] At that time, he was genuinely puzzled by the Soviet decision, fully aware that Washington had done very little to force a retreat. President Truman recalled in 1952 that he had threatened Stalin, but since the documents have been open, historians have been unable to find any evidence of this.[14] Perhaps a letter was sent and simply is yet to be found, but all the evidence to date suggests the president by 1952 had fully learned what Deborah Larson might call the "cold war" script and embellished his recollection.[15] In the script, Soviet retreats are caused by our strength so there must have been some display of our resolve.[16] In fact, however, Washington was encouraging compromise and, rather than threatening Stalin, it was reassuring him.

I suspect many readers will resist my suggestion that U.S. threats were not significantly responsible for Stalin's withdrawal. They will find it implausible and prefer to believe that Truman did send the message and that historians simply have not found it. But, of course, even if such a message does exist the traditional interpretation is still romantic. A piece of paper will not change the balance of forces on the ground in Iran. American analysts in Iran and Washington knew they could do nothing to enhance Iran's ability to resist Soviet pressure.[17] There were no available forces that could credibly compel Stalin. American military aid to Iran would not even begin to arrive until two years later.[18] Moreover, if Truman did make a threat, why was it secret? If it was secret because it would create an outcry of opposition in the United States (recall this is long before the Truman Doctrine), then how credible would it be to Stalin? And why should anyone believe that a tongue lashing at the United Nations would compel a ruthless dictator like Joseph Stalin to run for cover?

The Iranian case is very instructive. We are reluctant to question the credibility of the American threat and may cling to it as our explanatory variable even when the circumstances ought to make us suspicious. The alternative interpretation is hard to accept despite its congruence with the evidence. Marshal Shulman has argued that Stalin was committed to consolidating wartime gains and was worried about encirclement.[19] In Iran, Stalin may have feared the U.S.S.R.'s exclusion and the creation of an Anglo-American anti-Soviet outpost. George Kennan thought this might be the case.[20] Nikita Khrushchev recalled that it was.[21] If so, then the British willingness to divide Iran leaving Soviet influence in the north in exchange for British domination of the south plus the American policy of encouraging Tehran to grant oil concessions to Moscow, may have persuaded Stalin that withdrawal was safe. Moreover, Iranian Prime Minister Qavam was described by some Americans as a Soviet puppet. He was not, but he did have credibility in Moscow as a nationalist, and his appointment as prime minister might have convinced the Soviets that a nonaligned option was possible or that at least it was worth experimenting with a conciliatory gesture, especially one that would consolidate Soviet defenses.[22]

I have belabored the Iranian case because I want to emphasize the potency of cold war motivational assumptions. As we consider Gorbachev's decision to withdraw from Afghanistan, we ought to keep in mind our own proclivities for romance as well as naiveté. Many Americans believe that Leonid Brezhnev drew the wrong conclusions about American strength and resolve from our experience in Vietnam. Expecting American acquiescence he presided over a series of Third World adventures that produced a substantial American backlash and destroyed the political basis for detente. As we examine Moscow's retreat from Kabul, we need to avoid making the same mistake.

The Detente Hypothesis: Reassurance Works

We should balance the explanation of Gorbachev's retreat that postulates the key variables of Soviet weakness at home, American pressure abroad, and the mujahadeen's heroism in Afghanistan with a second hypothesis that emphasizes the ascendence in Moscow of new world views and strategic beliefs. The withdrawal could be a product of a reduced perception of threat. After all, a number of well-informed Americans argued that the original intervention was motivated by Soviet concerns about competition with the United States, intense rivalry with China, and fear of Islamic fundamentalism.[23] Gorbachev might believe that the American threat has been overblown in Moscow and that Third World conflicts are better understood in regional terms than in terms of assets and pawns in some great strategic game. In fact, he might believe that Third World allies are very expensive and not very important. In this case, he may have lowered the threshold of acceptable commitment much more dramatically than American aid or the mujahadeen raised the actual level of costs.

Gorbachev might also believe that in 1980 Washington could have staged a comback in Iran, but by 1987 have concluded that this was very unlikely. Rather than being compelled by American missiles in the hands of the mujahadeen and deterred by American aid to Pakistan, he might be reassured by the general failure of American policy toward Iran and Islam. At the same time, he might also suspect that an action–reaction dynamic has prevailed in Soviet-American relations and that fear of the U.S.S.R. actually does motivate American policy.

In this case, he would believe that the threat can be defused with enlightened Soviet behavior.[24] At the same time, he might envision a fairly optimistic future for Sino-Soviet rapprochement and conclude that the Sino-American axis that seemed united by anti-Soviet purposes in 1980 has come substantially unglued. He might also be advised by regional experts who see the Soviet occupation of Afghanistan as a terrible albatross around their necks. In this case, the withdrawal may not be a retreat at all but the beginning of a new diplomatic offensive in the Islamic Middle East that will strengthen Soviet influence.

Can Deterrence and Reassurance Work Together?

The cold war interpretation of the Soviet withdrawal and the alternative reduction of perceived threat hypothesis are not mutually exclusive. As long as the American aid is seen by Soviet leaders as simply a tactical move targeted exclusively to the Afghan bargaining situation and coupled to an overall strategic reduction in cold war competition, it is possible to marry the two sets of variables in a common interpretation. On the other hand, if the American military aid and pressure is seen in Moscow as very substantial and as part of a global recommitment to containment, then it is hard to imagine how Soviet leaders would perceive this as a reduced external threat. At that level, the two hypotheses really are competitive and may lead to the sort of polemical struggle I suggest when I use terms like romantic and naive. I have no pretensions that I can definitively prove which perspective is the correct one, but I do hope to shake those interpretations that claim they already have.

Soviet Perceptions and the Decision to Intervene

American Sovietologists have known for a long time that different points of view compete in Moscow and that referring to a single set of Soviet strategic beliefs is a significant simplification. This was true in the Brezhnev era and became undeniably obvious with Gorbachev's policy of *glasnost*. We can speak of a prevailing view, but it is important to keep in mind that Soviet sources cannot be used interchangeably. Parts of one article and parts of another may not add up to a single image but be components of quite different and competitive perspectives and policy preferences. Moreover, we can never be sure if the explanations for policy that leaders give are reflections of the perceptions on which the choices were made or simply the self-conscious manipulation of public impressions. We all wish there were an ingenious way to penetrate the Soviet decisional process, unmask the true perceptions of the most critical leaders, and then outline accurately how multiple views compete and are politically negotiated into a resultant decision. Unfortunately, there is not. The best we can do is make choices about how to infer Soviet perceptions from verbal and policy outputs and make a judgment about how many different points of view it is useful to describe.

I belive that decisions are made in the context of a situation. Defining the situation is perhaps the most critical determinant of decision making and the central activity in many political struggles.[25] I presume that Soviet politicians and commentators construct pictures of global and regional affairs both to influence the process in Moscow and to justify policy lines already in place. I have argued elsewhere that the types of images that are used to justify policy are not randomly or haphazardly constructed.[26] They follow identifiable scripts that are very revealing. The imperial image is such a script. It is the classic justification for intervention and domination.[27] My argument is that precisely because it is so self-serving and morally self-righteous those who evoke it are likely to believe in its veracity. We can expect to see this pattern when Soviet leaders perceive great opportunities in regional situations. We would be naive to believe that the content of this stereotypical imagery is accurate, but we would not be softheaded to assume that the appearance of the image is indicative of Soviet perceptions that they can and should dominate another country.

The enemy image is also a stereotype and like the imperial pattern should be expected to appear in progaganda. The enemy image, however, does not mask perceived opportunity. Instead it reveals very substantial fear. It can justify an aggressive and confrontational policy but is rooted in perceived threat. It is quite different than the image Hitler's propaganda used to justify the conquest of France, a policy I presume was based on perceived opportunity. Hitler characterized his victims as decadent and degenerate and hardly the highly aggressive monolithic juggernaut that the enemy image implies.[28] My contention is that we can infer a great deal about Soviet strategic beliefs from the images they evoke in their propaganda. Enemy images signal a concern with a threatening adversary and may stimulate a very competitively pursued strategy for containing that threat. Features of a degenerate stereotype may lead to some of the same aggressive actions but signal a confidence that opportunities can be exploited and revisionist aspirations achieved.

The cold war and detente hypotheses that I introduced at the outset of this chapter can be translated into hypotheses about Soviet perceptions. The first contends that Soviet leaders see little threat and move when they perceive opportunity. The second argues that perceived threat explains the most aggressive Soviet actions. My intention is to look at the Brezhnev decision to intervene in Afghanistan and the Gorbachev decision to withdraw in terms of these propositions. How did they describe the situation and what images were used to justify the decisions? I plan to look at three questions in particular for each episode. First, what was the basic picture of the United States and which image did it resemble? Second, how was the regional situation described and what role was ascribed to the United States in the region? Third, how was the internal situation in Afghanistan described and did it resemble an imperial image?

Because I am interested in the role that changing strategic beliefs may have played in the decision to withdraw, I intend to use the views that prevailed during the Brezhnev days and led to the intervention as a base line. I do not plan to discuss the other competing views that existed in Moscow in 1980. I also will assume that after the decision to intervene was taken, the Soviet media was mobilized to justify the attack and reflected the prevailing images. Consequently, I will stress what is common across articles. In the Gorbachev period, I plan to consider competing perspectives and pay much greater attention to differences across articles. The main reason for this is to search for a correlation between different perceptions of the strategic situation and support for the decision to withdraw. The Gorbachev period also demands greater differentiation because the range of views openly expressed is wider and, more importantly, because Soviet influence in Afghanistan is still very active and it is not clear which or what mix of the competing views will ultimately prevail.

Strategic Images of Washington and Brezhnev's Decision to Intervene

The late 1970s were a frustrating and alarming period for many Americans. Cambodia, Vietnam, Laos, Angola, Ethiopia, Iran, Nicaragua, and South Yemen seemed like an endless string of revolutions and setbacks for American diplomacy. Conservative Americans believed that their leaders had lost the will and determination to protect American interests and were sure that Soviet observers had reached the same conclusion.[29] Brezhnev's decision to occupy Afghanistan only reinforced their suspicions.

Brezhnev's cohort certainly saw the string of American setbacks. They talked about them constantly and argued that they demonstrated the great strength of the socialist community and the national liberation movement.[30] Picturing the progressive forces of peace and socialism as on the move and achieving ever new heights of glory was standard Soviet propaganda. So was the depiction of the United States as suffering one defeat after another as it tried to bolster and preserve its hegemonic and imperial domination over most of the world. The critical aspect of this propaganda imagery, as far as strategic beliefs are concerned, is the description of American motives and will power. In the prevailing image the United States had been defeated. It had been compelled to abandon aggressive and imperialistic policies and was being forced to deal with Moscow as an equal.[31] It did not lack will and had not given up its imperial aspirations and self-aggrandizing motives. To the contrary, its ambitions and arrogance vastly outstripped its capabilities. It was still a dangerous and expansionist enemy, but one that had been successfully contained by the resolute will of the socialist community and the heroic defiance by the forces of national liberation.[32]

The strategic conception evident in the Brezhnev imagery implied that Soviet strength produced American restraint. It followed the traditional pattern of the cold war and concluded that deterrence and compellence would work. There seemed to be little concern with escalation or any recognition that Soviet-American relations might follow an action–reaction pattern. Soviet observers rarely attributed defensive motives to Washington and regularly explained that American "ruling circles" did not really see the "Soviet threat" as endangering Western security, but only used it to mobilize mass support for militaristic policies.

Some academic experts at the Institue for the Study of the U.S.A. and Canada had more complicated pictures of American foreign policy. Henrik Trofimenko, for instance, took American perceptions more seriously. Nevertheless, he concluded that Washington was driven by imperial motives and had been defeated in the Third World; it had not restrained itself.[33] He also highlighted the continuing American commitment to "a policy of strength," which, he argued, was evident in the United State's policies in the Middle East—with the exclusionist and anti-Soviet nature of the Camp David Accords, the open playing of the China card, and the modernization of NATO tactical air and land based nuclear missiles. Other analysts at the institute, like Viktor Kremenyuk and V. Lukin, concentrated on Washington's troubles in the Third World and detailed what they saw as a changing American approach.[34] The changes they described, however, were entirely tactical. The goals were the same. The only effect the string of defeats had had was to force Washington to devise a more clever and diplomatically sophisticated way to retain hegemonic control.

I note the prevalence of the basic enemy conception in the academic writings not because they determined policy. Rather, my point is that the basic logic of the cold war was still thoroughly ingrained even in the institute that many assumed was one of the most vocal advocates of detente. In Soviet eyes, the American government was as committed as ever to hegemony. It was launching new offensives to reverse the setbacks it had suffered in the Third World. Consequently, American leaders would once again have to be taught the bitter lessons that observers like Trofimenko had hoped were learned in Vietnam.[35] In any case, the prescription was obvious. Demonstrate the will and resolve to block American advances and force Washington to recognize its overextension. This is how progress, justice, and peace would be promoted in the world.

Regional Images and the Decision to Intervene

Both the revolution in Iran and the seizure of power in Kabul by the Khalq party were seen in Moscow as positive events. The Soviet Union had not engineered either of these events and by all available evidence seemed to be caught off guard by both of them.[36] Once they were under way, however, Soviet observers saw the geostrategic implications and encouraged the anti-American, anti-imperial, and antimonarchist trends.[37] Soviet relations with the shah's Iran had been good, but the collapse of the American presence would be even better. Soviet enthusiasm for the Islamic revolution rose and fell with the anti-American emphasis of the revolt. In early 1979 Soviet observers celebrated the Islamic victory and took substantial credit for having deterred an American intervention.[38] Later in the year, when the Bazargan government began to explore new arrangements with Washington for military spare parts and the like, commentators like Aleksander Bovin began to express the disappointment and alarm with the course of the revolution.[39] Once American hostages were seized and anti-American sentiment in Iran again reached fever pitch, Soviet images once again took a positive tone and emphasized the importance of revolutionary unity against liberal and any other pro-American bourgeois forces.[40]

There may have been some Soviet analysts who perceived a chance to use revolutionary Islam against the United States. Others may have even seen the possibility of a leftist Islamic regime someday coming to power in Tehran.[41] But none of these ambitions prevailed. Soviet behavior made it clear that the bottom line in Moscow was to insure that the United States did not stage a comeback in Iran. The collapse of the American presence on the U.S.S.R.'s southern frontier was sufficient to satisfy Soviet motives. The possible threats to Soviet security had been reduced and, not surprisingly, Soviet leaders were loath to let Washington reestablish an outpost for encirclement, espionage, and anti-Soviet military development. Almost everyone in Moscow assumed that Washington would try to recover its previous influence in southwest Asia and were primed to interpret American actions in this way.

In the prevailing Soviet image, Washington did not let the shah fall. The shah was overthrown despite Washington's best effort to save him.[42] The Carter administration had tried everything, including plans for a coup d'état and military intervention, and had simply been forced to accept defeat.[43] The social and political forces inside Iran were simply too powerful. The popular base of the revolution was too wide for serious plans of military intervention and the hatred for American imperialism so deep that any American embrace for a new regime would delegitimate it immediately.[44] Washington, the Soviet observers continued, had run into the rising power of nationalism and once again had been forced to see the limits to the imperial use of force and the costs of sustaining puppets who were hated by their own people.[45] American ruling circles, they explained, refused to face these truths and instead turned to violence and aggression to vent their anger.[46] Judging from Soviet policy in Afghanistan, Soviet leaders were equally reluctant to learn comparable lessons. They also continued to link enemy conceptions of the cold war with imperial images of change in the Third World.

Prevailing Images of Afghanistan and the Expectations for Intervention

When the April 1978 revolution brought a communist regime to power in Kabul the Soviet decision to offer aid was an easy one. The new regime was even more openly friendly than the previous one. It was committed to social and economic reforms that Soviet ideology considered progressive, and it would side with Moscow in both the Soviet-American and Sino-Soviet contests. By late 1979, circumstances had changed and what had seemed like such an easy and attractive choice was heavily burdened with complications. The revolutionary regime had provoked strong internal resistance and had proved unable to establish a strong mass base. It had pursued rapid change, and when the Soviet Union advised moderation and gradualism, the Taraki regime was not very responsive. After September 1979, Taraki was dead and Hafizullah Amin, who many considered the main engine of the uncompromising stance on rapid social and political change, was in power and beyond Soviet control. And while the resistance had grown larger and stronger, the Soviet commitment had grown deeper and more directly tied to strategic concerns. Major concerns about credibility were now on the line. If Moscow could not defend its influence directly on its borders, where could it protect its interests and who would take its threats to do so seriously?

As it became increasingly clear that Amin's regime would fall, the Soviet dilemma grew more intense. The instability not only threatened Soviet credibility but also presented, at least in Soviet eyes, a potential opportunity for the United States and China. Sino-American rapprochement was reaching new heights as each played the other as a "card" against Moscow, and both had ties to Pakistan, although Washington's were quite strained.[47] The revolution in Iran had stimulated new American interest in Pakistan, and as argued above, most Soviet observers expected Washington to stage, or at least try to mount, a comeback in southwest Asia either in Iran directly or through Pakistan.[48] The loss of control in Afghanistan only gave the imperialists another option to pursue against Moscow. Perceived in this context, Afghanistan was described by most Soviet observers in nearly stereotypical imperial terms.

The prevailing Soviet images of Afghanistan described a dichotomized local scene.[49] There were progressive "good guys" committed to national development, freedom, and modernization, and then there were reactionary "bad guys" who personified evil. These "bandits" opposed civilized behavior and clung to xenophobic and fanatically extreme practices. They were opposed to national progress and were driven exclusively by personal greed. Moreover, they were not nationalists. To the contrary, they were the instruments of Washington, Beijing, and Islamabad. To the degree there was any complexity in the prevailing view it came with an occasional recognition that the bandits had indigenous roots and were simply being used by the outside powers rather than created by them. In the end, however, even Hafizullah Amin was accused of being CIA controlled. The definition of the situation justified the Soviet occupation in the classic terms of counterimperialism and patronizing concern for the poor backward and defenseless childlike Afghans who needed Soviet protection and tutelage.

In 1988, rumors in Moscow claimed that there had been three points of view on the intervention in 1980.[50] One view held that intervention was both unnecessary and unwise. It obviously did not prevail.[51] A second view claimed that intervention was necessary and that military victory would follow quickly.[52] The use of decisive force would deter further American mischief and "pacify" the restless natives. The agitating bandits and CIA agents would quickly be defeated, and the progressive national elite would win over the "hearts and minds" of the masses. A third view, reportedly strongest in the Ministry of Defense, agreed with the need to intervene but not with the optimistic forecast about quick success.[53] They shared the enemy image of the United States but had more complex images of the Afghans. Recalling the history of Soviet Central Asia, they expected a long fight, perhaps thirty years, and a gradual process of co-optation.

The point of the rumor about this threefold classification in 1988 was to argue that voices in the military were unhappy with the decision to withdraw, feeling that politicians had deluded themselves from the outset and were now giving up prematurely. My point in relating the rumor here is not to say that it has any validity but only to suggest that in 1980 there were competing views of Afghanistan and that some were more complicated than the classic stereotype. The dominant view in the party theoretical journal *Kommunist,* for instance, emphasized economic and political roots of the instability in Afghanistan.

Pavel Demchenko blamed foreign interference first but also attacked the Afghan regime's "excessive haste" and unwise and unrealistic efforts to "accelerate" the evolution to socialism without adequate preparation and concern for popular support.[54] He also criticized the regime's repression, alienation of the clergy, and inability to unite with other national forces. In this image Soviet strategy had to be multidimensional. A military presence to stop the foreign interference was required, but so were political reforms on the part of Babrak Karmal. An amnesty for political prisoners, an invitation to Afghan refugees to come home, and new laws to make the respect for Islam obligatory were all immediately enacted after the intervention.[55] Large scale economic and humanitarian aid also continued in an effort to win popularity for the Soviet-supported government.[56]

The military aspects of Soviet policy overshadowed its other dimensions, but they were there. The prevailing strategic beliefs were slightly more complex than the imperial stereotype would suggest. In the stereotype, only military force would be considered since foreign instigation would be seen as the major cause of trouble.[57] Internal reforms would not be emphasized because domestic politics in the stereotype are not taken seriously. In the prevailing Soviet views of Afghanistan some aspects of domestic politics were recognized, but the importance of nationalism was ignored almost completely. The prevailing image continued to assume that a regime brought to power with foreign forces could establish popular legitimacy. And even if it could not, the bipolar nature of the world required the Soviet Union to quell instability on its perimeter and eliminate opportunities that would invite American and Chinese advances.

The Soviet invasion of Afghanistan is not hard to understand. It was driven by a set of images and logic that has been well rehearsed in the postwar era. What is more interesting is the decision to withdraw. As I explained at the beginning of this chapter, cold war perspectives have a ready answer to the question of withdrawal. The Soviet Union was defeated, the costs grew too great, and a threshold was crossed. Moscow was taught a lesson about the limits of the political utility of force in an era of nationalism. This explanation, of course, would be more convincing if Soviet casualities had been very high or significantly rising, if Afghanistan were 10,000 miles away from the Soviet Union rather than right next-door with well-protected logistic access, and if it were not so self-serving and seductively reassuring for Americans.

If Soviet geostrategic interests and credibility were seen as requiring intervention in 1980, what changed in 1988 that redefined these interests or relieved the worries about undermining Soviet credibility? Why did the priority granted to Afghanistan drop, and what strategic images justify the pullback? Have they "learned their lesson" only with regard to costs, or have enemy and imperial images undergone fundamental change and led to new strategic beliefs that will have generalized effects? These are questions I want to take up as I look at the images of the United States, southwest Asia, and Afghanistan that compete in the Gorbachev era.

Soviet Perceptions and the Decision to Withdraw

Strategic Images of Washington and Gorbachev's New Thinking

In 1986 Mikhail Gorbachev called for "new thinking" with respect to international relations. After examining much of this new political thinking, Stephen Meyer concluded that "the most outstanding difference between the new thinkers and the old thinkers is their divergent perceptions of threat posed by the United States and NATO."[58] The new thinkers see less threat from the United States. Advocating new thinking and changing actual security policies and military preparations are not synonymous, and Meyer makes this very clear. Yet even though new thinking did not produce instantaneous and radical change in concrete Soviet deployments, it did have a major effect on the image of Washington that prevails in Moscow.

It is important to stress that Soviet new thinking represents a more complex image of Washington that is less driven to stereotypical extremes by intense fears and perceived threats. This is critical because it flies in the face of the cold war hypothesis, which contends that Moscow has finally learned its lesson and that resolute American policy forced Moscow to pull in its horns. It is hard to imagine why an effective American policy of pressure and military buildup would lead to a reduced perception of threat in Moscow. I cannot digress here into the sources and evolution of Soviet new thinking, this would require another chapter entirely. What is important here is that the new image of Washington, if one actually does prevail, is hard to attribute to the reaffirmation and reinforcement of America's policy of containment. Consequently, I intend to treat the change in Soviet perceptions as an independent causal variable related to the decision to withdraw.

Gorbachev has legitimated a picture of Washington's foreign policy that emphasizes defensive motives. Soviet analysts have always recognized that the "Soviet threat" is used in the United States to mobilize mass support but have traditionally disparaged its actual motivating power among the "ruling circles." Gorbachev's conception of "mutual security" has revised this pattern and has allowed Soviet analysts to argue that Washington's leaders are actually afraid of Soviet intentions and do pursue a policy that may have military and imperial effects but is motivated by concerns for security.[59]

This new picture of the United States's intentions leads directly to an action–reaction conception of the cold war and a concern over unnecessary spirals of escalation.[60] At the theoretical level, it also raises doubts about the widsom of an excessive focus on deterrence. Gorbachev insists on analyzing the interests of both sides, thereby implying that showing will and resolve in order to deter the adversary is not sufficient as a strategy.[61] The adversary is not seen as unconditionally aggressive nor is it waiting to seize every opportunity. In the new view, actions designed to deter may in fact provoke a defensive counteraction. Recognizing the security dilemma, the advocates of new thinking have announced a policy designed to deflate the enemy image of the U.S.S.R. that they say prevails in Washington.[62] A series of tactical unilateral concessions and unexpected diplomatic flexibility is presented by these advocates as a way to stimulate a de-escalatory cycle. They have put the primary emphasis on initiatives in bilateral arms control but have also recognized the importance of defusing regional conflicts.[63]

One irony of the cold war is that Third World allies that both sides have spent so much to cultivate and secure have rarely had much intrinsic value to either superpower. Their value has been the perceived role they could play in the geostrategic competition. Their value, in other words, has been almost entirely dependent upon the beholder's perception of the other great power. Take away the perceived threat from the enemy, and the value of the Third World ally is drastically reduced. If the perceived importance of the ally drops, so will the superpower's willingness to commit scarce resources or to sacrifice other cherished objectives in order to control the ally. It should not be surprising that new thinkers in Moscow often express a "Soviet Union first," sometimes even a Russia first, sentiment.[64]

Gorbachev faces stiff opposition to his domestic plans for *perestroika*. Many people do not agree with his political vision and his plans threaten the personal vested interests of many powerful players throughout the Soviet system. The ideas I have described as central to the new thinking in foreign policy are not part of a new consensus. To the contrary, in the era of *glasnost* the argument over foreign policy and the rejection of the new image of Washington is clearly evident. General Dmitri Volkogonov, a regular contributor to foreign policy debates in the Soviet military media, for instance, has declared that "new thinking is not a new world view."[65] He angrily rejects the notion that "unilateral disarmament," the label he gives to initiatives that proponents of new thinking call diplomatic flexibility, will lead to American restraint. Washington, he explains, is still ruled by the old militaristic and highly aggressive thinking of the cold war and no amount of wishful thinking on Moscow's part will change this.

Other important officials like Vadim Falin, who is the head of the Central Committee's Department for International Relations, reject with vigor the historical revisionism that is visible in Moscow. The revisionist view claims that the cold war was caused by Stalin and his expansionist great power ambitions and that the "second cold war," associated with the early days of the Reagan administration, was stimulated by Brezhnev's miscalculations and incompetence.[66] For Falin the cold war was imposed on the Soviet Union by American leaders who were hypnotized by a belief in irresistible "supremacy."[67] His view of Washington has not undergone a major change nor does he articulate an action–reaction notion of the interaction. It is impossible to know exactly how important Falin's views are but they surely are not isolated. Some evidence suggests that they are common among military analysts.[68] They are likely to constrain policy efforts to appease Americans.

Regional Images and the Decision to Withdraw

The debate evident at the highest level of strategy effects definitions of the regional context in southwest Asia as well. At this level three points of view compete. One perspective continues to describe a very aggressive and dangerous American policy and promotes a bipolar and East–West interpretation of regional events. A second view partially reflects the new thinking about American policy and de-emphasizes the geostrategic importance of regional events. The third point of view emphasizes the threat Islamic fundamentalism poses but does not connect this threat to Washington's machinations. Instead, it suggests joint Soviet-American action to contain Islamic movements.[69] This last perspective has added strength to proponents of the second view by de-emphasizing the American threat and by highlighting the independence of Islamic movements. It may emerge as more influential in the future but in 1988 the struggle in Moscow was mostly between advocates of the first two conceptions of the regional context.

In the early 1980s there were Soviet analysts who felt revolutionary Islam might serve Soviet geostrategic purposes.[70] Perhaps they even felt that the Left in Iran could effect the direction of revoluationary developments, although most evidence suggests that no one with serious area competence had much optimism for these scenarios.[71] By 1988 there still were geostrategically minded cold warriors in Moscow, but they had changed their minds on the role revolutionary Islam would play.[72] They still denied that it could a "third force" and pursue a genuinely nonaligned policy outside of the central global struggle, but they had concluded that instead of helping Moscow, revolutionary Islam would serve Washington's interests. Washington was trying to use Islamic movements against Moscow and was having some success.[73]

The American-Iranian arms deal that caused so much embarrassment for the Reagan administration was interpreted by these observers as perfectly predictable and indicative of Washington's determination to reestablish its influence in the area.[74] Moving through the most extreme fundamentalist Islamic groups, Washington was pursuing a classic strategy that had been first practiced by the British. The threat of an American-Iranian rapprochement was taken seriously, as was the Islamic threat that al-Dawah posed in Iraq, that the Moslem Brothers posed in Syria, and that the mujahadeen represented in Afghanistan.[75] A few observers even implies that Washington was stoking disturbances in Central Asia and blamed the CIA for direct subversion inside the U.S.S.R.[76]

In this geostrategic vision the withdrawal from Afghanistan was a risky move. It might allow the Soviet Union to improve its image in the Islamic world, but it also risked exciting further American pressure and bolstering Islamic confidence. The withdrawal, for advocates of this perspective, was possible only because of Pakistan's agreement to stop further aid to the mujahadeen and Washington's agreement to guarantee the Geneva Accords. The accords for this group were more than a face-saving way to pull out and give up the regime in Kabul. The accords represented a diplomatice victory that would insulate the process of political change in Afghanistan from American and Pakistani interference. The

Soviet Union would withdraw on its own terms and leave behind a transition process in which their influence remained substantial.

While concerns about American plans to use Islam against the Soviet Union were clearly evident in Moscow in 1987 they did not prevail. They may have constrained policy but did not determine it. The dominant view associated with Gorbachev explicitly criticized the East–West interpretation of regional events.[77] The new thinking described a reduced American threat and described Afghanistan as a bleeding wound that had to be healed.[78] Washington had tried to stage a comeback in southwest Asia but had failed. Washington was using the Gulf war as a pretext for building up its naval presence in the area, but it was seen as very unlikely to reestablish significant political influence over Iran.

Afghanistan, in this view, was not described as an important asset blocking Washington's efforts to exploit Islamic anticommunism, but rather as an expensive burden that was of marginal significance. In this context, the main concern about the regional conflicts both in the Gulf and in Afghanistan was that they might draw the superpowers into a clash that would undermine the burgeoning detente.[79] When Kuwait initiated the reflagging competition between Washington and Moscow, Gorbachev took the bait in the first iteration but quickly tried to dampen the spiral once the Americans reacted and the dynamics of the escalation trap were clear. In Afghanistan the emphasis also shifted away from trying to block American intrigue and expansion and toward trying to find some form of national reconciliation that would allow Moscow to put this issue aside. The shift in strategic beliefs abouoot Soviet-American relations had significantly reduced Kabul's geostrategic importance to Moscow. More than an asset in the cold war, it now stood as an obstacle to detente.

I do not want to exaggerate the distinctions between the traditional bipolar view of the region and the conception associated with new thinking. Soviet views ranged across a continuum with people at both extremes, as I have outlined them. Key leaders like Gorbachev are not easy to classify. Their speeches reflected a good deal from both points of view and surely were designed to build a coalition for policy action.[80] Most likely, these speeches represented a residual policy agreed on after domestic negotiations or reflected the duality in Soviet perceptions.[81] Cold war assumptions are so well learned they might even be called instincts. New thinking, if it is emerging, is likely to coexist with the old understandings for a long time.[82] This is true even for the learning associated with a single individual much less the process of change inside a huge bureaucracy. Soviet behavior suggests that both strategic conceptions had a significant influence over the decision to withdraw. The second perspective provided the impetus to change course and the first constrained the conditions under which the withdrawal would take place.

The Perception of Afghan Politics and the Decision to Withdraw

Moscow's strategy toward Afghanistan had been multidimensional even in 1980. The imperial image of the scene defined foreign interference as the main cause of instability and was used to justify the heavy use of force against what were dismissed as foreign-inspired fanatic bandits and agitators. Perceived economic and political causes of instability also received academic attention and, as argued above, stimulated a three-pronged Soviet strategy. This strategy, along with military intervention, included financial, medical, and developmental assistance and Soviet pressure for political reforms that aimed to broaden the base of popular support. In 1986, after a major review of the Afghan situation initiated by Gorbachev when he took office in 1985, aspects of the imperial image still prevailed in the Soviet daily press, but the political dimensions of the strategy took on new importance. When Babrak Karmal resisted the UN efforts to discuss withdrawal of Soviet forces within the context of the indirect proximity talks, he was removed. His dismissal in May 1985 signalled a new flexibility in Moscow's definition of an acceptable postintervention Afghan government and marked the beginning of a steady trend away from imperial assumptions and toward a formula that might better satisfy Afghan national demands. It is important to note that this took place before the major increase in American aid to the mujahadeen.[83]

While the Soviet press continued to blame foreign interference for Afghanistan's troubles, Soviet behavior suggested that there had finally been a recognition in Moscow that Afghan nationalism was the real source of continued resistance.[84] Babrak Karmal could never establish his legitimacy in an era of nationalism given the way he had come to power.[85] Perhaps Najibullah would be perceived as less of a Soviet creation. Of course this tactical adjustment is not much of a concession to nationalism and still derives from the logic of an imperial stereotype, but it was a step in the redefinition of the local problem. In December, Gorbachev promised Najibullah that the Soviet Union would not desert him but he made it clear that it was time for change.[86] In early January 1987, Eduard Shevardnadze and Anatoliy Dobrynin went to Kabul. As Foreign Minister Shevardnadze left Afghanistan, he explained that a "turning point in the history of the new Afghanistan" had been reached.[87] He said that Soviet-Afghan relations were "today acquiring completely different parameters from a qualitative point of view." Shortly thereafter, Najib announced that the government would honor a unilateral cease-fire beginning in mid-January and accelerate the process of national reconciliation.

During the year, Gorbachev implied that a coalition government should replace the existing regime and that nationalist leaders like Zahir Shah might play critical leadership roles. This fell far short of Pakistan's desire to have Islamic fundamentalist leaders like Gulbuddin Hikmatyar take power, but nevertheless, indicated a signficant move in a bargaining process over an issue that previously Moscow had dealt with as if it were nonnegotiable.[88] Najib extended an amnesty to mujahadeen in Iran and Pakistan and worked diligently to co-opt prominent elements of the clergy. By the end of the year, he organized a *Loya Jirgah* (traditional national congress) ostensibly to plan a process by which a new government could be created and national reconciliation achieved.[89]

In January 1988 Eduard Shevardnadze again went to Kabul, this time following by a month a visit to Washington by Mikhail Gorbachev. Shevardnadze announced that the Soviet Union now had the American agreement to stop aid to the mujahadeen, and therefore, Soviet forces could be withdrawn.[90] They would leave, he said, with a "clear conscience and awareness that we have done our duty." National reconciliation, he explained, had provided a way for the opposition to participate in the governing of the country without armed struggle.[91] The foreign minister implied that the decision to withdraw hinged on the American guarantee, but not on what sort of government would prevail in Kabul.

Moscow accepted the notion that a new government would emerge in Kabul but remained committed to influencing the course of events. While the political dimensions of Soviet strategy received greater emphasis, the military component was not ignored. Finally recognizing the importance of nationalist appearances, Moscow launched its own version of what we might call 'Afghanization' of the war. Soviet troops would pull back, but advisors would stay with Afghan units. Economic support and aerial bombardment would increase as Moscow substituted technology for manpower and reduced its physical presence while trying to manage the transition in political authority.[92] Just prior to the signing of the Geneva Accords, Moscow transferred $1 billion in military installations and equipment to Kabul and in early November surprised the American government by deploying SCUD missiles and Mig-27 and SU-24 aircraft to Kabul.[93] These strike forces surely had a tactical purpose related to compelling Pakistan's acceptance of the Soviet interpretation of the Geneva Accords, but they also signalled Moscow's seriousness about not abandoning Kabul to a fate that many in Moscow would see as American orchestrated.[94] The constraints imposed by still powerful cold war concerns were obvious.

In the summer of 1988, during the first phase of the Soviet withdrawal, the prevailing Soviet position was that Pakistan was flagrantly violating the agreement.[95] Military sources usually blamed Washington for Pakistan's continued support for the mujahadeen, but other dailies were careful to blame Pakistan and criticize Washington only for not fulfilling its role as guarantor of the agreement.[96] The differences between the two images may have been subtle but reflected the larger strategic debate. When the scene was described in mostly regional terms, emphasizing Pakistan's role independent of Washington, the view of the Afghan mujahadeen also was more complicated.

While no one defended the mujahadeen, many Soviet observers described them as much more complicated than simple bandits and creations of the CIA. Differences among the various factions inside the alliance of the seven main external groups of mujahadeen were explored as were the differences between these groups and other mujahadeen leaders inside the Afghanistan.[97] The Soviet pictures of the motives of these groups also became more complicated, mixing in some legitimate national and religious aspirations with the desires for power, personal wealth, and fanaticism that Soviet observers had traditionally said motivated the mujahadeen.[98] In the fall of 1988, Moscow dispatched Yuli Vorontsov to Kabul as ambassador. Given Vorontsov's reputation as a highly regarded diplomat, this may have been another signal of Moscow's willingness to expand the boundaries for a negotiated settlement and thus be behavioral evidence that the prevailing elite in Moscow were moving away from imperial assumptions.[99]

The fighting in Afghanistan continued and in many ways increased as the Soviet Union withdrew its forces. Those Soviet leaders who did not evoke the classic imperial stereotype and who did not argue that the mujahadeen were acting on orders from Washington, nevertheless, did hold Washington responsible for not restraining the mujahadeen and Pakistan. When President Zia dismissed Prime Minister Junejo in May 1988, the residual strength of bipolar and imperial images in Moscow was clear. The prevailing interpretation of this event was that Zia was moving to extricate himself from the constraints of the Geneva Accords.[100] It was a move, according to Soviet images, taken with Washington's complicity and designed to circumvent the Geneva agreement on noninterference in Afghanistan by eliminating Pakistani leaders who were committed to their implementation. The regional interpretation of this event, which stressed Junejo's challenge to the Pakistani military and Zia's decision to protect his own rule, were given much less play. A bipolar assumption dominated Soviet interpretations and read this move by Zia as partial evidence of Washington's bad faith.

President Zia's move could be read not as a move in the old bipolar cold war, but rather as indicative of the cold war's demise. Zia dismissed the government for several reasons, foremost of which was probably to protect his own influence in the military. He also reportedly disagreed with Junejo on Afghan policy and favored backing a very rapid Islamic victory in Kabul. He wrapped his own decision to dismiss the Pakistani government in the symbols of Islam.[101] He argued that Junejo had not implemented the Islamic codes that were necessary in an Islamic Republic. Rather than serving as a cold war puppet of Washington, as he was described in Moscow, he might have been trying to bolster his regional legitimacy by emphasizing his commitment to Islam and his independence from Washington's "concessions" at Geneva.[102]

Zia may have felt that, with Soviet forces withdrawing from Afghanistan, Washington would be less willing to commit resources to Pakistan, especially given Pakistan's nuclear programs and its role in the Islamic world, which threatens Israel. Zia had tacitly aligned with Iran in regard to the war in Afghanistan, but the regional relationship was uneasy because of Iran's strong commitment to nonalignment and Islamabad's close ties to Washington. Once the Russians left Afghanistan, Zia would have to survive in the area as an independent Islamic nationalist. He had to protect his own regional image and possibly prepare for a future in which superpower influence in the area would be far less important than the influence of Islamic and nationalist movements. In this case, his actions may have been to begin a process of distancing himself from Washington's embrace and reinforcing regional identities and ties. His symbolic manipulation of Islamic symbols and his open advocacy of an Afghan victory for the most fundamental of the mujahadeen groups would serve this purpose.

Strategic Images and Regional Complexities: The Rimland and Detente

I cannot prove what Zia's motives were for dismissing his government; he surely had several, but it is clear that Soviet observer's quickly accepted an exclusively bipolar interpretation and read the act as indicative of a new American effort to reinforce containment by influencing the future in Afghanistan. If the act was

Zia's independent decision connected to his concern for his own survival at home and in the region, then it was a move away from the logic of superpower competition. The mismatch between regional events and the conclusions drawn by elites in the superpowers in this case would be not only ironic but tragic. It would portend a rejuvenation of cold war images at a time when they were most inappropriate. The ideologies driving Islamic and national movements in southwest Asia oppose the extension of either superpower's influence. These movements will certainly continue to resist Soviet and American "imperialism," and they probably will fight among themselves. If leaders in a superpower cling to out-of-date assumptions about bipolarity and the weakness of regional actors, they will try to sustain their control where it is geostrategically unnecessary. The result will be to enflame the regional violence directed against the superpower and perpetuate a cold war with the global adversary.

The 1980s have been a tragic period for the Afghans. The national anguish is far from over and the effects will certainly be felt for years to come. My conclusion in this paper is that enemy and imperial images in Moscow played a critical role in fueling this tragedy and that the misfortune is doubly painful because much of it had no real basis. I in no way want to minimize the divisions inside of Afghanistan or pretend that the violence there is only a function of the cold war. The entire thrust of this chapter is that leaders in Moscow and Washington have greatly exaggerated the East–West aspects of the internal struggle. The point is that enemy images led Soviet leaders to conclude that political change and instability in Afghanistan was highly threatening because it represented an inviting opportunity for Washington and Beijing. Imperial images led Soviet leaders to conclude that an Islamic alternative could not be nonaligned and could be easily stopped. The enemy image led to a misunderstanding of American policy that accelerated a new escalatory cycle with Washington, much of it through Third World peoples. The imperial image turned out to be grossly inaccurate. National groups resisted, the pro-Soviet governments were never able to establish national legitimacy, and the violence and suffering reached tragic levels.

Many Americans misread the Soviet invasion of Afghanistan. They exaggerated Moscow's expansionist ambitions and underestimated the role security considerations played in Brezhnev's calculations. Americans may also misread the Soviet withdrawal from Afghanistan, if they overestimate the effectiveness of American pressure and underestimate the importance of new Soviet strategic beliefs. The evidence concerning Soviet perceptions does not conform to the expectations of the cold war hypothesis, while it does fit fairly well with the detente proposition that I raised at the outset. This evidence suggests that the withdrawal is related to a reduction in the perceived threat from the West as much, if not more, than it is a result of Soviet weakness and effective American pressure.

Americans should be cautious about exaggerating the magnitude of the Soviet retreat, especially when it reinforces a romantic image of their own effectiveness and control. On the heels of the final Soviet troop withdrawal from Afghanistan, Soviet Foreign Minister Eduard Shevardnadze launched a major diplomatic mission to the Middle East.[103] He accomplished the complete normalization of relations with Egypt and announced a "turnabout and change" in Soviet relations with Iran.[104] By late June 1989, Hashemi-Rafsanjani, Iran's most powerful leader after the death of Ayatollah Khomeini, arrived in Moscow for a major state visit involving economic and military relations.[105] The Soviet withdrawal was clearly not associated with a major strategic retreat from the region, but to the contrary, with a new diplomatic engagement.

In Afghanistan, the withdrawal was also not correlated with a complete abandonment of Soviet interests or positions. The Soviet press continued to call for a coalition government in Kabul and insisted that the People's Democratic Party of Afghanistan (PDPA), being the "biggest and best organized" force in Afghan society, had to be a central element in any regime.[106] Gorbachev suggested in December 1988 that Moscow and Washington cut off all military supplies to their respective allies in Afghanistan, but this came at a time when American government analysts estimated that the Najib regime had a substantial edge in equipment. The offer was rejected in Washington on the grounds that it would simply let the Soviet-installed regime in Kabul persevere and force the mujahadeen to accept Kabul's terms for settlement.[107] Najib continued to exploit the leverage he could gain by playing on the differences within the mujahadeen, offering, for example, to set up regional administrations in return for locally negotiated cease-fires.[108] And when the mujahadeen did attack Jalalabad, the Soviet Union did not let its ally down. Soviet weapons including SCUD missiles poured into Kabul, and Afghan soldiers, who many in the West had expected to simply collapse, fought with surprising tenacity and success.[109] When it looked like Pakistan, in return for new American weapons, would join the United States in insisting that Najib's regime must not be part of any future coalition, Moscow responded with a threat to deliver MIG 29s and other very advanced weapons to Kabul.[110]

The Soviet Union has now withdrawn its troops from Afghanistan, but it has not accepted complete political defeat. It reduced some of its costs in Afghanistan but has not fled the scene, and it would be dangerously romantic for Americans to conclude too quickly that our superior strength has simply pinned them to the mat. We must also avoid the simplifications of the regional scene that mislead Soviet leaders a decade ago. We should avoid dichotomized pictures of Afghans as either good guys or bad guys with the forces on our side sure to win with a quick knockout blow if only we give them the backing to carry it off. The scene in Afghanistan is very complicated and the divisions within the regime and within the mujahadeen are based on a variety of ethnic, religious, and tribal criteria and are very real and very deep. Soldiers on many sides, including the army serving the regime in Kabul, are likely to fight intensely for quite some time.[111] Moscow has reduced its costs in Kabul but it has not cut and run. Nor can costs alone explain the Soviet decision to withdraw. Moscow, after all, continues to provide massive assistance and has agreed to halt aid only under circumstances that would insure that its allies in the PDPA have a substantial chance to play a major role in the future coalition.

In the 1980s, both superpowers have suffered defeats at the hands of Islamic and nationalist movements and have been confronted with a serious challenge to their traditional bipolar assumptions. The Soviets were quick to see local causes and nationalism in Iran and terribly slow to see them in Afghanistan. Americans, on the other hand, knew immediately why Babrak Karmal had no legitimacy or chance of becoming popular and were slow to recognize the shah's problem with legitimacy and Khomeini's popular appeal. It is to be hoped that the defeats that Moscow and Washington have suffered will shake their imperial images of change in southwest Asia and not simply refuel their cold war fears of each other. If both enemy and imperial simplifications give way to more complex and multidimensional strategic beliefs, then a stable Soviet-American detente that encompasses the Asian rimland may be possible.

Notes

1. "Transcript of President's Interview with Frank Reynolds on Soviet Reply," *New York Times,* Jan. 1, 1980, A4.

2. Nathan Leites, *A Study of Bolshevism* (New York: Free Press, 1953).

3. For a sophisticated presentation of this theory see Seweryn Bialer, *The Soviet Paradox: External Expansion Internal Decline* (New York: Alfred Knopf, 1986).

4. See, for instance, Peter Rodman, "The Case for Skepticism," *The National Interest,* no. 12 (Summer 1988): 83–90; and Zalmay Khalilzad, "Afghanistan: Anatomy of a Soviet Failure," *The National Interest,* no. 12 (Summer 1988); 101–8.

5. Soviet commentators like Nikolay Shishlin report Soviet casualities as over 13,000 dead, over 35,000 wounded, 311 prisoners, and 312 missing. Vsevolod Ovchinnikov, Nikolay Shishlin, and Aleksey Vasilyev, "Repercussions," Moscow Television (July 26, 1988), *FBIS-SOV-88-144,* 6–13. Western sources put the casualty figures at 15,000 dead. *New York Times,* Feb. 16, 1989, 1.

6. Many signs suggest that Yuri Andropov did not share Brezhnev's or Chernenko's commitment to Afghanistan. Andropov saw the war as harmful to Soviet-American relations, Sino-Soviet relations, Soviet relations with the Muslim world, and Soviet relations in the Third World in general. He also felt it was too costly in terms of internal Soviet needs and made a number of diplomatic moves in the direction of compromise. See Selig Harrison, "Inside the Afghan Talks," *Foreign Policy* no. 72 (Fall 1988): 31–60.

7. See William Zimmerman and Robert Axelrod, "The 'Lessons' of Vietnam and Soviet Foreign Policy," *World Politics* 34 (October 1981): 1–24.

8. G. A. Trofimenko, "The Lessons of Vietnam," *SShA,* no. 6 (May 1975): 76–80; *FBIS-SOV-75-123.*

9. See Zimmerman and Axelrod, "'Lessons' of Vietnam."

10. On the enemy image see Ole Holsti, "Cognitive Dynamics and Images of the Enemy," in *Enemies in Politics,* ed. D. Finlay, O. Holsti, and R. Fagen (Chicago: Rand McNally, 1967), 25–96; and Richard Cottam, *Foreign Policy Motivation: A General Theory and a Case Study* (Pittsburgh: Univesity of Pittsburgh Press, 1977), 65. Also see Brett Silverstein, "Enemy Images: The Psychology of U.S. Attitudes and Cognitions Regarding the Soviet Union," *American Psychologist* 44:6 (June 1989): 903–13.

11. See William Taubman, *Stalin's American Policy: From Entente to Detente to Cold War* (New York: Norton, 1982), 131–32; and Bruce Kuniholm, *The Origins of the Cold War in the Near East: Great Power Conflict and Diplomacy in Iran, Turkey, and Greece* (Princeton, N.J. Princeton University Press, 1980), 303–82.

12. See Richard Cottam, *Iran & the United States: A Cold War Case Study* (Pittsburgh: University of Pittsburgh Press, 1988), 66–81; and Mark Lytle, *The Origins of the Iranian-American Alliance: 1941–1953* (New York: Holmes & Meier, 1987).

13. R. Cottam, *Iran & the U.S.* 70–3, 78.

14. For a transcript of Truman's interview, see Stanley Jados, *Documents on Russian American Relations* (Washington, D.C.: Catholic University Press, 1965). Contemporary studies that have searched the declassified documents and doubt Truman's memory see James Bill, *The Eagle and the Lion: The Tragedy of American-Iranian Relations* (New Haven, Conn.: Yale University Press, 1988), 37–38; Rouhollah Ramazani, *Iran's Foreign Policy 1941–1973: A Study of Foreign Policy in Modernizing Nations* (Charlottesville: University of Virginia Press, 1975), 138–39; John Oneal, *Foreign Policy Making in Times of Crisis* (Columbus: Ohio State University Press, 1982), 133–34; Cottam, *Iran & the U.S.*, 70; and Lytle, *Origins of Iran-U.S. Alliance,* 161.

15. Larson argues that cold war assumptions about Soviet foreign policy were not well defined in 1946. By 1952, however, the enemy image dominated American perceptions. Deborah Larson, *Origins of Containment: A Psychological Explanation* (Princeton, N.J.: Princeton University Press, 1985).

16. A script is a cognitive structure that organizes information into a sequence of activities. It is a general case that a subject is likely to use to interpret a specific incident. The learned sequence can "fill in" information that is not immediately evident in the specific empirical case. See Robert Abelson, "Psychological Status of the Script Concept," *American Psychologist* 36 (1981): 715–29; and S. Fiske and S. Taylor, *Social Cognition* (Reading, Mass.: Addison-Wesley, 1984), 141–79.

17. The State Department at the time concluded that there was nothing the U.S. could do to appreciably enhance Iran's ability to resist. See Cottam, *Iran & the U.S.*, 70–73, 78.

18. On the lack of material American support for Iran in 1946–1947, see Ramazani, *Iran's Foreign Policy,* 153–57.

19. Marshal Shulman, *Stalin's Foreign Policy Reappraised* (New York: Atheneum, 1966), 258.

20. Ramazani, *Iran's Foreign Policy,* 106–107.

21. See *Khrushchev Remembers: The Last Testament,* trans. and ed. Strobe Talbott (Boston: Bantam, 1974), 335–36.

22. Lytle, *Origins of Iran-U.S.Alliance,* 149.

23. See Raymond Garthoff, *Detente and Confrontation: American-Soviet Relations From Nixon to Reagan* (Washington, D.C.: Brookings Institution, 1985), 887–965. Also see George Kennan, "Was This Really Mature Statesmanship?" *New York Times,* Feb. 1, 1980, A27; and Selig Harrison, "Dateline Afghanistan: Exit through Finland?" *Foreign Policy* no. 41 (Winter 1980–1981): 163–87.

24. Jack Snyder has argued that whether or not the threat from the West is seen as contingent or unconditional has historically been a central dimension dividing different Soviet strategic ideas. See Jack Snyder, "The Gorbachev Revolution: A Waning of Soviet Expansionism?" *International Security* 12:3 (Winter 1987–1988): 93–131.

25. On the importance of defining the situation see Herbert Simon, "Human Nature in Politics: The Dialogue of Psychology with Political Science," *American Political Science Review* 79 (1985): 293–304.

26. R. Herrmann, *Perceptions and Behavior in Soviet Foreign Policy,* 22–49.

27. In the imperial image the situation is defined as one involving a backward people who are politically inattentive, culturally primitive, and technologically and economically inept. These "children" are seen as needing the tutelage of more advanced societies to progress domestically and to protect themselves from international actors who are

aggressive. The image simplifies the local scene into a dichotomy between "good guys," those who will cooperate with us, and "bad guys," those who will not. It describes the politics in another country as entirely derivative of great power concerns and as suspectable to control. It describes "agitators" and "uppity" natives who refuse to cooperate with the great power instruments of the enemy great power. The imperial image is analyzed best by Richard Cottam in *Foreign Policy Motivation: A General Theory and a Case Study* (Pittsburgh: University of Pittsburgh Press, 1977), 67–70. Cottam's case study of the British in Egypt illustrates the historical role the image has played (151–309). Hans Morgenthau argued that the most widely used justification for imperialism has always been counter-imperialism. See Hans Morgenthau, *Politics Among Nations: The Struggle for Power and Peace* (New York: Alfred Knopf, 1973), 95. I have developed the theory behind the imperial image as well as its characteristics elsewhere, e.g., see Richard Herrmann, "The Empirical Challenge of the Cognitive Revolution: A Strategy for Drawing Inferences about Perceptions," *International Studies Quarterly* 32 (1988): 175–203.

28. See *Hitler's Secret Conversations 1941–1944,* trans. Norman Cameron and R. H. Stevens (New York: Farrar, Straus and Young, 1953); and *Hitler's Secret Book,* trans. Salvator Attanasio (New York: Alliance, Longmans Green, 1939).

29. See Harry Gelman, *The Brezhnev Politburo and the Decline of Detente* (Ithaca, N.Y.: Cornell University Press, 1984); and Adam Ulam, *Dangerous Relations: The Soviet Union in World Politics, 1970–1982* (New York: Oxford University Press, 1983).

30. For an example of Brezhnev's images, see L. I. Brezhnev, *Our Course: Peace and Socialism* (Moscow: Novosti, 1977). For a convenient summary of the prevailing Soviet arguments, see V. Nekrasov's yearly year-end articles in *Kommunist*. V. Nekrasov, "God 1977-ee: Obzor Mezhdunarodnoy Zhizni," (The Year 1977: Survey of International Life) *Kommunist* no. 18 (December 1977): 89–102; and V. Nekrasov, "God 1978-ee: Obzor Mezhdunarodnoy Zhizni," (The Year 1978: Survey of International Life) *Kommunist* no. 18 (December 1978): 105–18.

31. See, for example, G. A. Trofimenko, "SSSR–SShA: Mirnoye Sosushchestvovaniye Kak Norma Vzaimootnosheniy," (U.S.S.R.–U.S.A.: Peaceful Coexistence as the Norm of their Relations) *SShA* no. 2 (February 1974): 3–17; G. A. Trofimenko, "Voprosy Ukrepleniya Mira i Bezopasnosti v Sovetsko-Amerikanskikh Otnosheniyakh," (Problems of Peace and Security in Soviet-American Relations) *SShA* no. 9 (September 1974): 7–18.

32. My evidence and argument about prevailing Soviet perceptions of the U.S.A. in the Brezhnev period is presented in R. Herrmann, *Perceptions and Behavior in Soviet Foreign Policy,* 114–65.

33. G. A. Trofimenko, "Amerikanskiy Podkhod k Mirnomu Sosushchestvovaniyu s Sovetskim Soyuzom Istoriya i Perspektivy," (The American Approach to Peaceful Coexistence with the Soviet Union [History and Perspective]) *SShA* no. 6 (June 1978): 18–31 and pt. 2 *SSHA,* no. 7 (July 1978): 38–53.

34. V. A. Kremenyuk, "Vashington i Razvivayushchiyesya Strany: Rol' Kontseptii 'Politicheskogo Razvitiya," (Washington and the Developing Countries: The Role of the 'Political Development Conception) *SShA* no. 1 (January 1979): 9–21; and V. P. Lukin, "SSHA, Razvivayushchiyesya Strany i Protsess Razryadki," (The U.S.A., the Developing Nations and the Process of Detente) *SShA* no. 11 (November 1979): 16–26.

35. See G. A. Trofimenko, "The Lessons of Vietnam."

36. See Muriel Atkin, "The Islamic Republic and the Soviet Union," in *The Iranian Revolution and the Islamic Republic,* ed. N. Keddie and E. Hooglund (Syracuse, N.Y.: Syracuse University Press, 1986), 191–207; and Louis Dupree, "Afghanistan Under the Khalq," *Problems of Communism* 28 (July 1979): 34–50; and R. Garthoff, *Detente and Confrontation,* 895–937.

37. See, for example, Aleksandar Bovin, "Iran: Consequences and Reasons," *Literaturnaya Gazeta,* Oct. 25, 1978, 14, *FBIS-SOV-78-212,* F10–13; and A. Filippov, "Iran; Days of Tension," *Pravda,* Nov. 3, 1978, 5, *FBIS-SOV-78-216,* F3–5. Also see S. Kondrashov, "Around the Events in Iran," *Izvestiya,* Dec. 6, 1978, 3, *FBIS-SOV-78-237,* F1–3; and A. Akhmedzyanov, "Iran's Hot Winter," *Izvestiya,* Dec. 14, 1978, 5, *FBIS-SOV-78-244,* F4–7.

38. M. Stura, "His Majesty in Flight," *Izvestiya,* Jan. 25, 1979, 5, *FBIS-SOV-79-22,* F3–6; and A. Bovin, "Iran in the People's Hands: Inevitable Denouement," *Izvestiya,* Feb. 13, 1979, 4, *FBIS-SOV-79-033.* Also see Pavel Demchenko, "When the People Rise Up," *Pravda,* Jan. 24, 1979, 4, *FBIS-SOV-79-019,* F5–8; and Pavel Demchenko, "Krushenie Absolyutizma," (The Collapse of Absolutism) *Kommunist* no. 3 (February 1979): 76–83.

39. Aleksandar Bovin, "With Koran and Saber!!!" *Nedelya* 36 (Sept. 4, 1979):6, *FBIS-SOV-79-176,* H1–2.

40. See I. Belyayev, "The Tangle of American-Iranian Problems," *SShA: Ekonomika, Politika, Ideologiya* 2 (February 1980): 48–58; *JPRS 75485,* 58–71; and S. M. Aliyev, "The Iranian Revolution of 1978–1979 and the Working Class," *Rabochiy Klass I Sovremennyy Mir* 5 (September–October 1980): 104–111, *JPRS 77230,* 9–24.

41. S. M. Aliyev, "The Iranian Revolution." Also see Muriel Atkin, "Rethinking the Iranian Revolution," *Problems of Communism* 35:2 (March–April 1986): 86–92.

42. A. Bovin, "Iran in the People's Hands: Inevitable Denouement," *Izvestiya,* Feb. 13, 1979, 4, *FBIS-SOV-79-033.* Also see Pavel Demchenko, "Iran: Stanovlenie Respubliki," (Iran: The Making of a Republic) *Kommunist* no. 9 (June 1979): 110–16; and Igor Belyayev, "Surrounding the Iranian-Iraqi Conflict," *Literaturnaya Gazeta,* Oct. 1, 1980, 9, *FBIS-SOV-80-193,* A2–3; P. Demchenko, "Who Is Fueling the Conflicts?" *Pravda,* Oct. 18, 1980, 5, *FBIS-SOV-80-204;* D. Volskiy, "The Persian Gulf: Dreams and Reality," *Novoye Vremya,* no. 46 (Nov. 14, 1980): 1–11, *FBIS-SOV-80-228;* A. Kislow, "Washington and the Iraq–Iran Conflict," *SShA* 1 (January 1981): 51–56, *JPRS 77507.*

43. Pavel Demchenko, "The Collapse of Absolutism."

44. P. Demchenko, "Iran: The Making of a Republic." Also see D. Volskiy, "Kabul's Program and Its Opponents' Maneuvers," *Novoye Vremya,* no. 23 (June 6, 1980): 12–13, *FBIS-SOV-80-114,* D1–4.

45. See A. Bovin, "Iran in the People's Hands: Inevitable Denouement"; D. Volskiy, "The Persian Gulf: Dreams and Reality," *Novoye Vremya,* no. 46 (Nov. 14, 1980): 1–11, *FBIS-SOV-80-228;* and Kislov, A., "The Middle East and American Strategy," *SShA,* no. 6 (1980): 15–26, *JPRS 76190.*

46. The common image argued that Washington had not learned its lesson in Iran and was repeating the same mistakes in Pakistan as it tried to turn Pakistan into its instrument. See, for example, V. Roshchupkin, "Dangerous Pretensions," *Krasnaya Zvezda,* Feb. 16, 1980, 3, *FBIS-SOV-80-037,* D4–5; M. Rostarchuk, "Regarding Events in Pakistan," *Izvestiya,* July 10, 1980, 5, *FBIS-SOV-80-138;* S. Kondrashov, "Dangerous Relapses," *Izvestiya,* Sept. 3, 1980, 5, *FBIS-SOV-80-176;* V. Baykov, "Cold Winds Over Islamabad," *Pravda,* Feb. 24, 1980, 4, *FBIS-SOV-80-040;* V. Pustov, "The Pentagon Plugs the 'Gap,'" *Krasnaya Zvezda,* Mar. 5, 1979, 3, *FBIS-SOV-79-047.*

47. The Carter administration began to play the "China Card" in a obvious way with Zbigniew Brzezinski's visit to China in May 1978. Relations were normalized in January 1979. See Zbigniew Brzezinski, *Power and Principle: Memoirs of the National Security Adviser, 1977–1981* (New York: Farrar, Straus, Giroux, 1983), 196–233. Washington had traditionally supported Pakistan, and Pakistan had played a role in facilitating the Sino-American rapprochement. President Zia's seizure of power and arrest of Bhutto,

however, strained U.S.-Pakistani relations. Human rights issues were involved as were Pakistan's nuclear energy programs. In the wake of the Islamic revolution in Iran and Zia's alliance to Jamaat-i-Islami in Pakistan, American fears of an Islamic atomic bomb also complicated U.S.-Pakistani relations. A U.S. embargo on the delivery of military equipment to Pakistan was in place when the Soviets invaded Afghanistan.

48. A. Kislov, "The Middle East and American Strategy," *SShA,* no. 6 (1980) 15–26, *JPRS 76190;* A. D. Portnyagin, "Operating Through Islamabad," *SShA,* no. 5 (1980): 77–80, *JPRS-76054;* S. Kondrashov, "First Fitting of New Doctrine," *Izvestiya,* Feb. 7, 1980, 5, *FBIS-SOV-80-029;* D. Volskiy, "Turban or Helmet!" *Novoye Vremya* 20 (May 16, 1980): 18–20, *FBIS-SOV-80-102,* CC1–5; V. Pustov, "The Pentagon Plugs the 'Gap'," *Krasnaya Zvezda,* Mar. 5, 1979, 3, *FBIS-SOV-79-047;* V. Ovchinnikov, "The Gendarme's Fist," *Pravda,* Jan. 12, 1980, 4, *FBIS-SOV-80-010.*

49. Editorial, "Key to Political Settlement," *Pravda,* July 1, 1980, 1, *FBIS-SOV-80-129;* M. Mikhaylov, "Rebuffing the Intrigues of Imperialism: The Afghan Revolution Has Entered a New Stage," *Izvestiya,* Jan. 1, 1980, 4, *FBIS-SOV-80-003;* V. Svetlov, "Duplicity of Imperialist Propaganda," *Pravda,* Jan. 5, 1980, 4, *FBIS-SOV-80-005;* Yu. Glukhov, "Rebuffing Imperialist Aggression," *Pravda,* Jan. 8, 1980, 4, *FBIS-SOV-80-007.*

50. Personal interviews in Moscow, June 1988.

51. After the U.S.S.R. decided to withdraw its troops from Afghanistan it became quite common for commentators and leaders to argue that the initial decision to intervene was taken by a very small group of leaders and that area experts were ignored. For an example of this type of argument, which is highly critical of the area knowledge that govenment officials relied on in making their decisions, see Yu. V. Ganovskiy, "A Lesson Worth Learning. War in Afghanistan Through a Historian's Eyes," *Izvestiya,* May 5, 1989, 5, *FBIS-SOV-89-089.*

52. Alexander Bovin, who by 1988 had become an open critic of the intervention and who presented one of the most forthright anti-imperial arguments explaining that Soviet interference had mobilized Afghan nationalism, was one of the few Soviet commentators who admitted they had been persuaded by the logic of intervention in the first place. After the decision to withdraw had been taken, Bovin explained the decision to intervene this way:

> It is only possible to guess at two main motives. First, to help a friendly regime in its struggle against outside interference, which was perceived as the main destabilizing force. Second, to prevent what was seen as a perfectly possible U.S. military presence in a region that we considered to be so sensitive. It was evidently assumed that the tasks would be accomplished in a short period of time, after which Soviet troops would withdraw.
>
> . . . An exceptional decision under exceptional circumstances—this, more or less, was the way the issue was presented. I personally was convinced by it.

A. Bovin, "Afghanistan: A Difficult Decade," *Izvestiya,* Dec. 23, 1988, 5, *FBIS-SOV-88-247,* 24–26.

53. General of the Army, Valentin Varrenikov, explained after the withdrawal of Soviet troops had been completed that his objections to the decision to intervene in 1979 and the objections of the General Staff were overruled by Defense Minister Dmitri Ustinov. Varrenikov argued that Ustinov had been mislead by overly optimistic reports from advisers in Kabul. *New York Times,* Mar. 19, 1989, 18.

54. P. Demchenko, "Afghanistan Standing Guard over the People's Gains," *Kommunist* no. 5 (1980): 71–78, *JPRS 75780.*

55. TASS, "Karmal Addresses Conference of Ulema," July 9, 1980, *FBIS-SOV-8-131;* TASS, "Afghanistan: Clergy Approves and Supports the Government's Policy," July 9, 1980, *FBIS-SOV-80-134.*

56. L. Mironov, and I. Schedrov, "Afghanistan: Main Directions of Work," *Za Rubezhom,* no. 34 (Aug. 14, 1980): 12–13, *FBIS-SOV-80-165,* D37–7; K. Rashidov, "Afghan Reportage, 'Return,'" *Izvestiya,* Mar. 8, 1980, 5, *FBIS-SOV-80-050.*

57. For Soviet imagery that came close to this unidimensional stereotype, see Aleksey Petrov, "Position of Peace and Good Neighborliness," *Pravda,* May 25, 1980, 4, *FBIS-SOV-80-103;* and V. Matveyev, "Maneuvers by Enemies of the Afghan Revolution," *Izvestiya,* July 9, 1980, 5, *FBIS-SOV-80-135.*

58. Stephen Meyer, "The Sources and Prospects of Gorbachev's New Political Thinking on Security," *International Security* 13:2 (Fall 1988): 124–163, 157.

59. Mikhail Gorbachev, *Political Report of the CPSU Central Committee to the 27th Party Congress* Feb. 25, 1986 (Moscow: Novosti, 1986), 80. The general secretary also explained the need for mutual trust in action–reaction terms in an address welcoming Rajiv Gandhi to Moscow in July 1987 see *Pravda,* July 4, 1987, 2, *FBIS-SOV-87-128,* E8–11, E11.

60. See A. Bovin, "New Mentality . . . Requirements of the Nuclear Age," *Kommunist,* no. 10 (1986): 113–24, *JPRS-UKO-86-017,* 129–41; Ye. Primakov, "New Philosophy of Foreign Policy," *Pravda,* July 9, 1987, 4, *FBIS-SOV-87-134,* CC5-10; and V. Petrovskiy, "The Soviet Concept of General Security," *MEiMO* 6 (June 1986): 3–13, *JPRS-UWE-86-010,* 4–16.

61. Mikhail Gorbachev, "The Reality and Guarantees of a Secure World," *Pravda,* Sept. 17, 1987, 1–2, *FBIS-SOV-87-180.*

62. On the security dilemma, see Robert Jervis, "Cooperation Under the Security Dilemma," *World Politics* 30:2 (January 1978): 167–214.

63. Yevgeni Primakov, "U.S.S.R. Policy on Regional Conflicts," *International Affairs (Moscow)* 6 (1988): 3–9.

64. See, for instance, Alexei Izyumov and Andrei Kortunov, "The Soviet Union in the Changing World," *International Affairs (Moscow)* 8 (August 1988): 46–56.

65. D. Volkogonov, "Imperatives of the Nuclear Age," *Krasnaya Zvezda,* May 22, 1987, 2–3, *FBIS-SOV-87-107,* V4–9; and D. Volkogonov, "Speech to the Union of Writers," *Literaturnaya Gazeta* 19 (May 6, 1987): 3, *FBIS-SOV-87-103,* R9–11.

66. See Vyacheslav Dashichev, "East–West: Quest for New Relations. On the Priorites of the Soviet State's Foreign Policy," *Literaturnaya Gazeta* (May 18, 1988): 14, *FBIS-SOV-88-098,* 4–9.

67. Lev Bezmenskiy and Valentin Falin, "Who Unleashed the 'Cold War . . . ' Documentary Evidence," *Pravda,* Aug. 29, 1988, 6, *FBIS-SOV-88-169,* 6–11.

68. See R. Hyland Phillips and Jeffrey Sands, "Reasonable Sufficiency and Soviet Conventional Defense: A Research Note," *International Security* 13:2 (Fall 1988): 164–78.

69. A. Z. Arabadzhyan, "The Iranian Revolution: Causes and Lessons," *Aziya I Afrika Segodnya,* no. 3 (March 1986): 32–36; A. Z. Arabadzhyan, "The Iranian Revolution: Causes and Lessons," *Aziya I Afrika Segodnya,* no. 4 (April 1986): 19–22, 38, both in *JPRS-UIA-86-034,* 43–53, 77–83.

70. They argued that Islam could potentially play a progressive or reactionary role. In its anti-imperial and antimonarchist form it was described as progressive. See R. Ul'yanovskiy, "Iranskaya Revolutsiya i ee Osobennosti," (The Iranian Revolution and Its Peculiarities) *Kommunist,* no. 10 (July 1982): pp. 106–16; and I. Timofeyev, "Rol' Islama v Obshchestvenno-politicheskoy Zhizni Stran Zarubezhnogo Vostoka," (The Role of Islam in the Social-Political Life of Oriental Countries) *MEiMO* 5 (May 1982): 51–63.

71. Ye. A. Doroshenko, "The Political Traditions of Shi'ism and the Anti-Monarchist Movement in Iran (1978–1979)," *Nardoy Azii i Afriki* No. 6 (1980): 58–66, *JPRS*

77532, 7–16; Ye. Doroshenko, "Iran: Moslem (Shi'ite) Traditions and Modernity," *Aziya i Afrika Segodnya* 8 (August 1980): 59–61, *JPRS 76721*, 25–30; and Ye. Doroshenko, "The Shiite Clergy in Iran," *Nauka I Religiya*, 9 (Sept. 83): 54–56, *JPRS-84-019*, 23–32.

72. See R. Ul'yanovskiy, "Sud'by Iranskoi Revolutsii," (Iranian Revolution's Destinies) *Kommunist*, no. 8 (May 1985): 104–110; S. Agayev, "The Zigzag Path of the Iranian Revolution," *Voprosy Istorii*, no. 1 (1985): 43–59; *The Soviet Review* 28:1 (Spring 1987): 18–45; and S. Agayev, "On the Concept and the Essence of the Islamic Revolution," *Aziya I Afrika Segodnya* 5 (May 1984): 27–31, *JPRS-UPS-84-071*, 23–33.

73. See A. Kislov and R. Zimenkov, *The U.S.A. and the Islamic World* (New Delhi: Sterling Publishers, 1984).

74. See I. Belyayev, "Iranian Gambit," *Literaturnaya Gazeta* (Nov. 26, 1986): 9, *FBIS-SOV-86-228;* I. Belyayev, "Irangate and the Destroyers of Parity," *Literaturnaya Gazeta* (Dec. 10, 1986): 9, *FBIS-SOV-86-238;* and V. Pustov, "Put an End to the Mutual Destruction," *Krasnaya Zvezda* (Jan. 24, 1987): 5, *FBIS-SOV-88-020*.

75. See Ye. Primakov, "Volna «Islamskogo»: Fundamentalizma Problemy i Uroki, (The Wave of "Islamic Fundamentalism": Problems and Lessons) *Voprosy Filosofiye* 6 (1985): 63–73; and S. Agayev, "Live Bombs," *Nauka i Religiya*, no. 5 (May 1987): 44–47, *JPRS-NEA-87-092*, 85–94.

76. Igor Belyayev, "Islam and Politics," *Literaturnaya Gazeta* (May 13, 1987): 13, and "Islam in Politics: Part Two," *Literaturnaya Gazeta* (May 20, 1987): 12, *FBIS-SOV-87-113*.

77. M. Gorbachev, *Perestroika: New Thinking for Our Country and the World* (New York: Harper & Row, 1987), 173.

78. Mikhail Gorbachev, *Political Report of the CPSU Central Committee to the 27th Party Congress*, February 25, 1986 (Moscow: Novosti, 1986), 86.

79. See Yevgeni Primakov, "U.S.S.R. Policy on Regional Conflicts"; and P. Demchenko, "The Persian Gulf: Cruisers, Tankers, and the Road to Peace," *Pravda*, June 12, 1987, 4, *FBIS-SOV-87-116*. Also see "Soviet Government Statement," *Pravda*, July 4,, 1987, 3, *FBIS-SOV-87-128*.

80. Despite his criticism of East–West perspectives, when it came to the details of the conflict in the Persian Gulf, Gorbachev's imagery followed a traditional geopolitical cold war pattern with respect to the U.S. See M. Gorbachev, *Perestroika: New Thinking for Our Country and the World*, 176–77.

81. After presenting a fairly complex and detached analysis of Islam in Iran, Primakov, for instance, returns to the traditional image and agrees with Ul'yanovskiy that there are no grounds for Islamic revolutionaries to claim that they represent a "third way." He rejects the idea that they can be genuinely independent ideologically or politically. See Ye. Primakov, (The Wave of "Islamic Fundamentalism": Problems and Lessons).

82. The daily press, for example, continued to describe Pakistan in classic cold war terms as nothing more than an agent of Washington. Washington, most articles said, was responsible for Pakistan's Afghan policy as well as its pursuit of nuclear weapons. See V. Shurygin, "AWACS for Pakistan," *Pravda*, May 23, 1987, 5, *FBIS-SOV-87-109;* V. Soldatov, "About the 'Islamic Bomb': Washington and Pakistan's Nuclear Pretensions," *Izvestiya*, Apr. 28, 1987, 5, *FBIS-SOV-87-087;* S. Kazennov, "Who Helped to Produce the 'Islamic Bomb,'" *Sotsialisticheskaya Industriya*, Mar. 19, 1987, 3, *FBIS-SOV-87-056;* A. Ivanov, "In Thrall to Washington. Pakistan: Following the Course of Confrontation with Neighbors," *Krasnaya Zvezda*, Jan. 3, 1987, 5, *FBIS-SOV-87-006*.

83. American aid to the mujahadeen in 1984 was $120 million and in 1985, $250

million. In 1986 it jumped to $470 million and then to $630 million in 1987. If Gorbachev made his decision to find a way to pull back in 1985 or early 1986, then it predated the largest increases in American aid and predated the delivery of stinger missiles. See Harrison, "Inside the Afghan Talks."

84. For articles that mostly still blamed foreign meddling, see D. Meshchaninov, "Peace Formula," *Izvestiya,* Mar. 23, 1987, 3, *FBIS-SOV-87-056;* D. Meshchaninov, "Afghanistan—Ringleaders Settling Scores," *Izvestiya,* Dec. 17, 1987, 4, *FBIS-SOV-87-248;* V. Skosyrev, "Hopes and Doubts. Who Is 'For' and Who Is 'Against' a Political Settlement Around Afghanistan," *Izvestiya,* Dec. 27, 1987, 4, *FBIS-SOV-87-251;* V. Vinogradov, "Reconciliation: Supporters and Opponents," *Krasnaya Zvezda,* Mar. 21, 1987, 5, *FBIS-SOV-87-058;* and A. Oliynik, "Gamble on Stingers," *Krasnaya Zvezda,* Mar. 17, 1987, 3, *FBIS-SOV-87-053.*

85. After the withdrawal of forces, Soviet commentators confirmed that Soviet troops had taken part in the attack on the presidential palace when Amin was ousted in 1979. See e.g. Yu. V. Gankovskiy, "A Lesson Worth Learning. War in Afghanistan Through a Historian's Eyes," *Izvestiya,* May 5, 1989, 5, *FBIS-SOV-89-089.* The recognition of nationalism and the rejection of the core elements of the imperial image became more common in the Soviet press as the withdrawal of Soviet troops continued. In December of 1988, midway through the withdrawal, Alexander Bovin pushed a more complex view, arguing as follows:

> I am deliberately not emphasizing the role played by external counterrevolution. This is a well-elaborated topic, especially in the propaganda context. Outside interference in Afghanistan's affairs did play a significant and fateful role. Nevertheless, the main reasons why the peasants took up arms and joined the counterrevolutionaries were not external but rather domestic by nature.
>
> . . . taking a broad look at everything, the effect of the presence of Soviet troops and their participation in combat operations was negative. We ourselves presented the counterrevolution with a powerful means to influence mass awareness: Foreign interference engendered patriotism; the arrival of "infidels" set religious intolerance in motion. Against such a background even a draw would have been a miracle.

A. Bovin, "Afghanistan: A Difficult Decade," *Izvestiya,* Dec. 23, 1988, 5, *FBIS-SOV-88-247,* 24–26.

86. M. Gorbachev, "In a Friendly Atmosphere," *Pravda,* Dec. 14, 1986 1–2, *FBIS-SOV-86-240.*

87. E. A. Shevardnadze, "Interview," *Pravda,* Jan. 8, 1987, 5, *FBIS-SOV-87-005.*

88. Daily reporters continued to dismiss the leaders of the mujahadeen as nothing more than bandits and self-serving agents. See, for instance, Yu. Kornilov, "Hornets' Nest. Why a Soviet Journalist Was Unable to Visit Peshawar," *Izvestiya,* Apr. 23, 1987, 5, *FBIS-SOV-87-083;* and A. Oliynik and A. Melnik, "The Difficult Path Home: Who Is Preventing the Afghan Refugees' Return to Their Motherland?" *Krasnaya Zvezda,* Apr. 7, 1987, 3, *FBIS-SOV-87-071.*

89. TASS, "*Loya Jirgah* Session," *Izvestiya,* Dec. 1, 1987, 4, *FBIS-SOV-87-232;* and TASS, "*Loya Jirgah* Ends Its Work," *Izvestiya,* Dec. 2, 1987, 4, *FBIS-SOV-87 232.*

90. E. A. Shevardnadze, "Interview," Jan. 6, 1988, *FBIS-SOV-88-004.* Soviet commentators emphasized that the American agreement to stop interference was the critical change that made withdrawal possible. See Editorial "Horizons of Peace Opened Up in Afghanistan as a Result of the Signing of the Geneva Agreements," *Pravda,* Apr. 30, 1988, 1, *FBIS-SOV-88-084,* 30–31; Pavel Demchenko, "Success for Realism," *Pravda,* Apr. 14, 1988, 5, *FBIS-SOV-88-072,* 20–21; Konstantin Geyvandov, "From Positions of New Thinking," *Izvestiya,* Apr. 22, 1988, 4, *FBIS-SOV-88-079,* 39–41; V. Okulov,

"The Day After the Spring," *Pravda,* Apr. 26, 1988, 4, *FBIS-SOV-88-082,* 28–29.

91. The daily press reported that the policy of reconciliation was working. See D. Meshchaninov, "Qandahar Is Healing Its Wounds," *Izvestiya,* Dec. 5, 1987, 4, *FBIS-SOV-87-236;* and Vadim Okulov, "Following the Course of Reconciliation," *Pravda,* Dec. 2, 1987, 5, *FBIS-SOV-87-232.*

92. Moscow offered 400 million rubles in food and aid to Afghanistan in October 1988. This complemented other efforts to win over Afghan "hearts and minds" and along with continuing economic agreements, secured persisting Soviet influence. *New York Times,* Oct. 13, 1988, 5.

93. On the transfer of facilities and equipment announced by Soviet General Gromov, see statement by Michael Armacost, Under Secretary for Political Affairs, "Status Report on Afghanistan," U.S. Department of State, Current Policy #1087, June 23, 1988, 2. On the deployment of strike missiles and aircraft, see *New York Times,* Nov. 7, 1988, 6.

94. Moscow announced that it was suspending its withdrawal and warned that it might delay the pullout if the Geneva Accords were not observed. For the Soviet explanation of the suspension, see Soviet First Deputy Foreign Minister Aleksandr Bessmertnykh, *TASS,* Nov. 4, 1988, *FBIS-SOV-88-214,* 17–18.

95. "U.S.S.R. Foreign Ministry Statement," *Izvestiya,* May, 29, 1988, 5, *FBIS-SOV-88-104,* 27–29.

96. See Editorial, "Observing the Geneva Accords, Which Lend Powerful Impetus to the Solution of Regional Conflicts," *Pravda,* June 16, 1988, 1, *FBIS-SOV-88-116,* 14–15; V. Okulov, "Those Who Do Not Like Geneva. Pakistan Continues Interference in Afghan Affairs," *Pravda,* June 4, 1988, 5, *FBIS-SOV-88-110,* 34; M. Pushev, "Agreements Must Be Fulfilled. On the Legal Grounds for Settling the Afghan Problem," *Izvestiya,* July 5, 1988, 4, *FBIS-SOV-88-130,* 35–36. In *Krasnaya Zvezda,* Washington was described as still massively increasing its aid to the mujahadeen and as having never abided by the accords. At the time the accords were signed, when the other dailies were emphasizing how important the American agreement to not interfere was, *Krasnaya Zvezda* was emphasizing how American deliveries of weapons were increasing and implicitly how dangerous it was to pull back. See V. Vinogradov "Military-Political Commentary: Dangerous Policy," *Krasnaya Zvezda,* May 27, 1988, 4, *FBIS-SOV-88-110,* 33–34; V. Vinogradov, "Who Needs a 'Strong Pakistan'?" *Krasnaya Zvezda,* Apr. 7, 1988, 3, *FBIS-SOV-88-068,* 14–15; V. Vinogradov, "Observer's Opinion: Milan Missiles Now," *Krasnaya Zvezda,* Apr. 2, 1988, 5, *FBIS-SOV-88-071,* 23–34; and V. Vinogradov, "Putting Out the Flame of Regional Conflicts," *Krasnaya Zvezda,* Apr. 10, 1988, 3, *FBIS-SOV-88-076,* 32–33.

97. See, for example, A. Bovin, "Afghanistan: Counterrevolution Resists," *Izvestiya,* July 14, 1988, 5, *FBIS-SOV-88-136,* 21–23. Also see M. Yusin, "The Afghan Opposition: Who Is Who?" *Izvestiya,* Feb. 21, 1989, 5, *FBIS-SOV-89-035.*

98. See Alexander Prokhanov, "Afghanistan," *International Affairs (Moscow),* 8 (August 1988): 15–24. Prokhanov discusses anti-Sovietism and national resistance while also arguing that the mujahadeen is mostly driven by desire for money. In *Moscow News,* Aleksandr Mostovshchikov also broke the traditional stereotype by explaining that the mujahadeen he interviewed got their resources locally and were not tied to foreign supporters, see "Behind the Walls of the Pol-e Charki, *Moscow News,* no. 23 (June 5, 1988): 7, *FBIS-SOV-88-119,* 37–38. These sources have been leaders in new thinking and in publishing nontraditional views. Even though *International Affairs* has become the journal of the Foreign Ministry, it represents views more complex than those likely to prevail. Pavel Demchenko, in "Afghanistan: What Next?" *Pravda,* Aug. 18, 1988, 5, *FBIS-SOV-*

88-160, 15–16, also paints an increasingly complex and less imperial view by attributing the mujahadeen's strength to religious and national trends as well as to "outside support."

99. In late November Soviet officials began to talk directly to leaders of the mujahadeen. *New York Times,* Nov. 28, 1988, 1.

100. See Press Service, "Rabble-Rousers from Islamabad," *Izvestiya,* June 11, 1988, 4, *FBIS-SOV-88-115,* 25–26; and V. Shurygin, "Treachery," *Pravda,* June 11, 1988, 5, *FBIS-SOV-88116,* 15–16.

101. Mohammad Ziaul Haq, "Address to the Nation," June 15, 1988, *FBIS-NES-88-116,* 58–60; and Ziaul Haq, "Address on Regional Cooperation," *Islamabad Domestic Service,* June 28, 1988, *FBIS-NES-88-125,* 43–44.

102. The Islamic Unity Movement of mujahadeen in Afghanistan rejected the Geneva Accords immediately. See *FBIS-NES-88-075,* 54–55. Gulbuddin Hikmatyar, who among the seven leaders in the Islamic movement seemed to be Zia's favorite, rejected the accord strongly but was careful not to criticize Zia. See *FBIS-NES-88-095,* 45–47, and *FBIS-NES-88-093,* 29–30.

103. Shevardnadze was in the Middle East from February 21 to 27, 1989. He visited Syria, Jordan, Egypt, Iraq, and Iran. In Egypt he met with Israel's Foreign Minister Moshe Arens and the PLO's Yasir Arafat. See *FBIS-SOV-89-33, 34, 35, 36, 37, 38.*

104. See "Interview E. Shevardnadze," *Pravda,* Mar. 2, 1989, 4, *FBIS-SOV-89-040.*

105. Rafsanjani visited Moscow, Leningrad, and Baku in Soviet Azerbaijan. See *FBIS-SOV-89-118, 119, 120* for coverage of the visit.

106. See Yu. Glukhov, "Today We Complete the Withdrawal of Soviet Troops from Afghanistan: Summing Up," *Pravda,* Feb. 15, 1989, 1, *FBIS-SOV-89-030.*

107. *New York Times,* Feb. 18, 1989, 1.

108. *New York Times,* Mar. 31, 1989, 3.

109. The attack began in early March. Intensive Soviet airlifts to Kabul were under way by the middle of March as was the Afghan use of SCUD missiles. See *New York Times,* Mar. 9, 1989, 1; Mar. 14, 1989, 3; Mar. 16, 1989, 3; Mar. 19, 1989, IV, 3; and Mar. 24, 1989, 8. In the middle of April, Kremlin officials told the Western press that they were prepared to send "whatever weapons are necessary" to defend the cities in Afghanistan against the mujahadeen's attack. See *New York Times,* Apr. 14, 1989, 3.

110. The First Deputy U.S.S.R. Foreign Minster in the Information Directorate, Vadim Perfilyev, announced Moscow's readiness to counter American military aid to Pakistan by sending MIG 29s and other highly advanced weapons to Afghanistan. *TASS,* June 7, 1989, *FBIS-SOV-89-109,* 12.

111. Soviet area experts who are very critical of the Soviet decision to intervene are also critical of American officials who "nurture illusions" of a quick victory by the mujahadeen. While criticizing their own leaders for not being adequately informed about Afghan society, they also criticize American leaders who fail to see that the Afghan army has been completely reorganized and equipped with modern weapons; that the Party, which previously was badly divided, is now mostly unified; and that the government's supporters know they are fighting for their lives and the lives of their friends and relatives and, thus, are more highly motivated than often acknowledged in the West. Yu. V. Gankovskiy, "A Lesson Worth Learning. War in Afghanistan Through a Historian's Eyes," *Izvestiya,* May 5, 1989, 5, *FBIS-SOV-89-089.*

9

Russian and Soviet Strategic Behavior in Asia

MILAN HAUNER

Introduction: Early "Dominoes" or a Misnomer?

To understand more fully the contemporary Soviet strategic behavior along the rimlands of Asia, it might be helpful to examine certain lessons of the past, especially since the essential geostrategic parameters delineating the Russian and Soviet Eurasian superpower have not changed fundamentally since the political genius Halford Mackinder described it in 1904 as uniquely endowed with "a correlation between natural environment and political organization and unlikely to be altered by any possible social revolution."[1] The second purpose of this critical exercise is to examine the relevance of the domino theory against the most obvious cases of the Anglo-Russian rivalry in Asia during the nineteenth and early twentieth centuries.

It would be wrong to interpret the behavior of pre-1945 statesmen in terms of an alleged belief in the domino theory for two reasons. One is of historic nature; the domino principle, itself a raw product of the post-1945 cold war, cannot be transplanted retrospectively into a world that had not yet experienced the rigid ideological division of the globe into two hostile camps, as if poised for the final nuclear armageddon. For this reason alone the Anglo-Russian rivalry in Asia can never be regarded the archetype of a conflict guided by the domino principle; it was rather a tug-of-war relationship within the traditional international framework resting on the balance of power between half-a-dozen or so great powers. Hence diversion, not domino, was the preferred *modus operandi*.

The second fundamental flaw of using the domino principle stems from this Manichaean vision of the world divided into two rigid camps, one of the faithful and the other of the unfaithful (very much like the Islamic dichotomy between *Dar ul-Islam* and *Dar ul-Harb*), thereby visualizing the assumed communist threat in the 1950s as a monolithic phenomenon. Formulated at the height of the cold war and the delusive Sino-Soviet honeymoon, one might argue only that this simplistic vision seemed justified at the time (i.e., the Korean War): thus the domino principle, conceived as early as 1950 as part of the Western strategy of containing communism,[2] and epitomized in President Eisenhower's 1954 metaphor of falling dominoes,[3] must be seen as a reflection of the bipolar world view. However, what in the early 1950s appeared to most experts as a mere trifle, namely whether the victims of the combined domino push along the rimlands of

Asia would emerge as victims either of the Soviet *or* of the Chinese variant of communism, has become since the 1960s a rather important differentiation (e.g., in the Vietnam War and its ramifications in Laos and Cambodia).

With regard to the "Central Asian Question" throughout the nineteenth and part of the twentieth centuries, better known today under the catchword of the "Great Game," only in the most hyperbolic sense could the British Indian strategy be called domino; nor did the domino principle ever reach such a preponderance as to dominate the Russian official mind. Many Russian authors actually advocated the principle of "imperialist solidarity" with Great Britain rather than of ideological antagonism, maintaining that both colonial superpowers had identical interests vis-à-vis the subject peoples of Central Asia; that they should cooperate in fulfilling their *mission civilisatrice,* rather than antagonize each other while spreading the gospel of Western culture and material progress. This message is present in the works and utterances of the leading tsarist expert in international law, Professor F. F. Martens; the most prominent historian on the Central Asian Question, M. A. Terentiev; the editor of the influential *Moskovskie Vedomosti,* M. N. Katkov; the celebrated general and the cutthroat of the Turkmens, M. D. Skobelev—just to give a representative sample of the most visible Russian public figures who influenced the opinion at home and abroad.[4] Even the great Russian orientalist, V. V. Barthold (1869–1930), who managed to stay aloof from official tsarist as well as Bolshevik propaganda, was basically in agreement with the notion of historical necessity to create world empires in the shape of those set up by Alexander the Great, the Mongols, the Arabs, or the contemporary Russian Empire in Central Asia.[5]

Certain features of a rather rudimentary domino principle, however, did emerge in various Russian diversionary schemes to threaten India with invasion (e.g., the Duhamel and Skobelev plans). These Russian designs threatening British India usually combined a diversionary move with a flair for political subversion. The combination of military maneuver with political agitation was supposed to create the right explosive mixture to foment a chain-like reaction of uprisings among India's Muslim population against the Raj, with the ultimate aim of shaking up the foundations of the British Empire and eventually rumpling England itself.

The second instance worth examining, which could be said to contain the domino principle in its kernel, occurred during the latter part of the Russian civil war, when Lenin's world revolution, having stalled in Europe, turned to the East. This time the actual military potential available for diversion along the rimlands of Asia was negligible, which did not matter much since India's military posture was equally weak in the aftermath of the (third) Anglo-Afghan War. What the Bolsheviks lacked in military strength in Turkestan, they provided in revolutionary propaganda propped up by subversive activities. Epitomized in the slogan "setting the Orient ablaze,"[6] this new Bolshevik strategy had Lenin's benediction and full support of the Komintern, so that one might be tempted to conclude that during this period (1920–1923) the foreign policy of the Bolsheviks became the function of their utopian and messianic ideology—which was never the case during the tsarist era. In a nutshell, this strategy was extremely simple: through a series of anticolonial uprisings spreading from their epicentrum in British India, the entire system of Western colonialism in Asia was to collapse; ultimately the waves of social upheaval were to reach the shores of Western Europe and North America. Although after less than three years this "Eastern (Domino) Strategy" of the Bolsheviks had to be abandoned in Central Asia, it was pursued to some extent in China. As for Lenin, in spite of being overwhelmed with the urgent tasks of internal reconstruction of Russia, which compelled him to shelve for a while his ambitious dream of world revolution and to restore normal trade relations with England and other capitalist powers, he never seemed to have lost his faith that, "in the last analysis, the outcome of the struggle will be determined by the fact that Russia, India, China, etc., account for the overwhelming majority of the population of the globe . . . so that in this respect there cannot be the slightest doubt what the final outcome of the world struggle will be."[7]

The Central Asian Diversion

The notion of the Russian scare was created by the British administration in India as a by-product of the Great Game played over Central Asia. The Great Game itself was a much more exciting term than the neutral denominator for the Anglo-Russian rivalry, known as the Central Asian Question.[8] Until the appearance of Malcolm Yapp's massive study, *Strategies of British India,* it was widely believed that the external threat to India for much of the nineteenth century, first from the French and then from the Russians, was a real one, and that as a result of it the creation of British India's ever-expanding defensive perimeter was fully justified as a matter of self-defense. Yapp, however, argues that, viewed from India, the threat of Russian invasion was a chimera, meaningful only in the sense that Russia's threat of advancing to India via Iran and Afghanistan might arouse internal uprising, and that the *real* Russian threat to India was to foment unrest among the Muslims in the Indian Army.[9] These fears seemed to have been confirmed by the outbreak of the Great Indian Mutiny in 1857, which fortunately for the British, occurred after the signing of the Peace of Paris ending the Crimean War (1853–1856).

On the other hand, manifestations of external threat to British India were even more notorious and frequent. The first British invasion of Afghanistan (1838–1842), which ended in an unprecedented military disaster, was provoked by the Russian-supported Persian siege of Herat in 1837–1838, increased Russian diplomatic activities in the Central Asian khanates and Afghanistan, and by the news that General Perovsky was again on the march to seize Khiva. In 1856, when Persia recaptured Herat, Britain forced her to relinquish the conquest by declaring war on her and by intervening militarily in the Gulf.

The idea of using diversionary actions against the British along the Eurasian rimlands of the Russian Empire took a more definite shape during the Crimean War (1853–1856). This strategem was an ancient device, and the British, enjoying an undisputed naval supremacy, used it as a matter of course. During 1854–

1855, for instance, an Anglo-French fleet on several occasions attacked fortified Russian posts along the Pacific coast, with the intention of making St. Petersburg extremely nervous.[10] At the same time, having been forced to relinquish their naval power in the Black Sea, the Russians began to contemplate the possibility of restoring their lost supremacy by shifting the main thrust of their military expansion to Central Asia and by attempting to threaten India directly. With the appointment of Prince A. M. Gorchakov, a gifted diplomat, as Russia's foreign minister in 1856, an important shift in policy priorities occurred. In his first memorandum to the tsar, Gorchakov argued that there was little Russia could gain in Europe under the terms of the Treaty of Paris, and that her future must lie in Asia to carry out her *mission civilisatrice*. During Gorchakov's tenure of the next quarter century, Central Asia became the main focus of Russian expansion.[11]

It was during the Crimean War that three hastily drawn schemes emerged for a Russian invasion of India. Although devoid of serious logistical appreciation, they are good examples of how strategic diversion becomes an instrument of political vengeance for a lost war. General A. O. Duhamel, the Russian envoy to Tehran; Nikolai Chikhachëv, a future admiral; and General Stepan Khrulev, one of the heroes of the defense of Sevastopol, submitted memoranda calling for an advance against India via Asterabad, Meshed, Herat, and Kabul. The logistics of the campaign were visualized with almost the same naiveté as in the previous plans of Paul I and Napoleon.[12] Duhamel, for instance, surmised that a Russian army, marching with a steady pace of twenty-five versts a day (1 *versta* = 1.0668 kilometers), could cover the distance from Asterabad to Herat in thirty-three days, Herat to Kabul via Kandahar in forty-three, and Kabul to Peshawar in fourteen. Despite the enmity between the Persians and Afghans, epitomized by the disputed possession of Herat, the Russians speculated that the former could be won by mixture of "threats and intimidation, presents and pensions," combined with territorial concessions at the expense of the Ottomans, allied at the time with Britain. The Afghans, on the other hand, were to be won by the prospect of an overall Muslim uprising and encouraged to cooperate with the Sikhs, still outraged by the recent British annexation of the Punjab (1849), following the disintegration of the great Sikh kingdom after the death of Ranjit Singh in 1839.[13]

The uncertainty of Russia's choice along her four axes of expansions (Balkans/Black Sea/Mediterranean; Caucasus; Indo-Persian Corridor; Far East) was to puzzle her neighbors. That she could follow only one priority at a time soon became clear to the Russians themselves: her poor communications did not allow her to expand on all four fronts simultaneously. In January 1857, for instance, E. P. Kovalevsky, an extremely able head of the Asiatic department in the foreign ministry, alarmed by Lord Elgin's expedition against Peking and the recent British victory over Persia, declared that the British could not be allowed to take either Peking or Herat.[14] As the British became fully preoccupied with suppressing the mutiny in India during that year, scores of Russian agents began to penetrate Khiva, Bukhara, Khorasan, Afghanistan, and Kashgar in a systematic quest for commercial and military intelligence. However, it would be a mistake to conclude that St. Petersburg, notwithstanding its focus on Central Asia, advocated an invasion of India. When Prince Baryatinsky, the tsar's viceroy of the Caucasus, suggested in February 1857 to the war minister, Count D. A. Milyutin, that in order to forestall the alleged British drive to the Caspian, Russia's eastern policy in Persia and Afghanistan must become more aggressive, the war ministry prepared a memorandum ("On the Possibility of a Hostile Clash between Russia and England in Central Asia") that rejected the very idea of conquering India, which was also dismissed by the cautious Gorchakov.[15]

It was the completion of the military conquest of the Caucasus that literally gave the Russians new blood to press ahead with the advance into Central Asia. Once the legendary Imam Shamil, the spiritual leader of the mountain tribes, was captured in 1859, the 200,000–man garrison in the Caucasus with its overambitious officer corps became available for another venture across the Caspian Sea.[16] During the following years, the great cities of Central Asia—Chimkent, Tashkent, Khojend, and Samarkand—were taken in rapid succession. In 1867 the Russians created the Turkestan Province and Military District.

To justify the policy of further expansion and annexation, Prince Gorchakov sent out a circular dispatch to his ambassadors in 1864, in which he very skillfully defended his country's civilized mission against "barbarous raiders and pillagers" while promising to settle accounts with the sedentary and agricultural populations of Central Asia peacefully. But he did not give any hint as to future limitations of Russia's "Forward Policy" because Russia on her onward march in Central Asia, just like the United States in North America, France in Algeria, and England in India, experienced the greatest difficulty in knowing "where to stop."[17]

The Russian press warned its readers that the British had been hatching a diabolic plan aiming at the creation of an alliance between the three Uzbeg Khanates, Bukhara, Khiva, and Kokand, supported on the one side by Yakub Beg of Kashgaria, on the other by Persia, and backed by the Afghans. The British, of course, suspected the Russians of being involved in a similar plot. The remarkable Sir Henry Rawlinson[18] was the foremost exponent of the "Forward School," which argued that, in order to forestall successfully a Russian advance against India, the British must build up a strong position at Kandahar, enabling them to exercise control over both Kabul to the east and Herat to the west. Rawlinson was an extraordinary man of many talents: soldier, diplomat, politician, explorer, archaeologist, and scholar, who deciphered old Persian and Babylonian cuneiform scripts. As a geographer he served as president of the Royal Geographical Society and used this position to advocate his rather extreme views, which made him into the leading Russophobe of his days. He became particularly notorious because of his insistence on the British occupation of Herat, widely regarded as the gateway to India.

There was something obsessive about the assumed key strategic importance of Herat, shared by both the Russians and the British. In the eyes of Russophobes like Rawlinson, "Russia in possession of Herat," as was previously the case with Khiva and later with Merv, constituted the convenient *casus belli,* as she "would have a grip on the throat of India."[19] Before the coming of railways, the British

"Forward Strategy," exercised in the name of defending India, focused on one particular threat, namely that Persia would become the vehicle for the expansion of Russian influence into Afghanistan and thence to India. It was precisely in this "geographic domino context," if we may call it that way, that Herat emerged as a vital strategic location in the defense of India, a position Herat was to retain for many years, since all military writers agreed then that the route from the Oxus across the Hindu Kush to Kabul was impracticable for an invading force (the Salang Pass tunnel was not completed until the 1960s!) and that the only likely route was through Herat.[20] The formerly tsarist general A. E. Snesarev, about whom more will be said later, while lecturing to the future Red Army general staff officers and diplomats in the 1920s, liked to repeat the old saying: "He who rules Herat, commands Kabul, and he who rules Kabul, commands India."[21]

Rawlinson visualized Russia advancing toward India on the basis of a preconceived plan consisting of three stages. If the domino principle could be applied to an attacking army "opening parallels against a beleaguered fortress," as Rawlinson suggested in 1868 in his famous "Memorandum on the Central Asian Question," his version would amount to almost a perfect analogy to the falling dominoes scare. In Rawlinson's parable Russia was advancing toward India like an army investing a fortress: she had already laid the first parallel ("a mere line of observation") along the Orenburg–Irtyst fortified line, was ready to take up the next one (a "line of demonstration") from the Krasnovodsk Bay to the Oxus river and further to the Pamir plateau, and was planning to seize some day the third parallel, running from Asterabad to Herat and further to Kabul and Kandahar if she survived "revolution in Europe and catastrophe in Asia." "Established in full strength at Herat," Rawlinson went on, "and her communications secured in one direction with Asterabad through Meshed, in another with Khiva through Merv, and in a third with Tashkent and Bukhara through Maimana and the passage of the Oxus . . . her position would indeed be formidable . . . and all the forces of Asia would be inadequate to expel her."[22] Although it took more than a hundred years for the fulfillment of Rawlinson's prophecy, his image of Russia as an immense land fortress, pushing ahead her parallel lines against the distant Indian fortress, fascinated and inspired several Russian geographers.[23]

The most outspoken critic of Rawlinson's geographic domino determinism was the outstanding administrator of British India, Sir John Lawrence, appointed Viceroy in 1863. Since his views so obviously contradict Rawlinson's main thesis, it may be useful to present here at least a gist of Lawrence's argument, especially as the polarity between the two views on the seriousness of the Russian threat in Central Asia has been recently revived in connection with the 1979 Soviet invasion of Afghanistan.[24] Lawrence was the very successful initiator and practitioner of "masterly inactivity," which we might dub in today's jargon an "anti-domino" policy directed against the rumors of an imminent Russian invasion of India. Instead of venturing farther into Afghanistan in the fulfillment of the dubious Forward Policy, Lawrence believed that Britain should instead consolidate her existing Indian realm.

As for Russia's conquest of Turkestan and her civilizing mission in Central Asia, Lawrence's views, as outlined in an 1867 document, would be applauded today by those supporters of detente who prefer arrangements between two superpowers at the cost of the underdog. For he sincerely believed that the Russians might prove "a safer ally and a better neighbor than the Mahomedan races of Central Asia and Kabul." Why did Lawrence believe so? Because Russia, he argued, "would introduce civilization, she would abate the fanaticism and ferocity of Mahomedanism, which still exercises to powerful an influence on India." And if Russia should one day resort to attacking India? In the event of such a "very problematical" invasion of India, Lawrence quite sensibly argued that the long march across Afghanistan would decimate any invading army without the necessity to apply the Forward Policy:

> In that case let them undergo the long and tiresome marches which lie between the Oxus and the Indus; let them wend their way through difficult and poor countries, among a fanatic and courageous population . . . then they will come to the conflict on which the fate of India will depend, toil-worn, with an exhausted infantry, a broken-down cavalry, and a defective artillery. Our troops would have the option of meeting them either in the defiles of the mountains, or as they debouched from the passes, or at the passage of the Indus.

Lawrence was equally scornful of the prospect that Russia could use the weapon of subversion against British India, "of stirring up strife and hatred against us among all the mountain tribes," since such a move, he argued not unreasonably, might well become counterproductive to the Russians themselves:

> And if so, will she be able to do us more harm than we can inflict on her in such a struggle? The further she extends her power, the greater area she must occupy; the more vulnerable points she must expose; the greater the danger she must incur of insurrection; and the larger must be her expenditure.

As could be safely predicted, the policy of Masterly Inactivity found no support among the Russophobes like Rawlinson. With great skill he would dig into contemporary Russian sources like newspapers to demonstrate to the British public that his theory was right. Many points that Rawlinson made in an 1868 memorandum have validity when applied against the Soviet strategy of the pre-Gorbachev era. But Rawlinson's memorandum was rejected by the number one military authority in British India, General W. R. Mansfield, who not only rejected the entire concept of Forward Policy (i.e., sending troops into Afghanistan), but opposed rigorously the diplomatic maneuvers advocated in the memorandum, such as British support in forming a "Central Asian Confederacy," composed of Bukhara, Khiva, Kokand, and Kashgaria and supported by Persia and Afghanistan, to resist further Russian penetration.[25]

Meanwhile the process of Russian absorption of Central Asia proceeded relentlessly. After defeating Bukhara and Khiva, Russia turned them into vassals in 1868 and 1873, respectively, and in 1876 annexed the Khanate of Kokand to the Turkestan Province. The absorption of Transcaspia followed suit.

The next stage of diversionary actions took place during the Russo-Turkish War of 1877–1878, when the Congress of Berlin met to thwart Russian designs on the Bosphorus. Since the Russians had already reached the gates of Constantinople and were not likely to give up the precious prize, the Russians decided for a heavy, diversionary thrust in Central Asia, sending 20,000 troops in three columns onto the Afghan and Pamir border. Simultaneously, a diplomatic mission under General Stoletov was sent to Kabul to sign a secret agreement with the Amir. Furthermore, in response to the arrival of a British squadron in the Sea of Marmara, the Russians considered sending a military expedition into Tibet and their cruisers from Vladivostok into the Indian Ocean in order to test out British reaction.[26] The situation could not be closer to Rawlinson's vision of Russia crossing the "line of demonstration" and preparing to occupy the fateful third parallel.

At that point another domino scheme emerged. In 1877, the flamboyant General M. D. Skobelev put forward a plan for a rapid advance against India with 15,000 men from Russian Turkestan. Skobelev's plan consisted of three stages: first, a political agreement with the Amir of Afghanistan combined with an occupation of Kabul by Russian troops; next, subverting all "disaffected elements in Hindustan"; and last, culminating in "hurling masses of Asiatic cavalry upon India as a vanguard under the banner of blood and rapine, thereby reviving the times of Timur."[27]

This was more than the British could digest and the sum of Russian diversionary activities led to their second invasion of Afghanistan (1878–1882), which forced the Russians to abandon their short-lived Afghan alliance. Despite the continuing tension between the Russians and the British, highlighted by the Panjdeh incident of 1885, and further clashes in the Pamirs, both sides finally agreed in 1895 on the demarcation of Afghanistan's boundaries, but Great Britain was to control the latter's external relations until 1919.

From about 1885, however, Russia's Asian strategy was undergoing an important shift from Central Asia to the Far East, whence expansion into Manchuria was to take place. This can be documented by the steady flow of reinforcements to the Amur and Ussuri frontier, even before the completion of the Trans-Siberian Railway. Here, east of Lake Baikal, her military strength between 1892 and 1903 increased from twenty-three to eighty-nine battalions, from thirteen to thirty-five squadrons, and from eight to twenty-five batteries; whereas in western Asia, which mainly consisted of the Turkestan Military District, the increase was insignificant. At the same time, following the acquisition of Port Arthur, Russia's Pacific fleet became overnight the most powerful component of her naval forces. Even after the disastrous outcome of its 1905 war with Japan, Russia continued to maintain a formidable military strength in the Far East.[28]

The trauma of the *two-front war,* to be fought simultaneously at both extremities of the empire's latitude of some 15,000 kilometers connected with the inefficient and vulnerable Trans-Siberian Railway for most of its length, became one of the principal geopolitical factors inherited by Soviet Eurasian strategy. This factor is indispensable for understanding the U.S.S.R.'s policy of balancing between East and West before Hitler's attack, as well as the enormous Soviet military and naval buildup in the Far East since the 1960s. There is a striking parallel between the vast military buildup of the 1960s and 1970s and that undertaken under Stalin during the 1930s: in 1988 the Far Eastern "TVD" (Theater of Military Operations) was deploying between one-quarter and one-third of Soviet military manpower and material;[29] in 1940 the Special Far Eastern Army contained at least 600,000 men in thirty-four rifle, eight cavalry divisions, and eight mechanized brigades (compared with fifty-five, nine, and twenty in the West respectively). Because Japan decided to strike south, half of the Soviet Far Eastern contingent could be dispatched westward to save Moscow from the German onslaught.[30] Barely four years later, as the defeat of Hitler's Germany drew closer, the Stavka managed to swing the pendulum back and throw over 1.5 million men, over 5,500 tanks, 26,000 guns, and 3,400 aircraft, inflicting thereby a crushing defeat of the Japanese *Kwantung* Army in Manchuria.[31] To apply, however, the principle of "swing strategy" forty years later appeared unrealistic;[32] the massive buildup in the Far East, which had started already under Khrushchev, was an indication that the Soviet strategists were resigned to face here the worst-case eventuality of truly nightmarish proportions: namely a simultaneous outbreak of hostilities against the United States in Europe as well as in the Pacific, combined with the high probability of conducting a parallel war with one billion Chinese.

Subversion: Setting the Orient Ablaze

Like diversion, the idea of subversion is an ancient strategem as old as the art of politics itself. It can be found in most Russian invasion schemes. Although tsarist Russia was generally more successful in planting subversion among the Christian subjects of the Ottoman Empire, especially in the Balkans and in the Trans-Caucasus, she found numerous opportunities to make it part of her threat to India as well. When in 1801 Emperor Paul I ordered Ataman Orlov and his Cossacks to advance against India, he instructed him to be concerned solely with fighting the British and "to offer peace to all who are against them and assure them of Russia's friendship."[33] General Duhamel's memorandum, mentioned earlier, spells out the idea of subversion with unambiguous clarity:[34]

> Proceeding on this road [i.e., to Lahore and Delhi], the army will stir up the Mohammedan population and carry rebellion into the very heart of the English territory. Allured by the prospect of plunder and territorial aggrandizement, the Afghans are likely to follow in our wake. If we succeed in inducing the Sikhs likewise to make common cause with us, all the better; if not, the Afghans alone are enough for our purpose. The negotiation of an Afghan alliance cannot early enough be taken in hand. All is gained if that can be gained; for not to conquer India, but only to destroy or shake the English rule, must be our object in invading the country. A moderate force, just strong enough to form the nucleus of a general insurrection, would be sufficient to attain our end. . . . Russia must announce herself as the liberator of all the neighbors and subjects of England. . . . Terrible enemies will rise in and around the very heart of the country, and although England has hitherto been able to suppress local insurrections, and has even availed herself of them to strengthen her position, she may not be able to repress a simultaneous insurrection of the entire country.

General Skobelev's scheme of 1877 for invading India, mentioned earlier, is not only very explicit on strategic diversion, but puts a great emphasis on rebellions inside India, which "might even produce a social revolution in England."[35]

A truly aggressive pitch on the subversive scale was reached when imperial Germany inserted herself through her extended bridgehead of the *Bagdadbahn* into the Great Game between Russia and Britain. It was the Kaiser himself, inspired by the leading German orientalist, Max von Oppenheim, who believed in the importance of the growing Pan-Islamic movement and proclaimed himself the protector of 300 million Muslims in his famous Damascus speech of 1898.[36] As Fritz Fischer showed in his important work, the emperor embraced willingly the image of revolutionary possiblities that Islam might offer in the event of a global war, including the idea of *Jihad*:[37]

> England must . . . have the mask of Christian peaceableness torn publicly off her face. . . . Our consuls in Turkey and India, etc., must inflame the whole Mohammedan world to wild revolt against this hateful, lying, conscienceless people of hagglers; for if we are to be bled to death, at least England shall lose India.

Germany developed diversion cum subversion as an effective and legitimate means of strategic warfare on the eve of World War I. The promotion of revolution by strategic subversion, in which imperial Germany became the real pioneer, was an incredibly wide-ranging and systematic operation launched by her general staff in cooperation with the foreign office.[38] Their most successful machination, with quite unforseeable consequences, was, of course, the transfer of Lenin in 1917 across Germany to Russia in a sealed train. German planners developed no less than ten schemes for the Islamic world alone, ranging from Lahore to Casablanca. "Revolution in India and Egypt, and also in the Caucasus," wrote General von Moltke, Jr., chief of the general staff, "is of the highest importance . . . to awaken the fanaticism of Islam."[39] By using Indian revolutionaries residing in Germany, two expeditions were organized during 1914 and sent to Baghdad with the military assistance of the Turkish ally. Led by Werner Otto von Hentig and Oskar von Niedermayer, the Kaiser's messengers rode across Persia and reached Kabul in the fall of 1915, without really achieving their main political objective. In exchange for the verbal recognition of full independence and an unrealistic offer of military assistance, Germany wanted to draw Afghanistan into war with British India by inciting a mass tribal uprising in order to tie down most of the Indian Army on the North-West Frontier and to facilitate revolutionary subversion inside India itself.[40]

Operating from Baghdad and from Persia itself, another group of highly adventurous German agents wanted to achieve too many aims at the same time: an anti-Russian uprising in Azebaijan, Bukhara, and Khiva; the extension of the *Jihad* among the Shiites; and a promotion of Pan-Turanian ideas advocated by Enver Pasha, which the Shiites had no reason to welcome. The boldest scheme was put forward by Count von Kanitz, the German military attaché at Tehran. He proposed on several occasions during 1915 to liberate 50,000 German and Austro-Hungarian prisoners of war believed to have been held in Turkestan and to use them not only to foment unrest inside Central Asia, but to isolate Turkestan from the rest of the Russian Empire by taking control of the railway network between the Caspian Sea and Orenburg. Furthermore, Kanitz proposed to take control of the bridges across the Irtysh and Ob rivers, and suggested that an operation against India be launched via Afghanistan.[41]

The Bolsheviks, especially Lenin and Trotsky, were keen to adapt the German revolutionary strategy with its subversive tactics vis-à-vis what is today called the Third World. To undermine the political cohesion of the Entente powers and their colonial empires, Wilhelmine Germany had pursued a radical revolutionary strategy with greater consistency than Hitler's Third Reich.[42] After all, was not the transfer of Lenin and his companions to Russia after the February Revolution of 1917 a sufficient demonstration of Germany's cynical determination to promote revolution in order to paralyze Russia and get rid of the two-front war problem? As for the subversive schemes to foment upheavals in India via friendly Afghanistan, this was by no means an original Bolshevik idea. They were copied from the earlier tsarist scenarios, as documented in this chapter, and amplified by the fresh German experience gathered during World War I. The first Bolshevik emissaries to Afghanistan, comrades Bravin and Surits, followed in the footsteps of their German predecessors, Herren von Niedermayer and von Hentig.

Turkestan in Turmoil

When Amir Amanullah of Afghanistan attacked British India in May 1919 (third Anglo-Afghan War), he was convinced that the Russian Bolsheviks would come fast to his side, but Lenin could offer only lofty promises of sending military aid and of recognizing Afghanistan's sovereignty, thereby merely conforming to the old German demands as stipulated in the Brest-Litovsk Peace Treaty. The primary cause of the abortive Afghan-Bolshevik coordination was failed communication: the Orenburg–Tashkent Railway remained for the most part of 1919 cut off, and although Tashkent could communicate with Moscow by radio, to and from Kabul only messengers on horse could be used.

The two Russian revolutions of 1917 caused great disruptions in the geopolitical framework of the tsarist empire, resulting in the cession of its borderlands (Finland, Baltic provinces, Poland, Bessarabia, temporarily the Ukraine and the Transcaucasion Federation); yet they could not fundamentally change the geopolitical foundations of the Anglo-Russian rivalry in Central Asia. Russian Turkestan, too, seemed to be drifting in the same irresistible direction of separation and disintegration. Bolshevik power rested solely on the maintenance of the only rail connection with central Russia via Orenburg, and as this was for most of the first two years of the civil war cut off, it remained confined to Tashkent, the only large Russified city in Turkestan. The central authority in Petrograd, and later in Moscow, could hardly reach Turkestan, which in any case occupied a low military priority in the eyes of the Bolshevik government struggling to survive against a multitude of internal uprisings and foreign interventions.

From early on, however, the Bolsheviks possessed two major advantages. First, they were the only force in Central Asia capable of maintaining, repairing, and using the railway network for their own military aims. Second, they seized the only professional force of military value available in Turkestan after the dissolution of the old Russian army. These were the prisoners of war, mostly Austro-Hungarians, estimated to number over 40,000 in the fall of 1917. As indicated earlier they constituted an important element in the calculations of German schemers as early as 1915 to unseat the British Raj in India by provoking a Muslim uprising.[43] In 1918 this remote threat became suddenly real. With a tacit agreement of the Bolsheviks under the terms of the Brest-Litovsk Peace Treaty, it was not impossible to imagine a Turco-German sweep originating from Transcaucasia across Transcaspia, northern Persia, and Afghanistan. As these prisoners of war, suffering from malnutrition and boredom, were volunteering in increasing numbers to join as *internationalists* the Red Guards in Turkestan, who constituted throughout 1918 the backbone of Bolshevik troops, the British became greatly alarmed watching "these potential recruits of an army of world revolution" getting loose in the direction of India.[44]

This was just one of many important factors that, during the period of great upheavals in Central Asia from 1917 to 1922, allowed the creation in this region of multiple political options, which could have shaped the future of Turkestan, as the core of Central Asia, in a different way from what we know today. This state of continuous flux in Central Asia created an unpredictable series of challenges and responses for all participants in the division of spoils. Since during the previous hundred years of Central Asian history there was no similar dramatic cleavage, it might be useful to sum up these options in a more or less chronological order:

1. German imperialists' designs concerned primarily with disrupting British control over India. By exploiting the Turkish connection they hoped to stir up the Muslim population of India via Afghanistan through a mass tribal uprising on the North-West Frontier tying down the British Indian Army, and thereby preventing troop reinforcements from India to reach other theaters of war. As a useful vehicle of religious and ethnic propaganda for Turkestan, the Germans hoped to exploit the Pan-Turanian movement (Enver Pasha). Although these German plans had been hatched in 1915 (e.g., the Henting–Niedermayer Expedition), preparations intensified after the Brest–Litovsk Peace Treaty in the short period between March and November 1918.[45]
2. British interventionists entered Baku at the end of the summer of 1918 to prevent the oil fields from falling into German hands and occupied Transcaspia between 1918 and 1919 to deny to the Turco-German forces the control of Russia's "south-east passage" toward India.

   Although some prominent Muslims, like the Aga Khan, urged the British Empire, already "the greatest Muslim power in the world," to include further Muslim states, "stretching from the Bosphorus to Chinese

Turkestan . . . ," the temptation was wisely avoided in London, because of fear that the effect of Pan-Islamism "might easily be paralyzing." If the former Russian Empire were to disintegrate, the India Office thought that Turkestan "should look rather to Omsk than to Petrograd or Moscow as its focus." If an Asiatic Russian government centered on Omsk, and controlling all the railway systems up to Orenburg, could survive the civil war, then Russian Central Asia, the India Office reflected, should be divided into four autonomous units under Siberian suzerainty.[46]

3. Intermittent centrifugal movements created with German encouragement within the disintegrating tsarist empire, such as a "Cossack South-Eastern Union," stretching from the Don region, Orenburg, to Semirechie, which might have significantly influenced events in Turkestan, pending the control and maintenance of the Orenburg–Tashkent Railway.[47]
4. The prospect of Balkanization of Central Asia, which might have led to the temporary extension of life for the ex-Russian protectorates, the khanates of Bukhara and Khiva.
5. Alternatively, the replacement of the conservative khanates by the forces of modern Islamic revival *(Jadids),* as epitomized by the short-lived existence of the "Provisional Government of Autonomous Turkestan" under Mustafa Chokaiev in Kokand, which claimed authority over Russian Central Asia in competition with the Bolshevik Tashkent government (all-European). The Kokand experiment was smashed savagely by the Red Guards dispatched from Tashkent in February 1918.[48]
6. An attempt to create a larger Islamic federation in Central Asia, led by the ambitious Amir Amanullah. Apart from Afghanistan, it was to consist initially of Bukhara and Khiva. Since Persia was too weak, it was assumed that it would have to accept Kabul's leadership. Amanullah was hoping that further disintegration of the Russian Empire would increase the chances of incorporating the rest of Turkestan. In the event of British power collapsing in India, Kabul would have undoubtedly tried to reclaim historic Afghan holdings across the Durand Line down to the Indus River to secure the integration of all Pashtun tribes (cf. the third Anglo-Afghan War of 1919 and the origins of "Pashtunistan"). An inseparable part of Afghan territorial claims against British India was the maritime province of Sindh with the port of Karachi as its center.[49]
7. A Muslim Pan-Turanist federation in Central Asia—a lifelong dream of Enver Pasha, who, after disastrously failing to lead Turkish troops to Central Asia through the Caucasus in 1915, would eventually arrive with Lenin's encouragement in Turkestan via Moscow in November 1921. But instead of helping to promote an anti-colonial revolution near the Indian border and to help the Bolsheviks consolidate their control over the Central Asian Turks, as he must have promised Lenin, Enver Pasha used the first opportunity to join the anti-Bolshevik guerrillas *(basmachi)*. Despite all his superb credentials (son-in-law of the last Turkish sultan, the *Khalif;* ex-minister of war, etc.), Enver's claim to overall leadership was never recognized by the *basmachi*. After his death amidst fighting in August

1922, the incoherent *basmachi* resistance would linger on into the 1930s, incapable, however, of providing a viable political alternative in Central Asia.[50]

8. A "Socialist Pan-Turan," as envisaged by the "red Tatar," Sultan Galiev, Stalin's confident in the Commissariat for Nationalities. This perspective was exploited by the Bolsheviks during the civil war, especially among the Tatars and Baskhirs. It was also useful as a propaganda vehicle for carrying anti-imperialist slogans to rally non-European revolutionaries.[51]
9. Finally, the option that materialized when all others had failed, the old *status quo ante bellum,* that is, the *reconquista*[52] of Turkestan by the Bolsheviks that terminated the interregnum in Russian Central Asia. Despite the protracted struggle with the *basmachi,*[53] the Bolsheviks did not want to postpone their anti-imperialist strategy and the promotion of world revolution through subversion from the Turkestan *place d'armes.* The failure of communist takeovers in Western Europe, which had been the prime goal of their previous strategy, gave advocates of anticolonial rebellions their chance to prevail with their own schemes, through which they could couple the civil war in Russia with cross-border subversions to undermine the colonial empires in Asia. The Bolsheviks showed no scruples in enlisting the assistance of every potential ally, including Amir Amanullah, who eagerly sought Soviet support in order to disentangle his country from British bondage; or Enver Pasha, still pursuing the grand Pan-Turanian dream. From the second Komintern Congress and the Congress of the Eastern Peoples in Baku, which took place in July and September 1920, respectively, the Bolshevik strategy seemed to have radically switched, at least temporarily, from pursuing revolutionary takeovers in the West, to supporting anticolonial uprisings in the East. Gregory Zinoviev, president of the Komintern who also chaired the Baku congress, urged the participants to declare "a true Holy War against the English and French robber-capitalists." "If Persia is the door," he went on, "through which one has to go in order to invade the citadel of the revolution in the entire Orient, that is to say India, we must foment the Persian revolution." This quasi-Rawlinsonian image, which Zinoviev used, received his finishing touch by invoking the parable of falling dominoes:[54]

> The Persian uprising will give the signal . . . for a series of revolutions that will spread through all of Asia and part of Africa. . . . All that is needed is an impulse from outside, an external aid, an initiative, and a resolute decision.

Ex Oriente Lux

Following the Komintern's decision, plans were made for scores of Indian revolutionaries and Muslim *muhajirs* to be trained and provided with weapons on Soviet territory. At a propitious moment they were to be launched via friendly Afghanistan to infiltrate the Indian border. At Tashkent, the prominent Indian Marxist, M. N. Roy, set up a military and propaganda training center.[55] Indian revolutionaries, who during the war had worked for the German emperor, were suddenly keen to transfer their allegiances to Lenin and conduct propaganda at the gates of India (e.g., Maulavi Barakatullah, V. N. Chattopadhyaya, and Raja Mahendra Pratap).[56] India now acquired a new dimension as the major external target for the Bolshevik strategy to enhance world revolution by striking at the most vulnerable spot in the edifice of British colonialism.

Both Lenin and Stalin were anticipating the great anticolonial upheaval in the East from as early as 1918, though they still seemed to consider Europe to be the major playground of the future world revolution. Dzhugashvili, alias Stalin, himself an Asiatic from the Caucasus, went beyond the official Bolshevik appeals stressing self-determination and renunciation of the former unequal imperialist treaties concluded by the tsarist government with its weaker neighbors. In the first anniversary article in *Pravda* of November 7, 1918, Stalin stressed that the October Revolution "built a bridge between the socialist West and the enslaved East . . . against world imperialism."[57] Two more articles followed suit in the journal of the Nationalities' Commissariat *(Narkomnats),* of which Stalin was in charge: "Do Not Forget the East" and "Light From the East."[58]

Did other Bolshevik leaders spread the same message? Nikolai Bukharin, for instance, expressed himself in March 1919 on the subject with cynical frankness: "If we propound the self-determination for the colonies, the Hottentots, the Negroes, the Indians, etc., we lose nothing by it. On the contrary, we gain."[59] Five months later, writing to the Central Committee, Trotsky exploited the idea of ideological diversion in terms of military strategy:[60]

> The sort of army, which at the moment can be of no significance in the European scales, can upset the unstable balance of Asian relationships, of colonial dependence, give a direct push to an uprising on the part of the oppressed masses and assure the triumph of such a rising in Asia. . . . One authoritative military official already some months ago put up a plan for creating a cavalry corps (30,000–40,000 riders) with the idea of launching it against India. It stands to reason that a plan of this sort requires careful preparation, both material and political. We have up to now devoted too little attention to agitation in Asia. However, the international situation is evidently shaping in such a way that the road to Paris and London lies via the towns of Afghanistan, the Punjab and Bengal.

This "authoritative military official" could well have been the ex-tsarist General A. E. Snesarev (1865–1937), selected by Trotsky to head the Academy of General Staff in Moscow between 1919 and 1921. Convinced of Russia's historic mission to reach the warm waters of the Indian Ocean, he did not think that the Bolshevik Revolution could have changed the fundamentals of Russia's geopolitical position in this region, as he had already laid out in his principal work, *India as the Main Factor in the Central Asian Question* (1906).[61] In the course of his lectures on the military geography of Central Asia, which Snesarev resumed in the autumn of 1919, he would exhort future Soviet general staff officers and diplomats: "If you want to destroy the capitalist tyranny over the world—beat the British in India!"[62]

However, such Bolshevik-sponsored invasion of India had never taken place in the early 1920s, when the political situation seemed to be most propitious. By 1923 the revolutionary enthusiasm, whether inspired by socialist ideas, Pan-Turanian beliefs, or Pan-Islamist beliefs, seems to have evaporated, and the Soviet government became more inward-looking, more cautious and calculating. They turned against the "Socialist Pan-Turan" movement, headed by Sultan Galiev, which they originally wanted to use as a springboard for launching communist agitators into the neighboring Islamic countries.[63] By the time of the Curzon Ultimatum (May 1923), the Bolshevik "Eastern strategy" directed against India and emphasizing the connection with Islam, was effectively terminated. The abolition of the Caliphate by Kemal Atatürk caused the *Khilafat* Movement in India to die a natural death.[64] In spite of the fact that Bolshevik forces did infiltrate Sinkiang and Outer Mongolia, trespassed on several occasions deep into Manchuria, and continued to fight against the *basmachi* guerrillas well into the 1930s, their main task was to consolidate Soviet power over the ex-tsarist territories of Central Asia rather than to confront the British inside Afghanistan by applying diversion cum subversion.

The Great Game and Cold War Compared

Notwithstanding the enormous geographical and logistical difficulties with which a Soviet-sponsored invasion of India would have had to cope in the 1920s and 1930s, at least five hypothetical preconditions would have had to be fulfilled, more or less simultaneously, to bring about the demise of the British Raj over India: (1) elimination of British naval supremacy in the Indian Ocean; (2) outbreak of civil rebellion inside India; (3) mutiny of the Indian Army; (4) external challenge in the form of a tribal uprising on the North-West Frontier supported by Afghanistan; and (5) collusion with an overland advance against India by a major power. Between 1918 and 1920, however, only two of these preconditions appeared to be fulfilled (2 and 4), but they did not occur simultaneously, and the Bolsheviks were either incapable of, because of the distance and logistics involved, or late in, exploiting them.

By contrast, between 1940 and 1942, when World War II created a series of parallel but not strictly analogous crises along the Eurasian rimland for the Western colonial powers, none of the serious challengers (i.e., the Soviet Union prior to June 1941, Nazi Germany, or Imperial Japan) were keen in shifting their priorities to Central Asia in order to exploit several unique opportunities, in spite of the fact that all five preconditions enumerated above seemed to have been to some extent fulfilled. Moreover, in addition to these five preconditions, the Axis powers could have been more efficient, as imperial Germany had been in 1917 when it sent Lenin from Switzerland to Russia, when transferring the outstanding Indian revolutionary, Subhas Chandra Bose, from Berlin to the Indian border (either to Afghanistan or Burma) in order to enhance decisively the collusion of all five elements needed to undermine the security of British India. When Bose finally arrived in 1943 on the Asian scene to take over the Japanese-sponsored Indian independence movement and the command of the Indian National Army (INA), it was too late, and all the five preconditions, which had still existed as late as the early part of 1942, either evaporated or turned in favor of the Allies.[65]

As for the domino principle transplanted onto the more than century-long Anglo-Russian Great Game, it did play a role, but limited and subsidiary, never for its own sake, but always in support of the principal idea of subversion and diversion. This idea, in the end, was to serve a limited political objective within the balance of power structure—not to change it radically by dividing multipolar world into two camps.

During the interim period between the two world wars when the Great Game was in transition to the Cold War, British administration in India regarded communist infiltration as the main external threat to British rule. In a confidential document prepared in 1933, the synopsis of communism in action comes very close to the domino parable: its escalation ladder counts five main stages (permeation—mobilization—revolution—sovietization—world revolution) and eighteen interstages.[66]

The military planners from the Indian General Staff and the War Office in London definitely viewed the Soviet Union as the number one enemy to the security of India. The *casus belli* clause of 1907, which stipulated that a Russian attack on Afghanistan was to be answered by a British declaration of war on Russia, was still retained in the Defence of India Plan ("War with Russia in Afghanistan"), drafted in 1928 by the War Office. During the previous year the Chiefs of Staff (COS) concluded that "the present policy of Soviet Russia towards India is identical with that adopted in the past by Imperial Russia."[67]

While the War Office scenario for a Forward Offensive Policy in the event of a Soviet invasion took the cooperation with the Afghan government and with the Frontier tribes for granted, the Indian General Staff believed in neither. Their own contingency plans for the period, carrying the codes "Blue," "Pink," and "Interim" (1927, 1931, 1938), anticipated a Russian penetration coupled with Afghan hostility and guerrilla actions of the cis- and trans-Frontier tribes against the British. Even when the Axis threat became predominant toward the end of the 1930s, the British planners could never entirely divert their attention from the assumed Soviet menace in Central Asia until June 1941.[68]

And yet, despite the deep ideological cleavage since 1917, the strategies applied in the pre-1945 world were not determined by the existence of the ultimate nuclear weapon. It would appear that the fear of Russian/Soviet expansionism, underlying in fact the entire period of the Anglo-Russian rivalry in Asia, posed in essence the same questions: Was the threat real? If we accept with the benefit of hindsight that the fear had no real foundation, then we must ask ourselves, was it then not rather absurd to harbor fears about it? Although a vocal minority of authors and decision makers at various stages of its evolution shared a disbelief about the nature of the fear, the very nature of the Anglo-Russian Great Game in Asia precluded a clear-cut answer about the genuine nature of fear; why?

One reason why the notion of fear became so ambivalent in Anglo-Russian rivalry was that the nature of the Great Game made terms "aggressive" and "defensive" mutually interchangeable.[69] While vis-à-vis each other the two great powers used extensively aggressive signaling without resorting to a major war, toward the minor powers along the Asiatic rimland they applied maximum coercion trying to turn them into pliable buffers (e.g., the rulers of Persia and Afghanistan were kept in power by cash allowances provided by the imperialist great powers).

The other reason for enhancing the power of the notion of a Russian threat was certainly the nightmarish experience the British colonial administration in India had with the Great Mutiny of 1857. Although the mutiny was not Russian-instigated, there was always the underlying fear that a hostile foreign power could in the future carry out subversive actions inside the subcontinent, especially among the Pashtun tribesmen and India's Muslim subjects.

Added to the psychological residual of fear was the historic dimension in the Russian threat, which the British-Indian official mind formed on the basis of the vast repository of past lessons—not just one irrelevant episode or superficial analogy, not even on account of Russian plans since the apocryphal testament of Peter the Great, but on four millenia of at least twenty large-scale invasions of India from the northwest.[70] Thus to argue that the Russian threat at that time, or the German one during World War II for that matter, was a mere chimera is not only wrong from the psychological point of view, but it betokens a great ignorance of historic precedents. The men who ruled India had a classical education; for them the smallest topographical and military details related to the campaigns of Alexander the Great,[71] or to Napolean's schemes against India, were just as fresh and relevant as the most contemporary blueprints of General Skobelev. It is, however, true that Napoleon's schemes and most of the early Russian ones (e.g., of Duhamel, of Khrulev) showed an appalling lack of logistical preparations. If they had been undertaken at their time, they would have been an almost certain failure—unless British India had been in turmoil and lying completely defenseless.

By contrast, with the arrival of the first strategic railroads on the Afghan border by the end of the nineteenth century, an era of a very sophisticated logistical planning entered the Great Game. Former adventurous amateurs, preferring to travel by horseback on their own, were pushed aside by professional geographers, surveyors, engineers, and quarter-master–generals, who carefully stocked rails and other construction materials at their prepositioned railheads. The Russians estimated that it would take them four-and-a-half months to reach Herat from Kushka by rail; their British counterparts calculated that they would need three months to bring a military train from Chaman to Kandahar.[72] These were, of course, short-range objectives, expanding the strategic buffer just over a few hills and ravines, but Herat and Kandahar were the two most sensitive locations, which neither the Russians nor the British could be expected to occupy on their own without risking a declaration of war.

The bureaucratic rivalry between New Delhi and Whitehall could have played an important, but not a decisive role, in exaggerating the Russian threat. There is plenty of evidence to show that London frequently viewed requests for money and troops on behalf of the government of India to improve defense and internal security against the Russian threat, as a form of blackmail—and turned them down. The result was that without the extra funds from the British Treasury, India's defenses deteriorated rapidly over the years, especially during the 1930s. Moreover, India's external defense commitments to send troops abroad had been steadily increased to cover the vast sector stretching from Egypt to Hong Kong.

With or without the notion of the Russian threat, with or without the imagery of falling dominoes, which the theory of subversion implied, India's defenses were in a catastrophic state in 1938. This was, more or less, the verdict that three special committees (named after their chairmen: Auchinleck, Pownall, and Chatfield) pronounced. They were set up in 1938 to look into the accumulated deficiencies of the Indian Army and to lay foundations for the creation of an "Imperial Reserve Force." The Auchinleck Report on modernization reported that the Indian Army in terms of modern equipment had fallen behind the forces of such states as Egypt, Iraq, and even Afghanistan. The bulk of its cavalry was still horsed, except for four regiments converted into armored car units and there were no tanks. The field artillery, mechanized only in part, remained equipped with obsolete guns. There were no antitank weapons, no fighter aircraft, and only eight antiaircraft guns in the whole of India. Judged by modern standards, the Auchinleck Report concluded, the Indian Army of 1938 was unfit to take the field against land or air forces equipped with up-to-date weapons.[73]

Was India threatened at the time by such a force? All military estimates are relative to the existing and potential strategic balance within a given space. Why should India have upgraded her defenses? A number of British strategists argued that the Red Army could line up such forces in the Turkestan Military District. Although the bulk of the Indian Army had been garrisoned along the Durand Line, its mobility and reserves were seriously jeopardized since 1936 by fighting a series of tribal uprisings in Waziristan.[74] At a time when India was practically defenseless against an air attack, the Soviet air force, according the M.I.2 comments in September 1939 (military intelligence branch in the War Office covering India), could easily concentrate on airfields near the Afghan border 400 modern bombers, whose radius of action would have sufficed to carry out bombing missions as far as Lahore. Although M.I.2 cautioned that the Red Army could not overrun the whole of Afghanistan because of the grand Hindu Kush massif,[75] it rightly concluded that the Soviet Union could occupy Afghanistan's northern provinces at any moment she chose: the Afghan garrison there was ridiculously weak, there were no armed tribesmen to serve as a second line of defense in this region, and even if the panic-stricken Afghan government invited the Indian Army—as they indeed were to consider during the coming weeks when the Russian threat loomed large over the horizon—the same Hindu Kush massif and the enormous logistical problems would have prevented the timely arrival of British military assistance to northern Afghanistan. M.I.2 did not believe that the renewed Russian threat had taken alarming proportions, but warned that it was more likely for the Soviets to cause diversion of the British war effort from its principal object to fight Germany, by stirring up trouble through subversive activities in Afghanistan and among the armed tribesmen on the North-West Frontier, which might bring about complete anarchy to India.[76]

Were there any signs during 1938 and 1939 of Soviet troops and bomber squadrons being concentrated along the Afghan border? There is no evidence of it. It would hardly make sense in the overall context of domestic and international problems the Soviet Union found itself at the time: Stalin was busy slaughtering most of his senior military commanders, and there was no logic in activating the Central Asian military theater when an undeclared war with Japan was being fought in the Far East, with a very high probability of the opening of a second front on the Polish border, 10,000 miles further west. It was not, however, the Soviet Union alone that posed a major threat to Afghanistan and India, but the far-reaching implications of Stalin's secret agreement with Hitler, known as the Non-Aggression Pact of August 1939, with its underlying assumption that a secret agreement between Germany and Russia must have been concluded on whose main purpose was the liquidation of the British Empire. Afghanistan thus resumed overnight its principal place in British Imperial strategic planning. The War Cabinet was suddenly confronted with an extremely awkward situation: Having just declared war on Germany, and realizing too well that in Central Asia the main threat to India was represented by the Soviet Union, how possibly could the British government seriously contemplate declaring war on the Soviet Union as well? Could Great Britain, together with France, stumble into that fantastic political folly, as she seemed to have come close to during the last weeks of the Soviet-Finnish War, of being simultaneously engaged in war with Nazi Germany and Communist Russia?

Nazi–Soviet cooperation made the possible invasion of Afghanistan a double threat to British India. First, in the form of a direct air and land attack carried out either exclusively by the Soviets, or in cooperation with the German *Luftwaffe* and paratroopers, whose transfer to Soviet Central Asia would have required minimal logistical preparations.[77] Second, the threat could have taken the form of subversive actions staged by an odd mixture of pro-Communist and pro-Axis fifth columnists. Third, it could have materialized as an aggregate of the two threats, as it did in the plans to restore Amanullah to his lost throne with the joint Nazi–Soviet assistance.[78]

Could the British government go as far as to guarantee Afghanistan's territorial integrity and thus commit itself, as in the Polish case, to restore that country to its present boundaries if it was plain to everybody that northern Afghanistan, like northern Iran, was indefensible against a Soviet attack? Furthermore, would such a British commitment involve the launching of a military campaign against Soviet Russia to hit her lines of communication and oil fields? Such questions were asked at the time, and however exaggerated they might sound today, the chiefs of staff in London believed during the early stages of the war that the most effective form of defense against any Russian advance was to bomb the Baku oil fields.[79] During the second half of 1940, however, the shadow of Soviet invasion of Afghanistan, with or without direct German assistance, began to recede, as

Soviet Russia was being pulled more into European affairs. It also became clear that Stalin's bargaining power vis-à-vis Hitler's Germany had been steadily declining, especially since the elimination of France as number one military power in Europe.

In summing up, the following lessons, covering the transition from the Great Game to the Cold War, can be drawn:

1. Who won the Great Game at the eve of the Great War in 1914? Although the British may be said to have given in to Russia, the latter power had only a limited capacity to exploit its geographic advantage. But it was obvious that Russian power was still on the increase and the British government had still found no means of halting it. It was Germany that was to bite twice for the ascendancy in Eurasia, and Germany twice came nearer to realizing it than any other power since Napoleonic France. It was only during the last year of World War I that the anti-German coalition of Great Britain, France, and the United States managed to thwart this bid and could look with satisfaction on the disappearance of four old empires in Eurasia. Suddenly, after forestalling the Bolshevik threat to the East, the exhausted British imperialists, behind a tier of old and new buffer states, appeared for a moment to have won the Great Game after all! Or was it a delusion?
2. Although the Bolsheviks emerged from the civil war substantially weakened in Europe by the loss of borderlands and buffers, in Asia, by contrast, they managed to shepherd peoples and territories of the tsars into the old imperial mould. The Great Game between the British and the Russians continued, but it became much less dramatic. There were several reasons for it. One was the unpredictable behavior in the new chain of much less reliable buffer states. Furthermore, in spite of the fact that the postitions of the two rival powers had become more entrenched because of ideology, the ensuing antagonism did not appear central after 1923 on the world stage; it became just one factor among many.
3. A mere twenty years after the establishment of the U.S.S.R., the Russians and British were compelled to become, with the Americans, allies once more against a renewed German bid for ascendance in Eurasia.
4. From the German point of view, however, the Japanese alliance and Soviet partnership were essential for the realization of the "Transcontinental Bloc" under German leadership, the favorite scheme of the German geopolitician Karl Haushofer. Although of hypothetical significance today, this scheme seemed to have a strong chance of succeeding during a brief but crucial period between 1939 and 1941, which might have radically changed the scope of events during the war, but even more after it.[80]
5. After the end of World War II, with Germany and Japan eliminated and following British withdrawal from India, the Soviet Union emerged as unquestionably the greatest single power in Eurasia, with seemingly far more capacity to influence events than either the British or Russian governments had had at their disposal. With the advent of thermonuclear weapons and China's emergence as a communist state in 1949, the world scene was set up for the worst-case scenario the cold war politicians could

think of: a global armageddon following a communist push to gain the definite sway over Eurasia. Only a few observers in those days warned that Soviet and Chinese communist objectives could never become identical.

Notes

1. H. J. Mackinder, "The Geographical Pivot of History," *The Geographical Journal* 23:4 (1904): 423, 436.

2. D. Macdonald, chap. 5, in this volume.

3. D. Macdonald, p. 112, in this volume.

4. F. F. Martens, *Rossiya i Angliya v Srednei Azii* (St. Petersburg, 1880); M. A. Terentiev: *Rossiya i Angliya v Srednei Azii* (St. Petersburg, 1875); *Rossiya i Angliya v bor'be za rynki* (St. Petersburg, 1876); *Istoriya zavoevaniya Srednei Azii,* 3 vols. (St. Petersburg, 1906); A. L. Narochnitskyi, *Kolonial 'naya politika kapitalisticheskikh derzhav na Dal' nem Vostoke, 1860–1895* (Moscow, 1956), 220; N. A. Khalfin, *Prisoedinenie Sradnei Azii k Rossii* (Moscow: Nauka, 1965), 19.

5. *Akademik Barthold-Sochineniya,* 2 vols. (Moscow: Izd. vostochnoi lit., 1963), I:13, 164–66, 345–50.

6. See Peter Hopkirk's highly romanticized and entertaining *Setting the East Ablaze: Lenin's Dream of an Empire in Asia* (London: John Murray, 1984).

7. "Better Fewer But Better," V. I. Lenin-Ulyanov, in *Pravda,* Mar. 4, 1923.

8. For the origins of the term, see H. W. C. Davis, "The Great Game in Asia, 1800–1844," The Raleigh Lecture on History, *Proceedings of the British Academy* (London, 1926); M. Hauner, "The Last Great Game," *The Middle East Journal* 38:1 (Winter 1984): 72–84.

9. M. E. Yapp, *Strategies of British India: Britain, Iran and Afghanistan, 1798–1850* (Oxford: Clarendon Press, 1980).

10. E. M. Zhukov, ed., *Mezhdunarodnye otnosheniya na Dal'nem Vostoke* (Moscow: Mysl, 1973) I: 94–95.

11. G. V. Chicherin, "Rossiya i aziatskie narody," *Vestnik NKID* 2, (Aug. 13, 1919), reprinted in "Rossiya i aziatskie narodny," *Stati i rechi* (Moscow, 1961), 86–98; see also M. Hauner, "Central Asian Geopolitics in the Last Hundred Years—A Critical Survey from Gorchakov to Gorbachev," *Central Asian Survey* 8:1 (1989): 1–19.

12. H. S. Edwards, *Russian Projects Against India from the Czar Peter to General Skobelev* (London: Remington, 1885).

13. General A. O. Duhamel, "The Road to India," India Office Records: Confidental Memoranda, L/P&S/18/C 9; Sir Louis Mallet, "Historical Summary of the Central Asian Question," April 30, 1874, ibid.

14. D. Gillard, *The Struggle for Asia, 1828–1914. A Study in British and Russian Imperialism* (London: Methuen, 1977), 105.

15. Khalfin, *Prisoedinenie* (1965), 97–98.

16. See Mallet, "Historical Summary"; Major-General Sir Henry Rawlinson "Confidential Report on Georgia" to the Secretary of State for India, November 14, 1859, reprinted in D. I. Lieven, ed., *British Documents on Foreign Affairs: Confidential Print, Russia,* vol. 1 (1859–1880) (University Publications of America, 1983), 1–13.

17. W. K. Fraser-Tytler, *Afghanistan:A Study of Political Developments in Central and Southern Asia* (London: Oxford University Press, 1967), 333–37.

18. Yapp, *Strategies,* 439–40; G. Morgan, *Anglo-Russian Rivalry in Central Asia: 1810–1895* (London: Frank Cass, 1981), 56–58.

19. H. Rawlinson, *England and Russia in the East. A Series of Papers on the Political and Geographical Condition of Central Asia* (London: John Murray, 1875), 379.

20. Morgan, *Rivalry,* 103–6; A. Vambery, *The Coming Struggle for India* (London: Cassell, 1885), chaps. 6 and 7; C. T. Marvin, *The Russians at the Gates of Herat* (New York: Scribners, 1885).

21. A. E. Snesarev, *Afganistan* (Moscow, 1921), 192, 219. For the criticism of Rawlinson's deterministic fixation on Herat as the gateway to India, see G. J. Alder, "The Key to India? Britain and the Herat Problem, 1830–1863," *Middle Eastern Studies* 10:2-3 (1974): 186–209, 287–311; and *British India's Northern Frontier 1865–1895* (London, 1963).

22. H. G. Rawlinson, "Memorandum on the Central Asian Question," July 20, 1868, India Office Records: L/P&S/18/C 3; see also Rawlinson, *England and Russia* (1875), 294–95.

23. A. N. Snesarev, *Anglo-Russkoe Soglashenie 1907 goda* (St. Petersburg, 1908), 14; P. N. Savitsky, "Geopoliticheskie zametki po russkoi istorii," in G. V. Vernadsky, *Nachertanie russkoi istorii* (Prague, 1927), 254–60. Certain strong residuals of the Herat fixation, I suspect, must have been present in the decision-making process of the Soviet leadership during 1979, which culminated in the full-scale invasion of Afghanistan by the end of the same year. Despite the absence of prima facie evidence from Soviet sources, there are strong indicators that the Soviets must have been extremely outraged by the anti-Russian uprising in Herat in mid-March 1979, during which an estimated 50 to 100 Soviet advisers along with members of their families were mercilessly massacred. In revenge, squadrons of Soviet bombers and numerous military personnel helped loyal Afghan troops to suppress the Herat rebellion. See E. Girardet, *Afghanistan: The Soviet War* (New York: St. Martin's, 1985), 115–16.

24. Sir John Lawrence, Minute on British Policy in Central Asia, Simla, October 3, 1867, India Office Records: L/P&S/5/260, reprinted in Morgan, *Rivalry,* 226–37.

25. Comments on Rawlinson's memorandum by Gen. W. R. Mansfield, December 24, 1868, read and annotated by Sir John Lawrence, the Viceroy; India Office Records: L/P&S/18/C 3.

26. A. L. Popov, "Ot Bosfora k Tikhomu Okeanu," *Istorik-Marksist* 3:37 (1934): 15–16.

27. "Indian Officer," *Russia's March Towards India,* vol. 2 (London: Sampson Low, 1894), 79–100; G. N. Curzon, *Russia in Central Asia in 1889 and the Anglo-Russian Question* (London: Longmans Green, 1889), 307, 322–30. In February of the same year a certain colonel Matveev was sent out by the Russian general staff to reconnoitre the future line of supply to Russian troops in the event of their advance from Herat to the Punjab. Matveev's study was published several years later in the *Sbornik geograficheskikh, topograficheskikh i statisticheskikh materialov po Azii,* published by the Imperial General Staff, vol. 5; W. B. Walsh, "The Imperial Russian General Staff and India: A Footnote to Diplomatic History," *The Russian Review* 16:2 (April 1957): 53–58.

28. *General Staff: The Military Resources of the Russian Empire* (1907), 188, confidential print, War Office Records: WO 33/419.

29. Department of Defense, *Soviet Military Power 1988* (Washington, D.C.: U.S. GPO); *The Military Balance 1987–1988* (London: IISS, 1987).

30. J. Erickson, *The Soviet High Command* (New York: St. Martin's, 1962), 767; A. D. Coox, *Nomonhan: Japan Against Russia, 1939,* vol. 1 (Stanford, Calif.: Stanford University Press, 1985), 84; J. Haslam, *Soviet Foreign Policy, 1930–33* (New York: St. Martin's, 1983), 71–96.

31. P. H. Vigor, *The Soviet Blitzkrieg Theory* (London: Macmillan, 1983), 102–21;

M. Sadykiewicz, "Soviet Far East Command: A New Developmental Factor in the U.S.S.R. Military Strategy Toward East Asia," *Asian Perspectives* 6:2 (1982): 29–71.

32. H. Gelman, *The Soviet Far East Buildup and Soviet Risk-Taking Against China*, R-2943-AF (Santa Monica, Calif.: Rand, 1982), 111; Gelman, "The Soviet Far East Military Buildup: Motives and Prospects," in *The Soviet Far East Military Buildup*, ed. R. H. Solomon and M. Kosaka,(Dover, Mass.: Auburn House, 1986), 53.

33. A. Lobanov-Rostovsky, *Russia and Asia* (New York: Macmillan, 1933), 101.

34. See note 13.

35. See note 27.

36. R. L. Melke, "Max Freiherr von Oppenheim: Sixty Years of Scholarship and Political Intrigue in the Middle East," *Middle Eastern Studies* 9 (1973): 81–93.

37. F. Fischer, *Germany's Aims in the First World War* (New York: Norton, 1967), 121.

38. T. G. Fraser, "Germany and Indian Revolution, 1914–1918," *Journal of Contemporary History* 12 (1977): 255–72.

39. Fischer, *Germany's Aims*, 126; M. Hauner, *India in Axis Strategy* (London and Stuttgart: Klett-Cotta, 1981), 161, 166, 236.

40. W. O. von Hentig, *Mein Leben eine Dienstreise* (Göttingen, 1962); O. von Niedermayer, *Im Weltkrieg vor Indiens Toren* (Hamburg, 1942); R. Vogel, *Die Persien—und Afghanistan—expedition Oskar Ritter v. Niedermayer 1915/16* (Osnabrück, 1976); see also Hentig's private papers: Aufzeichnungen 1934–69, 3 vols. (Institut für Zeitgeschichte, Munich); D. Dignan, *The Indian Revolutionary Problem in British Diplomacy 1914–1919* (New Delhi: Allied Publishers, 1983), 2.

41. U. Gehrke, *Persien in der deutschen Orient-politik whrend des Ersten Weltkriegs*, vol. 1 (Stuttgart: Kohlhammer, 1960), 137.

42. M. Hauner, "The Professionals and Amateurs in Nazi Foreign Policy: Revolution and Subversion in the Islamic and Indian World," in L. Kettenacker, ed., *The Führer State—Myth and Reality. Studies on the Structure and Politics of the Third Reich* (London and Stuttgart, 1980), 305–28.

43. See note 41. At the time of the October Revolution there were over two million prisoners of war in Russia, mostly Austro-Hungarians. In Siberia as much as 75 percent of the Bolshevik forces consisted in 1918, of foreign nationals. See V. M. Fric, *The Bolsheviks and the Czechoslovak Legion*, vol. 1 (New Delhi: Abhinav, 1978), 128–32.

44. Compiled from the *Journal of the Royal Central Asian Society*, vol. 6 (1919): 3–11, 119–36; vol. 7 (1920): 42–58; vol. 8 (1921): 46–69; vol. 9 (1922): 96–110.

45. W. Baumgart, *Deutsche Ostpolitik 1918* (Vienna: Oldenbourg, 1966).

46. See note 44. L. C. Dunsterville, *The Adventures of Dunsterforce* (London, 1920); F. M. Bailey, *Mission to Tashkent* (London: Cape, 1946). Quotes from "The Future of Russian Central Asia," memorandum by the India Office, December 3, 1918, India Office Records: L/P&S/18/C 186.

47. Anonymous, "Russia, Germany and Asia," *The Round Table* 8 (1917–18): 526–64.

48. M. Chokaiev, "Turkestan and the Soviet Regime," *Journal of the Royal Central Asian Society* 18 (1931): 403–420.

49. Ikbal Ali Shah, "The Federation of the Central Asian States," *Journal of the Royal Central Asian Society* 7 (1920): 29–49; L. W. Adamec, *Afghanistan 1900–1923. A Diplomatic History* (Berkeley: University of California Press, 1967), 108–68.

50. Essad Bey, *Die Vershwörung gegen die Welt* (Berlin, 1932); Azade-Ayse Rorlich, "Fellow Travellers: Enver Pasha and the Bolshevik Government 1918–1920," *Asian Affairs* (October 1982): 288–96.

51. A. Bennigsen and S. E. Wimbush, *Muslim National Communism in the Soviet Union. A Revolutionary Strategy for the Colonial World* (Chicago: University of Chicago Press, 1979).

52. Why the Spanish term *reconquista* fits better than any other is convincingly explained in Guy Imart's highly stimulating *The Limits of Inner Asia: Some Soul-Searching on New Borders for an Old Frontierland* (Bloomington: Indiana University Press, 1987), 14.

53. G. Fraser, "Basmachi," *Central Asian Survey* 6 and 2 (1987): 1–73 and 7–42.

54. *Baku: The Congress of the Peoples of the East, Baku, September 1920,* Stenographic Report, transl. and ed. B. Pierce (London, 1977), 36; R. A. Ulyanovsky et al., The Comintern and the East, 2 vols. (Moscow, 1969 and 1978).

55. M. N. Roy, *Memoirs* (Bombay, 1964); C. S. Samra, *India and Anglo-Soviet Relations* (Bombay, 1959); G. D. Overstreet and M. Windmiller, *Communism in India* (Berkeley: University of California Press, 1955), 33–44.

56. A. C. Bose, *Indian Revolutionaries Abroad* (Patna, 1971); H. Kapur, *Soviet Russia and Asia, 1917–1927* (Geneva, 1966).

57. E. H. Carr, *The Bolshevik Revolution 1917–1923* (London: Penguin, 1966), 236–37.

58. C. B. McLane, *Soviet Strategies in Southeast Asia* (Princeton, N.J.: Princeton University Press, 1966), 9.

59. Carr, *Bolshevik Revolution* (1966), 238.

60. J. M. Meijer, ed., *The Trotsky Papers, 1917–1919* (The Hague: Mouton, 1964), I: 623–25.

61. Snesarev, *Indiya kak glavnyi faktor v sredneaziatskom voprosye* (St. Petersburg: A. S. Suvorin, 1906), 7–13. See also Snesarev, *Afghanistan* (1921), 3–19.

62. Snesarev, *Afghanistan,* 243.

63. Bennigsen and Wimbush, *Muslim Communism* (1979), 66–68.

64. G. Minault, *The Khilafat Movement* (New York: Columbia University Press, 1982), 201–7.

65. Discussed in detail in Hauner, *India in Axis Strategy* (1981).

66. Sir Cecil Kaye, David Petrie, Sir Horace Williamson [all three men were Directors of Intelligence Bureau (D.I.B.) at the Home Department, Government of India, between 1919 and 1936], *Communism in India,* 3 vols. (Calcutta, 1971–1976); here vol. 3, 304–14.

67. B. Prasad, *Defence of India* (New Delhi, 1963), 15, 22–28, 28–33, 35–36.

68. Ibid. See also M. Hauner, "The Soviet Threat to Afghanistan and India 1938–1940," *Modern Asian Studies* 15 (1981): 287–309.

69. Gillard, *Struggle for Asia* (1977), 181–82.

70. For example, Snesarev, *Afghanistan* (1921), 205.

71. See, for instance, the masterly analysis of Alexander's campaign in Central Asia by Donald W. Engels, *Alexander the Great and the Logistics of the Macedonian Army* (Berkeley: University of California, 1978), 153–56.

72. India Office Records: L/P&S/10/1188; G. N. Curzon, *Persia and the Persian Question,* vol. 1 (London: Longmans Green, 1892), 236, 613–39; P. A. Rittich, *Zheleznodorozhnyi put' cherez Persiyu* (St. Petersburg, 1900), and *Otchët o poezdke v Persiyu i persidskiy Beludzhistan v 1900 g.* (St. Petersburg: General Staff, 1901).

73. Prasad, *Defence,* 6–12, 41, 45, 59–61. For a more comprehensive account see my three chapters, II-2, 3, 4, "The Defence of India, A Soviet Invasion of India and a British Guarantee to Afghanistan? The Amanullah Plan, in Hauner, *India in Axis Strategy,* (1981).

74. Hauner, *India in Axis Strategy,* II-2, "The Defence of India." On September 1, 1939, the strength of troops remaining in India was as follows: 43,500 British and 131,000 Indian, with an air cover of 6 RAF squadrons (none with fighters); Public Record Office: CAB 68/ W.P.(R) (39)5.

75. There was no Salang Pass Tunnel available then to facilitate the passage of Sovet troops across the Hindu Kush as in December 1979, although Soviet engineers had started work on the strategically important Salang Pass Road already during the early 1920s under King Amanullah's reign.

76. M.I.2 notes of September 29, 1939, on the Joint Planning Subcommittee memorandum (J.P.[39]38 and W.P.[39]55) of September 21, 1939, entitled "Russian Threat to India," prepared for the Chiefs of Staff (C.O.S.). See also the subsequent memoranda: W.P.(39)59, C.O.S.(40)249. For further details see Hauner, *India in Axis Strategy* chap. II-3, "A Soviet Invasion of India and a British Guarantee to Afghanistan."

77. CAB 66: W.P.(40)91, C.O.S.(40)252 of Mar. 8, 1940, entitled "Military Implications of Hostilities with Russia in 1940." See also *Stalin and His Generals, Soviet Military Memoirs of World War II,* ed. Seweryn Bialer (New York: Columbia University Press, 1969), 115–29.

78. See chap. II-4, "The Amanullah Plan" in Hauner, *India in Axis Strategy* (1981).

79. Report by the C.O.S. Committee of October 31, 1939, in CAB 66:W.P.(39)107, C.O.S.(39)102 and 105. See also the War Office and Admiralty files: WO 193/134 and ADM I/20034; L. Chassin, "Un plan grandiose: l'attaque des pétroles du Caucase en 1940," *Forces Aériennes Françaises* (1969): 821–49.

80. For further details see Hauner, *India in Axis Strategy* (1981), passim.

10

Conclusion

JACK SNYDER

The purpose of a volume like this one is not to close questions, but to open them up for further consideration. Consequently, the main aim of these conclusions will not be to summarize our findings. On the contrary, I will devote my main efforts to presenting qualifiers to the themes developed in the preceding chapters, counterarguments from different theoretical perspectives, and counterevidence from cases not considered by the other contributors. These remarks will address the five questions set forth in the introductory chapter:

1. What have statesmen believed about dominoes, bandwagons, the interdependence of commitments, and other forms of the cumulative gains argument?
2. Under what conditions do dominoes actually fall?
3. What have been the consequences of domino beliefs and policies based on them?
4. What are the causes of domino beliefs?
5. What prescriptions for the substance of American policy and for the process of American policymaking follow from this analysis?

Who Has Believed What About Falling Dominoes?

Several questions about the nature of domino thinking and domino thinkers were raised implicitly or explicitly in the preceding chapters, but require further comment. First, are domino beliefs peculiar to great powers that are on the defensive? Second, how strongly has the Soviet Union's behavior been motivated by the fear that its allies might fall like a row of dominoes? Third, is the perception of a powerful, expansionist opponent a necessary part of domino imagery? Fourth, is the domino theory primarily, if not exclusively, a sincere belief of the statesmen that espouse it, or is it a tactical argument used in policy debates?

First, are domino beliefs peculiar to great powers that are on the defensive? Four of our chapters are written largely from the standpoint of American containment strategy, and thus emphasize the domino fears of a power that sees itself as on the defensive. Moreover, Hopf's chapter minimizes Soviet hopes that its successes might create a favorable bandwagon effect, while Blum's sees a connection between orthodox Soviet ideology and the fear of unfavorable bandwagon effects. These results seem to fit with the earlier findings of a study of twentieth-century crisis diplomacy by Glenn Snyder and Paul Diesing. They contend that defending states have worried a great deal that backing down would tarnish their general reputation for resolve, whereas their aggressive opponents have rarely drawn the feared inferences. Hitler is the only clear exception to this rule, according to Snyder and Diesing.[1]

If this were true, and if the Soviet case adhered to this rule, this finding would have huge theoretical and policy implictions. Credibility and resolve, with which much of American deterrence theory is obsessed, would be beside the point, as would many of the arguments advanced by American policymakers in favor of interventionist international strategies. But neither the rule nor its application to the Soviet case are quite so clear cut.

Rising expansionist powers have often believed in bandwagon theories of one kind or another, and disbelieved in balancing theories. In fact, a bandwagon theory is necessary equipment for any expansionist who must explain how he expects to get away with it. Napoleon counted on a bandwagon developing behind his revolutionary political principles. The Bolsheviks thought that Warsaw workers, and eventually German workers, would flock to the side of the victorious German troops invading Poland in 1920. Wilhelmine Germany thought that increasing German power and belligerence would break apart the Entente and make England more accommodating, whereas it had the opposite effect.

The Soviets in the 1970s had a similar theory by which they rationalized the compatibility of detente and Third World expansion in authoritative statements at their Party Congresses. According to this theory, socialism's improved position in the correlation of forces strengthened the hand of realistic forces in the West and gave the West no alternative but to accept detente. Detente, in turn, made it harder for the United States to intervene militarily against progressive change, which would further shift the correlation of forces in favor of socialism. In this way, an irreversible bandwagon would be created.[2]

Looking at more detailed analysis by Soviet politicians and commentators, Hopf shows that optimistic bandwagon thinking was relatively short-lived and outweighed by expectations of resistance to Soviet gains. Such a disjunction between general strategic concepts and perceptions of specific situations is not unprecedented. Before World War I, for example, the German General Staff adhered to a generalized faith in the efficacy of offensive military strategies, yet their analysis of most specific military problems reflected a deep understanding of the operational advantages of the defensive.[3] The cult of the offensive was decisive for the development of the main outlines of German strategy, whereas the more defensive tactical and operational concepts had their impact on questions of how to implement the overall design.

In short, perceptions of cumulating gains and losses have not been peculiar to defending powers. Some of the most egregious bandwagon theorists have been expansionist statesmen. Soviet thinking in the 1970s manifested that view in a less egregious form. These relatively weak bandwagon hopes have dissipated still further, perhaps vanished, in recent years.[4]

Second, if the Soviets have hoped for the cumulative collapse of American positions around the world, have they also feared a similar collapse of their own positions? Sovietological folklore has typically denied that the Soviets harbor such fears. According to Nathan Leites's theory of "the operational code of the Politburo," for example, a Bolshevik "knows when to stop," takes "two steps forward, one step back," and "retreats before superior force."[5] There is, however, another side to the story. For example, Andrei Zhdanov's speech to the founding meeting of the Cominform in September 1947 is all about the Munich analogy and the domino theory. America has shown itself to be an aggressive imperialist power, much like Nazi Germany, Zhdanov says. Munich showed that the cardinal danger in facing such an opponent is to lose heart, remain passive, and try to appease him. Aggressive resistance will keep the aggressor off balance and prevent him from consolidating his forces, whereas passivity will lead to the cumulative unraveling of the socialist bloc through the instrument of the Marshall Plan.[6] Khrushchev, too, invoked the domino theory, warning for example about appeasing highwaymen.[7] Moreover, in 1956, 1968, and 1980, the Soviets feared that reformism in one East European country would spread to others. Blum's chapter in this volume finds similar fears arising among orthodox ideologues from the Afghan struggle.

Whether the Soviets fear domino consequences from their retreats in Eastern Europe and Afghanistan is a timely and important question. As Jervis's chapter shows, such retreats often engender a "never again" syndrome, which leaves the defeated power on the lookout for a Mayaguez incident to demonstrate his power and resolve. There is no indication that Gorbachev is at present seeking to use force gratuitously for this purpose. Rather, Gorbachev's activist diplomacy promoting arms control, a greater UN role, an international naval force for the Persian Gulf, and the like may be the functional equivalent, showing that the Soviets have not left the international stage despite their retreats. As a relatively benign alternative to "never again" aggression, the West might consider the advantage of playing along with some of these initiatives. The chapters by Blum and Herrmann show that Soviet "new thinkers" do not share the orthodox perception of the hand of imperialism orchestrating a globally interconnected campaign of rollback. Western policy should avoid discrediting this view.

A third question is what features of the international environment are most salient to domino thinkers. Are their beliefs dominated disproportionately by assessments of the inherent fragility of the target states, of one's own irresolute image, of the cumulativity of physical resources, or of the power and aggressiveness of the opponent? Though all of these considerations have entered into American domino thinking, our contributors stress the latter as particularly important.[8] If so, the demise of cold war enemy images might be expected to bring the demise of the domino theory.

Unfortunately, the facts to support such a conclusion are not quite so unambiguous. A variety of historical cases do indeed show that hostile images of the opponent are typical features in domino arguments. However, since proponents of domino theories tend to argue that "all of the above" factors make strategic positions precarious, it is difficult to establish which elements are most central.

British debates on the containment of Russia in the years before the Crimean War exemplify this pattern.[9] Part of the domino argument in favor of forward defense of India stressed the inherent fragility of Britain's regional positions, due to anti-British feelings among the Indians. Domino theorists also stressed the importance of perceptions of British resolve, due to the Persians' alleged eagerness to bandwagon with the strongest great power. Cumulativity of resources also came into play in assessments of the consequences for the Mediterranean naval balance of the loss of Constantinople, the joining of the Russian and Ottoman fleets, and the Russians' control of Greek sailors and Turkish timber.

Assessments of Russian power and intentions also played a key role. Domino theorists argued for aggressive, forward containment on the grounds that Russia was an insatiable expansionist power, dedicated to an inexorable course of expansion using gradualist "sap and mine" tactics, as in the methodical undermining of the defenses of a fortress. Opponents of a forward containment strategy, however, argued that Russia was not especially aggressive and also that Russian power was inherently greater in defense. The logistical, financial, and technological weaknesses of a backward power hindered the projection of Russian power abroad, they argued, whereas Russia's vast space and population made her formidable in self-defense.

Other bandwagon theorists have also emphasized the image of the adversary in their arguments, portraying the opponent as a paper tiger who is strong in offense but irresolute in self-defense.[10] Thus, German naval theorists argued that the British were so aggressive that they would strangle German trade if Germany lacked a fleet, yet so passive that they would not engage in a serious arms race in order to prevent the loss of their naval superiority. Japanese imperialists saw the United States as such a threat that an autarkic empire was needed for protection against her, yet so decadent that American will would collapse after the sharp rap at Pearl Harbor. Hitler's entire conception of international politics was couched in terms of the national character of various adversaries, typically explaining why they would fold under pressure.

However, these apparent connections between the image of the adversary and domino theorizing may be largely spurious. Domino and bandwagon theorists tend to put forward any and all rationalizations for how and why dominoes might fall. Thus, it is usually difficult to tell which elements are causal in domino arguments and which are merely brought into line in order to buttress the case, or put differently, to eliminate unsettling cognitive conflicts. Perhaps paper-tiger images come first and then images of regional dominoes follow, but perhaps it is the other way around. Another possibility is that the policy of forward containment comes first, and then is merely rationalized by a variety of domino and paper-tiger images.

This possibility raises the fourth question: Has domino imagery reflected sincere beliefs or merely opportunistic argumentation? In Chapter 5 Macdonald suggests that the two are often mixed in some indeterminate proportion, with the politics of overselling leading to the exaggeration of a strategic image, the kernel of which is sincerely held. Dean Acheson admitted, for example, that the domino imagery in NSC-68 "made our points clearer than the truth" in order to "bludgeon the mass mind of 'top government.' "[11]

Was this penchant for exaggeration caused by an unavoidable need to oversell a strategically essential policy, or was it due to the urge to rationalize a strategically dubious policy that was desired for other reasons? In the British case, these two sources of overselling are often hard to disentangle. Palmerston's diplomatic behavior in a number of contexts shows that he really believed in the need for an aggressive, forward approach to containing Russia as well as Britain's other enemies. At the same time, it is also clear that Palmerston saw his aggressive foreign policy as a domestic political expedient aimed at saving Britain's established order in an era of expanded political participation. "If the nation is overflowing with so much pugnacity," he said, "let us vent it on any and every other nation of the earth, let us not exercise a suicidal fury on ourselves."[12]

In a later period, the historians Robinson and Gallagher read archival documents and became convinced that the Victorian "official mind" scrambled for Africa because it saw a series of dominoes leading from various positions in the African hinterland back to the imperial cash cow, India. And yet a key force behind the scramble was Colonial Minister Joseph Chamberlain, a crucial makeweight in the Conservative-Unionist coalition who sought an expanded, autarkic empire to revive the economic fortunes of his hard-pressed Midlands industrial constituency.[13] These British examples may perhaps stand as a general model, in which sincere domino fears and political opportunism are mutually reinforcing and are not clearly distinguished in the mind of the statesman.

To sum up, both expansionist and status quo powers have held domino or bandwagon beliefs. The Soviets, though perhaps less prone to domino thinking than many historical states, have at least occasionally taken both favorable and unfavorable domino processes as matters for serious consideration. Paper-tiger images of the adversary have typically gone hand-in-hand with domino beliefs, but this may simply reflect the tendency of proponents of forward strategies of containment to invoke any and all rationales for their preferred policy.

When Do Dominoes Really Fall?

The contributors to this volume agree that the question is not *whether* dominoes fall in a cumulative fashion but *when* does this occur. Cumulative losses are more likely, they suggest, when (1) the targets are small, domestically weak, geographically contiguous, and lacking allies; (2) subsequent targets are analogous in important respects to the initial domino; (3) the first fallen domino is an important country; or (4) military technology favors the offense.[14]

Larsen's chapter shows that the 1930s were a period when states did bandwagon and significant gains did accumulate for Hitler, whose early gains strengthened his military position and economic base for further conquests.[15] The late 1940s, Larson suggests, may also have had some of these characteristics, requiring special American efforts to forestall domino processes. Nevertheless, it is important to point out that the overall pattern of great power politics is almost always the opposite of this. Balancing, not bandwagoning, is the norm, especially for the larger powers that count most. Aggressors like the Germans and Japanese in the two world wars have sometimes racked up cumulating gains at the outset of their wars, but the more they win, the more opposition they find ranged against them.[16]

Judging by the checklist provided by our contributors, bandwagon tendencies should be especially weak in today's conditions in the non-socialist world. All the major non-socialist powers have stable domestic institutions. Regional powers along the Eurasian rim have been growing in nationalism and military strength, making them unlikely candidates for bandwagoning. Though the great powers are increasingly disinclined toward direct military intervention, they continue to provide military and other assistance to clients who are pressed by external and internal enemies. The Afghan and Iran-Iraq wars, moreover, suggest that current military technology and organization make the defensive a force to be reckoned with. For all these reasons, current conditions work strongly against domino and bandwagon processes outside the formerly socialist bloc.[17]

Even in Eastern Europe, it might be unwarranted to say that the cascading collapse of communist governments constituted a true domino process, in the sense that the example of events in Poland and Hungary played a central role in causing subsequent transformations elsewhere. It seems more plausible to argue that the change of policy by the Soviet Union caused the changes in all of the countries, with domino-like spillover effects among the East European countries influencing merely the details of the process. On the other hand, since the Rumanian regime was not being propped up by Soviet power, spillover effects may offer the better explanation in that case.

Consequences of Domino Beliefs

Those who believe in the domino theory contend that "symmetric" strategies of containment have beneficial consequences.[18] By defending even peripheral dominoes, a clear signal of intent to resist aggression is sent to friends, foes, and neutrals, minimizing the costs of containment by stopping the juggernaut before it gains steam. This argument can be challenged even if one accepts the main assumptions of deterrence theory and the Realpolitik school of international politics.

First, it is by no means clear that a dedicated aggressor will be deterred by a show of resolve, especially in an arena of combat where the aggressor believes the defender to be weak. As Jervis's chapter points out, there is virtually no evidence that a strong Anglo-French demonstration of resolve in 1936 or 1938 would have resigned Hitler to accept the status quo. Consequently, for the Munich analogy to carry weight, it must be based on the argument that stopping the aggressor early, through what amounts to a preventative war, is *physically* easier and cheaper than stopping him later.

This leads to a second objection, which is that "symmetric" containment along the whole Eurasian perimeter actually weakens the defense by dispersing its resources and allowing the aggressor to fight on terrain and at times of his own choosing. In the Nazi case, it is probably true that Germany would have been easier to stop early, before Hitler took over the equipment of thirty Czech divisions and incorporated huge economic resources into the Reich.[19] But both the Korean and Vietnamese Wars were more costly for the United States than for the Soviet Union.

Even for those who argue that moral rather than material resources are the key issue, perimeter defense has drawbacks. If a defender makes global commitments, even to precarious allies, he runs the risk of losing even if he fights for them. If this happens, is his credibility helped because he shows the willingness to suffer in support of allies, or is it hurt because it shows up his lack of effectiveness?[20] After America's setback in Vietnam, the Soviets inferred that America was lacking *both* the capability *and* the resolve to win such conflicts.[21] Another moral advantage is that by resisting aggression later rather than earlier, the unlimited expansionist character of the opponent is demonstrated more clearly, making it easier to rally domestic public opinion and international allies to resist the aggressor.[22] For example, when the chief of the German General Staff urged a preventive war against France in 1867, Bismarck argued that Prussia had to wait for France to attack first so that world opinion would support Prussia as the aggrieved party.[23]

Causes of Domino Beliefs

Rational, cognitive, and domestic political explanations for the prevelence of domino thinking all have some merit. Any given case may have all three elements present in some varying proportion. Since domestic explanations have received only a little attention from most of the other contributors, I will stress the strengths of the domestic argument and point out the weaknesses of the others.

Rational Hedging

To minimize his maximum loss, a statesman may want to hedge against the unlikely contingency of a domino-like chain reaction of defeats.[24] The problem with this argument is that there are two equal and opposite ways in which states risk a maximum loss, overcommitment to the defense of the periphery and undercommitment to it. The fact that great powers typically hedge in favor of overcommitment, which is amply documented by Robert Gilpin and Paul Kennedy, suggests that something more than mere rational hedging is going on.[25] For example, Britain's scrambling for Africa in the 1880s and 1890s, ostensibly to keep the Suez and Cape routes to India out of hostile hands, got Britain embroiled with France and Germany and tied down in a costly land war against the Boers. This sucked funds from the naval budget, raised the specter of a grand coalition that would challenge Britain's naval supremacy, and made a successful Russian move on India more likely. Thus, by hedging against falling dominoes, Britain created a greater danger of suffering a "maximum loss" by provoking universal hostility. Britain was rational only in abandoning its strategy of hedging against unlikely domino contingencies.

Another test for the rationality of statesmen's domino fears is whether they have been sensitive to the conditions that make cumulative gains and defeats more or less likely. Here the picture is mixed. On the one hand, chapters in this volume indicate that American and Soviet thinkers did make some of the distinctions that Jervis suggests are appropriate, for example, that domino consequences are more likely when targets are geographically contiguous, domestically weak, and the like.[26] On the other hand, the point of the domino theory is always that eventually the chain reaction will affect large, noncontiguous, nonanalogous powers. American domino theorists held that America's commitment to far-flung points in the Asian periphery reflected, in some vague way, on America's commitment to Europe or on America's own security.[27]

Cognitive Explanations

The two strongest cognitive explanations for domino thinking hinge on formative lessons of the past and on differences in the perspectives of actors and observers.[28] While these two theories both fit some of the evidence presented in this book, neither qualifies as a powerful, general explanation for the prevalence of domino thinking.

A formative, salient lesson of the past, the Munich analogy, seems plausible as an explanation for American domino fears during the cold war.[29] It is hard to locate similar lessons, however, in other cases of domino or bandwagon thinking. Napoleon's string of victories, facilitated by irresolution on the part of the coalitions that should have resisted him, might have given rise to a domino obsession. Indeed, British domino theorists in the period before the Crimean War did occasionally analogize between Napoleon and Nicholas, but opponents of symmetric containment also drew on purported lessons from the Napoleonic struggles. To conservative appeasers like Lord Aberdeen, the lesson of the Napoleonic era was that a conflict spiral among the great powers would unravel the European Concert and unleash the forces of revolution.[30] Francophile Whigs like Lord Holland "learned" that Britain must align with progressive French political currents, rather than oppose them, to avoid costly wars that would play into the hands of reactionary forces within Britain.[31] Richard Cobden studied the wars against Napoleon and concluded that Britain could have ignored the Continental balance of power without jeopardizing her trade or security.[32] In each of these cases, the lessons supposedly drawn from the Napoleonic conflict were determined by a political ideology that had been shaped by extraneous values and traditions, some of which antedated Napoleon himself.

Other alleged historical lessons are equally spurious. Wilhelmine soldiers and statesmen often invoked Bismarck and the elder Moltke as models for their own big-stick diplomacy, bandwagon assumptions about alliance politics, and offensive military strategies. But Bismarck and Moltke themselves drew quite different lessons from the victories of 1866 and 1870—namely, that states balance against aggressive powers and that defensive military strategies enjoy some important advantages over offensive ones.[33]

In another case, Michael Barnhart argues that Japanese militarist thinkers learned from World War I that the security of medium-sized powers would henceforth depend on expanding to achieve an autarkic military-industrial resource base.[34] It is true that some militarist writers made this argument, but the connection is obviously spurious. Japanese militarists believed in security through expansion long before World War I. Germany's failed bid for an expanded economic base showed that other powers would balance against such an attempt, not bandwagon with it, as the Japanese militarist writers imagined. Moreover, Japan's own attempt at such a policy, its occupation of Siberia at the end of the war, was costly and fruitless. In this case as in the others, bandwagon lessons were spurious, being determined entirely by the preconceptions or ideology of the person drawing the lessons.

Even when they are not spurious, lessons may be short-lived when they conflict with the statesman's ambitions. Hitler initially learned from World War I that Germany should not build a fleet that would drive Britain into the opposing camp. But once it became clear that Germany could not recruit Britain as an ally in this manner, Hitler forgot the lesson and took up Admiral Tirpitz's old argument that Britain would be more accommodating the more Germany threatened her.[35]

The actor/observer theory also fails some important tests. This explanation hinges on the argument that cognitive biases give rise to exaggerated perceptions of the enemy as highly aggressive, purposeful, centralized, and cooperative only when physically restrained. This theory is challenged by evidence that states often use opposite images of the opponent to rationalize the same policy. Thus, Japanese expansionists thought (1) that they needed autarky because other powers, including the United States, were so aggressive; (2) that they could get away with their grab for autarky because American would not oppose them; (3) that they had to attack Pearl Harbor because, as it turned out, America *would* oppose them; and yet (4) that America was so irresolute that it would quit the war after receiving a bloody nose. Whether America was seen as acquiescent or resistant, the policy inference was always that expansion was necessary.[36] The fate of various military attachés and other analysts who reported inconvenient facts about the character of the opponent shows that this was not a matter of "actor/observer differences" but of the bureaucratic self-justification of expansionism.[37] Similarly, the Soviets rationalized the support of "progressive change" in the Third World in the mid-1970s on the grounds that "realists" in the imperialist camp would not effectively oppose it and in the late 1970s on the opposite grounds that there was a zero-sum competition with implacable imperialism.[38] Arkady Shevchenko and other sources identify the Central Committee International Department as a prime locus of these hydra-headed rationales for a militant Third World policy.[39]

Actor/observer differences are usually said to be driven by differences in the availability and salience of information. For example, the opponent seems monolithic because the observer simply does not know about splits in his camp. Thus, his aggressive acts seem highly purposeful, driven by a single will and plan, and intent on doing the utmost harm to the observer.[40] Following this reasoning, we might expect that the Dulles–Eisenhower domino theory about the consequences of losing Quemoy and Matsu was heightened by their monolithic view of communism, as expressed in their public statements. But in fact, we now know from private sources that Dulles was well aware of the Sino-Soviet rift and saw an assertive policy on the Taiwan Straits as a good way to exacerbate that split.[41]

Domestic Politics

Domestic political sources of domino thinking have received only sporadic mention in this volume. Consequently, this brief conclusion can only evaluate this type of explanation superficially. Whether militaries and imperialist economic interests are especially avid and effective proponents of bandwagon theories, for example, is far too complicated to address here.[42] What can be done, however, is to look briefly at different types of domestic political systems and the viability of bandwagon theories in each of them.

By far the worst cases of bandwagon theorizing are found in Germany and Japan, because of peculiar flaws in their domestic political systems. In their expansionist phases, the strategic beliefs of these states turned balance-of-power thinking on its head. They thought that security could be achieved only through expansion, that the profits of expansion would make further expansion even easier, that expansion would go unopposed, and once it *was* opposed, that threats would break apart encircling alliances. In particular, these two powers were distinctive in their perverse pattern of counterproductive learning from evidence that their beliefs were wrong. Thus, when the world failed to bandwagon with them, they learned not to cut their losses, but that war was needed to break the encirclement.

Victorian Britain, the United States, and the Soviet Union have all suffered from less egregious versions of the domino and bandwagon theories. Erroneous theories of this type pushed these powers into costly, but limited wars in Afghanistan, the Crimea, Vietnam, and elsewhere along the Eurasian rim. But these powers differed from Germany and Japan in that they reacted to these setbacks by cutting their losses and revising their strategic beliefs. After the Boer War, Britain moved away from interventionism, domino bogeys, and "splendid isolation," instead appeasing erstwhile imperial enemies who would be needed to balance German power.[43] After Vietnam, vestiges of the domino theory have been outweighed by Caspar Weinberger's prohibitive list of conditions that must be met before America can commit troops to combat abroad.[44] After Afghanistan, the Soviets have had little to say about the bandwagon of progressive change or about the role of the correlation of forces in forcing detente on the West.

The difference between Japan and Germany, on the one hand, and Britain, America, and the Soviet Union, on the other, is not just the ability of the latter to learn from their mistakes, but the domestic political systems that made this learning possible. Individuals who learned to doubt bandwagoning and domino theories lost their jobs in Germany and Japan, whereas they often eventually won strategic debates in the other three powers. In Germany and Japan, militarism and social imperialism were so deeply rooted in the fabric of the political order that accurate strategic evaluation was impossible. In the other states, such domestic pathologies were less virulent, so learning the truth about the domino theory was politically more feasible.[45]

Combining the Explanations

Each of the above explanations for domino thinking—rational, cognitive, and political—has some logical plausibility and empirical support. None is likely to account for all aspects of all cases all of the time. Consequently, we need hypotheses about when each is likely to predominate or how they may interact in a particular case. In my view, political causes were decisive in Germany and Japan, where political and organizational incentives for strategic mythmaking were overwhelming. Domestic politics should have less decisive effects in the Soviet and American cases. Cognitive forces should be more important when salient lessons about falling dominoes, such as the Munich analogy, were formative for key statesmen's strategic outlook. Rational inputs should be decisive when these factors are absent and when "smoking gun" evidence is available. Finally, Macdonald, in Chapter 5 of this volume, suggests that all three forces may interact in complex ways in a single case.

Policy Prescriptions

This book is not primarily an exercise in policy analysis. Nonetheless, the theoretical issues raised in most of the chapters have implications for the substance of American containment policy and for the process by which that policy is made.

As for substance, most of the contributors argue that American strategists and statesmen have exaggerated the danger of falling dominoes and consequently that the necessity for symmetrical strategies of containment has been oversold. On the other hand, they note that states might bandwagon when deprived of outside assistance. The implication is that a balance can and should be struck between heedless interventionism and equally heedless isolationism. Walt, in particular, suggests that fairly small American efforts may suffice to encourage balancing efforts by other states, though some other contributors appear to be less sanguine.

As for the policy process, our findings suggest a tension between the benefits of insulating the policymaking process from broader political pressures and debates, on the one hand, and increasing policymakers' accountability, on the other. The argument for greater insulation is that sensible policymaking elites may be forced to use exaggerated domino rationales to oversell necessary internationalist policies to a skeptical Congress or public. These arguments may then become part of the accepted wisdom of political discourse, provide ammunition to political opponents, and thus prevent policymakers from flexibly retreating when necessary. Some scholars have argued, for example, that the overselling of the Truman Doctrine, exploited politically by the China lobby and McCarthyites, led to the extension of the domino principle to cover even such indefensible and meaningless positions as the offshore islands in the Taiwan Straits.[46] If the makers of foreign policy could be insulated from politics of this kind, for example, through an effective bipartisan elite pact, exaggerated domino thinking might be controlled.[47]

An opposite argument stresses the value of increased accountability in minimizing erroneous strategic ideas. This could be effective whether the problem is cognitive bias or politically motivated rationalization. Cognitive psychologists have shown that perceptual biases and shoddy reasoning are far less common when decision makers know that their analyses will be held up to broad and critical scrutiny.[48] On the political side, a number of the domino and bandwagon theories that I have mentioned—ranging from the Fashoda dam concept to Tirpitz's risk theory—have hinged on a monopoly of information or analysis held by self-interested insiders, which outside critics had no way of challenging.[49] According to this logic, tighter public accountability would sharpen the decision makers' analytical process and tie the hands of intentional mythmakers.

A recent study by John Burke and Fred Greenstein shows how the Johnson administration made virtually irrevocable decisions to escalate the war in Vietnam without systematic analysis of key assumptions, like the domino theory, and without meaningful consultations within the government, with Congress, not to mention with the public. Though George Ball was writing memoranda decisively refuting the domino arguments being advanced by proponents of intervention, key decisions were made before Ball's analysis was allowed to reach the president. Systematic staff work and follow-up, which would have forced proponents of escalation to confront Ball's arguments in a systematic fashion, failed to happen. Moreover, influential senators who were wary of escalation in January 1965 were faced with a *fait accompli* by the escalation decisions of the following six months. In accord with the habits of the cold war consensus, they failed to speak out once American prestige was committed. By contrast, Eisenhower's decision not to intervene before the fall of Dienbienphu in 1954 was based on better staff work and broader discussion, according to Burke and Greenstein.[50] If this view is correct, better evaluation of strategic ideas like the domino theory will be served by greater accountability to rigorous standards of evidence and argument both within and outside the government.

In conclusion, beliefs and arguments about the cumulativity of gains and losses have played an important role in superpower strategy toward the Eurasian rimland. The contributors to this volume have tried to build on a small but sophisticated literature in venturing hypotheses about the nature, validity, causes, and consequences of these beliefs. While several of us have argued vehemently for one or another view, we see our task as opening up rather than closing questions for debate. If greater accountability in the field of strategic analysis is the desired goal, then such a debate will help achieve it.

Notes

1. Glenn Snyder and Paul Diesing, *Conflict among Nations* (Princeton, N.J.: Princeton University Press, 1977), 187.

2. For a balanced discussion, see Raymond Garthoff, *Detente and Confrontation* (Washington, D.C.: Brookings Institution, 1985), chap. 2.

3. Jack Snyder, *The Ideology of the Offensive* (Ithaca, N.Y.: Cornell University Press, 1984), chap. 4 and 5.

4. See the literature cited in George Breslauer, "Ideology and Learning in Soviet Third World Policy," *World Politics* 39:3 (April 1987): 429–48; See also Blum, chap. 7, and Herrmann, chap. 8, in this volume.

5. Nathan Leites, *A Study of Bolshevism* (Glencoe, Ill.: Free Press, 1953); Alexander George, "The 'Operational Code': A Neglected Approach to the Study of Political Leaders and Decisionmaking," *International Studies Quarterly* 13:2 (June 1969): 190–222.

6. Margaret Carlyle, ed., *Documents on International Affairs, 1947–1948* (London: Oxford University Press, 1949), 122–46.

7. Robert Jervis, *Perception and Misperception in International Politics* (Princeton, N.J.: Princeton University Press, 1976), 61.

8. See especially Jervis, chap. 2 in this volume, and Macdonald, chap. 5, on this point. For evidence of consideration of the full range of domino mechanisms by American decision makers, see John Lewis Gaddis, *Strategies of Containment* (New York: Oxford University Press, 1982), esp. chap. 4 and 8; Leslie Gelb with Richard Betts, *The Irony of Vietnam* (Washington, D.C.: Brookings Institution, 1979), 197–200; and Larry Berman, *Planning a Tragedy* (New York: Norton, 1982), 9–11, 16–17, 83, 130, 132.

9. These points are discussed in detail in Jack Snyder, *Myths of Empire: Domestic Politics and Strategic Ideology* (Ithaca, N.Y.: Cornell University Press, forthcoming in 1991). A summary of many of the following points can be found in John McNeill and David Urquhart, "The Diplomacy of Russia," *The British and Foreign Review* 1 (1835), 102–33; and John Howes Gleason, *The Genesis of Russophobia in Great Britain* (New York: Octagon, 1972).

10. Stephen Van Evera, "Causes of War" (Ph.D. diss., University of California, Berkeley, 1984), is especially good at showing how these bandwagon belief systems worked and revealing the contradictions in them.

11. Acheson, *Present at the Creation* (New York: Norton, 1969), 374–75.

12. H. F. Bell, *Palmerston,* vol. I (Hamden, Conn.: Archon, 1966), 79.

13. R. E. Robinson and J. A. Gallagher, *Africa and the Victorians* (London: Macmillan, 1961). Books including material on the domestic politics of British imperial policy in this period include Marvin Swartz, *The Politics of British Foreign Policy in the Era of Disraeli and Gladstone* (New York: St. Martin's, 1985); and Richard Jay, *Joseph Chamberlain* (Oxford: Clarendon, 1981).

14. See especially Jervis, chap. 2, in this volume.

15. Williamson Murray, *The Change in the European Balance of Power, 1938–1939* (Princeton, N.J.: Princeton University Press, 1984).

16. See the figures comparing the gross national product of opposing alliances in Paul Kennedy, *The Rise and Fall of the Great Powers* (New York: Random House, 1987).

17. For a discussion of contemporary balancing patterns, see Stephen Walt, *The Origins of Alliances* (Ithaca, N.Y.: Cornell University Press, 1987), chap. 8.

18. The term is from Gaddis, *Strategies of Containment.*

19. Murray, *Change.*

20. See Jervis, chap. 2, in this volume.

21. William Zimmerman and Robert Axelrod present evidence of both kinds of inferences in "The 'Lessons' of Vietnam and Soviet Foreign Policy," *World Politics* 34:1 (October 1981): 1–24.

22. Jervis, this volume, makes a similar point.

23. Snyder, *Ideology,* 128.

24. Macdonald, 66.

25. Gilpin, *War and Change in World Politics* (Princeton, N.J.: Princeton University Press, 1981); and Kennedy, *Rise and Fall.*

26. See especially the chapters by Larson and Hopf, 4 and 6.

27. For example, Gaddis, *Strategies of Containment,* 144, 240–41.

28. For discussion and citations, see my introduction, Chap. 1 of this volume.

29. Larson, 96; Macdonald, 133.

30. J. B. Conacher, *The Peelites and the Party System, 1846–52* (Hamden, Conn.: Archon, 1972), 84.

31. Gleason, *Genesis of Russophobia,* 231; and Leslie Mitchell, *Holland* (London: Duckworth, 1980).

32. Peter Cain, "Capitalism, War and Internationalism in the Thought of Richard Cobden," *British Journal of International Studies* 5 (1979): 229–47, esp. 236–37.

33. Snyder, *Ideology,* chap. 5.

34. Michael A. Barnhart, *Japan Prepares for War: The Search for Economic Security, 1919–1941* (Ithaca, N.Y.: Cornell University Press, 1987).

35. Eberhard Jaeckel, *Hitler's Weltansschauung,* (Middletown, Conn.: Wesleyan Univesity Press, 1972), 44.

36. See Van Evera, "Causes of War."

37. Asada Sadao, "The Japanese Navy and the United States," in *Pearl Harbor as History,* ed. Dorothy Borg and Shumpei Okamoto (New York: Columbia University Press, 1973), 225–60; Arthur Marder, *Old Friends, New Enemies* (Oxford: Clarendon, 1981), 335 and passim.

38. See Hopf, chap. 6, for background.

39. Shevchenko, *Breaking with Moscow* (New York: Knopf, 1985), 206, 262; Harry Gelman, *The Brezhnev Politburo and the Decline of Detente* (Ithaca, N.Y.: Cornell University Press, 1984).

40. Jervis, *Perception and Misperception,* chap. 2, 8, and 9.

41. David Allan Mayers, *Cracking the Monolith* (Baton Rouge: Louisiana State Univesity, 1986).

42. Van Evera, "Causes of War," discusses militaries' perceptions in detail. The following discussion is developed at length in Snyder, *Myths of Empire.*

43. Paul Kennedy, *Strategy and Diplomacy, 1870–1945* (London: Fontana, 1983), chap. 1 and 8.

44. Fiscal Year 1987 Department of Defense Annual Report, 78–9.

45. Snyder, *Myths of Empire,* elaborates on this idea and offers historical support for it. Van Evera, "Causes of War," presents a wealth of related hypotheses.

46. See the literature cited in chap. 1.

47. Larson, looking at Eisenhower's handling of foreign rather than domestic audiences during the Taiwan Straits Crisis, notes that rhetorical obfuscation can sometimes be an effective device to buffer policymakers when any clear choice would have adverse consequences.

48. Philip Tetlock, "Accountability: The Neglected Social Context of Judgment and

Choice," in *Research in Organizational Behavior,* ed. Barry Shaw and Larry Cummings, vol. 7 (Greenwich, Conn.: JAI Press, 1985), 297–332.

49. Kennedy, *Strategy and Diplomacy,* chap. 5, shows that the German naval staff withheld strategic information and analysis that would have exploded Tirpitz's whole risk theory had it been available for outside scrutiny.

50. John P. Burke and Fred I. Greenstein with Larry Berman and Richard Immerman, *How Presidents Test Reality: Decisions on Vietnam, 1954 and 1965* (New York: Russell Sage Foundation, 1989).

Index

12.00